RECIPES
– TO LOWER YOUR –
FAT THERMOSTAT

Second Edition

Vitality House International

RECIPES
– TO LOWER YOUR –
FAT THERMOSTAT

Second Edition

The Official Companion to
How to Lower Your Fat Thermostat
and
The New Neuropsychology of Weight Control

WRITTEN AND ILLUSTRATED
BY LARENE GAUNT

With flavor alternatives
by Chef Howard Gifford

Introduction by
Dennis Remington, M.D.
Garth Fisher, Ph.D.
Edward Parent, Ph.D.

**Vitality
House
International,
Inc.**

Copyright © 1992, 1984 by
Vitality House International, Inc.
1675 North Freedom Blvd. #11-C
Provo, Utah 84604

Telephone: 801-373-5100
To Order: Call Toll Free 1-800-748-5100

First Printing, Second Edition, February, 1992

Second Printing, March 1992

Third Printing, May 1993

Fourth Printing, July 1994

This cookbook is a collection of recipes which have been gathered from various sources. All recipes have been adapted to meet a low-fat, low-sugar, low-sodium criteria.

Library of Congress Catalog Card Number: 84-52705

ISBN 0-912547-10-3

Printed in the United States of America

Publisher's Cataloging in Publication
(Prepared by Quality Books Inc.)

Gaunt, LaRene.
    Recipes to lower your fat thermostat / written and illustrated
by LaRene Gaunt ; with flavor alternatives by Howard Gifford. —
2nd ed.
    p. cm.
    "The official companion to How to lower your fat thermostat and
The new neuropsychology of weight control."
    Includes index.
    ISBN 0-912547-10-3

    1. Low-fat diet--Recipes. 2. Cookery. I. Title.

RM 237.7.G38 1994   641.5'638
                                    QBI94-1417

This book is dedicated to
my mother,
Florence Porter,
who taught me how to cook
and
to my family,
David, Angela, Dennis, and Lisa,
for whom I now cook.
It represents a doorway through which we have
passed into a happier, healthier future of
low-fat eating.

TABLE OF CONTENTS

RECIPES

1. MAKING THE CHANGE 1

You may wonder how to incorporate low-fat eating into your lifestyle and into the lifestyle of your family. This chapter provides some suggestions. It gives ideas on ways to introduce these menus into your family's everyday eating as well as their special occasions. It even includes tips on snacking and "brown bagging it."

2. MENUS AND SHOPPING LIST 5

Menus and a shopping list for 14 days of low-fat eating. All menus use recipes found in this cookbook.

3. FABULOUS FLAVORS 19

Discover tasty, low-fat substitutes for sauces, spreads, and salad dressings in this chapter. These great recipes will keep your food flavorful and moist without the use of fats.

4. "WHAT SHALL I HAVE FOR BREAKFAST?" 41

This chapter contains recipes to help you enjoy this important meal.

5. "SOUP'S ON!" 57

Soups are a mainstay in your low-fat diet. These recipes will tempt your palate as well as give you ideas on how to create your own family favorites.

6. THE GARDEN SPOT 97

This chapter contains more than 40 salad recipes including bean, gelatin, fruit, and green salads.

7. "TO MEAT OR NOT TO MEAT?" 133

Enjoy the flavor of meat but not the fat with these recipes using small amounts of poultry, fish, or beef.

This important section is filled with vital information to help you master the art of low-fat cooking. Learn to sauté without oil; cook brown rice, beans, or chicken; and to make cottage cheese. You will enjoy the complete list of spices and seasonings, including Chef Howard Gifford's gourmet spices, to help you learn to season without salt. There is a guide for growing your own sprouts as well as guides to help you bottle, freeze, or dry your own fruits and vegetables. And there is much, much more!

2. HOW TO COMPUTE THE PERCENTAGE OF FAT . . 410
This section teaches you how to compute the percentage of fat in your own recipes and from the labels of commercial foods.

3. HOW TO COMPUTE REFINED CARBOHYDRATE UNITS (RCUs) AND FAT UNITS (FUs) 411
This section teaches you how to compute the number of RCUs and FUs in your own recipes.

4. RECIPES SUITABLE FOR USE WITH A YEAST-MANAGEMENT PROGRAM 412

5. SIMPLIFIED LIST OF FOODS 415
This section will help you identify at a glance the foods that fall within the suggested guidelines to lower your fat thermostat. The common foods from each food group are arranged into two columns. One column contains foods under 20 percent fat or with low RCUs. The other column contains foods over 20 percent fat or with high RCUs.

6. ABBREVIATIONS 417
This section contains a list of the abbreviations used in this book.

7. INDEX 418

ACKNOWLEDGEMENTS

To Dr. Edward Parent, for his encouragement, counsel, and the opportunity to write this cookbook.

To Sydette Parent, for her precise and careful work in putting this cookbook onto the computer. Also, for her long hours of proofreading with me, for her perceptive comments, and for her friendship that came as a result of working together.

To Borge Andersen Photography Studios for superior photography.

To Janet Schaap, food stylist, for her incredible talent and artistic eye. Each photograph became a masterpiece under her skilled hands.

To Michael Rogan, graphic designer, for his talented work with the cover design and layout of this cookbook.

To my family, who became my taste testers: my "meat and potatoes" husband who learned to love wok food; my daughters who willingly tried everything I cooked; and my "junk-food-loving" son who put every recipe to the ultimate test.

To those who contributed recipes goes a special thanks for your support. Also, thanks to those of you who tested many of the recipes for us.

To Jim Knight and Kathie Wysinger, for their help with our 1992 revision of this cookbook. To Jim for his subtle redesign of this cover, and to Kathie for her talents at the computer keyboard and her optimistic attitude.

To Chef Howard Gifford, who, with his understanding of spices and skillful use of them, suggested spice alternatives for most of the recipes included in our 1992 revision of this cookbook

To Dennis Remington (M.D.), Garth Fisher (Ph.D.), and Edward Parent (Ph.D.), for their outstanding research and book, *How to Lower Your Fat Thermostat*, which has changed so many lives.

WILD STRAWBERRY

PREFACE

I first read *How to Lower Your Fat Thermostat* in April 1983, and it literally changed my life. I read it again and again. The more I read it, the more I was convinced it was truth. The thing I liked best about it was that it was not a diet plan full of gimmicks. It was a sound, lifestyle change for long-range good health. As I began to incorporate its principles into my life, I was amazed at how good I began to feel.

After hearing Garth Fisher speak in August 1983, I began to get ideas for a low-fat cookbook. I thought how nice it would be to have a cookbook which would provide low-fat recipes with all the pertinent data already calculated on them. I put my ideas onto paper, showed them to Dr. Parent, and this cookbook is the result.

I spent nearly two years creating, collecting, adapting, and testing hundreds of recipes. I loved it! I hope you will love learning the principles of low-fat cooking as much as I have. Try these recipes and then adapt and create your own. It is one of the best things you'll ever do for yourself and for your family. The combination of exercise and proper eating is unbeatable and you'll feel healthier and happier right away.

I'd love to hear from you. Let me know which recipes you love, which ones you didn't, and how this program has worked for you and your family. Write to LaRene Gaunt, c/o Vitality House International, Inc., 1675 North Freedom Blvd., #11-C, Provo, Utah, 84604. Thanks and "bon appetit."

***

We trust you will find this book one of the most exciting and useful tools available for achieving a healthy and trim body. We would enjoy hearing of your successes. If you have any questions, take a moment and write to us.

If you would like to be on our mailing list for future publications, please tell us. It is likely that new discoveries will help specific types of weight problems. It is our intention to keep you informed of the latest advances in this area.

If you have not read our best-selling book, *How to Lower Your Fat Thermostat*, send $9.95 plus $2.50 for shipping and handling (a total of $12.45) and we will mail a copy to you.

Please write us at:

VITALITY HOUSE INTERNATIONAL, INC.
1675 North Freedom Blvd. #11-C
Provo, Utah 84604

INTRODUCTION

"Dieting is not effective in controlling weight; it has never worked, and it never will. Admittedly, you can get temporary weight loss with a diet, but each scheme ultimately gives way to weight gain, and subsequent losses become increasingly difficult. You become hungrier and more obsessed with food, frequently eating out of control. You get tired and weak, have poor endurance, and generally feel awful about yourself; worst of all you get progressively fatter on less and less food."

This is the beginning paragraph from the 1983 book entitled *How to Lower Your Fat Thermostat*, which ushered in an entirely new approach to weight management. Sybervision's audiotape series entitled *The New Neuropsychology of Weight Control* provides additional self-help materials. This book, *Recipes to Lower Your Fat Thermostat*, is designed to help you eat a variety of enjoyable dishes while applying the principles in the original book in order to lose weight, feel better, and improve your health. This introduction includes highlights from *How to Lower Your Fat Thermostat*, along with suggestions focusing the recipe book to best advantage.

SUMMARY OF HOW TO LOWER YOUR FAT THERMOSTAT

For many years scientists have taught that excess body fat is simply the result of eating more food than the body requires. Every calorie you eat counts against you, and every calorie you save by not eating counts for you in the overall energy balance. Reducing the caloric intake (dieting), and, if that doesn't work, reducing it even further, has been thought to be the only method that will cause weight loss.

Recent evidence suggests that the problems of weight control are much more complex than simply eating too much food. Many thin people eat huge amounts of food and yet remain thin, while many fat people eat very little and remain fat. The problem appears to be one of fat storage regulation. Thin people regulate their weight at a low level, and overweight people regulate their weight at a higher level, almost regardless of how much food is eaten. All of us have within our brains control mechanisms that regulate many body functions, including body temperature, acid base balance, electrolyte balance, and body fat stores. We have called the center that controls weight the weight-regulating mechanism, or the fat thermostat. Just as the thermostat in your home keeps the room temperature at the level to which it is set (setpoint), your fat thermostat tries to keep your body fat at its setpoint level.

The fat thermostat works by controlling hunger, and by directing a number of protective bodily functions that can either increase or reduce fat stores. If you eat less food than you need, within a few hours you begin to feel hunger, which becomes progressively worse with continued deprivation. After a short time of food reduction, the fat thermostat begins to direct your body to conserve energy, to protect fat stores, and to increase the rate at which fat is restored, once enough food becomes available. Thin people who can eat large quantities of food without gaining weight have fat thermostats that direct energy wasting, so that the excess calories are burned instead of deposited as fat.

The fat thermostat is basically a survival mechanism that allowed our ancestors to live through various famines and they passed these survival tools on to us. It helps to think of the fat thermostat as a powerful computer that analyzes a great deal of information coming from many sensors within your body, choosing a body weight that seems appropriate for your needs, and then working very hard to control your weight at that level. The weight level chosen gives you a nice balance between having plenty of fat storage to protect you from starvation in case of food shortage, yet leaving you mobile enough to run, fight, or migrate if those actions are indicated.

With this understanding, it is easy to see why dieting has been almost a total failure in controlling weight on a long-term basis. In response to dieting, the fat thermostat merely makes you very hungry, you get tired and weak, and you lack the drive to do anything physical as your body attempts to conserve energy. Although you may lose a few pounds temporarily, you soon gain it back as your more efficient body, with its enhanced ability to store fat, is again fed once you give in to relentless hunger. After an episode of dieting, the weight often returns to the previous setpoint. In many cases, it goes even higher, as the fat thermostat "decides" to put on another few pounds of fat to better protect you against the next episode of starvation.

The setpoint of the fat thermostat is not fixed for life, but varies from time to time based on certain conditions. The key to successful weight management is to understand which factors influence the setpoint of the fat thermostat, to stop doing those things that keep it too high, and to start doing those things that will cause it to go down to a lower level. Following are the main guidelines that, if followed, should lower your fat thermostat for permanent, comfortable weight loss.

1. Eat a wide variety of wholesome food on a regular basis. By providing your body with its complete requirements for calories, vitamins, minerals, and other essential nutrients on a regular basis, the starvation defenses (which are triggered by dieting) stop being stimulated. In response to the other guidelines, the setpoint is free to move downward.

2. Eat in harmony with the hunger drives from your fat thermostat. Eat when you are hungry, eat until completely satisfied, then stop eating until you are hungry again. Snacking is not only acceptable, but even encouraged in response to a genuine hunger drive. You should eat at least three times daily, but more often if needed. Eat at regular intervals, even if you are not very hungry at meal time. This will keep you from going too long between meals and triggering starvation defenses. It also encourages you to eat the more appropriate types of food usually available with a regular meal.

For many chronic dieters, this is a difficult concept to accept. They often believe that they must stay hungry to save every calorie possible. It makes them feel guilty to eat until satisfied, or even to eat the kinds of food we suggest. Many dieters have denied their hunger and starved themselves for so long that they don't even know when they are genuinely hungry, or when they feel satisfied. It does not take long, however, to get back into harmony with eating drives and to recognize hunger and satisfaction.

In one interesting study, several overweight subjects were given more food than required to satisfy hunger. These people felt stuffed for the entire sixteen-week duration of the study. They lost significant weight in spite of overeating, presumably because (1) they were doing the other things that lowered their fat thermostats, (2) they were filling up on foods that had a very low caloric density, and (3) they probably began using the same energy-wasting systems that thin people use to eliminate extra food energy. We probably all have these energy-wasting systems but may not have developed them well.

Some situations seem to interfere with natural hunger drives. Food addiction is often a serious problem: eating occurs, not because of a biological need for the food, but rather to satisfy an addictive need, or to keep from going through unpleasant withdrawal symptoms. The continued ingestion of high-calorie food to satisfy addiction often leads to the consumption of more food than your body can waste, leaving it no alternative except to store the extra calories as fat. If the addictive food is a type that tends to raise the fat thermostat, then the problem is even worse. If you have an addiction or strong cravings for certain foods, especially sugar, you are unlikely to succeed unless you stop eating those foods. It is best to completely eliminate foods to which you are addicted, go through the few days of withdrawal, and continue to avoid them for at least a few months. Once your body is functioning better, you might be able to eat those foods occasionally; keep in mind that many people start the addiction all over again by adding sugars or other addictive foods back into their diets.

Eating very sweet foods also seems to interfere with natural hunger drives. Artificial sweeteners, many times sweeter than sugar, may also increase your desire for sweet things, interfere with your enjoyment of healthy foods, and cause other physiological changes that may make you fatter. A recent study done by the manufacturer of NutraSweet showed that the group using Nutra-Sweet had a higher incidence of weight gain that a control group not using it. Our new audiotape/workbook program, *12 Steps to Lower Your Fat Thermostat*, outlines some of the problems associated with artificial sweeteners, sugar, caffeine, chocolate, and food addictions. It also provides powerful help to you as you incorporate this healthy weight loss program into your lifestyle.

Hypoglycemics, diabetics on insulin, and others with altered metabolic states may have some difficulty really knowing what their biological needs are. A hunger feeling may come from low blood sugar, and continued eating to satisfy those drives may well exceed your body's ability to waste the extra calories. However, by following the entire fat thermostat reprogramming plan, such people usually experience a dramatic improvement in these conditions and are able to eat in harmony with biological needs.

Diabetics on insulin must follow their doctor's recommendations regarding caloric intake to balance out their insulin. By changing the ratio of food eaten to that recommended here, and by following other aspects of the program, diabetics usually enjoy such an improvement in the diabetes that insulin must be reduced. It is useful for diabetics to be able to monitor their own blood sugar and insulin dose; if they can't, they need to keep in close touch with their doctor while following this program.

Chronic dieters often insist on eating an exact number of calories. In our program, no exact caloric guidelines are given. In fact, most people are successful who eat more calories than allowed with a traditional reduced-calorie diet program. The quality of food seems to be much more important than the quantity. As long as you eat regularly, in reasonable amounts, you are not likely to trigger starvation defenses.

You should never eat fewer than 1,200 calories, since anything below that is likely to trigger starvation defenses and make it difficult to obtain all the nutrients you need. Many people who eat 2,000 calories are still successful on the program. Men can often eat even more than that and still lose weight.

3. Decrease your consumption of fats. Dietary fats contain more than twice as many calories as carbohydrates, and are a major factor in raising the fat thermostat. Animals fed high-fat diets will increase their body fat by three or four times that of control animals fed the same number of calories of low-fat food. Reducing fat intake is an important factor in lowering the fat thermostat. Average people in our society ingest 40 to 45 percent of their calories as fat. This not only keeps most people fatter than ideal, but it is generally very unhealthy for many other reasons.

Ideally, between 10 and 20 percent of your calories should be in the form of fat. *How to Lower Your Fat Thermostat* and *The New Neuropsychology of Weight Control* both contain a number of ways to estimate fat intake. The Table of Food Composition section lists the percent of fat within each food item. You can see at a glance which foods are higher than 20 percent fat, and either eliminate those foods from your diet or eat them in small quantities.

A unique point system helps you quickly evaluate your adherence to the suggested guidelines without having to measure portions or count calories. This section describes a fat unit (FU), which is a measured amount of fat. If you restrict yourself to less than four fat units (FUs) if your ideal weight is less than 140 pounds, or less than five fat units (FUs) if your ideal weight is more than 140 pounds, then you will be getting about the right amount of fat in the diet. This recipe book lists the FUs for each recipe to help you better evaluate your fat intake.

Keep in mind that restricting fat intake too strictly is also unhealthy. Certain essential fatty acids and vitamins can be obtained in no other way than through fat-containing foods. Be careful not to restrict fat intake below 10 percent.

4. Reduce sugar intake. Experiments have shown that adding refined sugar to the diet of animals causes them to gain about 50 percent more fat than animals eating the same number of calories, but no sugar. In our society, the average person consumes about 126 pounds of sugar per year. This appears to be a major factor in causing obesity.

Sugar appears to cause problems for a number of reasons. Because it is highly refined, all the vitamins, minerals, and other complex food molecules have been removed. When much of your caloric intake consists of refined foods, you may feel a need to eat more food to obtain the required nutrients. Sugar is very sweet, and something about sweet foods seems to trigger excessive hunger.

A number of recent research articles have suggested that refined sugar is not that much different from complex carbohydrates in its effect on blood sugar and insulin and that eating sugar is perfectly acceptable. But there is much more to sugar than its effect on blood sugar and insulin, and anyone who has questioned people about the effects of sugar becomes very aware that a high percentage of them have real problems with it. Many people are either addicted to sugar or at least have very strong cravings for it. This usually leads to the ingestion of excessive sugar, which may raise the fat thermostat and cause other biological problems that result in excess weight.

Many people also develop unpleasant symptoms from eating sugar. If sugar is a regular part of your diet, you could be having chronic problems from it, yet not even be aware that sugar is the cause. Some new evidence suggests that these problems may be caused by yeast that feed on the ingested sugars, invade the lining of the intestinal tract, and put out toxic waste products like ethanol and acetaldehyde, which can inactivate various enzyme systems within your body. A wide range of unpleasant symptoms may result, including indigestion, heartburn, gas, bloating, alternating constipation and diarrhea, trouble thinking clearly, trouble concentrating, anxiety, sleep disturbance, depression, dizziness, headaches, fatigue, muscle soreness and stiffness, low blood sugar symptoms, food cravings, weight gain, and impairment of the immune system leading to repeated infections and the emergence of food and chemical allergies. A number of self-help books are available about this problem, including *Back to Health: A Comprehensive Medical and Nutritional Yeast Control Program* (Remington and Higa, 1986). Many of the recipes in *Recipes to Lower Your Fat Thermostat* are ideal for a yeast management diet, and a description of suitable recipes is listed on pages 412-414.

To lower your fat thermostat effectively, you should eat very little, if any, sugar. Hidden sugars are in most prepared foods, and you need to start reading labels to identify them. In *How to Lower Your Fat Thermostat* and *The New Neuropsychology of Weight Control* under the Table of Food Composition section, the refined carbohydrate units or RCUs for each food are listed, making it easy to detect problem foods. In the point scoring system, anything more than two RCUs daily is considered excessive, and points are deducted. This recipe book lists the RCUs for each recipe, making it easier for you to eat appropriately.

Drink water to satisfy thirst. Water is essential for life, and we all have a "built-in" thirst mechanism to tell us when we are in need of water. If we answer this thirst drive by drinking soda pop, alcohol, juice, milk, or other calorie-containing fluids, then we ingest unnecessary calories. Unless our energy-wasting systems are functioning well, we may experience an increase in fat.

It is very important to distinguish between hunger and thirst. If you are hungry, it is best to eat good nutritious food that contains fiber, vitamins, and minerals and that provides some chewing and eating satisfaction. If you are thirsty, it is important to satisfy that need with water. An exception to this general rule is to drink two glasses of skim or low-fat milk or use an equivalent amount of calcium in some other form.

5. Exercise effectively. Most overweight people have found exercise to be uncomfortable, and they do not enjoy it. This happens to anyone who tries to exercise while restricting food intake. With adequate eating, you should soon learn to really enjoy exercise. It can make you feel good if you follow just a few common-sense guidelines.

For years we have taught that the real reason for exercise is to burn calories. At about 100 calories a mile, it would take 35 miles of walking to burn even one pound of fat. Fortunately, exercise is much more effective than that. Exercise actually plays several major roles.

A. Exercise lowers the fat thermostat. Animals in the wild are lean; when caged, they get fat. Humans often get fatter during the times of inactivity and leaner when they exercise.

B. Exercise helps maintain lean body mass (muscle). Weight loss by diet alone often results in almost as much muscle loss as fat loss. Since fat is burned primarily in muscle, muscle loss is detrimental to our efforts to lower fat.

C. Exercise helps change muscle enzyme systems so that they burn fat more effectively. For instance, a long-distance runner would burn more fat than a nontrained person running with him.

D. Exercise has been shown to make people feel better. This effect is brought about by the release of brain chemicals called endorphines. Whatever the reason, it does feel good to exercise.

The rules for exercise for lowering the fat thermostat are similar to the rules for developing cardiovascular fitness, except that exercise must be done for a longer duration and more often to lower the fat thermostat. Both programs require the use of large muscles and rhythmic activity such as walking, jogging, riding an exercise bike, aerobic dancing, and swimming. These activities are more effective if done at a moderate rate. Exercise should be vigorous enough to cause heavy breathing, but not so hard that you feel breathless to the point of not being able to carry on a conversation. You should also exercise daily, starting at about 20 minutes a day and working up to 45 to 60 minutes. Don't increase the work load too rapidly. Shorter, more frequent exercise is an effective way to begin without injury.

6. Reduce stress in your life. For many people, stress has played a major role in initial weight gain, and it continues to play a role in preventing effective weight management. Stress seems to raise the setpoint and produce other undesirable biological changes. In our own clinical experience, most of the people who have problems with weight management are those who experience a great deal of stress in their lives.

Some of this stress may be due to inappropriate levels of stress hormones in the body, but much of it also comes from the way a person has learned to respond to life's problems. For most people, considerable improvement will come through effective exercise and good nutrition. For many people, however, additional lifestyle changes will be needed in order to reduce stress to a level that will allow the setpoint to lower and the other biological changes to occur, which will allow them to become naturally thin.

BENEFITS OF THE FAT THERMOSTAT REPROGRAMMING PLAN

Although effective weight loss almost always occurs with this program, we think of weight loss as only a pleasant side effect of a program designed for overall health maintenance. We have seen positive effects in the physical, emotional, and spiritual sides of many people.

Much research now shows that effective exercise and dietary fat reduction helps prevent heart disease. Although weight loss has been shown to protect against heart disease, the caloric restriction and decreased activity associated with most weight loss methods may greatly limit their effectiveness. Not only does the reprogramming plan protect against heart disease, it may even be effective in treating it. We have seen patients with severe heart pain (angina pectoris) who were able to entirely eliminate the pain and stop their medication under the direction of their doctor by following this program.

New evidence suggests that hypertension (high blood pressure — a major factor in causing heart disease and strokes) is strongly influenced by exercise and diet. People who eat more foods containing calcium, potassium, magnesium, and perhaps other minerals on a regular basis have a lower incidence of hypertension. Excess alcohol, sugar, fats, and proteins in the diet may all contribute to hypertension. The Reprogramming Plan seems to make many positive changes that should effectively reduce blood pressure. This program is also ideally suited for diabetes.

Recent evidence suggests that there is a relationship between diet and many types of cancer. The American Cancer Society has suggested a decrease in body weight and ingested fat, and an increase in complex carbohydrates (high-fiber food, vegetables, fruits, grains, etc.) to minimize cancer risk. The Reprogramming Plan fits in precisely with these guidelines, and following it should reduce the risk for developing many kinds of cancer.

Not only do the overweight suffer from a number of physical problems, but they often have a very high incidence of emotional problems. Many of them struggle with fatigue, irritability, anxiety, depression, and very poor self-esteem. The most exciting aspect of the Reprogramming Plan for us has been the dramatic improvement in the emotional state of these people. We are convinced that many emotional problems are related to the balance of brain hormones, and that prolonged or frequent dieting often exaggerates these problems. It is possible and even probable that following the principles outlined in *How to Lower Your Fat Thermostat* will dramatically improve the quality of your life. You should have a renewed zest for life and feel pride and dignity that you perhaps have never felt.

In addition to *Recipes to Lower Your Fat Thermostat*, Vitality House has published three other specialty recipe books that should also be of interest. *Desserts to Lower Your Fat Thermostat* (Higa, 1988) contains 200 delicious recipes for desserts, snacks, treats, and drinks. *Gifford's Gourmet De-Lites* (Gifford, 1988) contains 122 recipes for those with an interest in preparing and eating healthy gourmet foods. *Easy Gourmet Menus to Lower Your Fat Thermostat* (Gifford, 1991)

contains 210 recipes in menu form for healthy low-fat meals. The recipes in all four of these books are low in fat and sugar, and fit into the guidelines for *How to Lower Your Fat Thermostat* and *The New Neuropsychology of Weight Control*. These recipes are suitable for a low cholesterol diet, and also follow the recommendations of the American Heart Association, the American Diabetic Association, and the American Cancer Society.

Dennis W. Remington, M.D.
A. Garth Fisher, Ph.D.
Edward A. Parent, Ph.D.

ABOUT THE AUTHOR

LaRene Gaunt was born and reared in San Diego, California. She has a B.A. in art from Brigham Young University and has done post-graduate work at BYU, Ball State University, and Utah State University.

Her professional experience has been widely varied and includes teaching art in both junior high and high school, working as an interior decorator, and doing genealogical research. Currently, she is an assistant editor at the *Ensign* magazine in Salt Lake City, Utah.

She loves being with her husband and three children, writing, cooking, and walking.

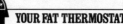

MAKING THE CHANGE

You never fail unless you fail to try.

MAKING THE CHANGE

INTRODUCING YOUR FAMILY TO LOW-FAT EATING

Low-fat eating will benefit everyone, so it is a good idea to feed your entire family in this way. Start with changes that usually meet with little resistance, like giving everyone a glass of water with his or her meal, preparing two vegetables, and serving fresh fruits as desserts or snacks.

Introduce a new recipe every other day and let your family try it. Let them vote; majority wins. As you find new recipes that your family enjoys, serve them more often. Space high-fat meals further and further apart. Adapt the family favorites to fit the guidelines. Some new recipes could share the spotlight with a family favorite as the main course, then everyone could eat a little of both. Keep the mood happy. Prepare and serve the food so that it looks attractive, and let your family know how much you enjoy the new recipe. Remember, as your family loses their taste for high-fat, high-sugar foods, they will accept and enjoy these changes.

Holiday and special occasion traditions may involve high-fat foods. Whenever possible, change the tradition by introducing low-fat food traditions. If that doesn't seem reasonable, modify the traditional recipe by reducing the amount of fats and sugars, or simply eat a smaller portion of the original recipes. It is probably a good idea to increase your exercise during the holidays, too.

To increase the convenience of low-fat cooking, prepare double recipes of soups, casseroles, and breads. Freeze one recipe that can be easily reheated on an especially busy day. A freezer and a microwave oven are a remarkable time-saving team. A freezer allows you to save prepared homemade foods and a microwave oven allows quick cooking of that food.

When grocery shopping, read the labels and learn exactly how many grams of fat and refined carbohydrates are in the foods you are eating. Buy "juice-packed" canned fruits and "water-packed" tuna. Look for the low-sodium canned goods such as green beans or tomato juice. Buy low-fat, low-sugar packaged cereals. Both bakeries and supermarkets have a good selection of nutritious breads such as rye, pumpernickel, or whole wheat. Learn which items can be purchased and make time to prepare the rest. Give these eating changes top priority, and you will be rewarded with more energy and better physical and mental health.

TIPS FOR SNACKS

Snacks are fine when eaten in response to genuine hunger and not for entertainment or pleasure. Drink a glass of water before you snack to be sure that you are not confusing hunger and thirst signals. This will also increase the satiety value of your snacks. If you are still hungry, eat any food in a small amount totaling fewer than 200 calories, except refined carbohydrates. Fruits, vegetables, whole wheat bread, or a small dish of cereal make excellent snacks. Avoid high-calorie snacks such as dried fruit, raisins, nuts, or peanut butter.

Behavior modification is of some importance if you have a problem with eating for reasons other than hunger (nondirected eating). Learning to recognize the stimuli that cause you to eat and then avoiding the stimuli or replacing eating with another activity can help. Certain TV programs, times of the day such as when children come home from school or bedtime, locations such as grandma's house or the movies, social occasions, and even certain friends can all be the stimulus for nondirected eating.

The list of possible behavior modifications is endless. Briefly, any change that will prevent the food from entering your mouth when you are not hungry is worth considering. Avoid the TV programs, crochet or knit instead of eating, or change the pattern of your day and be away from the house at problem times.

Other tips include:
1. Keep sliced fruit, as well as whole fresh fruit, available.
2. Keep prepared, raw vegetables available.
3. Keep a variety of low-fat breads, rolls, and muffins available.
4. Encourage snacking on low-sugar cereals, either dry or with milk.
5. Encourage snacking on plain, low-fat yogurt with fruit, cereal, or bread.
6. Make popsicles out of fruit juice.
7. See "Just for Fun!" on page 347 for other snack recipes.

EATING OUT

There may be times when you will need to eat out. The following are suggestions on how to meet this challenge:
1. For breakfast, ask for hot cereal or whole wheat toast without butter, a grapefruit, orange, or fresh juice.
2. For lunch, order a noncream soup or a salad with lots of chunky vegetables topped with lemon juice. Of course, you could always order some kind of baked fish or chicken with a baked potato and vegetables. Replace French fries with sliced tomatoes.
3. Choosing a low-fat dinner is easier than choosing a low-fat breakfast or lunch. Baked halibut, teriyaki chicken, soup, or salad are all good dinner choices. Vegetable plates or Chinese foods are usually low in fat, too. Avoid desserts.

BROWN BAGGING IT

Taking your own lunch is a good way to ensure that you will enjoy a low-fat meal. It is possible to carry almost anything, hot or cold, from home to your place of work. Today lunch boxes come in a wide variety of shapes and sizes. Thermoses come with traditional openings for liquids or with wide-mouth openings for chunky foods, stew, and soups. Many lunchrooms even have a refrigerator, microwave oven, or hot plate. All of these things make taking your lunch a convenient and popular option.

First, take a look at the suggested menus for lunches on pages 6 - 13. You will see that the menus fall into several general categories: sandwiches with a soup or salad; soup with homemade bread; a tossed green or fruit salad with muffins or bread; a meat salad with rolls; or a vegetable casserole. It is very simple to adapt these menus to the needs of the "brown bagger."

Sandwiches are easily transported to work. Pack lettuce, tomatoes, or pickles in a separate container and place them on your sandwich just before eating to prevent soggy sandwiches. Salads are also easily transported. Simply pack dressing separately, then pour over salad just before eating. Soups, stews, and casseroles can usually be transported in a thermos and kept warm. Even a thermos is unnecessary if you have access to a refrigerator and a microwave or hot plate. Homemade breads, muffins, and rolls all remain fresh in a plastic bag. Fresh fruits can be sliced and kept cold until lunch if you have access to a refrigerator. If not, bring whole fruit and slice it just before eating.

Working can also divide your day into regular patterns and sometimes bad eating habits become a part of it. Following are some suggestions to help change unwanted habits:

1. Bring fruit or an acceptable snack to enjoy while others are eating doughnuts or cookies.
2. Bring ice water or an acceptable drink to sip on during the day to replace soda pop.
3. Chew gum or brush your teeth so that you will not be tempted to put unnecessary food into your mouth.
4. If foods or friends sabotage your eating changes, go for a walk during lunch or eat in a different setting.

You will find the solution to your particular problem and when you do, stick with it. With a little practice, you will become an expert "brown bagger," enjoying all the benefits of fabulous low-fat meals.

WHITE WALNUT

BLACK WALNUT

MENUS AND SHOPPING LIST

"Good order is the foundation of all good things."

--Edmund Burke

MENUS AND SHOPPING LIST

Following are suggestions for 14 days of low-fat eating including breakfast, lunch, dinner, and snacks. All of the meals can be expanded by adding skim milk, fruit, vegetables, salad, or low-fat sauces. As you try the various recipes, note your own and your family's reaction to them. Let your family's favorites become mainstay meals; replace their "not-so-favorites" with new recipes. Gradually, you will develop a long list of low-fat menus suited to your own family's taste.

Day One:

Breakfast:
Hot Cracked Wheat Cereal (p. 44)
Sliced apples
Whole Wheat Toast

Snack:
Frozen Fruit Shake (p. 371)

Lunch:
Tuna Sandwich
Snow White and Rose Red (p. 122)

Snack:
Raw vegetables

Dinner:
Baked Fish Filets (p. 145)
Sourdough Bread (p. 341)
Green Beans with Mushrooms Galore (p. 190)
Sunburst (fruit salad) (p. 125)

Day Two:

Breakfast:
Swiss Fruit Cereal with chopped pears (p. 46)

Snack:
Choice of fruit

Lunch:
Basic Baked Potatoes and Toppings (p. 230)
Perfectly Cooked Broccoli (p. 176)
Corn on the cob

Snack:
Low-sodium vegetable juice and whole wheat crackers

Dinner:
Haystacks (p. 285)
Steamed green peas
Fresh Fruit Salad (p. 127)

Day Three:

Breakfast:
Whole Wheat Pancakes (p. 52)
Apple or Pear Butter Topping (p. 49)

Snack:
Yogurt and fruit

Lunch:
Tomatoes stuffed with Chunky Chicken Salad (p. 111)
Eleven Variation Dinner Rolls (p. 330)

Snack:
Crunchy Munchies (p. 374)

Dinner:
Souper Chicken (p. 152)
Steamed mixed vegetables
Peachy Perfect Gelatin (p. 117)

Day Four:

Breakfast:
Cinnamon French Toast (p. 55)
Fantastic Fruit Sauce (p. 47)

Snack:
Banana

Lunch:
Marvelous Minestrone (p. 96)
Dilly Bread (p. 310)

Snack:
Raw vegetables

Dinner:
Hamburger Spaghetti Sauce (p. 164)
San Francisco Sourdough Garlic Bread (p. 342)
Dark Green Salad Toss (p. 103)
Creamy French Dressing (p. 31)

Day Five:

Breakfast:
Orange sections
Raisin-Molasses Bread (p. 323)

Snack:
Fruit Snow (p. 371)

Lunch:
Crunchy Tomato Teaser (p. 372)
Sourdough English Muffins (p. 343)

Snack:
Raw vegetables and whole wheat crackers

Dinner:
Pineapple Ham Stir-Fry (p. 223)
Oriental Salad Toss (p.106)

Day Six:

Breakfast:
Vegetable Omelet (p. 56)
Potato Crisps (p. 242)

Snack:
Whole Wheat Bread Sticks (p. 308)

Lunch:
Tico Taco Salad (p. 108)
Salsa (p. 27)
Sliced Cantaloupe
Snack:
Apple
Dinner:
Vegetable Fugue Casserole (p. 206)
Whole Wheat Carrot Bread (p. 318)
Fresh Fruit Salad (p. 127)

Day Seven:
Breakfast:
Crepes (p. 358)
Fresh strawberries and yogurt
Snack:
Choice of fruit
Lunch:
Hawaiian Chicken Salad (p. 110)
Bran Muffins (p. 334)
Snack:
Tortilla Triangles (p. 363) and Salsa (p. 27)
Dinner:
Grilled Hamburgers (p. 163)
Hamburger Buns (p. 321)
Watermelon Basket (p. 131)
Suit Yourself Potato Salad (p. 238)

Day Eight:
Breakfast:
Cold cereal (Shredded Wheat, bran cereal,
or other low-fat, low-sugar cereals) and skim milk
Sliced bananas
Snack:
Raw vegetables and Cucumber Dip (p. 29)

Lunch:
Pita Bread Sandwiches (p. 306)
Vegetable Cocktail Bouillon (p. 61)

Snack:
Crunchy Munchies (p. 374)

Dinner:
Turkey (p. 156)
Apple Stuffing (p. 304)
Basic Bouillon Gravy (p. 22)
Sweet Potatoes and Fruit Juice (p. 200)
Steamed green peas

Day Nine:

Breakfast:
Hot oatmeal with skim milk
Fresh fruit
Whole Wheat Bagel (p. 332)

Snack:
Low-sodium vegetable juice and whole wheat crackers

Lunch:
Easy Chili (p. 255)
Golden Corn Bread (p. 294)
Traditional Tossed Salad (p. 106)
Thousand Island Dressing (p. 32)

Snack:
Sliced Apples

Dinner:
Beef Kabobs on Wild Rice (p. 166)
Extra Special Asparagus (p. 175)
Waldorf Salad (p. 126)

Day Ten:

Breakfast:
Applesauce (p. 362)
Applesauce Muffins (p. 339)

Snack:

Slice of whole-grain bread

Lunch:

Lovely Layered Lunch (p. 108)

Creamy Italian Dressing (p. 32)

Bran Cereal Batter Bread (p. 324)

Snack:

Popcorn

Dinner:

Pizza (p. 167)

Springtime (fruit salad) (p. 124)

Day Eleven:

Breakfast:

Frozen Fruit Slush (p. 367)

Crunchy Banana Muffins (p. 335)

Snack:

Low-sodium vegetable juice and whole wheat crackers

Lunch:

Zesty Three-Bean Salad in Tomatoes (p. 114)

Surprise "No Oil" Rolls (p. 327)

Snack:

Choice of fruit

Dinner:

Good Old Goulash (p. 68)

Basic Whole Wheat Bread (p. 311)

The 3-C Salad (p. 116)

Day Twelve:

Breakfast:

Arctic Sunshine (p. 367)

Fast and Easy Whole Wheat Bread (p. 309)

Snack:

Choice of fruit

Lunch:
Tostadas (p. 263)
Refried Beans (p. 261)
Sliced honeydew melon sprinkled with lime juice

Snack:
Rainbow Raw Vegetables (p. 100)

Dinner:
Crab and Shrimp Casserole (p. 142)
Seven-Layer Salad (p. 104)

Day Thirteen:

Breakfast:
Hash Browns (p. 243) with sautéed mushrooms
and pineapple chunks

Snack:
Applesauce

Lunch:
Veggie Stir-Fry (p. 215) with brown rice
Fresh Pineapple Basket (p. 130)

Snack:
Muffin

Dinner:
Turkey Enchiladas (p. 158)
Traditional Tossed Salad (p. 106)
Low-fat Ranch Dressing (p. 34)

Day Fourteen:

Breakfast:
Favorite Buckwheat Pancakes (p. 52)
Tutti Fruitti Topping (p. 50)

Snack:
Yogurt and fresh fruit

Lunch:
Mozzarella Sprout Sandwich (p. 346)
Crunchy Onion Rings (p. 193)

Snack:
Choice of fruit

Dinner:
Best Meat Loaf Ever (p. 165)
Stuffed Potato Boats (p. 245)
Sunshine Carrots (p. 182)
Crazy Coleslaw Gelatin (p. 121)

Following are some guidelines to help you create your own menus. Breakfast, lunch, and dinner menus can be grouped into several general combinations:

Breakfast:
Cereal (cold or cooked) and fruit.

Pancakes or French toast with fruit topping.

Muffins or hearty whole-grain breads and fruit.

Omelet and hash browns.

Even soup and toast or a baked potato can be eaten for breakfast.

Remember, a glass of skim milk or a slice of whole-grain toast is a welcome addition to any breakfast.

Lunch:
A sandwich with soup, salad, or fruit. To make a low-fat sandwich, simply use whole-grain bread, omit the butter or mayonnaise, and fill it with a low-fat filling such as water-packed tuna. Tomatoes, pickles, and lettuce will help keep your sandwich moist as will many of the spreads in Fabulous Flavors (p. 19).

Soup and homemade bread.

A tossed salad, meat salad, or a fruit salad with a muffin or a slice of bread.

A vegetable casserole makes a good lunch.

These lunches can be filled in with a glass of skim milk,
a dish of yogurt, fresh fruit, raw vegetables, or homemade bread,
if you are still hungry.

Dinner:

Soup, salad, and bread is a surefire combination.
Almost any soup, salad, and bread trio served with a glass of milk will
provide a nourishing meal.

There are some low-fat options for the traditional
"meat and potatoes" family. See Rolled Flank and Dressing on page 169.

Casseroles easily combine vegetables, grains,
and a small amount of meat. Team them up
with muffins or rolls, a glass of milk,
and a salad or vegetable side dish.

Stir-fry over rice is a great choice for low-fat eating.

Mexican dishes use beans, corn, and rice in combination
with salads, fruits, or small amounts of meat.
Just make sure you don't use much cheese, meat, or fat.

Sometimes it's fun to serve just a vegetable meal.
Choose three or four steamed vegetables, add bread or rolls,
a glass of skim milk, and fruit in season.

If you want to end your meal with a refreshing finish,
enjoy sliced fresh fruit or a whipped fruit
drink. See Just for Fun! on page 347.

This shopping list*, built from the fourteen-day menu plan above, includes most of the basics for low-fat cooking. Amounts were determined from the recipes as they appear in this cookbook, so you will have enough ingredients to make any of the suggested recipes. (Note that the number of servings varies from recipe to recipe.)

As you incorporate low-fat cooking techniques into your meal preparations, you will gradually replace many of your basic food items with their low-fat equivalent. This shopping list will get you started. Remember to check your kitchen for items on the shopping list before you go to the store.

Ingredient	Quantity	Measure
Meats		
Chicken	2	lbs.
Chicken breasts	6	each

Ingredient	Quantity	Measure
Crab	2	6 ½ oz. cans
Fish filet	16	oz.
Ham, lean	6	oz.
Hamburger, lean	3	lbs.
Round steak	12	oz.
Shrimp	1	4 ½ oz. can
Turkey	1	12-14 lbs.

Produce

Ingredient	Quantity	Measure
Alfalfa sprouts	3	cups
Apples	33	each
Bananas	8	each
Bean sprouts	8	oz.
Broccoli, fresh	36	oz.
Cabbage	1	head
Cantaloupe	1	each
Carrots	19	each
Cauliflower	1	med. head
Celery	26	stalks
Cherries	1	cup
Corn, fresh	4	ears
Cucumbers	5	each
Grapefruit	1	each
Grapes	2	cups
Green beans, fresh	1	lb.
Green onions	24	each
Green peppers	13	each
Honeydew melon	1	each
Lemons	1	each
Lettuce, iceberg	4	heads
Lettuce, romaine	1	head
Mushrooms, chopped	5	lbs.
Mushrooms, canned	1	6 oz. can
Mushrooms, whole	16	each
Onions	16	each
Onions, Bermuda	2	each
Oranges	6	each
Peaches, fresh	13	each
Pears	6	each
Pineapple, fresh	1	each
Potatoes	28	each
Radishes	12	each
Red cabbage	1	sm. head
Spinach, raw	½	lb.
Strawberries	1	pint
Sweet potatoes	1	lb.
Tomatoes	23	each

Ingredient	Quantity	Measure
Tomatoes, cherry	4	lbs.
Watercress	1	cup
Watermelon	1	each
Yellow squash	1	each
Zucchini	2	lbs.

Dairy

Buttermilk	48	oz.
Cheddar cheese	2	T
Eggs	3	dozen
Low-fat cottage cheese	7	lbs.
Low-fat yogurt	4	lbs.
Mozzarella cheese, skim	10	oz.
Parmesan cheese	2	T
Skim milk	3	quarts
Skim milk, evaporated	4	oz.
Swiss cheese	2	oz.
Yellow cheese	6	T

Frozen

Apple juice, frozen concentrate	6	6 oz. cans
Asparagus, frozen	2	10 oz. pkgs
Green beans, frozen	1	9 oz. pkg
Mixed vegetables, frozen	1	12 oz. pkg
Orange juice, frozen concentrate	2	6 oz. cans
Peas, frozen	4	12 oz. pkgs

Flours/Powders/Starches

Barley	1/3	cup
Bran	6	oz.
Brown rice, uncooked	5	cups
Buckwheat flour	2	cups
Cheerios	1	cup
Corn Chex	1	cup
Corn meal	1	cup
Corn tortillas	32	each
Cornstarch	11	T
Cracked wheat	3	cups
Dry buttermilk powder	1	cup
Kidney beans, uncooked	8	oz.
Kidney beans	1	16 oz. can
Malted milk powder	1	T
Nonfat dry milk	7	T
Pinto beans, uncooked	1	lb.
Pretzel sticks	2	cups
Raisin Bran cereal	4	cups
Rice Chex	2	cups
Rolled oats	5	cups

Ingredient	Quantity	Measure
Unbleached flour	14	cups
Wheat Chex	2	cups
Wheat germ	3	cups
Whole bran cereal	3	cups
Whole wheat bread	1	loaf
Whole wheat bread crumbs	2	oz.
Whole wheat crackers	1	box
Whole wheat flour	25	lbs.
Whole wheat macaroni, elbow	1	16 oz. pkg
Whole wheat spaghetti	1	32 oz. pkg
Wild rice	1	16 oz. pkg

Miscellaneous Groceries

Ingredient	Quantity	Measure
Almonds	6	each
Applesauce, unsweetened	56	oz.
Beef broth, or	52	oz.
Beef bouillon granules	1	jar
Brown sugar	2	T
Butter Buds® Sprinkles	1	pkg
Catsup	8	oz.
Chicken broth, or	128	oz.
Chicken bouillon	1	jar
Chili sauce	2	T
Dill pickle, whole	1	8 oz. jar
Dry onion soup mix	1	pkg
Dry yeast	14	T
Gelatin, unflavored	6	env.
Green beans	1	8 oz. can
Green chilies	4	oz.
Honey	13	T
Imitation bacon bits	2	T
Lemon juice	14	oz.
Lime juice	1	T
Low-calorie mayonnaise	1	T
Molasses	2	oz.
Oil	11	oz.
Pimento	11	T
Pineapple, chunks	44	oz.
Pineapple juice	34	oz.
Pineapple, crushed	26	oz.
Popcorn, popped	2	cups
Prepared mustard	5	T
Raisins	14	oz.
Red wine vinegar	4	oz.
Sugar	12	T
Tomato juice	40	oz.
Tomato paste	2	6 oz. cans

Ingredient	Quantity	Measure
Tomato sauce, smooth	3	8 oz. cans
Tomato sauce, chunky	4	8 oz. cans
Tomatoes, stewed	5	16 oz. cans
Tuna fish, water-packed	1	can
Vegetable juice, low-sodium	32	oz.
Vinegar	7	oz.
Walnuts	1	T
Water chestnuts, sliced	1	cup
Wax beans	1	8 oz. can

Spices and Seasonings

Ingredient	Quantity	Measure
Allspice	1	tsp.
Baking powder	12	tsp.
Baking soda	9	tsp.
Basil	4	tsp.
Black pepper	4	tsp.
Chili powder	8	tsp.
Chives	1	tsp.
Cinnamon	3	tsp.
Cumin	5	tsp.
Dill seed	2	tsp.
Dry mustard	2	tsp.
Garlic	9	cloves
Garlic powder	3	tsp.
Garlic, minced	5	T
Ginger	1	tsp.
Italian seasoning	2	T
Nutmeg	1	tsp.
Onion powder	3	tsp.
Oregano	2	tsp.
Paprika	4	tsp.
Parsley, flakes	15	T
Red hot taco sauce	0	tsp.
Rosemary	1	tsp.
Sage	1	tsp.
Salt	12	tsp.
Soy sauce	3	T
Tabasco sauce	1	dash
Tarragon	1	tsp.
Thyme	1	tsp.
Vanilla extract	1	tsp.
Worcestershire sauce	5	T

To order Gifford's Six Spices, see form in the back of this book.

*Remember, items on this shopping list will vary according to the recipes you choose to actually use. Depending on the season, adjustments may need to be made on produce.

FABULOUS FLAVORS

"What is a weed? A plant whose virtues have not yet been discovered."

--Ralph Waldo Emerson

FABULOUS FLAVORS

"Hmmm! This tastes so good!" Isn't that what we like to hear when others eat our cooking? Well, this chapter is filled with tasty low-fat sauces, gravies, spreads, dips, and salad dressings. They can be used in an incredible number of ways. Most of them replace common high-fat items such as mayonnaise, salad dressings, gravies, white sauces, sour cream, or cheese sauces. But many of them can be used as a base sauce from which you can build your own soups, casseroles, or toppings to be combined with potatoes, rice, grains, or meats. Even the salad dressings perform double duty when they are used as a sandwich spread, marinade, or seasoning.

The biggest complaint with low-fat cooking is that it is dry. Well, don't worry any longer. Keep your breads, grains, and casseroles moist with these terrific sauces, spreads, and dressings.

Read and experiment with the recipes in this chapter, then brace yourself for the raves over your low-fat cooking. You are only limited by your imagination and willingness to try because "this is where the taste is."

Fruit sauces, see:
"What Shall I Have For Breakfast?" on page 41
"Just For Fun!" on page 347
Additional salad dressings, see:
The Garden Spot on page 97

CREAMY ORANGE DRESSING

What could be faster than this creamy, sweet dressing? Use it with tossed spinach greens or over your favorite fruit salad.

½	C	low-fat yogurt*
½	C	low-fat cottage cheese,* blended
½	C	orange juice concentrate*

Gifford's Alternatives: Add:

1	tsp.	*orange flavor extract*
½	tsp.	*pure vanilla*
1	tsp.	*Schilling® Orange Peel*

1. Combine yogurt, cottage cheese, and orange juice concentrate. Chill before serving.

Yield: 1½ C = 24 T

* See "Cooking Methods" section

	RCU	FU	Cal	%Ft	P	F	C	Na
Per Tablespoon	0	0	17	16	1	T	3	13

BASIC BUTTER SPREAD

This basic butter-flavored spread has a smooth, mild flavor. Try it or one of its variations on whole wheat bread.

½	C	low-fat cottage cheese*
2	T	nonfat dry milk*
2	tsp.	Butter Buds® Sprinkles or Molly McButter®

Gifford's Alternatives: Add:
¼	tsp.	*ground turmeric*

1. Blend cottage cheese, nonfat dry milk, and Butter Buds® Sprinkles until smooth.

2. Chill.

3. For a variety of spreads, add 1 of the following: 3 tablespoons well-drained crushed pineapple, 1 teaspoon grated orange rind, 1 tablespoon finely chopped parsley, or 1 teaspoon finely chopped chives.

Yield: ½ C = 8 T

* *See "Cooking Methods" section*

	RCU	FU	Cal	%Ft	P	F	C	Na
Per Tablespoon	0	0	14	T	2	T	1	32

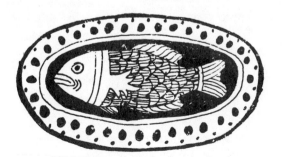

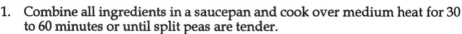

BASIC BOUILLON GRAVY

This recipe is much lower in fat than other gravies. It also makes a perfect base for soups and stews.

3	T	cornstarch*
3	C	beef OR chicken bouillon*
to taste		seasoning without salt*

Gifford's Alternatives: Add:
1	T	*onion powder*
½	tsp.	*thyme or basil -OR-*
1	T	*Gifford's Basic Spice®*

1. Whisk cornstarch into cool bouillon. Season to taste. Heat until mixture becomes thickened. Serve.

Yield: 3 C = 6 servings

* See "Cooking Methods" section

	RCU	FU	Cal	%Ft	P	F	C	Na
Per Serving	0	0	18	26	1	1	1	201

GOLDEN GRAVY

This thick golden gravy is wonderful over beef, bean, or rice casseroles.

1	C	yellow split peas	½	tsp.	salt
3	C	water			

Gifford's Alternatives: Add:
1	T	*Gifford's Basic Spice®*
1	tsp.	*onion powder*
1	tsp.	*ground mustard*
¼	tsp.	*sage*

GARLIC

1. Combine all ingredients in a saucepan and cook over medium heat for 30 to 60 minutes or until split peas are tender.

2. Pour mixture into a blender and blend until smooth.

3. Return to saucepan. Adjust consistency with water or chicken bouillon, if necessary. Season and serve.

Yield: 4 C = 8 servings

	RCU	FU	Cal	%Ft	P	F	C	Na
Per Serving	0	0	87	2	6	T	16	128

MUSHROOM ONION GRAVY

This makes a fabulous gravy for beef dishes or a base for soups, stews, and casseroles.

1	pkg	dry onion soup
2	C	water
2	T	cornstarch*
1	3 oz. can	mushrooms, sliced

1. Combine onion soup mix and water.

2. Whisk in cornstarch.

3. Add mushrooms.

4. Heat, stirring constantly, until thickened. Serve.

Yield: 2 C = 4 servings

* See "Cooking Methods" section

	RCU	FU	Cal	%Ft	P	F	C	Na
Per Serving	0	0	24	19	1	1	5	190

BARBECUE SAUCE

Keep this ready in your refrigerator to use at a moment's notice.

¾	C	catsup
¾	C	water
2	T	vinegar
¼	tsp.	black pepper
1	tsp.	chili powder
1	tsp.	paprika
1 ½	T	Worcestershire sauce

Gifford's Alternatives: Add:

2	T	*peach juice concentrate*
1	tsp.	*ground mustard*
2	drops	*Wright's® Liquid Smoke OR*
1	tsp.	*Gifford's Mexican Spice®*
1	tsp.	*Gifford's Basic Spice®*
½	tsp.	*Gifford's Dessert Spice®*
		OMIT chili powder

GARLIC

1. Combine all ingredients and heat.

2. Use over chicken, baked potatoes, or as a seasoning.

Yield: 2 C = 8 servings

	RCU	FU	Cal	%Ft	P	F	C	Na
Per Serving	0	0	25	T	0	T	7	107

BASIC TOMATO SAUCE

Use over stuffed cabbage or stuffed green peppers. There are many uses for this basic sauce.

1	C	onion, diced	⅛	tsp.	black pepper
2	cloves	garlic, minced	½	tsp.	oregano
1	28 oz. can	tomatoes,* stewed	½	tsp.	basil
			1		green pepper, diced
3	T	tomato sauce*	½	C	mushrooms

Gifford's Alternatives: Add:

1	T	*peach juice concentrate*
1	tsp.	*onion powder*
½	tsp.	*beef bouillon granules* OR*
2	tsp.	*Gifford's Italian Spice®*

OMIT black pepper, oregano, basil, onion powder, beef bouillon granules

1. Combine all ingredients.

2. Bring to boil. Then reduce heat and simmer for 20 minutes. Serve.

Yield: 4 C = 8 (½ C) servings

* See "Cooking Methods" section

	RCU	FU	Cal	%Ft	P	F	C	Na
Per Serving	0	0	42	9	2	T	7	202

SPICY TOMATO SAUCE

There are so many uses for this valuable tomato sauce. Use it in soups, stews, and with meats.

1	C	tomato sauce*
1	T	vinegar
1	T	prepared mustard
2	tsp.	Worcestershire sauce
¼	tsp.	onion powder
1	dash	Tabasco sauce
¼	tsp.	garlic powder

Gifford's Alternatives: Add:
1   tsp.   *Gifford's Italian Spice®*

1. Combine and bring to a boil.

2. Turn heat down and simmer about 8 minutes. Serve.

Yield: 1 C = 16 T

* See "Cooking Methods" section

	RCU	FU	Cal	%Ft	P	F	C	Na
Per Tablespoon	0	0	7	T	T	T	1	18

PIZZA SAUCE

Use this in place of Basic Tomato Sauce for added zip.

½	C	onion, chopped
3	T	celery, chopped
3	T	green pepper, chopped
¼	C	mushrooms, chopped
1	C	tomatoes,* stewed
6	T	tomato paste
1	tsp.	oregano
⅛	tsp.	basil
⅛	tsp.	black pepper
¼	tsp.	rosemary

TOMATOES

Gifford's Alternatives: Add:
2   tsp.   Gifford's Italian Spice®
OMIT oregano, basil, black pepper,
rosemary

1. Sauté* onion, celery, green pepper, and mushrooms until tender.

2. Add tomatoes and tomato paste. Stir in seasonings.

3. Cook over low heat for about 30 minutes, stirring occasionally. Use immediately or refrigerate.

Yield: 1½ C = 6 servings

* *See "Cooking Methods" section*

	RCU	FU	Cal	%Ft	P	F	C	Na
Per Serving	0	0	33	5	1	T	7	81

BLACK PEPPER

OLE! OLE! SALAD DRESSING

Spice up a green salad with this unusual dressing.

½	C	low-calorie Italian dressing
½	C	tomato juice
3	T	parsley, chopped
1	tsp.	ground cumin

Gifford's Alternatives: Add: ¾ *tsp.* *Gifford's Mexican Spice®*
OMIT cumin

1. Combine ingredients in a covered jar. Shake well.

2. Store in the refrigerator. Shake before using.

Yield: 1 C = 16 T

	RCU	FU	Cal	%Ft	P	F	C	Na
Per Tablespoon	0	0	5	T	T	T	1	35

SALSA

Use freely with Tortilla Triangles (p. 363) or on Taco Salad (p. 108).

2	large	tomatoes, peeled and chopped
1	med.	onion, chopped
1	4 oz. can	diced green chilies
¼	C	lemon juice
1	clove	garlic, pressed

Gifford's Alternatives: Add:
| 1 | tsp. | *Gifford's Mexican Spice®* |
| ¼ | tsp. | *Gifford's Dessert Spice®* |

HOT PEPPERS

1. Combine all ingredients and store in refrigerator until ready to use.

Yield: 2½ C = 40 T

	RCU	FU	Cal	%Ft	P	F	C	Na
Per Tablespoon	0	0	3	T	T	T	T	T

SAUCY SEAFOOD SAUCE

Great with shrimp!

1	C	tomato juice
1	tsp.	horseradish
1	tsp.	lemon juice
½	tsp.	Worcestershire sauce
½	tsp.	parsley, chopped

Gifford's Alternatives: Add:
1	tsp.	*white grape juice concentrate*

1. Cook tomato juice to half its volume.
   Stir in additional ingredients and serve.

Yield: ½ C = 8 T

	RCU	FU	Cal	%Ft	P	F	C	Na
Per Tablespoon	0	0	6	T	T	T	1	64

TARTAR SAUCE

Serve this with broiled fish.

½	C	low-fat yogurt*
¼	C	carrot, finely chopped
1	T	dill pickle, finely chopped
1	tsp.	onion, finely chopped
1	tsp.	parsley, minced
1	tsp.	pimento
1	tsp.	lemon juice

Gifford's Alternatives: Add:
1	T	*white grape juice concentrate*
½	tsp.	*chicken bouillon granules**
¼	tsp.	*dill weed*

1. Combine all ingredients. Chill and serve.
Yield: 12 T

* *See "Cooking Methods" section*

	RCU	FU	Cal	%Ft	P	F	C	Na
Per Tablespoon	0	0	7	20	T	T	1	60

LIME DRESSING

This is especially nice over a tossed spinach salad. The overall percentage of fat will be reduced when this is combined with a salad.

1	tsp.	sesame seeds
1/2	tsp.	lime peel, grated
4	tsp.	lime juice
1/4	tsp.	dry mustard
2	T	water

1. Combine all ingredients in a small, screw-top jar. Cover and shake well.

2. Chill before serving.
Serves 1

	RCU	FU	Cal	%Ft	P	F	C	Na
Per Serving	0	0	21	42	T	1	2	T

CUCUMBER DIP

Use as a garnish or a dip.

1		cucumber
1	C	low-fat yogurt*
to taste		garlic powder
1	dash	Worcestershire sauce
1	tsp.	lemon juice

Gifford's Alternatives: Add:

	1 1/2	T	apple juice concentrate
	1/4	tsp.	ground cinnamon
if desired:	1/2	tsp.	Gifford's Basic Spice®
	1/8	tsp.	Gifford's Gourmet Spice®

CUCUMBER

1. Scrub cucumber. Grate unpeeled cucumber and drain until almost dry.

2. Combine with other ingredients. Chill before serving.
Yield: 1¾ C = 24 T

* See "Cooking Methods" section

	RCU	FU	Cal	%Ft	P	F	C	Na
Per Serving	0	0	6	25	T	T	T	6

CURRIED VEGETABLE DIP

A different dip for vegetables.

1	lg.	head cauliflower, broken into florets
1		onion, chopped
½	C	water
1	T	cornstarch*
1	C	skim milk*
¼	tsp.	ground ginger
1	tsp.	lemon juice
1	tsp.	curry powder

CAULIFLOWER

Gifford's Alternatives: **Add:**
2   tsp.   *Gifford's Basic Spice®*

1. Bring cauliflower, onion, and water to a boil. Reduce heat and simmer until tender, 15 to 20 minutes.

2. Blend in blender on medium speed until smooth.

3. Whisk cornstarch into milk. Heat until thickened, stirring constantly.

4. Add remaining ingredients.

5. Chill before serving.

Yield: 2 C = 32 T

* See "Cooking Methods" section

Per Serving	RCU	FU	Cal	%Ft	P	F	C	Na
	0	0	12	6	1	T	2	8

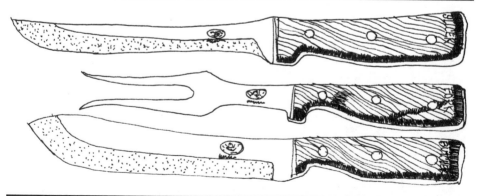

BASIC CREAMY SALAD DRESSING

A whole wardrobe of salad dressings!

1	C	low-fat cottage cheese*
1/3	C	buttermilk*
1	tsp.	lemon juice

1. Blend all ingredients in a blender until smooth and creamy. Chill before serving.

Yield: 1⅓ C = 21 T

* See "Cooking Methods" section

	RCU	FU	Cal	%Ft	P	F	C	Na
Per Tablespoon	0	0	11	15	1	T	T	28

VARIATION: CREAMY FRENCH

1	tsp.	paprika	1/4	tsp.	garlic powder
1	tsp.	dry mustard	1/2	C	tomato juice*
1	tsp.	Worcestershire sauce	1	recipe	basic dressing
1/4	tsp.	onion powder			

Gifford's Alternatives:	*Add:*	2	*T*	*tomato purée*
		2	*T*	*peach juice concentrate*
		1/2	*tsp.*	*Gifford's Basic Spice®*
		1	*pinch*	*Gifford's Dessert Spice®*

1. Combine all ingredients. Chill before serving.

* See "Cooking Methods" section

	RCU	FU	Cal	%Ft	P	F	C	Na
Per Tablespoon	0	0	12	14	1	T	T	41

31/FABULOUS FLAVORS

VARIATION: CREAMY ITALIAN

¼	tsp.	oregano	¼	tsp.	onion powder
¼	tsp.	garlic powder	1	recipe	basic dressing

Gifford's Alternatives: **Add:**

			½	tsp.	*lime juice*
			1	T	*white grape juice concentrate**
		if desired:	1	tsp	*Gifford's Italian Spice®*
					OMIT oregano, garlic, onion powder

*Unsweetened pear juice is a good substitute for white grape juice, if not available.

1. Combine all ingredients. Chill before serving.

	RCU	FU	Cal	%Ft	P	F	C	Na
Per Tablespoon	0	0	11	15	1	T	T	28

VARIATION: HORSERADISH

1	T	grated horseradish	1	recipe	basic dressing

Gifford's Alternatives: **Add:**

	1	T	*Butter Buds® or Molly McButter®*
	1	T	*peach juice concentrate*
	½	tsp.	*lime juice*
	1	pinch	*Gifford's Dessert Spice®*

1. Combine all ingredients. Chill before serving.

	RCU	FU	Cal	%Ft	P	F	C	Na
Per Tablespoon	0	0	11	14	1	T	T	29

VARIATION: THOUSAND ISLAND

2	T	chili sauce
to taste		dry mustard
1	recipe	basic dressing

Gifford's Alternatives: Add:

	1	tsp.	*prepared mustard*
	1	T	*dill pickle, finely chopped*
	¼	tsp.	*celery seed, ground*
	1	T	*apple juice concentrate*
if desired:	1	tsp.	*Gifford's Basic Spice®*

1. Combine all ingredients. Chill before serving.

	RCU	FU	Cal	%Ft	P	F	C	Na
Per Tablespoon	0	0	12	13	1	T	T	37

VARIATION: DILL

1	tsp.	dried dill		1	recipe	basic dressing

Gifford's Alternatives:	*Add:*	2	*tsp.*	*dill pickle juice*
		½	*tsp.*	*chicken bouillon granules**
		⅛	*tsp.*	*Gifford's Gourmet Spice®*

1. Combine all ingredients. Chill before serving.

*See "Cooking Methods" section

	RCU	FU	Cal	%Ft	P	F	C	Na
Per Tablespoon	0	0	11	15	1	T	T	28

HOT DILL SAUCE

This sauce is good served on many kinds of vegetables.

1	C	water
⅓	C	nonfat dry milk*
3	T	cornstarch*
1	T	prepared mustard
¼	tsp.	dill seed

1. Combine all ingredients. Beat with an electric mixer.

2. Cook over medium heat, stirring constantly, until thickened. Serve hot.

Serves 4

*See "Cooking Methods" section

	RCU	FU	Cal	%Ft	P	F	C	Na
Per Serving	0	0	48	14	3	1	8	75

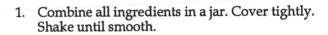
LOW-FAT RANCH DRESSING

This will keep in the refrigerator for a week, if tightly covered.

1	C	buttermilk*
1	T	prepared mustard
1	tsp.	minced onion
⅛	tsp.	dried dill
1	tsp.	dried parsley
½	tsp.	garlic powder
¼	tsp.	black pepper
½	C	low-fat yogurt*

1. Combine all ingredients in a jar. Cover tightly. Shake until smooth.

2. Chill. Shake well before serving.

Yield: 1½ C = 24 T

* *See "Cooking Methods" section*

	RCU	FU	Cal	%Ft	P	F	C	Na
Per Tablespoon	0	0	7	11	T	T	T	23

SIMPLE SWEET-AND-SOUR SAUCE

Delicious with Oriental dishes.

5	T	lemon juice
¾	C	water
1	T	soy sauce
1	clove	garlic, in pieces
1	tsp.	sugar*
1	T	pimento, chopped

Gifford's Alternatives: Add:

½	tsp.	*Gifford's Chinese Spice®*
¼	tsp.	*Gifford's Dessert Spice®*

1. Combine all ingredients and cook for 10 minutes, uncovered.

2. Discard garlic. Store in refrigerator until served.

Yield: 1 C = 16 T

*See "Cooking Methods" section

	RCU	FU	Cal	%Ft	P	F	C	Na
Per Tablespoon	0	0	4	3	T	T	T	83

LOW-FAT SANDWICH SPREAD

There are many uses for this tasty spread. Use it in place of mayonnaise on sandwiches and in salads.

1	T	cornstarch*
2	tsp.	dry mustard
1	C	water
2		egg whites
4	T	lemon juice
2	T	white vinegar
1	T	sugar*

1. Mix cornstarch and dry mustard in the top of a double boiler.

2. Slowly add water and egg whites that have been lightly beaten together. Stir constantly.

3. Cook over simmering water for 5 minutes, stirring constantly.

4. Slowly stir in lemon juice and vinegar. Cook for another 10 minutes.

5. Remove from heat. Add sugar and blend well.

6. Cool and store in refrigerator.

Yield: 1 ½ C = 24 T

* See "Cooking Methods" section

	RCU	FU	Cal	%Ft	P	F	C	Na
Per Tablespoon	0	0	5	7	T	T	1	3

35/FABULOUS FLAVORS

CHEESE SAUCE STAND-IN

This is an acceptable cheese sauce substitute, if used sparingly.

½	C	nonfat milk powder	1	dash	cayenne
1	C	skim milk*	1	dash	dry mustard
2	T	sharp cheddar cheese, grated			

Gifford's Alternatives: Add:

2	tsp.	*Butter Buds® Sprinkles*
1	tsp.	*onion powder*
½	tsp.	*ground turmeric*
½	tsp.	*chicken bouillon granules**

1. Shake milk powder and skim milk together in a tightly covered jar until smooth.

2. Pour into saucepan and heat.

3. Add cheese. Stir until melted.

4. Remove from heat. Add cayenne and mustard to heighten the cheese flavor. Serve warm.

Yield: 1 C = 16 T

* See "Cooking Methods" section

	RCU	FU	Cal	%Ft	P	F	C	Na
Per Tablespoon	0	0	10	24	T	T	1	14

RUSSIAN DRESSING

Luscious!

2	small	carrots, thinly sliced
½	C	water
½	med.	tomato
2	T	lemon juice
½	C	vinegar
¼	C	onion, finely chopped
1	tsp.	paprika

Gifford's Alternatives: Add:

3	T	*tomato purée*
2	T	*pear juice concentrate*

1	tsp.	orange flavor extract
2	tsp.	Butter Buds® Sprinkles
1	tsp.	chicken bouillon granules*

1. Simmer carrots in water until tender.

2. Purée tomato in blender or food processor. Add cooked carrots and water, and blend with remaining ingredients until smooth. Chill before serving.

Yield: 2 C = 16 T

*See "Cooking Methods" Section

	RCU	FU	Cal	%Ft	P	F	C	Na
Per Tablespoon	0	0	8	T	T	T	1	5

LOW-CALORIE ITALIAN DRESSING

There are so many places this low-calorie dressing will perk up the taste besides salads. Spread it on chicken before barbecuing for a real treat.

½	C	red wine vinegar
½	tsp.	fruit juice concentrate*
½	tsp.	oregano
¼	tsp.	basil
¼	tsp.	tarragon
½	tsp.	dry mustard
¼	tsp.	black pepper
½	tsp.	garlic, minced
¾	tsp.	Worcestershire sauce
½	C	vinegar

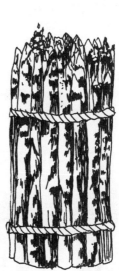

1. Combine all ingredients in blender and blend at top speed for 2 minutes. Chill before serving.

Yield: 1 C = 16 T

* See "Cooking Methods" section

	RCU	FU	Cal	%Ft	P	F	C	Na
Per Tablespoon	0	0	1	T	T	T	0	3

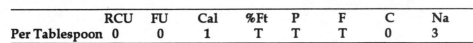

MINUTE MAGIC SAUCE

It's as good as magic! Use this to replace sour cream, as a creamy salad dressing base, a dip, or a spread.

2	C	low-fat cottage cheese*
1	T	lemon juice
1/3	C	skim milk*

1. Blend all ingredients until creamy. Chill before serving.

Yield: 2 C = 32 T

* See "Cooking Methods" section

	RCU	FU	Cal	%Ft	P	F	C	Na
Per Tablespoon	0	0	7	T	1	T	T	22

VARIATION: ONION

2	tsp.	dry onion soup mix
1	tsp.	green onion, finely chopped
1	C	basic recipe

1. Mix and chill before serving.

	RCU	FU	Cal	%Ft	P	F	C	Na
Per Tablespoon	0	0	7	T	1	T	T	22

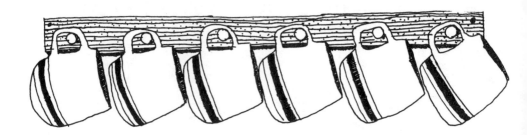

BASIC LOW-FAT WHITE SAUCE

You may sprinkle Butter Buds® or butter flavoring into this for a more buttery taste.

1	T	cornstarch*
1	C	skim milk*
to taste		seasoning without salt*

1. Whisk cornstarch into milk.

2. Heat until mixture becomes thickened, stirring constantly.

3. Season, if desired.

4. For a thicker white sauce, use 2 tablespoons cornstarch. (This will increase calories to 145 per cup and percentage of fat to 12%.)

5. HERB SAUCE: Add chives, basil, dill, thyme, mint, parsley, or rosemary.

6. CURRY SAUCE: Add 1 teaspoon curry powder.

7. HORSERADISH SAUCE: Add 1 tablespoon horseradish.

8. MUSTARD SAUCE: Add 1 tablespoon prepared mustard.

Yield: 1 C

See "Cooking Methods" section

	RCU	FU	Cal	%Ft	P	F	C	Na
Per Cup	0	0	115	8	10	1	20	123

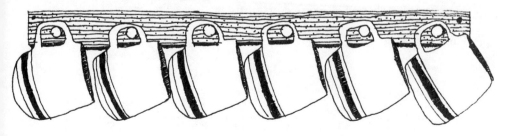

SURPRISE MUSTARD DRESSING

Toss this with raw cabbage or potato salad. It is also good as a vegetable dip.

1	C	low-fat cottage cheese*
1	tsp.	vinegar
2	tsp.	prepared mustard
4	T	skim milk

1. Blend in blender until smooth and creamy, about 3 minutes. Chill before serving.

Yield: 1 C = 16 T

* See "Cooking Methods" section

	RCU	FU	Cal	%Ft	P	F	C	Na
Per Tablespoon	0	0	14	T	3	T	T	51

SIMPLE SOUR CREAM SUBSTITUTE

Another sour cream substitute can be made by pouring homemade yogurt into a muslin-lined strainer and allowing it to drain at room temperature for several hours.

1	T	cornstarch*
½	C	skim milk*
½	C	low-fat yogurt*

1. Whisk cornstarch into milk and yogurt.

2. Heat until thickened, stirring constantly.

3. Chill before serving.

Yield: 1 C = 16 T

* See "Cooking Methods" section

	RCU	FU	Cal	%Ft	P	F	C	Na
Per Tablespoon	0	0	9	20	T	T	1	8

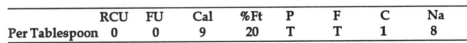

"WHAT SHALL I HAVE FOR BREAKFAST?"

"Nothing is worth more than this day."

--Johann W. Goethe

"WHAT SHALL I HAVE FOR BREAKFAST?"

Breakfast is an important meal. Since your system slowed down while you were asleep, breakfast will give your body fuel to get started for the day. Many people skip breakfast and say that they just aren't hungry. Studies have shown that obese people have many eating habits in common, one of which is skipping breakfast.

A study was done with a group of rats that shows why it is important to eat three meals a day and refrain from long periods of hunger. The rats were allowed to eat as much food as they wanted, whenever they were hungry. As soon as the amount of food they regularly ate each day had been established, the group was divided in half. The first group maintained the same pattern, but the second group was only allowed to eat for 30 minutes a day. Even though the second group was given exactly the same type and amount of food as the first group, they became fatter. Why? They were essentially fasting for 23½ hours a day. That long period of hunger caused their bodies to raise their setpoint and conserve fat.

It is important to eat low-fat, high-fiber foods so that you can feel full without consuming too many calories. The possibilities are endless. Experiment with the various whole-grain hot cereals and match them up with your favorite fruits for one of the best breakfasts available. There are even several commercial cold cereals that are low in fat and sugar and are perfectly acceptable for breakfast. See page 410 to learn how to calculate the percentage of fat and the refined carbohydrate units from the information on the package.

Gifford's Dessert Spice® is a wonderful topper for all cereals. Also peach juice concentrate is a nice substitute for sugar or artificial sweeteners. Butter Buds® Sprinkles or Molly McButter® adds a nice flavor, as well as Schilling® Orange Peel. A drop or two of vanilla extract, banana extract, or black walnut extract is recommended.

Combine any of the pancake toppings with the various pancake recipes. Your favorite fresh fruit with yogurt and any of the tasty breads or rolls in The Bread Spread (p. 297) make a super breakfast. Or for variety, try an omelet with whole wheat bread or potatoes.

They all sound tempting, don't they? So give them a try and learn to eat breakfast. Before long you'll be saying with a smile, "What shall I have for breakfast?"

GRANOLA

This is only one of more than 200 no-sugar, low-fat recipes in Desserts to Lower Your Fat Thermostat *by Barbara Higa.*

4	C	rolled oats
4	C	rolled wheat
1	C	wheat germ
1	C	unroasted sunflower seeds, optional
¾	C	frozen unsweetened apple juice concentrate*, thawed
2	tsp.	vanilla
¾	C	chopped dates
¾	C	raisins
¾	C	dried apples, cut into bite-sized pieces
1-2	C	slivered almonds, optional

1. Mix together oats, rolled wheat, and wheat germ. Add nuts, if desired.

2. Combine apple juice concentrate and vanilla.

3. Blend apple juice mixture into oats mixture and put into a 9" x 13" cake pan.

4. Bake at 275° for 1 hour.

5. After taking granola out of the oven, add the dried apples, dates, and raisins.

6. Use as a cold cereal or mix with nonfat plain yogurt and fruit for a delicious breakfast. This recipe also makes a great fruit cobbler topping.

Yield: 16 (¾-cup) servings

* See "Cooking Methods" section

	RCU	FU	Cal	%Ft	P	F	C	Na
Per Serving	0	0	263	9	8	3	55	9

CRACKED WHEAT CEREAL

A superior breakfast!

1	C	cracked wheat
3	C	boiling water
1/8	tsp.	maple flavoring

Method 1: Cook wheat and water in saucepan for 30 minutes, stirring frequently.

Method 2: Cook in a double boiler for about 1 hour.

Before serving, add maple flavoring and desired fruit. Top with skim milk.

Yield: 2 C = Serves 4

	RCU	FU	Cal	%Ft	P	F	C	Na
Per Serving	0	0	88	5	4	1	19	2

WHOLE KERNEL CEREALS

Each of these makes an especially nourishing breakfast.

| 1 | C | whole wheat |
| 2 | C | water |

Yield: 2 C = 4 servings

	RCU	FU	Cal	%Ft	P	F	C	Na
Per Serving	0	0	151	3	5	1	32	1

| 1 | C | rolled oats |
| 2 | C | water |

Yield: 2 C = 4 servings

	RCU	FU	Cal	%Ft	P	F	C	Na
Per Serving	0	0	83	16	4	2	14	9

| 1 | C | brown rice |
| 2 | C | water |

Yield: 2 C = 4 servings

	RCU	FU	Cal	%Ft	P	F	C	Na
Per Serving	0	0	167	4	4	1	36	5

This beautiful array of fresh fruits provides us with nutritious snacks and salads.

| 1 | C | corn meal |
| 3 | C | water |

Yield: 3 C = 6 servings

	RCU	FU	Cal	%Ft	P	F	C	Na
Per Serving	1	0	77	7	2	1	15	1

| 1 | C | barley |
| 2 | C | water |

Yield: 2 C = 4 servings

	RCU	FU	Cal	%Ft	P	F	C	Na
Per Serving	0	0	175	2	4	1	39	3

ORANGES

Double Boiler Method:

1. Soak the wheat for 24 hours, drain. The rest of the grains do not need to be soaked.

2. Place soaked wheat or other grain in top of double boiler with ½-inch water. Put kettle over boiling water and cook until water in top of double boiler is boiling and producing steam. Reduce heat to simmer and cook until tender, for 30 to 60 minutes; drain off water. Rolled oats will cook in 5 minutes.

3. Serve hot with skim milk.

4. Store in covered container in refrigerator. Can be reheated in microwave or on the stove with a small amount of water and then drained.

Popcorn, Crunchy Munchies (p. 374) and a Frozen Fruit Shake (p. 371) all make great snacks.

SWISS FRUIT CEREAL

Rosette Krahenbuhl

This is known as "Muesli" in Switzerland. It also makes a great snack.

2	C	quick rolled oats, raw
1	T	sugar* or honey*, optional
1	C	skim milk*

1. Mix all ingredients together.

2. Let mixture stand until oatmeal absorbs the milk. DO NOT COOK.

3. Add any fruits in season, such as grated apples, sliced bananas, a few raisins, crushed pineapple, sliced peaches, mandarin oranges, grapes, applesauce, or berries. Serve.

Yield: 3 C = 4 servings

* See "Cooking Methods" section

	RCU	FU	Cal	%Ft	P	F	C	Na
Per Serving	1	0	198	14	10	3	30	47

CRUNCHY WHEAT CEREAL

This cereal is similar to grape-nuts.

3½	C	whole wheat flour
1	C	buttermilk*
½	tsp.	salt
½	C	molasses
1	tsp.	baking soda
2	tsp.	baking powder
¼	C	wheat germ
2	T	malted milk powder, optional

1. Combine all ingredients and stir well.

2. Press onto a nonstick* baking sheet to about ½-inch thickness. It will not fill the pan.

3. Bake at 350° for 30 to 35 minutes, until firm. Turn off oven.

4. Cut into 1-inch by 2-inch strips. Turn them over and allow them to dry out in the turned off oven.

5. Grind dried strips in a food grinder using a course disk. Store in an airtight container until served.

Serves 18

* See "Cooking Methods" section

	RCU	FU	Cal	%Ft	P	F	C	Na
Per Serving	1	0	103	5	3	1	22	133

FANTASTIC FRUIT SAUCE

Replace orange juice with one cup of your favorite juice for a delicious change.

2	T	cornstarch*
1	C	water
1	C	orange juice
½	tsp.	lemon juice
to taste		nutmeg
to taste		artificial sweetener*, optional

1. Whisk cornstarch into water, orange juice, and lemon juice.

2. Heat until thickened, stirring constantly.

3. Add nutmeg and sweetener, if desired.

4. Serve hot over whole wheat pancakes, or cool and serve at room temperature with fresh fruit.

5. Store in refrigerator.

Yield: 4 C = 6 servings

* See "Cooking Methods" section

	RCU	FU	Cal	%Ft	P	F	C	Na
Per Serving	0	0	30	10	1	T	7	1

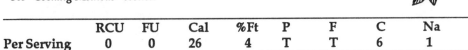
FRUIT AND SPICE AND EVERYTHING NICE

A natural fruit topping for pancakes—wonderful!

1	16 oz. can	peach slices, diet-pack	¾	C	strawberries, halved
2	tsp.	cornstarch*	¼	tsp.	cinnamon
2	T	water	⅛	tsp.	allspice

Gifford's Alternatives: Add:
| 1 | tsp. | **Gifford's Dessert Spice®** |

OMIT cinnamon, allspice

1. Drain peaches. Reserve juice. Whisk cornstarch into water. Add reserved juice and heat until thickened.

2. Stir in peaches, strawberries, cinnamon, and allspice. Heat thoroughly and serve.

3. Store in refrigerator. This can be served either hot or cold.

Serves 8

* See "Cooking Methods" section

	RCU	FU	Cal	%Ft	P	F	C	Na
Per Serving	0	0	26	4	T	T	6	1

BANANA TOPPING

Scrumptious over pancakes.

3	T	orange juice concentrate
2		bananas, sliced very thin
3	T	water

1. Simmer 2 to 3 minutes. Serve.

Serves 4

	RCU	FU	Cal	%Ft	P	F	C	Na
Per Serving	0	0	93	T	1	T	22	1

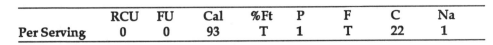

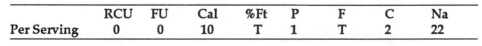

APPLE OR PEAR BUTTER

Always keep a jar of this in your refrigerator to use at a moment's notice.

4	qts.	fruit, peeled and cored
1/4	C	apple juice
1	tsp.	cinnamon
1/2	tsp.	nutmeg
1/2	tsp.	allspice or cloves

Gifford's Alternatives: Add:

3	T	*Butter Buds® Sprinkles*
1	T	*Gifford's Dessert Spice®*
		OMIT all other spices

1. Put fruit into large pan. Add apple juice. Simmer until soft.

2. Mash with potato masher or with electric mixer. Add the spices. Serve over pancakes or on whole wheat toast.

Yield: 16 C = 64 servings

	RCU	FU	Cal	%Ft	P	F	C	Na
Per Serving	0	0	16	9	T	T	4	T

CINNAMON SPREAD

Spread on French toast, pancakes, or whole wheat toast.

1	C	low-fat cottage cheese*
1	tsp.	lemon juice
2	T	skim milk*
1	tsp.	cinnamon
1	T	sugar*

1. Blend all ingredients together until creamy.

2. Chill before serving.

Yield: 1 C = 16 T

* See "Cooking Methods" section

	RCU	FU	Cal	%Ft	P	F	C	Na
Per Serving	0	0	10	T	1	T	2	22

TUTTI FRUTTI TOPPING

This is a delicious snack with a little cereal sprinkled in it.

2	C	applesauce
½	C	crushed pineapple, drained
¼	C	raisins
½	tsp.	cinnamon
12	T	low-fat yogurt*

Gifford's Alternatives: Add:
1	med.	red delicious apple, cored, diced
2	T	Butter Buds® Sprinkles
½	tsp.	vanilla extract
1	tsp.	Gifford's Dessert Spice®
		OMIT cinnamon

1. Combine all ingredients except yogurt in a bowl. Chill for 4 hours. Use this as a topping for pancakes. Garnish with 1 tablespoon yogurt.

Serves 12

* See "Cooking Methods" section

	RCU	FU	Cal	%Ft	P	F	C	Na
Per Serving	0	0	40	5	T	T	8	10

FRESH FRUIT TOPPING

There are so many places a low-calorie topping like this can be used. Try it over pancakes, with yogurt, or in a Grape-Nuts Pie Shell (p. 350).

2	C	fresh fruit: strawberries OR raspberries OR peaches OR other fruit
2	T	cornstarch*
½	C	water

Gifford's Alternatives: Sprinkle: Gifford's Dessert Spice®

1. Chop fruit into large pieces.

2. Whisk cornstarch into cool water and bring to a boil.

3. Add 1 cup fruit and bring to a boil again.

4. Immediately remove from heat and add remaining fruit. Do not cook. Serve.

Yield: 2 ½ C = 10 servings

* See "Cooking Methods" section

	RCU	FU	Cal	%Ft	P	F	C	Na
Per Serving	0	0	20	18	T	T	5	T

BLINTZES

These light, cottage cheese pancakes make a fancy breakfast for special occasions.

3		egg whites
1		egg yolk
1	C	dry-curd cottage cheese* OR
1	C	low-fat cottage cheese,* rinsed
⅓	C	skim milk*
¼	C	whole wheat flour
1	tsp.	vanilla

1. Beat egg whites until peaks fold over. Set aside.

2. In another bowl, beat the egg yolk. Add cottage cheese and beat until smooth.

3. Blend in milk, flour, and vanilla.
4. Fold in egg whites and let batter stand for 5 minutes.

5. Heat nonstick* griddle or frying pan. Use ¼ cup batter per blintz and cook until top is bubbly. Turn once.

6. Serve immediately with yogurt and fresh fruit.
Yield: 8 blintzes

* See "Cooking Methods" section

	RCU	FU	Cal	%Ft	P	F	C	Na
Per Serving	0	0	47	19	7	1	4	17

WHOLE WHEAT PANCAKES

Edward Parent

Try a sprinkle of shredded zucchini or sliced bananas in these while they are cooking.

3	C	whole wheat flour
½	C	dry buttermilk powder*
½	tsp.	baking soda
2	tsp.	baking powder
2 ¾	C	skim milk*
4	tsp.	oil*
3		egg whites

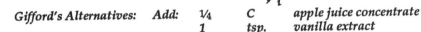

Gifford's Alternatives: **Add:**

¼	C	apple juice concentrate
1	tsp.	vanilla extract

1. Mix all ingredients together until smooth. Ladle pancake batter onto medium to hot griddle in ¼ cup measurements. Turn when bubbles form on pancake. Serve.

2. Use this recipe for waffle batter by adjusting the consistency with water or whole wheat flour. Pour it into nonstick* waffle iron. Cook, and serve.

Yield: 24 pancakes. 6 C batter = ¼ C per pancake

* See "Cooking Methods" section

	RCU	FU	Cal	%Ft	P	F	C	Na
Per Serving	0	0	69	14	4	1	11	84

FAVORITE BUCKWHEAT PANCAKES

BUCK-EYE

These are so light and fluffy they are worth waiting for.

2	T	brown sugar*	2	C	buckwheat flour
2	C	warm water	½	C	wheat germ
1	T	dry yeast	1	C	skim milk*
½	C	whole wheat flour			

1. Dissolve sugar in warm water. Sprinkle yeast over the top. Set aside for 10 minutes.

2. Combine flours and wheat germ. Add to yeast. Stir in milk and beat until smooth. Cover and let rise for 1 hour.

3. Stir down and cook on a nonstick* griddle. Serve.

Yield: 24 pancakes

* See "Cooking Methods" section

	RCU	FU	Cal	%Ft	P	F	C	Na
Per Serving	0	0	51	9	3	1	10	6

SOURDOUGH PANCAKES

See page 340 to learn how to make a sourdough starter.

½	C	sourdough starter
1	C	evaporated skim milk*
1	C	water
2	C	whole wheat flour
2		egg whites
1	T	sugar*
1	tsp.	baking soda

1. Combine sourdough starter, evaporated skim milk, water, and whole wheat flour in a bowl. Let sit overnight at room temperature.

2. In the morning, add egg whites, sugar, and soda.

3. Cook on nonstick* griddle or pan. Serve.

Yield: 12 6-inch pancakes

* See "Cooking Methods" section

	RCU	FU	Cal	%Ft	P	F	C	Na
Per Serving	0	0	86	3	5	T	17	33

APPLESAUCE TOPPING

Margaret Stevenson

Delicious over whole wheat pancakes.

1	qt.	sugar-free applesauce
½	6 oz. can	frozen orange juice concentrate
1	tsp.	vanilla
1	tsp.	orange extract
to taste		cinnamon and nutmeg

Gifford's Alternatives: Add: *to taste*   *Gifford's Dessert Spice®*

1. Combine all ingredients. Store in refrigerator until served.

Yield: 8 (½ cup) servings

	RCU	FU	Cal	%Ft	P	F	C	Na
Per Serving	1	0	46	T	T	T	11	1

FABULOUS FRUIT DRINK

A wild breakfast for those on the go! A great dessert, too.

1		peach, pitted and peeled
1	C	apple juice
1		banana, very ripe
1		orange, peeled
3		ice cubes

1. Combine all ingredients in a blender until smooth. Enjoy!

Serves 2

	RCU	FU	Cal	%Ft	P	F	C	Na
Per Serving	1	0	174	T	2	T	43	3

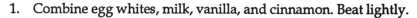

CINNAMON FRENCH TOAST

This is so tasty that you may not want a topping.

2		egg whites
2	T	skim milk*
1/4	tsp.	vanilla extract
1/8	tsp.	cinnamon
2	slices	day-old whole wheat bread

1. Combine egg whites, milk, vanilla, and cinnamon. Beat lightly.

2. Heat nonstick* griddle until hot (400°).

3. Dip bread slices in the egg white mixture and cook on both sides until golden brown and crisp.

4. Serve with applesauce or other fruit topping.

Serves 2

* See "Cooking Methods" section

	RCU	FU	Cal	%Ft	P	F	C	Na
Per Serving	0	0	80	T	6	T	12	178

APPLESAUCE CINNAMON TOAST

You will reduce RCUs and calories if you use unsweetened applesauce.

1	C	applesauce
to taste		cinnamon
4	slices	whole wheat bread

1. Spread applesauce and a sprinkle of cinnamon on each slice of bread. Toast under the broiler. Serve.

Serves 4

	RCU	FU	Cal	%Ft	P	F	C	Na
Per Serving	1	0	115	T	3	T	24	143

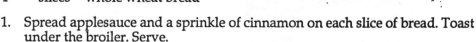

VEGETABLE OMELET

You can enjoy an occasional omelet if you omit two egg yolks.

2		egg whites	2	T	onions, chopped
1		egg	2	T	green pepper, chopped
1	T	cold water	½		tomato, chopped
½	C	bean sprouts	1	slice	whole wheat toast
2	T	mushrooms, sliced			

Gifford's Alternatives: Add: **1** *tsp.* ***Gifford's Basic Spice®***

1. Whisk egg whites, egg, and water together until foamy.

2. Heat a nonstick* omelet pan very hot (water drops will pop out of pan when sprinkled over it).

3. Spray with vegetable cooking spray. Pour in eggs and tilt pan so that the bottom is covered evenly. Use a nonscratch pancake turner to pull the edge of the omelet into the center and tilt pan so that the uncooked egg flows onto the pan. Repeat all around the omelet until the eggs are cooked.

4. Fill the left side of the omelet with chopped vegetables. Lift the right side of the omelet carefully with the pancake turner so that it folds the omelet in half.

5. Carefully slide the omelet onto a plate and serve with a slice of whole wheat toast.

Yield: 1 omelet

* See "Cooking Methods" section

	RCU	FU	Cal	%Ft	P	F	C	Na
Per Serving	0	1	257	21	22	6	28	262

"SOUP'S ON!"

*"When love and skill work together,
expect a masterpiece."*

--John Ruskin

"SOUP'S ON!"

Hmmmm! You'll love everything about these soups. Your mouth will water as you catch the aroma of a robust bean soup or the delicate fragrance of gazpacho. You'll delight in the colorful collections of yellow corn, bright carrots, and green beans with rice or potatoes. And the flavorful combination of homemade soup and warm bread will satisfy your palate and fill you up. No matter how you look at it, soups should become a mainstay in your low-fat diet. They make nutritious, filling, inexpensive, convenient, and memorable meals for your family.

Nutrition comes naturally to soups since they are made from the best of foods: vegetables, grains, beans, milks, and meats. For a main meal, soup should contain some basic staple foods such as potatoes, rice, barley, beans, peas, lentils, or even tomatoes. They can be served meatless or with a small amount of meat. They can be kept low-fat by skimming the fat off of homemade stock, by trimming all visible fat off meats, and by using skim milk.

Soups are a great friend to your pocketbook, too. Soup fixings are inexpensive and are a smart, natural way to use up leftovers. Save the water from cooked vegetables (including canned, fresh, and frozen vegetables) to use as stock in your next soup. This adds a great deal of variety to the flavor and will improve the nutritional content. Celery tops, outer salad green leaves, vegetables that have lost their freshness, and most leftovers can be added to your soups. It won't be long until you'll be creating your own family favorites. The possibilities are endless, and your homemade soups will be far more nutritious and tasty than soups you buy at the store.

Convenience is soup's middle name. Soup can be made days ahead and be reheated to be served with a salad or bread for a delightfully easy dinner. Or double your recipe and freeze part of it in a foil-lined loaf pan. After it is frozen, dump it out of the pan, wrap it in the foil and replace it in your freezer. It will be waiting for you when you need a quick meal. Simply peel off the foil, place it in a bowl, and cook it in your microwave or place it in a pan and heat it on your stove top.

Microwave ovens add to the convenience of meal preparation for our busy lives. Soupmaking is no exception. Onions and other vegetables can be sautéed without oil in a microwave oven by simply cooking them in a few tablespoons of water. Meats can be cooked and drained of fats before adding them to soups. Potatoes, carrots, and other slow-cooking vegetables can be cooked quickly in the microwave and then added to your soup.

Soups can be taken conveniently to work in a thermos for a savory, low-fat lunch. Eat them with a piece of fruit and homemade bread, and you'll have plenty of energy to keep you going through the rest of the day.

So enjoy yourself. Meals built around a soup tureen filled with steaming soup on a snowy day or a cool summer soup after a swim are full of fun, nutrition, and memories. So what are you waiting for? "Soup's on!"

Additional Soup Recipes, see:
   "To Meat or Not To Meat?" on page 133
   The Bean Bag on page 251
   The Sweep of the Scythe on page 269
   Bizarre Bazaar on page 375

CREATE-YOUR-OWN SOUP STOCK

Soup stocks can be homemade, canned, made from bouillon cubes, or be a combination of simple, but flavorful ingredients. The choice is yours. Take a look at the following examples and use the one that is most convenient for you: Homemade Stock, Magic Tomato Bouillon, Tomato Onion Soup Base, or Vegetable Cocktail Bouillon.

Remember that soup stocks can be thickened with either cornstarch or flour. One cup of liquid to 1 tablespoon of thickening is a good combination. Cornstarch must be mixed with cold or cool liquids, but flour can be mixed with water and poured into hot liquids.

HOMEMADE STOCK

Keep this frozen in small quantities to use in place of oil, to sauté onions, or to use in your wok.

Homemade beef or chicken stock can be made by cooking chicken parts (for chicken stock) or beef bones (for beef stock) in about 2 quarts of water, so that meat is covered. Onions or celery can be added to the meat as it cooks. Bring to a boil, then simmer for 2 to 3 hours.

Remove from heat, strain, and cool. Skim remaining fat from top of cooled stock. The stock is now ready to use in soups or stews. Store in refrigerator or freezer.

MAGIC TOMATO BOUILLON

This can be a warm, soothing drink, a light soup, or a base for a robust stew.

3	C	tomato juice*
1	10 ½ oz. can	condensed beef broth,* diluted
1	T	lemon juice
1	tsp.	Worcestershire sauce
¼	tsp.	basil
¼	tsp.	thyme

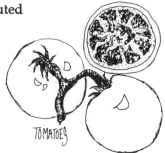

TOMATOES

Gifford's Alternatives: Add:
to taste   *Gifford's Basic Spice®*
                OMIT basil and thyme

1. Combine all ingredients in saucepan and bring to a boil. Simmer, covered, 5 minutes.

2. Use as a soup base, or ladle into bowls and garnish with a thin lemon slice. Serve hot.

Serves 6

* See "Cooking Methods" section

	RCU	FU	Cal	%Ft	P	F	C	Na
Per Serving	0	0	30	T	2	T	6	384

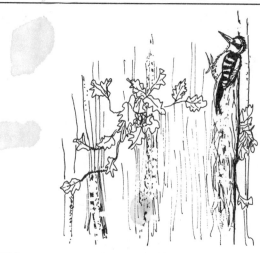

TOMATO ONION SOUP BASE

You can use this in place of recipes calling for beef stock.

1	T	cornstarch*
3	C	water
1	pkg	dry onion soup
1	C	tomato sauce*

1. Whisk cornstarch into water until smooth. Heat until thick and shiny.

2. Add dry onion soup and tomato sauce.

3. Add your favorite vegetables or leftovers. Heat thoroughly. Serve.

Serves 6

* See "Cooking Methods" section

	RCU	FU	Cal	%Ft	P	F	C	Na
Per Serving	0	0	24	9	1	T	5	48

VEGETABLE COCKTAIL BOUILLON

Use this as a soothing drink or a soup stock.

1	10 oz. can	beef broth*
1	soup can	water
1	C	low-sodium vegetable juice*

Gifford's Alternatives: Add:
to taste   Gifford's Basic Spice®

1. Combine all ingredients. Simmer for 5 minutes. Serve hot.

Serves 4

* See "Cooking Methods" section

	RCU	FU	Cal	%Ft	P	F	C	Na
Per Serving	0	0	21	2	2	T	3	578

CREAMY BEAN SOUP

Corn bread is the perfect partner for this creamy soup.

2	C	navy beans*, dried
4	oz.	lean ham, cooked and cubed
½	C	mashed potatoes
3	C	celery, chopped
4	med.	onions, chopped
3	T	fresh parsley, chopped
1	clove	garlic, minced
½	C	skim milk*
½	C	carrots, diced
to taste		black pepper

Gifford's Alternatives: Add: ¼   C   *catsup*
    2   T   *apple juice concentrate*
    if desired: 1   tsp.   *Gifford's Basic Spice®*

1. Cover beans with water and soak overnight in soup pot. Drain.

2. Add ham. Cover with water again and bring to a boil. Reduce heat and simmer 1 hour.

3. Add remaining ingredients. Simmer 1 more hour or until beans are tender. Serve hot.

Serves 12

* *See "Cooking Methods" section.*

	RCU	FU	Cal	%Ft	P	F	C	Na
Per Serving	0	0	170	12	5	2	12	75

TACO BEAN SOUP

Rene Mortensen

Add to the "south-of-the-border" taste by serving Tortilla Triangles (p. 363).

6	C	pinto beans,* cooked
1		onion, chopped
2	cloves	garlic, chopped
¼	tsp.	black pepper
½	tsp.	cumin seed

1	4 oz. can	taco sauce
1	4 oz. can	green chilies, diced
2	C	tomatoes,* stewed

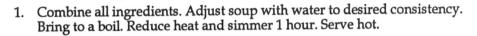

Gifford's Alternatives: Add:
| 1 | tsp. | Gifford's Mexican Spice® |
| | | OMIT cumin |

1. Combine all ingredients. Adjust soup with water to desired consistency. Bring to a boil. Reduce heat and simmer 1 hour. Serve hot.

Serves 12

* See "Cooking Methods" section

	RCU	FU	Cal	%Ft	P	F	C	Na
Per Serving	0	0	149	4	8	T	27	103

SIMPLE BLACK BEAN SOUP

Quick and convenient.

1	16 oz. can	black beans*
1	C	beef broth
2	tsp.	onion, minced
1	tsp.	lemon juice
½	tsp.	salt

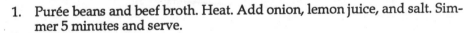

Gifford's Alternatives: Add:
¼	tsp.	ground sage
⅛	tsp.	ground caraway
1	tsp.	Kitchen Bouquet®

1. Purée beans and beef broth. Heat. Add onion, lemon juice, and salt. Simmer 5 minutes and serve.

Serves 4

*See "Cooking Methods" section

	RCU	FU	Cal	%Ft	P	F	C	Na
Per Serving	0	0	56	8	3	1	10	237

SIX-BEAN MINESTRONE

This soup freezes well and it's a good thing it does. This soup will become a family favorite. You'll want a good supply on hand.

½	C	pinto beans,* dried
½	C	northern white beans,* dried
½	C	lima beans,* dried
½	C	pink beans,* dried
½	C	red beans,* dried
10	C	water
½	C	garbanzo beans, canned
1		onion, chopped
1	clove	garlic, minced
2	C	celery, chopped
¼	C	parsley, chopped
4	C	tomatoes,* stewed
2	C	cabbage, shredded
5	C	zucchini, thinly sliced

Gifford's Alternatives: Add: 3   T   Gifford's Italian Spice®

1. Soak all beans except garbanzos overnight in 10 cups of water. Add more water as necessary.

2. Before cooking beans, drain off old water and replace with clean water until beans are covered.

3. Cook beans 2 to 3 hours or until done. Add garbanzos and heat thoroughly.

4. Sauté* onion, garlic, celery, and parsley. Add to cooked beans.

5. Add tomatoes. Simmer, covered, for 45 minutes.

6. Add cabbage and zucchini. Add enough water to equal 7 ½ quarts of soup. Cook until cabbage and zucchini are tender. Serve hot.

Serves 30

* See "Cooking Methods" section

	RCU	FU	Cal	%Ft	P	F	C	Na
Per Serving	0	0	69	6	4	1	13	16

CREAMY LIMA BEAN SOUP

Save out one cup of lima beans to put in the soup after it is puréed, if you like.

4	C	water	*Gifford's Alternatives:*		*Add:*
1	C	lima beans,* dried	1	tsp.	chicken bouillon granules*
½	C	celery, finely chopped	1	tsp.	onion powder
1		onion, finely chopped	⅛	tsp.	ground white pepper
2	C	beef bouillon*			
1	C	low-fat yogurt*			

ONIONS

LIMA BEANS

1. Boil water. Add beans and boil 2 minutes.

2. Remove from heat. Cover and let stand 1 hour.

3. Sauté* celery and onion. Add to beans.

4. Strain soup and return liquid to the soup pot.

5. Purée vegetables and return to soup pot.

6. Add bouillon.

7. Put yogurt in a bowl. Remove 1 cup soup broth and add to yogurt. Mix well. Return to soup pot and stir until blended.

8. Cover and simmer. Serve hot.

Serves 6

* See "Cooking Methods" section

	RCU	FU	Cal	%Ft	P	F	C	Na
Per Serving	0	0	58	10	3	1	9	237

BRUNSWICK STEW

Spoon this over cooked brown rice or try it with a slice of dark homemade bread.

16	oz.	chicken, cooked
4	C	water
1	C	onion, sliced
2	C	tomatoes,* stewed
1	10 oz. pkg	frozen lima beans

1	17 oz. can	corn, whole kernel
1	dash	cayenne pepper, optional
2	cloves	garlic, crushed
1/4	tsp.	black pepper
3	T	whole wheat flour*
3	T	skim milk*

Gifford's Alternatives: **Add:** 1 1/2 tsp. *Gifford's Basic Spice®*
                                1/4 tsp. *Gifford's Gourmet Spice®*

1. Cover chicken with 4 cups water and cook 30 to 40 minutes until it is tender. Reserve liquid. Skin and debone chicken. Cut into bite-sized pieces. and set aside.

2. Stir onion, tomatoes, lima beans, corn, and seasonings into 1 cup of reserved chicken broth. Cook 30 minutes.

3. Whisk flour into milk until smooth. Pour into stew and stir until slightly thickened.

4. Add meat. Adjust consistency with additional chicken broth. Simmer for 10 minutes. Serve hot.

Serves 8

* See "Cooking Methods" section

	RCU	FU	Cal	%Ft	P	F	C	Na
Per Serving	0	0	165	10	19	2	18	158

GREEK LENTIL SOUP

Complete this meal with pocket bread sandwiches, and you'll feel like you are on vacation in the Mediterranean.

2	C	lentils,* dried
4	C	cold water
1	C	onion, chopped
1	clove	garlic, crushed
4	C	beef broth*

1/2	C	celery, chopped
2	C	tomatoes,*stewed
1		bay leaf
1	C	carrots, chopped
3	T	parsley, chopped

¼	tsp.	black pepper	½	tsp.	oregano
			2	T	vinegar

1. Wash lentils and drain well. Combine lentils with all ingredients except vinegar. Bring to a boil.

2. Lower heat. Cover and simmer 2 hours or until lentils are tender.

3. Add vinegar and simmer another 30 minutes. Remove bay leaf. Serve.

Serves 8
* See "Cooking Methods" section

	RCU	FU	Cal	%Ft	P	F	C	Na
Per Serving	0	0	138	2	10	T	24	232

"WHAT'S A GARBANZO BEAN?" SOUP

Garbanzos are also called chickpeas. They are high in fiber and protein and an important addition to your low-fat diet.

2	15 oz. cans	garbanzo beans
1	C	water
1	C	carrots, grated
½	C	celery, chopped
¼	C	parsley, chopped
1	tsp.	curry, optional
4	T	low-fat yogurt*

CHICKPEA

Gifford's Alternatives: Add:	3	T	catsup
	1	T	Butter Buds® Sprinkles
	1	tsp.	Schilling® Orange Peel
for added flavor:	1	tsp.	Gifford's Basic Spice®

1. Blend all ingredients except yogurt in blender. Pour into a soup pot and heat thoroughly. Garnish with a tablespoon of yogurt before serving.

Serves 4
* See "Cooking Methods" section

	RCU	FU	Cal	%Ft	P	F	C	Na
Per Serving	0	0	132	15	6	2	21	41

GOOD OLD GOULASH

Claudia Hiatt

You'll never have leftovers with this old favorite. For color and variety, add an assortment of vegetables.

½	lb.	lean hamburger
1	med.	onion, chopped
1	8 oz. can	tomato sauce
1	6 oz. can	tomato paste
1	pint	tomatoes,* stewed
2	tsp.	chili powder
¼	tsp.	garlic powder
1	C	whole wheat elbow macaroni* OR Whole Wheat Noodles* (p. 305)

Gifford's Alternatives: Add:

1 ½	tsp.	*Gifford's Basic Spice®*
¾	tsp.	*Gifford's Mexican Spice®*
⅛	tsp.	*Gifford's Dessert Spice®*

1. Brown* hamburger and drain well. Add onions and cook until onions become transparent.

2. Add tomato sauce, tomato paste, and stewed tomatoes.

3. Season with chili powder and garlic powder.

4. While this is simmering, cook macaroni or noodles until tender. Drain and add to soup. Stir well. Heat and serve.

Serves 8

* See "Cooking Methods" section

	RCU	FU	Cal	%Ft	P	F	C	Na
Per Serving	0	0	232	17	15	5	29	228

HEARTY SPLIT PEA SOUP

This stouthearted soup is wholesome and nourishing enough to be the main course. Round out your meal with whole wheat bread sticks and a salad.

2	C	split peas,* dried
2	oz.	lean ham, diced
6	C	water
1	C	carrots, chopped
½	C	onion, chopped
½	C	celery, chopped
¼	C	celery leaves, chopped
1	T	parsley flakes
1	tsp.	basil
¼	tsp.	allspice
¼	tsp.	thyme
1		bay leaf

Gifford's Alternatives: Add:

1 ½	tsp.	Gifford's Basic Spice®
½	tsp.	Gifford's Italian Spice®
¼	tsp.	Gifford's Dessert Spice®
		OMIT parsley, basil, thyme, allspice, bay leaf

1. Place split peas and ham in large soup pot. Add water.

2. Sauté* carrots, onion, and celery until tender. Add to split peas.

3. Stir in remaining ingredients. Bring to a boil. Cover and simmer 30 minutes. Remove bay leaf. Serve soup.

Serves 8

* See "Cooking Methods" section

	RCU	FU	Cal	%Ft	P	F	C	Na
Per Serving	0	0	90	17	6	2	13	32

VARIATION: GREEN ON GREEN

1	C	frozen green peas	1	recipe	Hearty Split Pea Soup

1. Add peas to Hearty Split Pea Soup 30 minutes before serving.

	RCU	FU	Cal	%Ft	P	F	C	Na
Per Serving	0	0	104	15	7	2	16	32

DRY SOUP MIX 1

This mix is easy to store, easy to make, and easy to eat.

BARLEY

1	16 oz. pkg	green split peas, dried
1	16 oz. pkg	whole wheat macaroni*
1 ¾	C	barley
1	16 oz. pkg	lentils, dried
2 ½	C	brown rice,* raw
4	C	dried onion

1. Mix all ingredients in a large container.

2. Store in a dry 1-gallon jar with a tight lid.

Serves 15

* See "Cooking Methods" section

	RCU	FU	Cal	%Ft	P	F	C	Na
Per Cup	0	0	534	4	24	3	105	30

HAMBURGER SOUP

This recipe is just one of the many ways to use the Dry Soup Mix.

1 ⅓	C	Dry Soup Mix 1 (see above)
2	qt.	water
1	C	carrots, chopped
1	C	celery, chopped
1	C	cabbage, shredded
1	C	tomato sauce*
8	oz.	lean hamburger, browned*

1. Bring water and soup mix to a boil, then simmer 1 to 2 hours. Add remaining ingredients and simmer 20 minutes more. Serve hot.

Serves 8

* See "Cooking Methods" section

	RCU	FU	Cal	%Ft	P	F	C	Na
Per Serving	0	0	187	17	13	4	22	45

DRY SOUP MIX 2

You'll want to keep this dry soup mix on hand so you can make thick, tasty soup anytime.

1	C	split peas*, dried
1	C	lentils*, dried
1	C	black-eyed peas*, dried
1	C	barley, raw
1	C	brown rice,* raw

1. Mix together and store in airtight container.

Makes 5 cups

*See "Cooking Methods" section

	RCU	FU	Cal	%Ft	P	F	C	Na
Per Cup	**0**	**0**	**589**	**3**	**28**	**2**	**117**	**33**

HAM LEGUME SOUP

Beans and peas are classified as legumes.

1	C	Dry Soup Mix 2 (see above)	1		bay leaf
½	C	dried onion flakes	1		dried hot chili pepper
4	C	tomatoes,* stewed	½	C	lean ham cubes
3	C	chicken stock*			

1. Combine all ingredients except ham. Cover and simmer for 1 to 1½ hours until thick.

2. Add ham cubes 15 minutes before serving. Simmer 10 to 15 minutes. Remove bay leaf and hot chili pepper.

Serves 8

* See "Cooking Methods" section

	RCU	FU	Cal	%Ft	P	F	C	Na
Per Serving	**0**	**0**	**126**	**19**	**6**	**3**	**20**	**232**

CHICKEN-NOODLE SOUP

Whole wheat noodles add so much nutrition to this old soup favorite.

16	oz.	chicken	1		carrot, chopped
2	qt.	water	¼	C	parsley, chopped
6	oz.	Whole Wheat	4	oz.	mushrooms, sliced
		Noodles,* (p. 305)	½	tsp.	basil
2		stalks celery, chopped	¼	tsp.	black pepper
1		onion, chopped	1		bay leaf

Gifford's Alternatives: Add:

2	tsp.	chicken bouillon granules*
1	T	onion powder
½	tsp.	dry ground mustard
2	T	Butter Buds® Sprinkles

1. Cook chicken and pick meat off the bones. Cut the meat into bite-sized pieces.

2. Strain water in which chicken was cooked and measure out 2 quarts. Cook noodles until tender in the 2 quarts of water.

3. Add remaining ingredients and cook until vegetables are tender. Remove bay leaf before serving soup.

Serves 6

* See *"Cooking Methods"* section

	RCU	FU	Cal	%Ft	P	F	C	Na
Per Serving	0	0	223	9	25	2	26	69

CREAM OF CHICKEN SOUP

This is also good as a topping over rice or whole wheat biscuits.

2		chicken breasts	2	T	cornstarch*
½	C	celery, chopped	5	C	chicken stock*
½	C	onion, chopped	1	C	skim milk*
½	C	mushrooms, chopped			

Gifford's Alternatives: Add:

2	T	Butter Buds® Sprinkles
1	T	onion powder
1	tsp.	rubbed sage
⅛	tsp.	ground white pepper

1. Cook chicken until tender. Remove meat from bones and cut into bite-sized pieces to make 1 cup.

2. Sauté* celery, onions, and mushrooms.

3. Whisk cornstarch into cool chicken stock. Add milk, chicken, and vegetables. Heat until thick and creamy, stirring constantly. Serve.
Serves 6

* See "Cooking Methods" section

	RCU	FU	Cal	%Ft	P	F	C	Na
Per Serving	0	0	91	10	12	1	8	61

SOUTH-OF-THE-BORDER SOUP

You can increase or decrease the amount of green chilies according to how "fiery" you like your food.

16	oz.	chicken	1	6 oz.	tomato paste
1 ½	qt.	water		can	
1		onion, studded with 2 or 3 whole cloves	1	4 oz. can	green chilies, chopped
3	cloves	garlic, crushed	1	T	chili powder
1		bay leaf	1	tsp.	basil
2	C	kidney beans,* cooked	½	C	corn

Gifford's Alternatives: Add: 1   T   Gifford's Mexican Spice®
1   tsp.   Gifford's Basic Spice®
1   tsp.   Gifford's Dessert Spice®
OMIT 3 cloves, chili powder, basil

1. Cook chicken in 1 ½ quarts water with onion, garlic, and bay leaf until chicken is tender, about 45 minutes.

2. Remove chicken, reserving the broth. Pick meat off the bones.

3. Skim fat from reserved broth. Remove cloves from onion and chop up onion. Remove bay leaf.

4. Combine all ingredients and heat thoroughly. Serve with cooked rice or Tortilla Triangles (p. 363).
Serves 8

* See "Cooking Methods" section

	RCU	FU	Cal	%Ft	P	F	C	Na
Per Serving	0	0	170	6	19	1	18	118

MULLIGATAWNY

This chicken curry soup comes to us from India.

¼	C	onion, chopped
¼	C	celery, chopped
¼	C	carrot, diced
2		tart apples, sliced
¼	C	chicken stock*
¼	C	whole wheat flour*
1	tsp.	curry powder
6	C	chicken stock*
1	C	tomatoes,* stewed
½		green pepper, minced
1	T	parsley, minced
⅛	tsp.	black pepper
⅛	tsp.	mace
2		cloves
1	C	chicken, cooked and diced
1	C	brown rice,* cooked

1. Sauté* onion, celery, carrots, and apple slices in chicken stock.

2. Stir in flour and curry powder.

3. Gradually add chicken stock, stirring constantly.

4. Stir in tomatoes, green pepper, parsley, black pepper, and mace. Cook until vegetables are tender.

5. Strain soup. Purée vegetables in blender and return to soup pot.

6. Add cloves and chicken. Heat.

7. Add hot cooked rice. Serve.

Serves 8

* See "Cooking Methods" section

	RCU	FU	Cal	%Ft	P	F	C	Na
Per Serving	0	0	104	8	7	1	16	34

THICK CHICKEN-TOMATO STEW

Serve this with a plate of steaming whole wheat muffins. Hmmm!

16	oz.	chicken
2		onions, chopped
1 ½	C	carrots, chopped
1 ½	C	celery, chopped
4	oz.	mushrooms, sliced
1		bay leaf
2	C	tomato sauce*
4	T	parsley, chopped
1	8 oz. can	corn, drained
to taste		seasoning without salt*

Gifford's Alternatives: Add:
2	tsp.	Gifford's Basic Spice®

1. Cook chicken in 2 quarts water.

2. Strain water and reserve 6 cups of chicken stock.

3. Pick meat off the chicken and cut into bite-sized pieces.

4. Combine all ingredients in chicken stock and cook until vegetables are tender. Remove bay leaf. Serve.

Serves 6
* See "Cooking Methods" section

	RCU	FU	Cal	%Ft	P	F	C	Na
Per Serving	0	0	201	7	22	2	20	207

OKRA

TURKEY SURPRISE SOUP

What will surprise you is how much meat is left on those turkey bones!

1		turkey carcass
2	qts.	water
1	C	lentils, dried
2		onions, sliced
½	C	carrots, thinly sliced
½	C	celery, thinly sliced
4	oz.	mushrooms, thinly sliced
to taste		seasoning without salt*

Gifford's Alternatives: Add:

2	*tsp.*	*chicken bouillon granules**
2	*tsp.*	*onion powder*
2	*tsp.*	*Butter Buds® Sprinkles*
½	*tsp.*	*ground mustard*
½	*tsp.*	*Gifford's Basic Spice®*
to taste		*pepper*

1. Put as much of the turkey carcass as you can in a deep soup pot and fill with water to within a few inches of the top. Let cook until meat falls easily off the bones, about 1 hour.

2. Remove carcass and pick all of the meat off it.

3. Reserve about 2 quarts of the turkey broth. Add the meat and remaining ingredients. Cook until vegetables and lentils are tender. Serve hot.

Serves 8

* See "Cooking Methods" section

	RCU	FU	Cal	%Ft	P	F	C	Na
Per Serving	0	0	121	7	15	1	13	46

CRAB COCKTAIL

This can be used as an appetizer or a cool, summer soup.

1	6 ½ oz. can	crab meat	1 ½	C	catsup, low-sodium
			3		lemons, juiced
½	C	grapefruit sections, canned	1		dash Tabasco sauce
1	qt.	tomato juice			

Don't pass up breakfast when you can have Whole Wheat Pancakes (p. 52) with Fantastic Fruit Sauce (p. 47), milk and fresh fruit.

Gifford's Alternatives: Add at step #3:

1	tsp.	*Gifford's Basic Spice®*
½	tsp.	*Gifford's Gourmet Spice®*

1. Drain and shred crab meat.

2. Drain grapefruit and shred. Toss together with crab meat.

3. Combine tomato juice, catsup, lemon juice, and Tabasco. Pour over crab and grapefruit mixture.

4. Chill and serve.

Serves 6
* See "Cooking Methods" section

	RCU	FU	Cal	%Ft	P	F	C	Na
Per Serving	0	0	141	4	6	1	29	293

CREAM OF CELERY SOUP

Match this soup up with Dilly Bread (p. 310) for an unparalleled combination.

2	C	celery, diced
1		onion, diced
4	T	cornstarch*
4	C	chicken stock*
¾	C	skim milk*
to taste		seasoning without salt*
garnish		parsley

1. Sauté* celery and onions.

2. Whisk cornstarch into cool chicken stock until smooth.

3. Add milk, celery, and onions to chicken stock. Heat until thickened.

4. Season to taste. Garnish with parsley. Serve.

Serves 5
* See "Cooking Methods" section

	RCU	FU	Cal	%Ft	P	F	C	Na
Per Serving	0	0	65	11	3	1	14	75

A cold soup like Cool As a Cucumber (p. 92) thick soup like Marvelous Minestrone (p. 96) or a light soup like Magic Tomato Bouillon (p. 60) all taste great with Whole Wheat Bread Sticks (p. 308) or Croutons (p. 302).

NEW ENGLAND CHOWDER

Snuggle up in front of the fire with a steaming mug of this chowder. It'll taste great after a long, cold day outside.

4	med.	potatoes, cubed
1 ½	C	onions, diced
⅛	tsp.	black pepper
to taste		seasoning without salt*
2	C	boiling water
1	lb.	haddock filets, frozen or fresh, cut in ¾-inch cubes
2	C	skim milk* MIXED WITH
6	T	nonfat dry milk
1	T	parsley, chopped
sprinkle		paprika

Gifford's Alternatives: Add:

2	T	Butter Buds® Sprinkles
1	T	onion powder
½	tsp.	chicken bouillon granules*
½	tsp.	thyme
½	tsp.	ground mustard

1. Cook the potatoes, onion, and seasoning in 2 cups boiling water for about 10 minutes or until vegetables are tender.

2. Add fish and cook 10 minutes more.

3. Stir in milk. Simmer 15 minutes longer. Do not boil.

4. Garnish with chopped parsley and sprinkle with paprika. Serve.

Serves 6

* See "Cooking Methods" section

	RCU	FU	Cal	%Ft	P	F	C	Na
Per Serving	0	0	212	17	22	4	24	159

TUNA

SEAFARING CHOWDER

Easy and elegant! This chowder will please your seafood-loving friends. Serve it by candlelight with crusty French bread.

3	small	potatoes, diced
1		sweet Spanish onion, thinly sliced
¾	C	celery, chopped
¼	C	green pepper, chopped
2	cloves	garlic, minced
¼	tsp.	black pepper
¼	tsp.	thyme
¼	tsp.	marjoram
2	C	clam-tomato juice
2	C	tomatoes,* stewed
4	T	parsley, chopped
8	oz.	halibut, fresh or frozen

Gifford's Alternatives: Add:

2	T	*peach juice concentrate*
1	tsp.	*lime juice*
1	T	*Butter Buds® Sprinkles*
1	pinch	*cardamon*

1. Simmer everything together except the halibut. Add water, if necessary.

2. When potatoes are tender, add halibut. Cover and simmer until fish is cooked.

3. Sprinkle with parsley. Serve.

Serves 8

* See "Cooking Methods" section

	RCU	FU	Cal	%Ft	P	F	C	Na
Per Serving	0	0	117	19	9	3	15	251

LUCK O' THE IRISH POTATO SOUP

This takes on a wonderful creamy texture when thickened with mashed potatoes. This soup is also nice with cooked broccoli added.

4	med.	potatoes, diced
½	C	onion, minced
3	C	chicken broth*
to taste		seasoning without salt*
1	C	celery, diced
⅛	tsp.	black pepper
2	C	skim milk*
1	T	chives, minced

Gifford's Alternatives: Add:

1	T	Butter Buds® Sprinkles
2	tsp.	onion powder
1	tsp.	Worcestershire sauce
½	tsp.	ground nutmeg

1. Combine all ingredients except milk and chives in a saucepan. Cover and simmer about 15 minutes or until potatoes are tender.

2. Add milk. Simmer uncovered another 15 minutes. Garnish with chives. Serve.

Serves 4

* See "Cooking Methods" section

	RCU	FU	Cal	%Ft	P	F	C	Na
Per Serving	0	0	144	T	8	T	25	66

VARIATION: APPLE CURRY IRISH SOUP

1		apple, diced
½	tsp.	curry powder
1	recipe	Luck O' the Irish Potato Soup
		apple wedges for garnish

1. Add diced apples and curry powder to potato soup the last 5 minutes of cooking time. Garnish with apple wedges instead of chives just before serving.

	RCU	FU	Cal	%Ft	P	F	C	Na
Per Serving	0	0	164	T	8	T	30	66

CHILI POTATO SOUP

These two old favorites combine to create a sporty new soup. Delicious with corn bread.

1		onion, chopped
3		potatoes, diced and cooked
2	C	water, boiling
2	C	skim milk*
½	C	tomato sauce*
1	tsp.	chili powder
¼	tsp.	oregano
⅛	tsp.	garlic powder
1	C	kidney beans,* cooked

Gifford's Alternatives: Add: 2 tsp. *Gifford's Mexican Spice®*
OMIT chili powder, oregano, garlic powder

1. Combine all ingredients and cook until tender. Serve.

Serves 6

* See "Cooking Methods" section

	RCU	FU	Cal	%Ft	P	F	C	Na
Per Serving	0	0	124	T	7	T	23	59

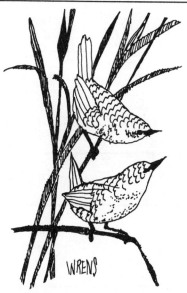

WRENS

FRENCH ONION SOUP

This soup is a perfect way to begin your meal but you use low-sodium beef bouillon.

2 ½	C	onions, sliced
6	C	beef bouillon*
6		slices French bread
1	T	parmesan cheese, grated

Gifford's Alternatives: Add:

1 ½	tsp.	*Gifford's Basic Spice®*
1	tsp.	*Worcestershire sauce*
½	tsp.	*Kitchen Bouquet®*
¼	tsp.	*thyme*
¼	tsp.	*paprika*

1. Sauté* onions until transparent.

2. Combine with beef bouillon in soup pot. Cover tightly and simmer for 1 hour.

3. Ladle into soup bowls and top with a piece of toasted French bread. Sprinkle with 1 teaspoon grated parmesan cheese. Serve.

Serves 6

* See "Cooking Methods" section

	RCU	FU	Cal	%Ft	P	F	C	Na
Per Serving	1	0	95	4	4	T	18	199

OLD-FASHIONED BEEF STEW

What tastes better on a cold winter's night than a thick, hot stew?

1	tsp.	Worcestershire sauce
2		bay leaves
1	clove	garlic, minced
½	tsp.	paprika
dash		ground cloves
¼	tsp.	black pepper
2	C	carrots, quartered
4	med.	potatoes, quartered
3	med.	onions, quartered
1	T	cornstarch*
8	oz.	lean hamburger, browned*

Gifford's Alternatives: Add:
1	*T*	*Gifford's Basic Spice®*
½	*tsp.*	*ground celery seed*
2	*T*	*tomato purée*
1	*tsp.*	*Kitchen Bouquet®*
1	*C*	*frozen peas, thawed*

1. Combine Worcestershire sauce, bay leaves, garlic, paprika, cloves, 1 ½ cups water, and black pepper in a soup pot.

2. Add vegetables. Cook, covered, for 30 to 40 minutes.

3. Drain, reserving liquid. Set aside vegetables and remove bay leaves.

4. Add water to reserved liquid to equal 1 ¼ cups. Return to soup pot.

5. Whisk cornstarch into ¼ cup cool water until smooth. Pour slowly into soup pot. Heat, stirring constantly, until thickened.

6. Add meat and vegetables to soup pot. Heat thoroughly. Serve.

Serves 8

* See "Cooking Methods" section

	RCU	FU	Cal	%Ft	P	F	C	Na
Per Serving	0	1	145	20	10	3	16	37

CABBAGE PATCH SOUP

This basic soup with its variation gives you two distinctive flavors.

4	C	cabbage, shredded
2	T	water
1		onion, sliced thin
6	C	beef or chicken stock*
dash		black pepper
1/8	tsp.	nutmeg, optional
1 1/2	C	brown rice,* cooked

CABBAGE

Gifford's Alternatives: Add:

2	*T*	*lemon juice*
2	*T*	*pineapple juice concentrate*
1	*tsp.*	*Gifford's Chinese Spice®*
1/4	*tsp.*	*Gifford's Dessert Spice®*

1. Cook cabbage, water, and onion, covered, over low heat until golden brown and half-done. Stir frequently.

2. Add stock, black pepper, nutmeg, and rice. Cover and simmer for 10 minutes. Serve hot.

Serves 6

* See "Cooking Methods" section

	RCU	FU	Cal	%Ft	P	F	C	Na
Per Serving	0	0	93	T	4	T	10	16

VARIATION: FARMER MacGREGOR'S CABBAGE SOUP

1 1/2	C	celery, chopped
2		green onions, chopped
1	C	carrots, chopped and cooked
2	C	white beans,* cooked
1	recipe	Cabbage Patch Soup, without rice

1. Sauté* celery and green onions.

2. Add all ingredients to cabbage soup and simmer for 10 minutes. Serve.

	RCU	FU	Cal	%Ft	P	F	C	Na
Per Serving	0	0	185	2	9	T	20	60

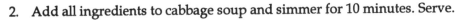

CAULIFLOWER SOUP

Purée cooked vegetables and rice to make creamy cauliflower soup.

1/3	C	brown rice,* uncooked
2	C	cauliflower, cut in pieces
5	C	chicken stock*
1/2	C	celery, chopped
4	T	cornstarch*
1	C	skim milk*
1/4	tsp.	black pepper
to taste		seasoning without salt*
garnish		chives, parsley, or watercress

CAULIFLOWER

Gifford's Alternatives:

Add:	2	tsp.	*Gifford's Basic Spice®*
	3/4	tsp.	*Gifford's Gourmet Spice®*
Topping:	1/4	C	*grape-nuts , ground*
	1	T	*Butter Buds® Sprinkles*
	1/2	tsp.	*paprika*
	1/2	tsp.	*fresh chopped parsley*

Mix together and sprinkle over top of soup when serving, if desired.

1. Cook rice and set aside.

2. Bring cauliflower, chicken stock, and celery to boil. Reduce heat and simmer until cauliflower is tender-crisp, about 10 minutes.

3. Whisk cornstarch into milk until smooth. Add to soup, stirring constantly. Heat until thickened.

4. Add seasoning and rice. Garnish with chives, parsley, or watercress. Serve.

Serves 6

* See "Cooking Methods" section

	RCU	FU	Cal	%Ft	P	F	C	Na
Per Serving	0	0	63	9	4	1	11	39

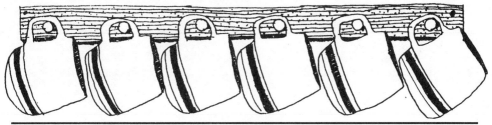

CORNY TOMATO SOUP

This soup is rich, warm, and wonderful. Try it with your favorite muffins or batter bread.

¼	C	onion, chopped
2	T	whole wheat flour*
2	C	tomato juice
1	16 oz. can	cream-style corn
2	C	skim milk*
garnish		parsley

1. Sauté* onions until transparent. Stir in flour.

2. Pour mixture into a blender with tomato juice and corn. Blend until smooth.

3. Pour tomato mixture into a 2-quart saucepan. Add milk. Place over moderately low heat and cook, stirring constantly, until thickened. Do not allow to boil.

4. Garnish with parsley. Serve.

Serves 6

* See "Cooking Methods" section

	RCU	FU	Cal	%Ft	P	F	C	Na
Per Serving	**0**	**0**	**114**	**5**	**5**	**1**	**23**	**224**

CREAM OF ASPARAGUS SOUP

A classic soup with a distinctive, refined flavor.

1	15 oz. can	asparagus with liquid
¼	C	onion, chopped
¼	C	celery, chopped
1	C	brown rice,* cooked
2	C	skim milk*
⅛	tsp.	black pepper
1	dash	nutmeg

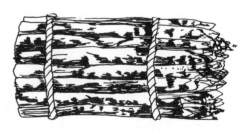

Gifford's Alternatives: Add: 3   T   *unsweetened crushed pineapple*
                                   ¼   tsp.   *lime juice*
                                   1   tsp.   *Gifford's Chinese Spice®*
                                   1   T   *diced pimentos*

1. Place canned asparagus and liquid in a blender with onion, celery, and cooked rice. Blend on low speed until puréed.

2. Pour into a saucepan. Stir in milk. Season and heat. Serve warm.

Serves 5

See "Cooking Methods" section

	RCU	FU	Cal	%Ft	P	F	C	Na
Per Serving	0	0	105	2	6	T	19	284

CREAMY BRUSSELS SPROUT SOUP

Delightfully different and delicious.

1   onion, sliced
2   10 oz. frozen brussels sprouts,
       pkgs   defrosted and cut in halves
2   C   chicken stock*
4   C   skim milk*
3   potatoes, diced
½   tsp.   basil
3   T   whole wheat flour*

1. Sauté* onions and brussels sprouts until sprouts turn a darker green, about 5 minutes.

2. Add chicken stock, milk, potatoes, and seasonings. Bring to a boil, then simmer 10 minutes or until sprouts are barely tender.

3. Combine flour and ⅓ cup cool water in a jar. Cover tightly and shake well. Add slowly to soup, stirring constantly, until slightly thickened. Heat thoroughly. Serve.

Serves 6

See "Cooking Methods" section

	RCU	FU	Cal	%Ft	P	F	C	Na
Per Serving	0	0	134	T	9	T	26	219

JACK-O'-LANTERN SOUP

This soup will warm up your little ones after a night of trick-or-treating.

½		onion, chopped
2	C	pumpkin, canned
2	T	whole wheat flour
¼	tsp.	ground ginger
2	C	skim milk*
4	C	chicken stock*
garnish		chives or parsley, chopped

Gifford's Alternatives: Add:
½	tsp.	Gifford's Chinese Spice®
½	tsp.	Gifford's Dessert Spice®
		OMIT ground ginger

1. Sauté* onion. Stir in canned pumpkin. Blend flour and ginger with ⅓ cup of milk. Stir into pumpkin mixture.

2. Add remaining milk and cook, stirring constantly, 5 to 10 minutes until thickened. Do not allow to boil.

3. Add chicken stock and adjust consistency with water, if needed. Heat almost to boiling.

4. Garnish before serving with chives or parsley to look like a jack-o'-lantern. Serve hot.

Serves 8

* See "Cooking Methods" section

	RCU	FU	Cal	%Ft	P	F	C	Na
Per Serving	0	0	55	4	3	T	10	33

RED SUNSET SOUP

Make large batches of this soup in the fall when tomatoes are in season. Then freeze it for use throughout the year.

8		tomatoes, quartered	1		bay leaf
1		onion, quartered	2	cubes	chicken bouillon*
¼	tsp.	black pepper	1	T	cornstarch*
¼	tsp.	cinnamon	1	C	skim milk*
⅛	tsp.	cloves			

*Gifford's Alternatives: Add: ½   tsp.   Gifford's Dessert Spice®
OMIT cinnamon, cloves*

1. Combine all ingredients except cornstarch and milk in a soup pot. Cook until vegetables are tender. Remove bay leaf.

2. Whisk cornstarch into milk. Add gradually to the soup. Heat until thickened. Serve hot.
Serves 4

* See "Cooking Methods" section

	RCU	FU	Cal	%Ft	P	F	C	Na
Per Serving	0	0	121	2	7	T	26	243

SUNSHINE SOUP

The rich, golden color of this soup made from squash warms up any autumn meal.

2	C	squash, cooked and mashed
3		onions, chopped
1	C	celery, chopped
1	clove	garlic, minced
½	tsp.	rosemary
1	qt.	chicken stock*
¼	tsp.	black pepper
2	C	skim milk*
garnish		nutmeg

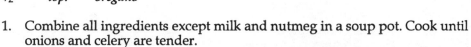

Gifford's Alternatives: Add:
3	T	orange juice concentrate
2	T	pineapple juice concentrate
1	tsp.	onion powder
½	tsp.	oregano

1. Combine all ingredients except milk and nutmeg in a soup pot. Cook until onions and celery are tender.

2. Remove from heat. Stir in milk. Sprinkle with nutmeg and serve immediately.
Serves 6

* See "Cooking Methods" section

	RCU	FU	Cal	%Ft	P	F	C	Na
Per Serving	0	0	66	T	5	T	13	69

CREAM OF MUSHROOM SOUP

This can be used as a soup base or as a delightful meal.

2	8 oz. cans	mushrooms, drained and minced
1 ½	C	chicken broth*
1	T	cornstarch*
1 ½	C	skim milk*
½	tsp.	Worcestershire sauce
garnish		paprika

Gifford's Alternatives: Add:

1	*tsp.*	*Gifford's Basic Spice®*
1	*T*	*diced pimentos*

1. Simmer mushrooms in chicken broth for 5 minutes.

2. Whisk cornstarch into cool milk until smooth. Pour slowly into broth. Heat, stirring constantly, until thickened.

3. Add Worcestershire sauce. Garnish with paprika. Serve.

Serves 4

* See "Cooking Methods" section

	RCU	FU	Cal	%Ft	P	F	C	Na
Per Serving	0	0	62	4	6	T	10	62

VARIATION: CRUNCHY CREAM OF MUSHROOM SOUP

½	C	peas, cooked
3		water chestnuts, diced
½	C	mushrooms, raw, sliced
1	recipe	Cream of Mushroom Soup

1. Add peas, water chestnuts, and mushrooms to Cream of Mushroom Soup. Heat and serve.

CHESTNUT

	RCU	FU	Cal	%Ft	P	F	C	Na
Per Serving	0	0	85	T	7	T	14	68

FARMER'S MARKET DELIGHT

Run all or part of this through your blender to give an interesting change of texture to this popular soup.

8	oz.	lean hamburger*
1	C	carrots, finely chopped
2	C	cabbage, shredded
1	C	celery, finely chopped
1	med.	onion, chopped
4	C	tomatoes,* stewed
3	C	beef stock*
3	C	water
3	med.	potatoes, diced
½	C	peas
1	C	green beans, cut
½	C	corn
4	oz.	mushrooms, sliced
⅓	C	barley, raw

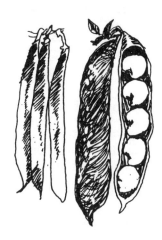

Gifford's Alternatives: Add:
1	T	Gifford's Basic Spice®
¼	tsp.	ground caraway seed
1	drop	Wright's® Liquid Smoke
1	tsp.	low-sodium soy sauce

1. Brown* hamburger and drain.

2. Combine all ingredients together in a soup pot.

3. Bring to a boil. Reduce heat, cover, and simmer until all vegetables are tender. Serve hot.

Serves 10

* See "Cooking Methods" section

	RCU	FU	Cal	%Ft	P	F	C	Na
Per Serving	0	0	155	16	10	3	25	273

CREAMY CARROT SOUP

Any of the following foods will provide delicious surprises to this unique soup—cooked brown rice, a few raisins, diced potatoes, celery, or apples.

1	med.	onion, diced
2	C	raw carrots, thinly sliced
4	C	chicken stock*
1	C	nonfat dry milk *

1. Sauté* onions until transparent. Remove and place in blender. Do not run.

2. Sauté* carrots until tender-crisp. Reserve 1 cup carrots. Put remaining carrots with the onions in the blender. Add 1 cup chicken stock, and purée.

3. Dissolve milk powder in remaining 3 cups of chicken stock.

4. Combine milk, purée, and remaining carrots in the top of a double boiler or in a microwave oven. Heat. Garnish with parsley or dill before serving.

Serves 6

* See "Cooking Methods" section

	RCU	FU	Cal	%Ft	P	F	C	Na
Per Serving	0	0	115	T	10	T	14	151

COOL AS A CUCUMBER

This soup will help cool you off on a warm summer evening.

1	qt.	buttermilk*
1	C	cucumber, peeled, seeded, and shredded
2	T	parsley, chopped
2	T	green onion, sliced
1	dash	black pepper

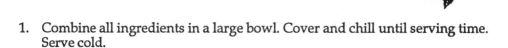

1. Combine all ingredients in a large bowl. Cover and chill until serving time. Serve cold.

Serves 5

See "Cooking Methods" section

	RCU	FU	Cal	%Ft	P	F	C	Na
Per Serving	0	0	75	T	T	T	11	248

CREAMY ZUCCHINI SOUP

This soup is a delicious way to use all your fresh zucchini. Make several batches and freeze them for later use.

1½	C	beef stock*
2	C	water, boiling
3	C	zucchini, peeled and sliced
½	C	onion, chopped
⅛	tsp.	garlic powder
to taste		seasoning without salt*
3	C	skim milk*
garnish		chives or parsley, chopped

SQUASH

Gifford's Alternatives: Add:
1½	tsp.	Gifford's Basic Spice®
2	T	pineapple juice concentrate

1. Cook all ingredients, except milk and garnish, until zucchini is tender. Strain soup, reserving the liquid.

2. Purée zucchini mixture in a blender or put it through a food mill. Return to reserved liquid.

3. Add milk and stir until smooth. Heat, but do not boil. Garnish with chives or parsley before serving.

Serves 6

See "Cooking Methods" section

	RCU	FU	Cal	%Ft	P	F	C	Na
Per Serving	0	0	66	T	6	T	12	164

CURRIED ASPARAGUS BISQUE

This elegant soup can be served hot or cold.

2	10 oz. pkgs	frozen cut asparagus
3 ½	C	water
1	med.	onion, minced
2	T	lemon juice
4	oz.	fresh mushrooms, sliced
4	C	chicken stock*
1-2	tsp.	curry powder
1	dash	black pepper

1. Combine all ingredients in saucepan and bring to a boil. Reduce heat. Cover and simmer for 8 to 12 minutes or until asparagus is tender.

2. Place half the asparagus mixture in the blender and blend until smooth.

3. Combine blended and nonblended mixtures in saucepan.

4. Heat and serve hot, or chill for 4 hours and serve cold.

Serves 6

* See "Cooking Methods" section

	RCU	FU	Cal	%Ft	P	F	C	Na
Per Serving	0	0	38	T	3	T	6	274

GAZPACHO

Cool and crunchy! This is like having a garden salad in a soup bowl.

1		tomato
½	C	green pepper
½	C	celery
½	C	zucchini
¼	C	onion
1	T	green onion, green only
1	T	parsley
2	cloves	garlic
2 ½	T	Tarragon wine vinegar
½	tsp.	salt
¼	tsp.	black pepper
½	tsp.	Worcestershire sauce
2	C	tomato juice*

ROSEMARY

Gifford's Alternatives: Add:
2	T	*apple juice concentrate*
1	tsp.	*lemon juice*
1	tsp.	*lime juice*
½	tsp.	*Gifford's Mexican Spice®*

1. Finely chop all vegetables.

2. Combine all ingredients and chill. Serve cold. Pass Croutons (p. 302) separately for sprinkling on each bowlful.

Serves 6

* See "Cooking Methods" section

	RCU	FU	Cal	%Ft	P	F	C	Na
Per Serving	0	0	31	4	2	T	7	333

SPICE RACK

MARVELOUS MINESTRONE

Double this recipe and freeze part of it to use later.

2	C	onion, finely chopped	3	T	parsley, minced
1	clove	garlic, minced	1	T	basil
3	C	cabbage, finely shredded	½	tsp.	rosemary
2	C	carrots, finely diced	2	C	tomato purée
1	C	green beans, cut	4	C	beef bouillon*
2		potatoes, cubed	1	C	kidney beans,* cooked
2	C	zucchini, chopped	¾	C	whole wheat macaroni*
4	oz.	fresh mushrooms, sliced	⅓	C	barley, raw
2	C	tomatoes,* stewed			

Gifford's Alternatives: Add:
1	T	**Gifford's Italian Spice®**
½	tsp.	**Gifford's Basic Spice®**
¼	tsp.	**Gifford's Dessert Spice®**
		OMIT basil, rosemary

1. Sauté* onion until transparent.

2. Combine garlic, cabbage, carrots, green beans, potatoes, zucchini, mushrooms, and tomatoes in a large soup pot. Add sautéd onions and cook for 10 minutes.

3. Add parsley, basil, rosemary, tomato purée, and bouillon.

4. Purée ½ cup kidney beans in blender and add to soup. Add remaining ½ cup whole kidney beans. Bring to a boil. Reduce heat and simmer for 25 minutes.

5. Add macaroni and barley. Cook for 15 minutes longer. Serve hot.

Serves 10

*See "Cooking Methods" section

	RCU	FU	Cal	%Ft	P	F	C	Na
Per Serving	**0**	**0**	**161**	**2**	**8**	**T**	**37**	**240**

THE GARDEN SPOT

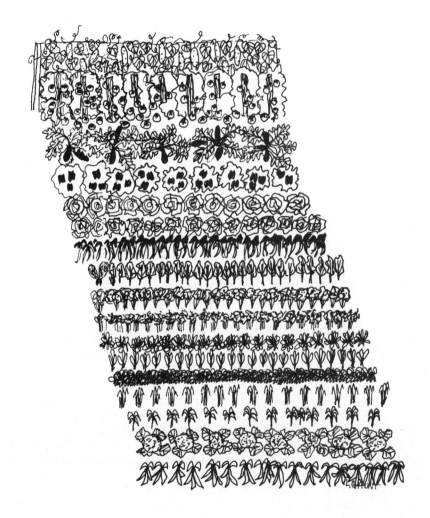

To everything there is a season.

---Ecclesiastes 3:1

THE GARDEN SPOT

Hungry? Well, it is nice to know that there are some foods that are naturally low in calories and fats yet naturally high in vitamins and fiber. What are they? "Salad fixin's," of course! And they should quickly become a substantial part of your low-fat diet.

There are as many salad combinations as there are ingredients. The only limitations are your own individual taste and imagination. These recipes provide delicious, basic salads, but you should feel free to adapt the ingredients according to what you have on hand, what is in season, or what your family enjoys most. Almost all fruits and vegetables are interchangeable. Be careful of avocados, nuts, seeds, olives, bacon, egg yolks, and cheeses, which are all high in fat.

Salad dressings are fine and add a marvelous variety of tastes and textures to your salad. But make sure that any dressings you buy or make are low in fat. Following are some suggestions to help you reduce the fat in your salad dressings. Try substituting blended low-fat cottage cheese, skim yogurt, or low-calorie mayonnaise for regular mayonnaise. Plain lemon juice makes a simple flavoring for salads. Oil and vinegar dressings can be diluted with water or the amount of oil can be reduced. Mixing one tablespoon of your favorite creamy, low-calorie dressing with one cup skim yogurt will greatly reduce the fat grams and calories but retain the flavor and consistency. Experiment with your favorite dressing to find a low-fat alternative. Also check Fabulous Flavors on page 19 for more low-fat dressings. Remember, it is a good habit to measure the amount of dressing used on a salad so you don't accidently turn a low-fat meal into a high-fat meal.

Leafy green salads are a traditional favorite. There are many types of lettuce available, such as iceberg, Bibb, romaine, endive, New York, and Great Lakes. Other greens add variety, such as spinach, mustard greens, beet greens, Swiss chard, and cabbage. Red cabbage provides color as well as crunch. For best results, keep greens dry and crisp after washing. By breaking them into pieces instead of cutting them with a knife, you can avoid a bitter taste and brown edges.

Sprouts add an interesting texture to a tossed salad. Alfalfa, mung bean, pea, bean, or wheat sprouts are all a delicious, nutritious change. Buy them or grow your own. See "Cooking Methods" section, on page 385.

Make a green salad the "King" of your meal by adding bits of protein like tuna, chicken, or beans. Then toss in some "crunchies" like imitation bacon bits, croutons, carrots, peas, celery, radishes, or corn. Serve hot muffins or whole wheat bread, and you have a healthful, low-fat meal.

Fruits make delightful desserts, convenient snacks, or colorful salads. They satisfy our desire for sweets without negative side effects. Fruits are highest in pectin and fiber when eaten raw, with the skins. Raspberries, blackberries, strawberries, plums, pears, apples, cherries, and bananas are especially high in fiber.

Canned fruits come packed in their own juices, light syrup, or heavy syrup. Buy canned fruits that are packed in their own juices. When you buy fruits packed in a sweet syrup, drain them, and rinse the fruit in a colander.

Fruits are a natural treat. Eat them fresh, frozen, alone, or mixed together. So enjoy them daily.

Gelatin salads add another dimension of creativity to salad making. They satisfy our aesthetic appetite because of the wide variety of shapes, sizes, colors, and textures that are possible. By using unflavored gelatin instead of sweet, flavored gelatins, you add protein and avoid unnecessary sugar. Following are some fun suggestions. Fill gelatins with fruit juice, fruits, cottage cheese, or even vegetables. Experiment with a variety of molds and artistic ways of serving gelatin salads. Add vegetable or fruit pieces to make faces or designs. Layer gelatin and cottage cheese or fruit in a parfait glass. Set gelatin in a 9" x 13" pan, then cut it into squares or triangles as finger food for children. Whip fruit juices set in gelatin, then freeze it for a cool summer treat. Let your imagination run wild!

So when hunger pangs start, turn to this section for relief. You'll always be safe instead of sorry when you choose a salad.

Additional fruit recipes, see:
    "Just For Fun!" on page 347

Potato salad recipes, see:
    "The Potato, Friend or Foe?" on page 227

Meat salads, see:
    "To Meat or Not to Meat?" on page 133

TURNIPS

HEAD LETTUCE

RAINBOW RAW VEGETABLES

These fancy vegetables will dress up the simplest sandwich or proudest main course. Keep some on hand for snacks, too.

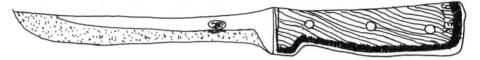

CUCUMBER WHEELS:

2   cucumbers, cold

1. Peel completely. Using a fork, pull tines down cucumber lengthwise. Repeat until ridges completely cover cucumber. Slice crosswise. Serve.

	RCU	FU	Cal	%Ft	P	F	C	Na
Per Serving	0	0	30	0	T	0	6	12

CARROT CURLS:

2   carrots

1. Peel carrots. Slice them paper-thin lengthwise with a vegetable peeler. Roll up and fasten with toothpicks. Leave in ice water until curled. Remove toothpick before serving.

	RCU	FU	Cal	%Ft	P	F	C	Na
Per Serving	0	0	60	0	2	T	14	68

CELERY CURLS:

2   stalks   celery

1. Wash and cut celery in short lengths. Feather the ends by slitting them into narrow strips, almost to the center. Chill in ice water until ends curl. Serve.

	RCU	FU	Cal	%Ft	P	F	C	Na
Per Serving	0	0	14	0	1	T	3	100

RADISH FLOWERS:

10   radishes

1. Wash and top radishes so that some white shows. Make 3 diagonal cuts lengthwise near the edge evenly spaced to resemble the petals of a flower. Chill in ice water until crisp. Serve.

	RCU	FU	Cal	%Ft	P	F	C	Na
Per Serving	0	0	20	0	T	T	5	20

CUCUMBER AND ONION MARINADE

Keep a bowl of this in your refrigerator for a snack or to serve as a side dish.

1	med.	cucumber, peeled and sliced
1	med.	onion, sliced and separated into rings
¼	C	vinegar
¼	C	water
1	dash	paprika
1	dash	black pepper

ONIONS

Gifford's Alternatives: Add:
2	*T*	*apple juice concentrate*
¼	*tsp.*	*ground nutmeg*
1	*pinch*	*allspice*

1. Combine all ingredients.

2. Chill before serving. Stir occasionally.

Serves 4

	RCU	FU	Cal	%Ft	P	F	C	Na
Per Serving	0	0	16	T	1	T	4	4

Choose firm medium-size CUCUMBERS with good green color. Avoid withered ends. Wash, dry, and store in the refrigerator. Use within one week.

CREAMY CUCUMBERS

Use your imagination! There are so many times when this recipe can be served.

1	lg.	cucumber, peeled and sliced
½	C	low-fat yogurt*
1	T	vinegar
2	T	chives, chopped
1	drop	Tabasco sauce
½	tsp.	dill seed
1	dash	black pepper

Gifford's Alternatives: Add:
1	med.	orange, peeled, quartered, sliced
2	T	orange-banana-pineapple juice concentrate
1	tsp.	Schilling® Orange Peel
½	tsp.	Gifford's Dessert Spice®, optional

1. Slice cucumbers into a bowl. Let sit 30 minutes, then drain any liquid off cucumbers.

2. Combine remaining ingredients and add to sliced cucumbers. Chill before serving.

Serves 4

* See "Cooking methods" section

	RCU	FU	Cal	%Ft	P	F	C	Na
Per Serving	0	0	21	22	1	1	2	18

CALICO COLESLAW

This basic salad is delicious with a sandwich for lunch.

4	T	skim milk*	8	oz.	low-fat cottage cheese*
2	tsp.	prepared mustard	6	C	cabbage, shredded
1	tsp.	vinegar	2	C	carrots, grated
⅛	tsp.	black pepper	2	T	onion, minced

Gifford's Alternatives: Add:
3	T	peach juice concentrate
1	tsp.	onion powder
½	tsp.	chicken bouillon granules*

1. Combine milk, mustard, vinegar, black pepper, and cottage cheese in blender. Blend about 3 minutes until dressing is smooth and creamy.

2. Toss cabbage, carrots, and onions together.

3. Add blended cottage cheese to cabbage mixture and toss until well mixed. Cover and refrigerate until ready to serve.

Serves 10

* See "Cooking Methods" section

	RCU	FU	Cal	%Ft	P	F	C	Na
Per Serving	0	0	43	2	5	T	6	100

CUCUMBER

DARK GREEN SALAD TOSS

Dark greens such as spinach, watercress, parsley, or endive are very nutritious and especially high in vitamin A.

1	C	carrots, shredded
1	C	cauliflower, sliced into ½-inch pieces
1	C	spinach or other dark greens torn into small pieces

1. Toss all ingredients together lightly.

2. Chill and serve with your choice of dressings. See salad dressing section of Fabulous Flavors on page 19.

Serves 4

	RCU	FU	Cal	%Ft	P	F	C	Na
Per Serving	0	0	23	T	2	T	4	39

SEVEN-LAYER SALAD

This unusual combination creates a great taste that even salad-haters will love. And the peas give it a delightful "crunch."

1	head	lettuce, shredded
1		green pepper, diced
5	stalks	celery, chopped
½		onion, chopped
1	10 oz. pkg	frozen peas
1	C	low-fat cottage cheese,* blended, OR
1	C	low-fat yogurt*
2	T	sugar
2	T	parmesan cheese, grated
2	T	imitation bacon bits*
2		tomatoes, wedged

LEAF LETTUCE

Gifford's Alternatives: *Sprinkle: Gifford's Dessert Spice® over top of salad when serving.*

1. Put shredded lettuce in a bowl. Layer diced green pepper, chopped celery, chopped onion, and peas on top of lettuce.

2. Spread yogurt or blended cottage cheese completely over the top of the salad.

3. Sprinkle with sugar, parmesan cheese, and bacon bits. Garnish with tomato wedges.

4. Cover tightly and chill, preferably overnight. Toss thoroughly before serving.

Serves 10

* See "Cooking Methods" section

	RCU	FU	Cal	%Ft	P	F	C	Na
Per Serving	0	0	65	14	4	1	11	95

FANCY FROZEN FRUIT SALAD

Serve on special occasions and listen to the raves.

1	8 oz. can	pineapple, crushed
1	8 oz. can	mandarin oranges
½	C	apples, chopped
1	lg.	banana, sliced
2	C	cottage cheese*
1	C	orange juice concentrate*
¾	C	cranberries, whole

1. Combine pineapple, oranges, apples, banana, cottage cheese, and ½ cup orange juice concentrate. Pour into a nonstick* loaf pan and freeze.

2. Prepare cranberry sauce by boiling cranberries and remaining orange juice concentrate for 10 minutes. Cool.

3. To serve, thaw frozen fruit salad enough that it will slide out of the loaf pan. Slice into 8 pieces. Top with cranberry sauce and enjoy.

Serves 8

See "Cooking Methods" section

	RCU	FU	Cal	%Ft	P	F	C	Na
Per Serving	T	0	162	1	8	2	27	122

TRADITIONAL TOSSED SALAD

You are always safe with a salad for lunch or dinner. Make sure you use low-fat dressings; then eat heartily.

½	lb.	romaine lettuce
½	lb.	fresh button mushrooms
1	lb.	cherry tomatoes
1	sm. head	cauliflower, broken into florets
½	C	carrots, grated
½	lb.	iceberg lettuce, torn into pieces

LEAF
LETTUCE

1. Wash all vegetables under cold running water. Drain well.

2. Place inner leaves of romaine upright, around the sides of a deep round salad bowl. Arrange remaining ingredients attractively in the center. Chill until serving time.

3. Serve with your favorite salad dressing from Fabulous Flavors (p. 19).

Serves 8

	RCU	FU	Cal	%Ft	P	F	C	Na
Per Serving	**0**	**0**	**69**	**4**	**6**	**T**	**13**	**33**

Choose large, round, solid heads of iceberg LETTUCE that "give" slightly when squeezed. Boston and Bibb lettuce are best in smaller heads with light green leaves. Romaine lettuce leaves should be crisp and dark green in a loosely folded head. All greens can be washed, drained well, and stored in the refrigerator crisper for three to five days.

ORIENTAL SALAD TOSS

Reduce soy sauce in order to lower sodium content.

½	C	raw spinach leaves, coarsely broken
½	C	salad greens, broken into small pieces
½	C	bean sprouts,* drained
½	C	celery, thinly sliced on the diagonal
½	C	water chestnuts, thinly sliced
½	C	fresh mushrooms, thinly sliced lengthwise
½	C	green pepper, thinly sliced lengthwise

RED CABBAGE

½	C	red cabbage, thinly sliced
½	C	watercress

DRESSING:

1	T	soy sauce
to taste		garlic, pressed
1	T	Low-Calorie French Dressing (p. 31)
½	C	low-fat yogurt*

Gifford's Alternatives: Add:
1	T	*tomato purée*
1	T	*cherry juice concentrate*
1	tsp.	*Gifford's Chinese Spice®*
½	tsp.	*dry ground mustard*

1. Combine all salad ingredients in a large bowl.

2. Make dressing. Toss salad and dressing together just before serving.

Serves 4

* See "Cooking Methods" section

	RCU	FU	Cal	%Ft	P	F	C	Na
Per Serving	0	0	71	15	3	1	12	460

CRISP APPLE SALAD

Apple salad tastes marvelous any time. Try this for lunch, dinner, snack, or a dessert.

½	C	crushed pineapple, juice-packed
2		apples, diced or sliced
¼	C	celery, diced
1	T	walnuts, chopped

1. Toss pineapple, apples, and celery together gently. Chill.

2. Spoon onto a lettuce leaf. Top each serving with 1 teaspoon walnuts.

Serves 3

	RCU	FU	Cal	%Ft	P	F	C	Na
Per Serving	0	0	87	16	T	2	18	14

LOVELY LAYERED LUNCH

Salads also make scrumptious snacks.

CHERRY
TOMATOES

1	sm. head	lettuce, torn into pieces
2	sm.	Bermuda onions, thinly sliced and separated into rings
2	C	zucchini, thinly sliced
2	C	cherry tomatoes, halved
4	oz.	low-fat cottage cheese, blended
1	tsp.	Worcestershire sauce
½	tsp.	dry mustard
1	C	low-fat yogurt*

1. Layer lettuce, onion, zucchini, and cherry tomatoes in a large bowl.

2. Combine blended cottage cheese, Worcestershire sauce, and mustard. Stir in yogurt.

3. Spoon over layered vegetables. If desired, sprinkle with paprika.

4. Cover and refrigerate 4 to 6 hours or overnight. Toss just before serving.

Serves 8

* See "Cooking Methods" section

	RCU	FU	Cal	%Ft	P	F	C	Na
Per Serving	0	0	72	10	6	1	12	69

Choose TOMATOES that are smooth, firm, and plump with an overall rich, red color. Avoid tomatoes with green or yellow areas, cracks near the stem, or depressed areas. Store tomatoes in a cool, dark place and use as soon as possible. Unripe tomatoes will ripen if kept away from direct sunlight at room temperature. They are in season all year.

TICO TACO SALAD

Enjoy the flavor of tacos without the fat.

1	head	lettuce, shredded	to taste	Salsa (p. 27)
3		tomatoes, chopped	¼ recipe	Tortilla Triangles
¾	C	chicken, cooked and diced		(p. 363)
¼	C	onion, chopped		
3	oz.	cottage cheese,* dry or drained		

Gifford's Alternatives: *Add to chicken when cooking:*

1 ½	tsp.	*Gifford's Mexican Spice®*
½	tsp.	*Gifford's Dessert Spice®*

1. Arrange each ingredient in separate containers.

2. Build your salad in this order: lettuce, tomatoes, meat, onions, and cottage cheese. Top with Salsa and Tortilla Triangles.

Serves 6

* See "Cooking Methods" section

	RCU	FU	Cal	%Ft	P	F	C	Na
Per Serving	0	0	109	12	10	2	13	133

SPINACH-APPLE TOSS

Apple pieces add so much to this variation of a favorite salad.

1	lb.	spinach, raw
2		tart red apples
¼	C	imitation bacon bits*
1	recipe	Creamy Orange Dressing (p. 20)

SPINACH

1. Wash spinach. Break into bite-sized pieces.

2. Core and slice apples. Toss with spinach.

3. Sprinkle with bacon bits.

4. Prepare Creamy Orange Dressing. Toss with salad immediately before serving.

Serves 8

* See "Cooking Methods" section

	RCU	FU	Cal	%Ft	P	F	C	Na
Per Serving	0	0	87	12	5	1	15	79

Choose SPINACH that has crisp, green leaves. Avoid coarse stems or soft yellowing leaves.

FAVORITE SPINACH SALAD

This fresh spinach salad makes a refreshing change from lettuce salads in the summer. To reduce percentage of fat, omit the egg yolk.

3	C	fresh spinach, torn
1	C	fresh mushrooms, sliced
½	C	radishes, sliced
1		hard-cooked egg, sliced
1	recipe	Lime Dressing (p. 29)

1. Combine spinach, mushrooms, radishes, and egg slices. Shake dressing, pour over spinach mixture, and toss before serving.

Serves 4

	RCU	FU	Cal	%Ft	P	F	C	Na
Per Serving	0	0	73	24	6	2	8	95

HAWAIIAN CHICKEN SALAD

What a treat! Luscious alone or with a steaming whole wheat muffin.

2	C	chicken OR turkey, diced
2		apples, diced
1	C	pineapple chunks, drained
3	T	low-fat cottage cheese,* blended
6	leaves	lettuce
6	med.	almonds, whole

1. Toss together all ingredients, except almonds and lettuce leaves. Spoon individual portions onto lettuce leaves. Garnish with 1 chopped almond per serving.

Serves 6

* See "Cooking Methods" section

	RCU	FU	Cal	%Ft	P	F	C	Na
Per Serving	0	0	138	18	16	3	15	51

CHUNKY CHICKEN SALAD

This salad makes a delicious filling for whole, hollowed-out tomatoes.

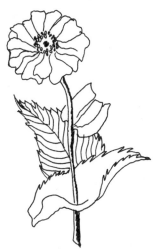

2	C	chicken OR turkey, white meat chunks
½		cucumber, peeled and diced
½	C	celery, diced
½	C	water chestnuts, drained and sliced
¼	C	green pepper, diced
¼	C	pimento, chopped
6		green onions, sliced
¼	C	low-fat cottage cheese,* blended
6	leaves	lettuce
sprinkle		paprika

Gifford's Alternatives: Add:
1	T	*peach juice concentrate*
1	tsp.	*onion powder*
½	tsp.	*chicken bouillon granules**
½	tsp.	*Gifford's Dessert Spice®*

1. Toss meat, cucumber, celery, water chestnuts, green pepper, pimento, and green onions with blended cottage cheese.

2. Serve on lettuce leaves with a sprinkle of paprika.

Serves 6

* See "Cooking Methods" section

	RCU	FU	Cal	%Ft	P	F	C	Na
Per Serving	0	0	107	15	15	2	6	5

VARIATION: TITILLATING TUNA SALAD

2	6 ½	water-packed tuna
	oz. cans	

1. Replace chicken or turkey with tuna. Proceed as directed above.

	RCU	FU	Cal	%Ft	P	F	C	Na
Per Serving	0	0	107	4	18	7	6	48

BELL PEPPER "FILL-UPS"

Fill 'em up with rice, salad, or thick stews. After you "fill 'em up," then "eat 'em up."

6	sm.	green peppers
5	C	water

1. Core green peppers.

2. Boil for 3 minutes in water.

3. Drain and put immediately in ice water. Let stand for 15 minutes.

4. Drain well. These are now ready to fill with your favorite low-fat tuna or chicken salad. Serve.

Serves 6

	RCU	FU	Cal	%Ft	P	F	C	Na
Per Serving	0	0	13	T	T	T	3	10

Choose PEPPERS that are firm and heavy for their size with a glossy bright green color. Avoid soft peppers with thin walls or watery spots on the sides. Wash, dry, and store in refrigerator crisper. Use within one week. They are available all year.

"DILLY" OF A SHRIMP SALAD

Beautiful enough to serve to company.

1	lb.	shrimp
½		onion, peeled and sliced
1	15 oz. can	water chestnuts, sliced
4	T	Low-Calorie Italian Dressing (p. 37)
1	tsp.	dill, dried OR
2	T	fresh dill, chopped
1	head	romaine lettuce
3		tomatoes
4	oz.	mushrooms, sliced
garnish		parsley

1. Drain and chill shrimp. Toss shrimp, onion, water chestnuts, and dressing. Sprinkle with dill.

2. Serve on romaine lettuce. Surround with sliced tomatoes and mushrooms. Garnish with parsley.

Serves 10

	RCU	FU	Cal	%Ft	P	F	C	Na
Per Serving	0	0	85	7	12	1	7	124

TEMPTING TUNA SALAD

Wrap each serving in an iceberg lettuce leaf and secure with a toothpick for a delightful luncheon.

1	6 ½ oz. can	tuna, water-packed
2	T	sweet pickle relish
¼	C	low-fat cottage cheese,* blended
1	T	onion, minced
¼	C	peas
to taste		seasoning without salt*

1. Drain tuna.

2. Toss all ingredients together.

3. Serve chilled as a salad, use as a stuffing for tomatoes, or use as a filling for a sandwich.

Serves 8

* See "Cooking Methods" section

	RCU	FU	Cal	%Ft	P	F	C	Na
Per Serving	1	0	43	9	8	T	7	40

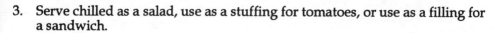

ZESTY THREE-BEAN SALAD

Add garbanzo beans for an instant four-bean salad.

1	8 oz. can	green beans, drained
1	8 oz. can	wax beans, drained
1	16 oz. can	kidney beans, rinsed and drained
1	T	fruit juice concentrate*
½	C	onion, chopped
2	T	parsley, chopped
1	C	Low-Calorie Italian Dressing (p. 37)
1	clove	garlic, crushed

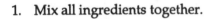

Gifford's Alternatives: Add:
2	tsp.	*Gifford's Italian Spice®*
¼	tsp.	*Gifford's Dessert Spice®*

1. Mix all ingredients together.

2. Refrigerate for at least 3 hours before serving. This also makes a delicious stuffing for hollowed-out tomatoes.

Serves 8

* *See "Cooking Methods" section*

	RCU	FU	Cal	%Ft	P	F	C	Na
Per Serving	0	0	73	1	4	T	14	142

SPROUT DUPLEX: A SALAD OR A SANDWICH

Lentil sprouts taste a lot like fresh peas.

¼	C	fresh mushrooms, sliced
½	C	lentil sprouts*
½	C	alfalfa sprouts*
½	head	lettuce, finely sliced
2	lg.	tomatoes, sliced
1		green onion, sliced

Gifford's Alternatives: *Add:*   *to taste*   *Gifford's Gourmet Spice®*

1. Toss all ingredients together.

2. Top with your favorite low-fat dressing. See Fabulous Flavors on page 19.

3. This is also a fancy filling for a pita bread sandwich.

Serves 6
* See "Cooking Methods" section

	RCU	FU	Cal	%Ft	P	F	C	Na
Per Serving	0	0	51	3	3	T	10	10

CRUNCHY TOMATO ASPIC

Joyce Nixon
Mariteresa Bergerson

What a spicy companion to a turkey sandwich.

CLOVES

¼	C	onion, chopped
1 ¼	C	celery, chopped
2		bay leaves
4	whole	cloves
4	C	tomato juice,* low sodium
2	env.	gelatin, unflavored
3	T	lemon juice

1. Simmer onion, ¼ cup celery, bay leaves, cloves, and 2 cups tomato juice for 5 minutes. Strain.

2. Dissolve unflavored gelatin in 1 cup cold tomato juice. Add to hot tomato mixture.

3. Add 1 cup tomato juice and lemon juice.

4. Cool to lukewarm, then add 1 cup chopped celery.

5. Pour into a mold or ring. Refrigerate to set. Unmold onto lettuce leaves and serve.

Serves 8
*See "Cooking Methods" section

	RCU	FU	Cal	%Ft	P	F	C	Na
Per Serving	0	0	37	T	3	T	7	37

THE 3-C SALAD: CUCUMBERS, CARROTS, AND COTTAGE CHEESE

This salad is cool, crunchy, and crisp.

1	env.	gelatin, unflavored
1 ½	C	chicken broth*
1	T	lemon juice
1 ½	tsp.	horseradish, optional
¼	C	cucumber, thinly sliced
1 ½	C	low-fat cottage cheese,* dry
⅓	C	carrot, shredded
⅓	C	cucumber, seeded and shredded
2	T	green onion, chopped
2	T	green pepper, chopped

HORSERADISH

Gifford's Alternatives: Add at step #2:

1	*T*	*Butter Buds® Sprinkles*
1	*T*	*peach juice concentrate*
½	*tsp.*	*lime juice*
½	*tsp.*	*Gifford's Basic Spice®*
1	*pinch*	*rubbed sage*

1. Soften gelatin in chicken broth.

2. Combine lemon juice and horseradish. Add to gelatin mixture and stir over low heat until gelatin is dissolved.

3. Cool. Arrange cucumber slices in 1-quart mold. Pour ½ cup gelatin mixture into mold and chill until almost firm.

4. Combine remaining ingredients and pour into mold. Chill until firm. Serve.
Serves 6

* See "Cooking Methods" section

	RCU	FU	Cal	%Ft	P	F	C	Na
Per Serving	0	0	63	T	11	T	3	274

PEACHY PERFECT GELATIN

Trim with fresh peach slices — perfect!

2	env.	gelatin, unflavored
1	tsp.	ginger, ground
½	C	water
1	C	apple juice
8		fresh peaches, peeled and pitted
2	T	lemon juice
1	C	low-fat cottage cheese*

Gifford's Alternatives: Add:
½	C	peach juice concentrate
1	tsp.	ground cinnamon
		OMIT ½ cup water

1. In small saucepan combine gelatin, ginger, and water. Stir over low heat until gelatin is dissolved.

2. Remove from heat and add apple juice.

3. Purée enough peaches to make 2 cups. Stir into gelatin. Add lemon juice.

4. Chill until partially set.

5. Chop enough of the remaining peaches to make 1 cup. Fold into gelatin mixture along with cottage cheese. Pour into a 5-cup mold. Chill 5 to 6 hours or overnight. Serve.

Serves 8

* See "Cooking Methods" section

	RCU	FU	Cal	%Ft	P	F	C	Na
Per Serving	0	0	88	13	6	1	19	63

   Choose PEACHES that are slightly soft and avoid those that are green, hard, or have large bruises. They ripen at room temperature. The peak season is June through September.

GLISTENING GREEN GELATIN

Tossed salad doesn't ALWAYS need to be tossed. This one is set in gelatin. Nice change.

1	env.	gelatin, unflavored	6		green onions, chopped
1	T	sugar	2	C	spinach, raw, shredded
1¾	C	water	1	C	celery, chopped
3	T	vinegar	1	C	carrot, coarsely grated
1	T	lemon juice	1	T	green pepper, minced

1. Combine gelatin and sugar in saucepan. Add ¾ cup water. Heat, stirring constantly, until gelatin is dissolved. Remove from heat.

2. Stir in remaining water, vinegar, and lemon juice.

3. Chill mixture until partially set. Then fold in remaining ingredients.

4. Pour into a 1-quart mold or 7 individual molds. Chill until firm. Serve.

Serves 7

	RCU	FU	Cal	%Ft	P	F	C	Na
Per Serving	0	0	29	3	2	T	5	55

VARIATION: CHICKEN-FLAVORED GELATIN SALAD

1¾   C   chicken broth*

1. Replace sugar, water, and vinegar with chicken broth.

See "Cooking Methods" section

	RCU	FU	Cal	%Ft	P	F	C	Na
Per Serving	0	0	22	4	2	T	0	154

SPARKLING APRICOT GELATIN

A shimmering side dish.

1	16 oz. can	unsweetened apricot halves
1/2	C	water
1	env.	gelatin, unflavored
1	T	lemon juice
1/2	C	water

Gifford's Alternatives: Add:

1/2	C	*white grape juice concentrate,*
1	tsp.	*Butter Buds® Sprinkles*
1	tsp.	*Gifford's Dessert Spice®*
		OMIT 1/2 cup water

1. Drain and purée apricots in blender or through a sieve. This makes about 1 cup of purée.

2. Combine water and gelatin in saucepan. Heat until gelatin is thickened. Remove from heat.

3. Add lemon juice and apricot purée. Mix well.

4. Add water and mix gently.

5. Divide equally into 4 molds or serving dishes. Chill until set. Serve.

Serves 4

	RCU	FU	Cal	%Ft	P	F	C	Na
Per Serving	0	0	48	T	2	T	10	1

Choose APRICOTS that are plump and fairly firm. They will ripen in a paper bag kept in a warm room. Peak season is June through July.

PUSSY WILLOW

SUNSET GELATIN SALAD

This salad has the warm, streaked colors and textures of a sunset.

2	env.	gelatin, unflavored
1	C	water
1/4	C	orange juice
1/4	C	pineapple juice
1	C	crushed pineapple, drained
1	C	carrots, grated

1. Soften gelatin in cool water. Heat to boiling. Cool slightly.

2. Add fruit juices.

3. Chill until slightly thickened.

4. Fold in remaining ingredients and pour into 1-quart bowl or individual molds.

Serves 6

	RCU	FU	Cal	%Ft	P	F	C	Na
Per Serving	**0**	**0**	**53**	**T**	**3**	**T**	**11**	**9**

ASPARAGUS IN APPLE GELATIN

You can use cooked, fresh, or frozen asparagus in place of canned.

2	env.	gelatin, unflavored
1/2	C	cold water
1	C	apple juice
1	C	water
1	T	onion, minced
2	T	lemon juice
1	10 oz. can	asparagus, cut
2	T	pimento, diced
1	15 oz. can	water chestnuts, sliced
1	C	celery, chopped

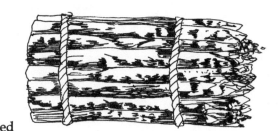

1. Dissolve gelatin in 1/2 cup cold water.

2. Add apple juice and 1 cup water. Bring to a boil. Remove from heat. Add onion and lemon juice.

3. Allow to cool. Add asparagus, pimento, water chestnuts, and celery.

4. Pour into a 1 ½-quart mold and chill until set. Serve.

Serves 10

	RCU	FU	Cal	%Ft	P	F	C	Na
Per Serving	0	0	60	5	3	T	12	99

CRAZY COLESLAW GELATIN

Crunchy cabbage in an apple juice gelatin. Crazy? Sure! And I'll bet you'll love being crazy about this salad.

2	env.	gelatin, unflavored
½	C	cold water
1	C	water
1	C	apple juice
2	T	lemon juice
3	T	onion, chopped
1	C	cabbage, shredded
1	C	celery, diced
3	T	pimento, chopped
3	T	green pepper, chopped

CABBAGE

1. Soften unflavored gelatin in ½ cup cold water.

2. Add 1 cup water. Heat to boiling. Cool slightly. Add apple juice and lemon juice. Continue cooling until mixture starts to thicken.

3. Fold in onion, cabbage, celery, pimento, and green pepper. Pour into a 1-quart mold and chill until set. Serve.

Serves 8

	RCU	FU	Cal	%Ft	P	F	C	Na
Per Serving	0	0	33	T	2	T	6	27

FRUIT WHIRL

This salad is as good to look at as it is to eat. Try serving it as a dessert.

2		oranges OR
1		grapefruit
2		apples, unpeeled
4		leaves lettuce
4	tsp.	unsweetened coconut, grated, optional

Gifford's Alternatives: Add to grated coconut:
1   tsp.   *Gifford's Dessert Spice®*

1. Peel and separate oranges or grapefruit into segments. Core unpeeled apples and slice into wedges.

2. Alternate citrus fruit and apple wedges on lettuce leaf to form a pinwheel. HINT: Apples and oranges could be sliced crosswise in thin circles and alternated to form another colorful pattern.

3. Sprinkle a small amount of grated coconut over fruit before serving.

Serves 4

	RCU	FU	Cal	%Ft	P	F	C	Na
Per Serving	0	0	84	6	1	1	16	4

Choose firm, heavy ORANGES or GRAPEFRUIT with finely textured skin. Greenish color or dark speckling over the skin does not affect the quality of the fruit. Avoid oranges or grapefruit with rough or dull, dry skin or with soft spots. Refrigerate or store at room temperature. Use within two weeks. Oranges are available all year, while grapefruits are only in season from January through May.

SNOW WHITE AND ROSE RED

Sydette Parent

This will dress up a quiet luncheon with friends or an elegant dinner for two.

1	fresh	tomato
½	C	low-fat cottage cheese*
2	T	celery, diced
⅛	tsp.	parsley, snipped
1/16	tsp.	garlic powder
1/16	tsp.	onion powder

Gifford's Alternatives: Add: 1   tsp.   Gifford's Gourmet Spice®

1. Wash and stem the tomato. Then cut it into 6 wedges, but only cut ¾ of the way through so that it resembles a flower.

2. Combine remaining ingredients and fill the tomato with the cottage cheese mixture. Chill before serving.

Serves 1

See "Cooking Methods" section

	RCU	FU	Cal	%Ft	P	F	C	Na
Per Serving	0	0	143	2	22	T	14	360

ALPINE SUMMER

Fresh fruit over a snowy mount of cottage cheese. Fast and fabulous! Serve with homemade bread and reduce the overall fat percentage.

1	C	low-fat cottage cheese*
1		pear, sliced OR
1		peach, sliced or diced OR
¾	C	crushed pineapple, juice-packed

1. Spoon fruit over the top of the cottage cheese or mix together. Chill. Serve on lettuce leaves.

Serves 2

See "Cooking Methods" section

With Pear	RCU	FU	Cal	%Ft	P	F	C	Na
Per Serving	0	0	162	24	15	4	16	242

With Peach	RCU	FU	Cal	%Ft	P	F	C	Na
Per Serving	0	0	131	30	15	4	8	241

With Pineapple	RCU	FU	Cal	%Ft	P	F	C	Na
Per Serving	0	0	146	27	15	4	12	242

Choose fairly firm PEARS with yellowish color. Dark speckling over skin does not affect quality of the fruit. Avoid shriveled pears with dull skin or those that are soft near the stem. Ripen in a paper bag at room temperature until stem end yields to pressure, then refrigerate. Use within three to five days. Bartlett pears are in season from August through November.

INDIAN SUMMER

This makes a colorful side dish with dinner on those warm autumn evenings.

½	C	crushed pineapple, juice-packed
2	C	carrots, shredded
¼	C	raisins

Gifford's Alternatives: Add:
| 1 | tsp. | *orange flavor extract* |
| ½ | tsp. | *ground cinnamon* |

1. Toss all ingredients together gently.

2. Chill and serve on a lettuce leaf.

Serves 4

	RCU	FU	Cal	%Ft	P	F	C	Na
Per Serving	0	0	64	T	T	T	14	28

SPRINGTIME

This would be charming layered with cottage cheese in a parfait glass.

1	C	crushed pineapple, juice-packed
2		apples, diced or sliced
¼	C	raisins

Gifford's Alternatives: Add:
| 1 | tsp. | *black walnut extract* |
| ½ | tsp. | *Gifford's Dessert Spice®* |

1. Toss all ingredients together gently.

2. Chill and serve in a decorative iced bowl or glass.

Serves 4

	RCU	FU	Cal	%Ft	P	F	C	Na
Per Serving	0	0	93	T	T	T	20	4

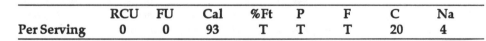

CARROT CABBAGE HAYSTACKS

Serve this stacked lightly on a lettuce leaf with your favorite sandwich.

½	C	crushed pineapple, juice-packed
1	C	carrots, shredded
2	C	cabbage, shredded

Gifford's Alternatives: *Add:*

¼	tsp.	coconut flavor extract
¼	tsp.	pure vanilla extract
½	tsp.	Schilling® Orange Peel
1	pinch	ground nutmeg

CABBAGE

1. Toss all ingredients gently. Chill.

Serves 4

	RCU	FU	Cal	%Ft	P	F	C	Na
Per Serving	0	0	35	T	T	T	7	23

SUNBURST

Kids and adults will delight in the beauty of this fruit salad.

¼	C	crushed pineapple, juice-packed
1		orange
1		grapefruit

ORANGE SEGMENT

1. Section fresh orange and grapefruit.

2. Arrange sections in an alternating pattern to form a sunburst on a lettuce leaf.

3. Spoon crushed pineapple onto the center of the sunburst. Chill before serving.

Serves 2

	RCU	FU	Cal	%Ft	P	F	C	Na
Per Serving	0	0	97	T	2	T	23	2

WALDORF SALAD

If you leave out the walnuts, this salad is only 11 percent fat.

2	T	lemon juice
2	C	apples, unpeeled, diced
1	C	celery, diced
½	C	seedless grapes, halved
½	C	pineapple tidbits, juice-packed, liquid drained and reserved
½	C	low-fat cottage cheese*
2	T	nonfat dry milk*
1	T	walnuts, chopped, optional

Gifford's Alternatives: Add to blender in step #2:.
1	T	apple juice concentrate
1	small	ripe banana, peeled
½	tsp.	black walnut extract
½	tsp.	Gifford's Dessert Spice®

1. Sprinkle lemon juice on diced apples to keep them white. Toss apples, celery, grapes, and pineapple together gently.

2. Place cottage cheese, nonfat dry milk, and 1 tablespoon drained liquid from pineapple tidbits in blender. Blend until creamy smooth.

3. Pour over apple mixture and toss until thoroughly mixed. Chill. Serve on lettuce leaves. Sprinkle ½ teaspoon walnuts over each serving, if desired.

Serves 6

* See "Cooking Methods" section

	RCU	FU	Cal	%Ft	P	F	C	Na
Per Serving	0	0	76	19	5	2	11	81

Choose APPLES that are firm and crisp with good color. Avoid fruit that is discolored or soft. Store in a plastic bag in the refrigerator. Apples are available throughout the year.

RING-A-ROUND THE ROSY

This makes an exquisite dessert as well as an elegant salad.

CANTALOUPE

1		cantaloupe
1	pint	strawberries

1. Cut melon crosswise into rings 1-inch thick. Remove seeds.
2. Place slices on individual plates and cut around the slice ¼ inch from the rind. Do not remove rind but slice the melon into bite-sized pieces, leaving rind intact.
3. Rinse strawberries, but do not hull. Arrange 5 or 6 strawberries in the center of each melon slice. Serve.

Serves 5

	RCU	FU	Cal	%Ft	P	F	C	Na
Per Serving	0	0	54	6	1	T	13	13

Choose CANTALOUPE that has a yellowish cast to the rind, with thick, coarse veining. Ripe cantaloupes have a pleasant odor and give slightly at the blossom end when pressed gently. Avoid melons with bruises or soft areas. Ripen at room temperature, then refrigerate. Use as soon as possible. Peak season is from May through September.

Choose firm, dry, full-red STRAWBERRIES with a bright luster and green caps still attached. Avoid berries with large seedy areas or a sunken appearance. Store in refrigerator unwashed with caps intact. Hull and wash just before serving. Peak season is from April through June.

MIX-AND-MATCH FRESH FRUIT SALADS

There are no hard and fast rules for fruit salads. Just make sure the fruit is fresh and ripe and cut into bite-size pieces. Try to vary the colors and the texture of the fruit, including some crisp and some soft fruits. Since fresh fruit is naturally low in fat, it makes perfect snacks, salads, or desserts. Experiment with your favorite fresh fruit combinations.

HINT: Toss apples, pears, and bananas in a little lemon juice to prevent them from browning.

SOME SUGGESTED FRUIT SALAD COMBOS

Dilute nonfat yogurt with pineapple or orange juice, and drizzle it over sliced fruit for an easy fruit dressing.

APPLE, PEACH, ORANGE, AND GRAPES

1		apple
1		peach
1		orange
½	C	grapes

Serves 4

	RCU	FU	Cal	%Ft	P	F	C	Na
Per Serving	0	0	57	3	1	T	17	1

MELON, GRAPEFRUIT, PEAR, AND PINEAPPLE

2	C	melon
½		grapefruit
1		pear
1	C	pineapple

Serves 4

	RCU	FU	Cal	%Ft	P	F	C	Na
Per Serving	0	0	73	T	T	T	18	8

RASPBERRIES, PEARS, APRICOTS, AND GOOSEBERRIES

1	C	raspberries
1		pear
3		apricots
1	C	gooseberries

Serves 4

	RCU	FU	Cal	%Ft	P	F	C	Na
Per Serving	0	0	74	3	1	T	18	2

TANGERINE, BANANA, APPLE, AND BLUEBERRIES

1		tangerine
1		banana
1		apple
1	C	blueberries

Serves 4

	RCU	FU	Cal	%Ft	P	F	C	Na
Per Serving	0	0	66	T	1	T	17	1

STRAWBERRIES, MELON, CHERRIES, AND APPLES

1	C	strawberries
2	C	melon
1	C	cherries
1		apple

CHERRIES

Serves 4

	RCU	FU	Cal	%Ft	P	F	C	Na
Per Serving	0	0	70	3	1	T	17	8

Choose plump, firm GRAPES that are securely attached to green pliable stems. Avoid wrinkled or leaking berries and those with bleached areas around the stem. Refrigerate and use as soon as possible. Peak season is from July through November.

Choose bright, clean RASPBERRIES with uniform good color. Refrigerate immediately and use as soon as possible. Peak season is from June through August.

Choose TANGERINES that are heavy for their size and have a deep yellow or orange color. A puffy appearance and feel are normal. Refrigerate and use as soon as possible. Peak season is from December through January.

BANANAS should be firm and plump. Color ranges from green to brown, but best eating quality is reached when skin is solid yellow specked with brown. Avoid bruised or grayish yellow fruit. Ripen at room temperature and use as soon as possible. Bananas are available all year.

Choose plump, firm BLUEBERRIES. Color should be dark blue with a silvery bloom. Avoid bruised or leaking fruit. Pack loosely, cover, and refrigerate. Use as soon as possible. Peak season is from May through September.

CHERRIES should be plump, glossy, and firm, but not hard. Color should be dark and range from deep red to black. Avoid dried stems or shriveled, leaking fruit. Cherries will ripen at room temperature. Refrigerate and use within two days. Peak season is from May through August.

PINEAPPLE BASKET

FRESH PINEAPPLE BASKET

A unique, edible centerpiece for a party or special occasion.

This is not so much a recipe as a method of serving fresh pineapple, making it attractive and easy to eat.

Halve the pineapple lengthwise, or, if it is very large, quarter it lengthwise, including the leaves.

Using a very sharp grapefruit knife, penetrate the flesh of the pineapple just underneath the hard center core. Cut all the way along, then down and along the bottom edge, just inside the prickly skin.

Turn the half pineapple around and do the same to the other side.

When this is done, it should be possible to remove all the fruit in one piece. But do not do this. Instead, cut it into bite-size pieces, but leave it looking like it is still intact.

When the pineapple has been eaten, you are left with a basket shape that is made up of all the inedible parts of the fruit—the center core, prickly skin, and leaves.

For a special party effect, you could remove three or four of the cubes of pineapple and replace them with perfect whole strawberries or huge black grapes.

OR

Dice the pineapple flesh and remove from basket. Toss with other favorite fruits such as grapes, melon, orange segments, blueberries, strawberries, or apples. Fill hollowed pineapple basket with this fruit mixture. Serve chilled.

	RCU	FU	Cal	%Ft	P	F	C	Na
Per Serving	0	0	81	T	T	T	21	2

Choose a PINEAPPLE that is plump, firm, heavy for its size, and has a rich, sweet smell. The leaves or spikes should pull out easily. Avoid fruit that is watery, dull, or yellowish green in color. Ripen at room temperature and then store in refrigerator, always crown side down. Use as soon as possible. Peak season is April through May.

FRUIT-FILLED WATERMELON BASKET

This makes the perfect centerpiece for any summer gathering. It can be used as the salad or the dessert.

Select a ripe watermelon that has a flat bottom to keep it stable. You may cut a thin slice to form a flat bottom, if necessary.

Outline a handle, 3 inches wide, in the center of the short width of the melon. Bring handle line half way down the side of the melon, then bring the line out from the bottom of the handle to the ends of the melon so that it will form a basket with a handle. When you are sure that you have it well placed, cut it out with a sharp knife and remove the sections.

Hollow out the melon under the handle but leave it at least ½ inch thick. Hollow out the rest of the melon with a melon baller. Drain the juice.

Decorate the rim of the basket with a sawtooth pattern.

Fill the basket with melon balls and other fruits of your choice that have been cut into bite-sized pieces. Try cantaloupe, bananas, oranges, pineapples, peaches, blueberries, strawberries, cherries, grapes, apples, or whatever is in season.

Choose a WATERMELON that is firm and smooth with red, juicy flesh. Avoid stark-white or greenish colored undersides and white streaks in the flesh. Store at room temperature or refrigerate. Use within three to five days. Peak season is June through August.

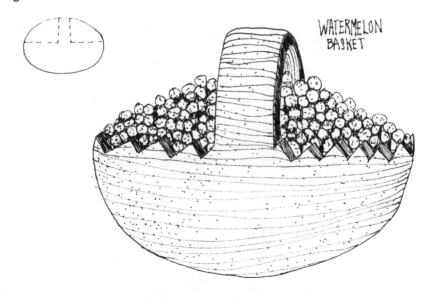

WATERMELON BASKET

MACARONI SALAD

Picnics and parties are perfect places for this macaroni salad.

1	C	whole wheat macaroni,* uncooked
2	T	low-fat cottage cheese,* blended
2	T	low-calorie mayonnaise
1	T	vinegar
1	tsp.	prepared mustard
¾	C	celery, chopped
6		green onions, sliced
2	T	sweet pickle relish
1	T	pimento, chopped

Gifford's Alternatives: Add:
1 ½ tsp. Gifford's Basic Spice®

1. Cook and drain macaroni.

2. Mix blended cottage cheese, low-calorie mayonnaise, vinegar, and mustard in a large bowl.

3. Add remaining ingredients and toss together. Chill before serving.

Serves 8

* See "Cooking Methods" section

	RCU	FU	Cal	%Ft	P	F	C	Na
Per Serving	1	0	132	15	6	2	27	53

"TO MEAT OR NOT TO MEAT?"

Give a man a fish, you've fed him once; teach him to fish,
you've fed him for a lifetime.

---Old Proverb

"TO MEAT OR NOT TO MEAT? THAT IS THE QUESTION!"

Whether or not to eat meat has become a controversial question and a complicated issue in recent times. At one end of the scale, you have vegetarians that totally abstain from meat for reasons ranging from ecology and economics to health and religion. At the other end of the scale, you have those who indulge in eating large amounts of meat with pride for reasons ranging from status and flavor to habit and health. Our position is in between these two extremes, leaning more toward the vegetarian side. We do not advocate total abstinence from meat, but we do suggest that you reduce your intake of meat to two to four ounces a day. This simple change will greatly decrease the overall percentage of fat in your daily diet. It will also allow you to replace those calories with low-fat, high-fiber complex carbohydrates such as beans and grains. This is the single most important change you can make to achieve the benefits of a low-fat diet.

It is important to know something about the various types of meats so that you can make a wise decision about which meats to eat. The main groups of meat are beef, ham, processed meats, poultry, and fish. Eggs and cheese can also be included in our discussion of meats since they are animal products with complete proteins and are often used as meat substitutes.

Beef is an American favorite. Steak dinners have become the ultimate reward when celebrating anniversaries, birthdays, business deals, or personal successses. Fast food chains give us hamburgers and roast beef sandwiches at a moment's notice. Many people eat strictly "meat and potatoes." We serve expensive cuts of beef when we want to impress company. The list goes on. For some, it may be difficult to give up or alter these practices, but the evidence against a high-fat diet is overwhelming. Somehow these lifestyle changes need to be made. Learn to celebrate by eating low-fat meals when eating out (see p. 3); eat fresh fruits for lunch when you are in a hurry instead of stopping at a fast food chain; learn to enjoy the wonderful soups, stews, casseroles, and breads available in place of strictly "meat and potatoes"; and impress your guests with steaming hot loaves of homemade breads instead of expensive meats.

These recipes are designed to reduce the amount of fat in the meat dishes you prepare, but it is very difficult to keep beef recipes under the 20 percent standard. These recipes are much lower in fat than they would be normally, but many of them are between 20 percent and 30 percent fat. Compensate for this by eating small servings and adding lots of vegetables or salads to your meal to reduce the overall fat percentage to 20 percent.

The cuts of beef that you eat are very important. Most people know that the most tender, flavorful, and expensive cuts of beef are those that are "marbled." This means that they are streaked with fat. As a result, a sirloin tip is 75 percent fat, corned beef is 74 percent fat, spareribs are 80 percent fat, filet mignon is 80 percent fat, and a club steak is 83 percent fat. The leanest cuts of beef are the

flank, round, and rump, which are between 33 percent and 53 percent fat. These cuts of meat are not very tender nor are they very flavorful, so they are best cooked by using moist heat. These methods include boiling, pressure cooking, simmering, stewing, casseroling, or wrapping in foil. All of the recipes use lean cuts of beef or lean hamburger and incorporate these moist heat methods of cooking. These lean cuts of beef can be used interchangeably with each other or lean hamburger in most of the recipes. There are also many other meat recipes under 20 percent fat that can be found in the chapters on soups (p. 57), grains (p. 297), beans (p. 251), or salads (p. 97).

Ham comes in wide ranges of fat content, anywhere from 47 percent to 74 percent. Always buy the leanest cuts of ham and trim away all visible fat. Ham is commonly teamed up with beans or added to a tossed green salad. All of the ham recipes are found in the chapters on beans (p. 251) or on salads (p. 97). Bacon is 77 percent fat and has little place in a low-fat diet. Imitation bacon bits are made from soybeans and give the enjoyment of a bacon garnish but with reduced fat.

Processed meats such as salami, bologna, lunch meats, hot dogs, sausage, or liverwurst are convenient and tasty, but they are 70 percent to 80 percent fat and laced with preservatives. It is best to avoid these on a low-fat diet.

The poultry group consists of chicken, turkey, goose, duck, and pheasant. Goose, duck, and pheasant are all high in fat, ranging from 43 percent to 77 percent fat. The dark meat of chicken and turkey are higher in fat than the white meat. Chicken dark meat is 25 percent fat and the light meat is 12 percent fat. Turkey dark meat is 35 percent fat and the white meat is 18 percent fat. It is always best to remove the skin from chicken or turkey before eating it since there is a layer of fat between the meat and the skin that can then be eliminated. As a rule, the white meat of both chicken and turkey are good choices for meat on a low-fat diet and they can be used interchangeably in most cases. There are many recipes in this chapter as well as in the chapters on soups (p. 57), grains (p. 297), and salads (p. 97).

Fish is the meat with the lowest percentage of fat: cod has three percent fat; tuna, six percent; flatfish, 10 percent; shrimp, 10 percent; scallops, 13 percent; sole, 11 percent; and crab, 21 percent. Salmon is 68 percent fat when raw and reduces to 61 percent when canned. Tuna becomes 67 percent fat when canned and packed in oil. Some of the fat can be reduced in oil-packed fish by dumping the fish into a colander and rinsing it with very hot water. Fish is an excellent meat choice on a low-fat diet. Do not increase the percentage of fat in fish by cooking or dipping it in butter or by spreading high-fat tartar sauce over it. See page 28 for a low-fat tartar sauce recipe. Use Butter Buds® Sprinkles for a low-fat butter substitute.

Eggs and cheese are often used as protein substitutes for meat. However, both are high in fat, and eggs are also high in cholesterol. The yolk is the source of fat in the egg. There are six grams of fat in one egg yolk, which makes an egg 68 percent fat. If eggs are used at all, they should be used sparingly. If they are eaten in combination with complex carbohydrates, such as bread, then the overall percentage of fat in the meal will be reduced. Most recipes are fine if you replace a whole egg with two egg whites.

Cheeses range in their level of fats from skim cottage cheese, which is three percent fat, to Edam or cream cheeses which are both more than 90 percent fat. But even cottage cheese can range from three percent to 36 percent fat, so always buy dry curd, skim, or two percent cottage cheese. Higher-fat cottage cheese can be rinsed off in a strainer to lower its fat content. White or yellow hard cheeses are between 60 percent to 75 percent fat. Some white cheeses are made with skim milk, which lowers their fat percentage. Processed cheese is 69 percent to 73 percent fat. All cheeses, except cottage cheese, must be used sparingly, if at all, on a low-fat diet.

Meat salad recipes, see:
The Garden Spot on page 97

Meat soup recipes, see:
"Soup's On!" on page 57

Meat casserole recipes, see:
The Bean Bag on page 251
The Sweep of the Scythe on page 269

APPLE TUNA TOSS

Joyce Nixon
Mariteresa Bergerson

This salad makes a cool, nutritious meal on a hot summer day.

4	C	lettuce, broken into pieces
2	C	apples, unpeeled and diced
1	6 ½ oz. can	water-packed tuna, drained
1	C	orange sections
½	C	low-fat yogurt*
2	tsp.	soy sauce
1	tsp.	lemon juice

1. Toss lettuce, apples, tuna, and oranges together.

2. Mix yogurt, soy sauce, and lemon juice together.

3. Pour over salad, toss, and serve.

Serves 6
See "Cooking Methods" section

	RCU	FU	Cal	%Ft	P	F	C	Na
Per Serving	0	0	92	12	10	1	12	174

TERRIFIC TUNA CASSEROLE

Joyce Nixon
Mariteresa Bergerson

Carrots or corn also make a colorful addition to this casserole.

2	6 ½ oz. cans	water-packed tuna, drained
1	C	low-fat yogurt*
2	T	dried onion
1	10 oz. pkg	frozen peas
½	tsp.	garlic powder
¼	tsp.	black pepper
3	C	whole wheat macaroni,* cooked

Gifford's Alternatives: Add:
1	tsp.	chicken bouillon granules*
2	tsp.	Butter Buds® Sprinkles
½	tsp.	dill weed
½	tsp.	thyme
to taste		white pepper

DILL

1. Combine all ingredients except macaroni.

2. Mix well and combine with macaroni.

3. Bake in nonstick* casserole at 350° for 30 minutes. Serve.

4. Other vegetables may be substituted for peas.

Serves 10

See "Cooking Methods" section

	RCU	FU	Cal	%Ft	P	F	C	Na
Per Serving	0	0	209	8	18	2	28	57

ORIENTAL TUNA

Chinese pea pods can be added for an oriental touch.

½	C	green onions, sliced	2	tsp.	cornstarch*
1	8 oz. can	bamboo shoots, sliced, drained	⅛	tsp.	garlic powder
			¼	tsp.	celery seeds
1	C	mushrooms, sliced	2	6 ½ oz. cans	water-packed tuna, drained
1	C	peas			
½	C	water	1		tomato, cut into wedges
¼	tsp.	chicken bouillon granules*	2 ½	C	brown rice, *cooked
			5	tsp.	soy sauce, optional

Gifford's Alternatives: Add: 1 ¼ tsp.   *Gifford's Chinese Spice®*

1. Sauté* onions, bamboo shoots, and mushrooms until tender-crisp.

2. Add peas.

3. Combine water, bouillon granules, cornstarch, garlic powder, and celery seeds.

4. Add to vegetables. Simmer 3 minutes or until thickened.

5. Stir in tuna and tomato wedges. Heat through.

6. Serve over ½ cup hot rice. Season with 1 teaspoon soy sauce, if desired.

Serves 5

* See "Cooking Methods" section

	RCU	FU	Cal	%Ft	P	F	C	Na
Per Serving	0	0	276	4	28	1	36	508

CREAMED TUNA ON BISCUITS

Make this a colorful, inviting meal by serving it with peas and carrots.

1		onion, chopped	1 ½	C	skim milk*
1	can	cream of mushroom soup	2	6 ½ oz. cans	water-packed tuna, drained
1	can	cream of celery soup			
1	soup can	water	20		Whole Wheat Biscuits (p. 334)

1. Sauté* onion in a nonstick* skillet.

2. Combine undiluted soups, water, skim milk, tuna, and onion. Heat thoroughly.

3. Serve over 2 whole wheat biscuits.

Serves 10

*See "Cooking Methods" section

	RCU	FU	Cal	%Ft	P	F	C	Na
Per Serving	0	0	254	21	16	6	28	674

TURKEY TOSS

Exchange the asparagus with your favorite vegetable, if desired.

1	10 oz. pkg	frozen cut asparagus
3	C	cooked turkey, cut into strips
½	C	chicken stock*
2	T	vinegar OR lemon juice
1½	C	brown rice,* cooked
1½	C	wild rice,* cooked
to taste		seasonings without salt*
12	med.	almonds, slivered

Gifford's Alternatives: Add:
1	T	*pineapple juice concentrate*
1	tsp.	*Gifford's Gourmet Spice®*

1. Cook asparagus and drain.

2. Add asparagus, turkey, chicken stock, and vinegar or lemon juice to cooked rice. Toss gently together.

3. Heat and season to taste. Garnish with slivered almonds before serving.

Serves 8

*See "Cooking Methods" section

	RCU	FU	Cal	%Ft	P	F	C	Na
Per Serving	0	0	189	19	22	4	17	76

BREADED FISH FILETS

For an exciting taste change, replace evaporated milk with one slightly beaten egg white, six tablespoons thawed orange juice concentrate, and two tablespoons soy sauce.

16	oz.	whitefish filets
2	C	flake cereal, corn or bran
to taste		seasoning without salt*
¼	C	evaporated skim milk*
2	T	lemon juice

Gifford's Alternatives: Add:
| 1 ½ | tsp. | Gifford's Basic Spice® |
| ¼ | tsp. | Gifford's Dessert Spice® |

1. Divide filets into 4 servings.

2. Roll flake cereal between waxed paper until it has become fine crumbs. Sprinkle seasoning into crumbs and mix thoroughly.

3. Dip filets into milk and then into crumbs.

4. Place on a nonstick* baking sheet. Sprinkle with lemon juice. Bake at 500° for 10 minutes. OR Broil until golden brown, turning once. Serve.

Serves 4
* See "Cooking Methods" section

	RCU	FU	Cal	%Ft	P	F	C	Na
Per Serving	0	0	169	5	21	1	14	153

"MUY BIEN" SOLE

This dish is bright and colorful in both appearance and taste.

½	C	onion, chopped
3	T	green chilies, diced
1		tomato, chopped
3	T	parsley flakes
1	T	lemon juice
¼	tsp.	oregano
2	6 oz.	sole filets
1		green pepper, sliced into rings
2	C	brown rice,* cooked

Perk up any meal with a fresh fruit salad like Fresh Pineapple Baskets (p. 130) or Sunset Gelatin Salad (p. 120) with Fantastic Fruit Sauce (p. 47).

Gifford's Alternatives: Add:		1 ¼	tsp.	*Gifford's Mexican Spice®*
		¼	tsp.	*Gifford's Dessert Spice®*
				OMIT oregano
For additional flavor add:		1	T	*peach juice concentrate*
		1	tsp.	*Worcestershire sauce*

1. Sauté* onion and chilies. Add tomato, parsley, lemon juice, and oregano.

2. Place sole in a nonstick baking dish and arrange green pepper rings on top.

3. Pour tomato mixture over fish and bake at 450° for 10 to 20 minutes or until fish flakes when picked at with a fork. Serve over hot rice and garnish with lemon wedges.

Serves 4
* See "Cooking Methods" section

	RCU	FU	Cal	%Ft	P	F	C	Na
Per Serving	0	0	208	3	18	T	31	81

FISH OR SHRIMP CREOLE

Substitute shrimp for the fish filets and enjoy shrimp creole.

½		onion, chopped	2	C	tomatoes, chopped
½	C	green pepper, chopped	2	T	parsley, snipped
1	clove	garlic, minced	16	oz.	fresh or frozen fish fillets
1	T	cornstarch*	3	C	brown rice,* cooked
1	tsp.	chili powder			

Gifford's Alternatives: Add:		1	T	*peach juice concentrate*
		¾	tsp.	*Gifford's Mexican Spice®*
		½	tsp.	*Gifford's Gourmet Spice®*
				OMIT chili powder

1. Sauté* onion, green pepper, and garlic until tender in a nonstick* skillet. Whisk in cornstarch and chili powder.Add tomatoes and parsley. Cook until thickened, stirring constantly. Simmer for 20 minutes.

2. Add shrimp or fish that has been cut into 1-inch cubes. Heat until thoroughly cooked. Serve over ½ cup hot rice.

Serves 6
* See "Cooking Methods" section

	RCU	FU	Cal	%Ft	P	F	C	Na
Per Serving	0	0	225	7	16	2	33	77

Seven Layer Salad (p. 104), Tico Taco Salad (p. 108) with Salsa (p. 27) or Spinach Apple Toss (p. 109) could all make a refreshing luncheon meal with friends.

CRAB AND SHRIMP CASSEROLE

Use fresh crab meat to reduce the sodium content in this seafood casserole.

1	tsp.	lemon juice
1	C	low-fat yogurt*
2	6 ½ oz. cans	crab, drained
1	4 ½ oz. can	shrimp, drained
1	10 oz. pkg	frozen peas, thawed
1 ½	C	brown rice,* cooked
¼	C	green pepper, chopped
2	T	parsley flakes

Gifford's Alternatives: Add:

1	T	*unsweetened pear juice*
1	tsp.	*lime juice*
1	tsp.	*onion powder*
½	tsp.	*chicken bouillon granules**
⅛	tsp.	*ground coriander*
1	pinch	*ground cloves*

1. Whisk lemon juice into yogurt.

2. Add remaining ingredients and toss lightly.

3. Bake at 350° for 1 hour in a covered 2-quart nonstick* casserole dish. Serve.

Serves 6

* See "Cooking Methods" section

	RCU	FU	Cal	%Ft	P	F	C	Na
Per Serving	0	0	191	12	20	3	21	800

CRAB MEAT SUPREME

Superb! You'll want to serve this to company with a tossed green salad.

1	T	green pepper, chopped
1	T	pimento, chopped
dash		paprika
1	C	skim milk*
1		egg white, slightly beaten
¼	tsp.	dry mustard
½	tsp.	Worcestershire sauce
3	T	cornstarch*
2	6 ½ oz. cans	crab meat, well-drained

1. Sauté* green pepper and pimento until tender.

2. Whisk in cornstarch, paprika, and milk, stirring constantly. Heat until thickened and smooth.

3. Add the egg white to the sauce, stirring slowly.

4. Fold in crab meat. (Use fresh crab meat to reduce sodium content.)

5. Divide into 3 individual serving dishes and bake at 350° for 30 minutes. Serve.

Serves 3

* See "Cooking Methods" section

	RCU	FU	Cal	%Ft	P	F	C	Na
Per Serving	**0**	**0**	**167**	**14**	**25**	**3**	**10**	**1173**

POACHED SKILLET FISH FILETS

A tossed green salad and sourdough bread will round out this meal.

16	oz.	white fish filets
3	C	chicken bouillon
to taste		seasonings without salt*
1		bay leaf
1	med.	onion, sliced
1	T	parsley flakes
1		lemon, sliced

Gifford's Alternatives: Add:
1 ¼   tsp.   *Gifford's Gourmet Spice®*

1. Divide filets into 4 servings.

2. Combine bouillon, seasonings, bay leaf, onion, and lemon slices in a non-stick* skillet. Simmer for 5 minutes.

3. Add filets and simmer about 5 minutes. Be careful not to overcook.

4. Remove from liquid and garnish with parsley.

Serves 4

* See "Cooking Methods" section

	RCU	FU	Cal	%Ft	P	F	C	Na
Per Serving	0	0	129	7	19	1	4	375

LEMONS

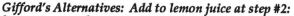

BAKED FISH FILETS

This is an easy method for preparing perch, whitefish, or cod. It will come out of the oven tender and flaky. Fish filets can also be brushed with lemon juice, seasoned, and broiled on each side until golden brown.

16	oz.	whitefish filets
1	T	lemon juice
½	C	mushrooms, sliced
1		onion, sliced
1		carrot, sliced lengthwise
1	T	parsley flakes
to taste		seasoning without salt*

Gifford's Alternatives: **Add to lemon juice at step #2:**

2	tsp.	honey
¼	tsp.	vanilla extract
		Blend well

Add to step #3:

1	med.	orange, peeled, quartered, sliced
to taste		Sprinkle Gifford's Basic Spice® over top

1. Divide filets into 4 servings. Place each serving in the center of a 12-inch square of foil.

2. Brush with lemon juice. Season.

3. Lay mushrooms, onions, and carrots on top of the fish. Seal the foil.

4. Bake at 450° for 25 or 30 minutes in a shallow pan.

5. Roll back foil, sprinkle filets with parsley and seasonings, then serve.

Serves 4

* See "Cooking Methods" section

	RCU	FU	Cal	%Ft	P	F	C	Na
Per Serving	0	0	138	6	20	1	4	88

LEMONS

HEN ON THE NEST

This dressy dish is good enough for guests.

3		chicken breasts
1	can	cream of chicken soup, undiluted
1	C	low-fat yogurt*
1	T	lemon juice, optional
½	C	mushrooms, chopped
1	stalk	celery, chopped
3	C	brown rice,* cooked
1 ½	C	frozen peas, cooked

1. Cook, skin, and cut up chicken.

2. Mix together undiluted cream of chicken soup with yogurt and lemon juice.

3. Saute* mushrooms and celery until tender.

4. Add mushrooms, celery, and cooked chicken to chicken soup mixture.

5. Layer brown rice on the bottom of a baking dish. Pour soup mixture over rice. Heat at 350° for 20 minutes until thoroughly warm.

6. Top with cooked peas. Serve.

Serves 6

* See "Cooking Methods" section

	RCU	FU	Cal	%Ft	P	F	C	Na
Per Serving	0	0	285	17	21	6	36	485

CHICKEN AND DUMPLINGS

Joyce Nixon
Mariteresa Bergerson

Warm and wonderful!

1		onion, chopped	1	clove	garlic, minced
1	C	carrots, chopped	2	qts.	chicken stock*
1	C	celery, chopped	1	10 oz.	frozen mixed
1 ½	C	peas		pkg	vegetables
1	C	broccoli	1	3 lb.	chicken, cooked and diced

Gifford's Alternatives: Add:	1	T	onion powder
	2	tsp.	(additional) chicken bouillon granules*
	½	tsp.	dry ground mustard
	⅛	tsp.	ground white pepper

1. Add onions, carrots, celery, peas, broccoli, and garlic to chicken stock. Cook until tender.

2. Add frozen vegetables. Cook 10 minutes.

3. Add chicken. Adjust liquid with water to cover chicken and vegetables, if necessary. Bring to a boil.

4. Drop dumpling batter (see below) on top of soup in heaping tablespoons.

5. Cover and cook on medium heat for 10 minutes. Don't peek.

6. Uncover and cook an additional 10 minutes. Serve immediately.
Serves 6

See "Cooking Methods" section

	RCU	FU	Cal	%Ft	P	F	C	Na
Per Serving	0	1	201	18	28	4	13	131

DUMPLINGS

2	C	whole wheat flour
1	T	baking powder
3	T	diet margarine
1	C	skim milk*

1. Combine flour and baking powder.

2. Cut in margarine thoroughly.   BROCCOLI

3. Add milk and stir. Always drop dumplings into boiling liquid.

Serves 6

See "Cooking Methods" section

	RCU	FU	Cal	%Ft	P	F	C	Na
Per Serving	0	0	159	20	6	4	27	282

CHICKEN IN THICK TOMATO SAUCE

Serve this on special occasions with peas, carrots, and corn.

1		tomato
¾	C	mushrooms, sliced
¼	C	onion, chopped
¼	C	green pepper, chopped
1	clove	garlic, minced
½	tsp.	oregano
2		chicken breasts
1		sprinkle paprika
2	tsp.	cornstarch*

Gifford's Alternatives: Add in step #1:
½	tsp.	Gifford's Mexican Spice®
¼	tsp.	Gifford's Italian Spice®
		OMIT oregano

Add in step #4:
¼	C	tomato purée, stir into skillet
		OMIT cornstarch

1. Cut up tomato in a pan. Add mushrooms, onions, green pepper, garlic, and oregano.

2. Skin and debone chicken breasts. Lay chicken on top of vegetables. Bring everything to a boil. Cover and simmer for 25 minutes.

3. Remove chicken. Sprinkle with paprika and keep warm.

4. Whisk cornstarch with 2 tablespoons cool water and stir into skillet mixture. Cook until thickened. Stir and cook for another minute.

5. Place chicken in serving bowl. Pour sauce over chicken. Garnish with parsley and serve.

Serves 4

* See "Cooking Methods" section

	RCU	FU	Cal	%Ft	P	F	C	Na
Per Serving	0	0	170	11	30	2	5	79

CHICKEN IN HERB SAUCE

This would make a good filling for the Rice Pie Shell (p. 292).

1	3 lb.	chicken, cut up
1	C	chicken stock*
2		onions, chopped
1	C	mushrooms, sliced
½	C	carrot, coarsely chopped
3	stalks	celery, cut in half
2	T	parsley
¼	tsp.	thyme, crushed
1	clove	garlic, minced
1		bay leaf

GARLIC

Gifford's Alternatives: Add:
1	tsp.	Gifford's Italian Spice®
½	tsp.	Gifford's Basic Spice®
		OMIT thyme, garlic, bay leaf

1. Skin chicken.

2. Combine all ingredients. Bring to boil, cover, and simmer 45 minutes.

3. Discard bay leaf and celery.

4. Remove chicken and vegetables and place in serving bowl. Keep warm.

5. Boil sauce until reduced to about ½ cup. Pour over chicken. Serve.

Serves 6

* See "Cooking Methods" section

	RCU	FU	Cal	%Ft	P	F	C	Na
Per Serving	0	1	159	22	25	4	5	166

MICROWAVE CHICKEN

Eat chicken as is, slice for sandwiches, or cut into bite-sized pieces for use in other recipes.

1	3 lb.	chicken, skinned
as desired		paprika

Gifford's Alternatives: Sprinkle, as you would the paprika, Gifford's Basic Spice®

1. Arrange chicken pieces in a round dish, thick pieces outside and thin pieces toward the center. Sprinkle with paprika.

2. Cover with paper towels and bake 7 minutes per pound. Turn over when half way done and sprinkle paprika on the other side.

Serves 10

	RCU	FU	Cal	%Ft	P	F	C	Na
Per Serving	0	0	82	25	14	2	0	40

PEERLESS POULTRY

Sydette Parent

There's nothing like this chicken. The unique sauce gives it a rich flavor and a deep caramel brown color.

1	6 oz. can	orange juice concentrate	3		chicken breasts, skinned
1	pkg	onion soup mix	3	C	brown rice,* cooked

1. Combine thawed orange juice concentrate and dry onion soup mix. Pour half of mixture in a nonstick* casserole.

2. Place chicken breasts meat side down in the casserole and top with remaining sauce.

3. Cover casserole with a lid or foil. Bake at 400° for 1 hour. Serve with rice and any remaining sauce from the casserole.

Serves 6

* See "Cooking Methods" section

	RCU	FU	Cal	%Ft	P	F	C	Na
Per Serving	1	0	251	6	17	2	40	103

OVEN FRIED CHICKEN

Use chicken breasts to reduce the percentage of fat since white meat is lower in fat than dark meat.

¼	C	whole wheat flour	3	T	water
2	T	parsley, minced	1		3 lb. chicken, cut up
1	T	Italian salad dressing mix			
½	tsp.	paprika			

Gifford's Alternatives: Add to flour mixture: 1 ¼ *tsp. Gifford's Basic Spice ®*

1. In a small bowl, stir together flour, parsley, salad dressing mix, and paprika. Blend in water.

2. Skin chicken. Spread flour mixture over chicken pieces. Place chicken in nonstick* baking pan. Bake 375° for 50 to 60 minutes. Do not turn. Serve.

Serves 8

* See "Cooking Methods" section

	RCU	FU	Cal	%Ft	P	F	C	Na
Per Serving	0	1	114	23	18	3	2	50

BROILED CHICKEN

Serve this hot for dinner or cold for a picnic.

4		chicken breasts
1	C	Barbecue Sauce (p. 24)

1. Remove skin and all visible fat from chicken. Place on a broiler pan and baste with Barbecue Sauce. Set chicken 4 to 6 inches away from broiler.

2. When the top of the chicken is browned, turn and baste the other side. Return to broiler.

3. Keep turning and basting chicken until it is cooked but not burned. Serve.

Serves 4

	RCU	FU	Cal	%Ft	P	F	C	Na
Per Serving	0	0	169	10	28	2	7	157

SOUPER CHICKEN

Florence Porter

Serve with fresh fruit salad or several vegetable side dishes.

1	can	cream of celery or
		cream of mushroom soup
1	C	chicken bouillon*
1	soup can	skim milk*
1	C	brown rice,* raw
1	C	mushrooms, whole or sliced
6		chicken breasts, skinned
1	pkg	dry onion soup mix

1. Mix soup and bouillon with milk. Add rice and mushrooms and pour into large nonstick* casserole pan.

2. Place chicken breasts meat side down. Sprinkle dry onion soup over the top.

3. Cover with aluminum foil and bake at 350° for 1 ½ hours. Serve.

Serves 6
* See "Cooking Methods" section

	RCU	FU	Cal	%Ft	P	F	C	Na
Per Serving	0	0	384	7	34	3	50	399

IT'S ALL GONDI

Sydette Parent

This is colorful and filling.

2		chicken breasts, skinned, cooked and diced
2	C	brown rice,* cooked
3		green onions, sliced
2	T	celery, diced
¼	tsp.	garlic powder
4	oz.	mushrooms, sliced
10	oz.	broccoli, frozen
1	T	lemon juice
4	T	low-fat yogurt

GARLIC

Gifford's Alternatives: Add:	1	*tsp.*	*chicken bouillon granules**
	1	*tsp.*	*onion powder*
	¼	*tsp.*	*ground black pepper*
	2	*tsp.*	*Butter Buds® Sprinkles*

1. Mix cooked chicken and cooked rice together.

2. Sauté* onions, celery, garlic powder, and mushrooms.

3. Cook frozen broccoli. Drain. Add to sautéed vegetables. Add 1 tablespoon lemon juice.

4. Serve vegetables over chicken-rice mixture. Top each serving with 1 tablespoon dollop of plain yogurt.

OTHER SERVING SUGGESTIONS:

1. Pat rice mixture into nonstick* bundt pan. Heat. Turn out on a platter. Fill center with broccoli mixture. Top with yogurt.

2. Layer rice mixture with vegetables in a 9" x 9" pan. Heat. Pass yogurt separately.

Serves 4

* See "Cooking Methods" section

	RCU	FU	Cal	%Ft	P	F	C	Na
Per Serving	0	0	191	10	19	2	24	416

SQUASH

SWEET-AND-SOUR CHICKEN

One of many exciting ways to cook chicken.

1	med.	onion, sliced	2	T	cider vinegar
1	lg.	green pepper, chopped	½	tsp.	ginger
6		fresh mushrooms, sliced	2	T	cornstarch
1	C	pineapple juice, drained from canned pineapple	1	can	water chestnuts, drained and sliced
¾	C	chicken bouillon*	2	C	cooked chicken, diced
2	T	soy sauce	1		20 oz. pineapple chunks
2	T	honey*			can
			3	C	cooked brown rice

Gifford's Alternatives: Add:

1 ¼	tsp.	*Gifford's Chinese Spice®*
½	tsp.	*Gifford's Dessert Spice®*
		OMIT ginger

1. Sauté* onion, peppers, and mushrooms in a nonstick* skillet for 3 minutes. Remove from heat and set aside.

2. Combine pineapple juice, bouillon, soy sauce, honey, vinegar, ginger, and cornstarch. Add to onion mixture and cook until thickened, stirring constantly.

3. Add water chestnuts, chicken, and pineapple. Simmer for 10 minutes. Serve over brown rice.

Serves 6

* See "Cooking Methods" section

	RCU	FU	Cal	%Ft	P	F	C	Na
Per Serving	1	0	128	T	3	1	31	246

BLACK PEPPER

BARBECUE CHICKEN KABOBS

The perfect treat for that summer barbecue. Try cooking these over an open grill. Yummy!

½	C	Barbecue Sauce (p. 24)
½	C	water
1	clove	garlic, minced
2		chicken breasts, raw, skinned and cut into 1-inch cubes
6	lg.	green onions, bias-sliced into 1-inch lengths
6	lg.	mushrooms, whole
4		cherry tomatoes

1. Combine barbecue sauce, water, and garlic. Boil 1 minute. Cool. Marinate chicken and green onions in mixture for 30 minutes at room temperature, stirring once to coat all pieces.

2. Drain. Reserve marinade.

3. Alternate chicken, mushrooms, and onion pieces on 4 skewers. Broil kabobs 4 inches from heat for about 5 minutes.

4. Place a cherry tomato on end of each skewer. Turn. Broil kabobs about 5 minutes longer, brushing occasionally with barbecue marinade. Serve immediately.

Serves 4

	RCU	FU	Cal	%Ft	P	F	C	Na
Per Serving	0	0	273	16	46	5	8	143

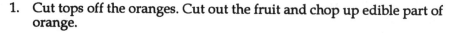
ORANGES A LA CHICKEN

This dish brings sunshine into your winter luncheons.

4	lg.	oranges
1	C	celery, thinly sliced
¼	C	low-fat yogurt*
1	T	green onion, thinly sliced
½	tsp.	celery seeds
2		chicken breasts, skinned, cooked, and diced

ORANGE SEGMENT

1. Cut tops off the oranges. Cut out the fruit and chop up edible part of orange.

2. Chill orange shells.

3. Toss chopped orange, celery, yogurt, onion, celery seeds, and chicken together.

4. Spoon chicken mixture into orange shells and serve.

Serves 4

* See "Cooking Methods" section

	RCU	FU	Cal	%Ft	P	F	C	Na
Per Serving	0	0	162	11	17	2	19	76

HOW TO COOK A TURKEY

Holidays shouldn't be the only time you cook a turkey.

Ready-To-Cook Weight

6-8 lbs.	=	6-8 servings
8-12 lbs.	=	8-12 servings
12-16 lbs.	=	12-20 servings
16-20 lbs.	=	20-28 servings
20-24 lbs.	=	28-32 servings

Thawing Your Turkey

1. NO-HURRY METHOD involves placing the turkey on a tray in the refrigerator. It will take two to three days for a 13-pound bird to thaw.

2. QUICK-DEFROST METHOD involves covering the turkey with cold water. Change the water frequently. Figure ½ hour per pound.

Preparing Your Turkey

1. Remove the plastic bag. Remove the neck and giblets from the body cavity.

2. Wash the turkey in cold water and pat dry. Stuff it, if you wish.

3. Insert meat thermometer into the center of the thigh next to the body but do not let it touch the bone.

Roasting Your Turkey

1. Place the turkey on a rack in a shallow roasting pan. Cook, uncovered, or in a foil tent at 325° according to the table.

Unstuffed Turkeys		Stuffed Turkeys	
6–8 lbs.	2 ½ - 3 hrs.	8-10 lbs.	2 - 2 ½ hrs.
8-12 lbs.	3 - 4 hrs.	10-12 lbs.	2 ½ - 3 hrs.
12-16 lbs.	4 - 5 hrs.	14-16 lbs.	3 - 3 ¼ hrs.
16-20 lbs.	5 - 6 hrs.	18-20 lbs.	3 ¼ - 3 ½ hrs.
20-24 lbs.	6 - 6 ½ hrs.	22-24 lbs.	3 ½ - 4 hrs.

Turkey is done when the meat thermometer reads 180° to 185°, or shake the drumstick and if it feels loose it is done.

Be sure to keep your turkey refrigerated. Do not allow it to sit around at room temperature. Remove the stuffing to refrigerate. You may refrigerate the turkey whole or cut the meat off the bones. The meat can be frozen by wrapping it in foil and it will keep two months. Stuffing may also be frozen but should be used within one month. After the meat has been stripped off the carcass, you can make soup with it. See "Soup's On!" for Turkey Surprise Soup on page 76.

TURKEY ENCHILADAS

A nice way to use leftover turkey.

1½	C	onions, chopped	2	C	turkey, cooked and diced
1½	C	green pepper, chopped	1	tsp.	oregano
4	cloves	garlic, minced	1	tsp.	onion powder
1	C	chicken bouillon*	8		corn tortillas
2	16 oz. cans	chunky tomato sauce*	2	C	lettuce, shredded
			6		green onions, chopped
½	C	canned green chilies, diced	1	C	nonfat yogurt*
2	tsp.	cumin			

Gifford's Alternatives: Add:

1 ½	*tsp.*	*Gifford's Mexican Spice®*
1	*T*	*peach juice concentrate*

1. Sauté* ¾ cup of onions, ¾ cup of green peppers, and 2 cloves of garlic in ½ cup of bouillon. Cook until tender.

2. Add tomato sauce, ¼ cup of green chilies, and 1 teaspoon of cumin. Simmer for 5 minutes. Remove from heat and set aside.

3. Mix remaining onions, green peppers, garlic, green chilies, turkey, and spices in a bowl.

4. Fill 8 corn tortillas with turkey mixture, and place rolled tortillas side by side in a 9" x 13" baking pan. Pour tomato sauce over tortillas and bake at 350° until tender, about 20 minutes.

5. Serve each tortilla topped with lettuce, green onions, and 2 tablespoons of nonfat yogurt.

Serves 8

* See "Cooking Methods" section

	RCU	FU	Cal	%Ft	P	F	C	Na
Per Serving	0	0	188	19	15	4	22	442

FLUFFY COTTAGE CHEESE SOUFFLE

Make sure to preheat the oven so that it is up to temperature as soon as you are finished preparing this dish.

4	slices	whole wheat bread, toasted
4	lg.	egg whites
1 ½	C	low-fat cottage cheese*
1 ¼	C	skim milk*
¼	C	nonfat dry milk
¼	tsp.	dry mustard
¼	tsp.	paprika
¼	tsp.	Worcestershire sauce
2	T	chives, chopped

1. Cut toast into cubes and place evenly over the bottom of an 8" x 13" non-stick* baking dish.

2. Beat egg whites until they stand in stiff peaks.

3. Beat cottage cheese in a blender until creamy. Add the remaining ingredients, except egg whites, and blend thoroughly.

4. Carefully fold this mixture into the stiffly beaten egg whites and pour into the baking dish.

5. Bake at 350° until a knife inserted in the center comes out clean, for 45 to 60 minutes. Serve.

Serves 6

* See "Cooking Methods" section

	RCU	FU	Cal	%Ft	P	F	C	Na
Per Serving	0	0	138	1	17	T	14	336

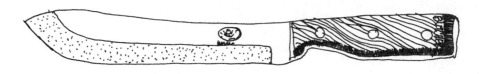

RODEO PIE

A hearty meat-and-potatoes pie.

1	med.	onion, chopped	1	8 oz. can	tomato sauce
1	med.	green pepper, chopped			
1/4	tsp.	garlic powder	1/2	tsp.	basil
1/2	lb.	lean hamburger	1/8	tsp.	black pepper
			3	C	mashed potatoes

Gifford's Alternatives: Add:

2	tsp.	**Gifford's Basic Spice®** OMIT basil, garlic powder, pepper

1. Sauté* onions and green peppers in a nonstick* skillet until transparent. Add garlic powder. Remove from heat and set aside.

2. Cook hamburger in a skillet. Drain off excess grease. Add hamburger to sautéed onions and green peppers.

3. Add tomato sauce, basil, and pepper. Simmer for 15 minutes, stirring occasionally.

4. In a nonstick* 9" x 13" baking pan, layer mashed potatoes with hamburger mixture in 3 layers, beginning with potatoes.

5. Bake at 450° for 20 minutes. Serve warm.

Serves 6

* See "Cooking Methods" section

	RCU	FU	Cal	%Ft	P	F	C	Na
Per Serving	1	1	186	24	13	5	18	482

BEEF STROGANOFF

The use of cubed lean beef raises this recipe to 25 percent fat.

½	lb.	lean hamburger OR
½	lb.	lean beef, cubed, rump, or round
½	C	fresh mushrooms, sliced
1	pkg	dry onion soup mix
1	T	whole wheat flour
1 ¾	C	water
2	C	whole wheat noodles,*cooked
8	T	low-fat yogurt*

1. Brown* hamburger and drain OR sauté* beef cubes. Add mushrooms.

2. Whisk dry onion soup and flour into water. Heat. Stir until thickened.

3. Combine thickened onion soup and cooked lean beef.

4. Serve over cooked whole wheat noodles. Garnish with a dollop of yogurt.

Serves 4

* See "Cooking Methods" section

	RCU	FU	Cal	%Ft	P	F	C	Na
Per Serving	0	1	402	20	28	9	43	120

QUICK HAMBURGER STEW

You may add rice or vegetables to this basic stew.

6	oz.	lean hamburger
4	T	cornstarch*
8	C	water
8		potatoes, cut up
½	C	barley
1	10 oz. pkg	frozen mixed vegetables OR
1 ½	C	fresh vegetables, cut up
1		onion, chopped
1	C	fresh mushrooms, sliced
to taste		seasoning without salt*

Gifford's Alternatives: Add:

2	T	*Butter Buds® Sprinkles*
1	T	*onion powder*
2 ½	tsp.	*beef bouillon granules**
¼	tsp.	*ground black pepper*

1. Brown* hamburger and drain well.

2. Whisk cornstarch into water.

3. Combine all ingredients and bring to a boil. Reduce heat, cover, and simmer until all vegetables are tender.

4. Serve hot with whole-grain bread.

Serves 10

* See "Cooking Methods" section

	RCU	FU	Cal	%Ft	P	F	C	Na
Per Serving	0	0	177	13	9	3	31	32

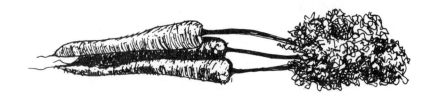

GRILLED HAMBURGERS

Serve these with Hash Brown Potatoes (p. 243) or Oven French Fries (p. 241) to lower the total fat percentage of this popular American meal. Omit the dill pickles to reduce the sodium level.

18	oz.	lean hamburger	1		onion, sliced
6		Whole Wheat Hamburger	3	T	prepared mustard
		Buns (p. 321)	3	T	catsup
1		tomato, sliced	18		slices dill pickles,
6		lettuce leaves			optional

Gifford's Alternatives: Add:

2	tsp.	*Gifford's Basic Spice ® OR*
2	tsp.	*Gifford's Italian Spice ® OR*
2	tsp.	*Gifford's Mexican Spice®*

1. Divide hamburger into 3-ounce patties. Grill over an outdoor barbecue or broil in your oven until thoroughly cooked.

2. Serve on homemade or commercial whole wheat buns with any or all of the remaining ingredients.

Serves 6

	RCU	FU	Cal	%Ft	P	F	C	Na
Per Serving	0	1	357	30	28	12	26	696

HAMBURGER SPAGHETTI SAUCE

This is also tasty over cauliflower.

½	lb.	lean hamburger
3	T	whole wheat flour*
1	7 ½ oz. can	tomato sauce*
1	16 oz. can	tomatoes,* puréed
1	6 oz. can	mushrooms and juice
1	T	parsley, minced
¼	tsp.	oregano
¼	tsp.	basil
½	tsp.	onion powder
½	tsp.	garlic powder
2	T	Italian seasoning
1	dash	black pepper
3	C	whole wheat spaghetti,* cooked

Gifford's Alternatives: Add:
1	T	Gifford's Italian Spice®
¼	tsp.	Gifford's Dessert Spice®

OMIT oregano, basil, onion powder, garlic powder, Italian seasoning

1. Brown* hamburger and drain.

2. Stir in whole wheat flour.

3. Return to heat. Add tomato sauce, puréed tomatoes, and undrained canned mushrooms.

4. Add parsley, oregano, basil, onion powder, garlic powder, Italian seasoning, and black pepper.

5. Simmer for 30 to 60 minutes.

6. Serve over whole wheat spaghetti.

Serves 6

* See "Cooking Methods" section

	RCU	FU	Cal	%Ft	P	F	C	Na
Per Serving	0	0	265	18	17	5	29	266

BEST MEAT LOAF EVER

Serve this with baked potatoes and green vegetables for a "best-ever" family dinner.

Filling:

1 ¼	C	beef stock*
⅓	C	brown rice,* raw
¼	C	onion, chopped
¼	C	celery, chopped
2	T	parsley, minced
2	T	wheat germ
1		egg white
½	tsp.	sage

Meat loaf:

½	lb.	lean ground beef
2		egg whites
½	C	skim milk*
¼	C	dried bread crumbs
2	T	wheat germ
1	C	oatmeal
¼		onion, chopped
½	tsp.	thyme
½	C	Tomato Sauce (p. 24)

1. Make filling by placing beef stock and brown rice in a small saucepan. Bring it to a boil, reduce heat, cover, and simmer until liquid has been absorbed, about 30 minutes.

2. Sauté* onion and celery and add to rice mixture. Add parsley, wheat germ, 1 egg white, and sage. Set aside.

3. Make meat loaf by combining lean hamburger, 2 egg whites, milk, bread crumbs, wheat germ, oatmeal, chopped onions, and seasonings. Mix well.

4. Pat half of the meat loaf mixture into a 9" x 5" x 3" loaf pan. Spread filling mixture evenly over the top. Cover with remaining meat loaf mixture. Then pour tomato sauce over the top and spread evenly.

5. Bake at 350° for 50 minutes. Serve.

Serves 8

* See "Cooking Methods" section

	RCU	FU	Cal	%Ft	P	F	C	Na
Per Serving	0	0	193	21	13	4	19	130

BEEF KABOBS ON WILD RICE

Elegant and versatile. These kabobs are perfect for a candlelight dinner or a barbecue.

12	oz.	round steak, good grade
2	C	Barbecue Sauce (p. 24)
16		mushrooms, whole
16		green pepper squares
16		cherry tomatoes, whole
16		onion wedges
1	C	brown rice,* cooked
3	C	wild rice,* cooked

1. Cut beef into 12 1½-inch cubes and marinate for 2 to 3 hours using the Barbecue Sauce (p. 24) or your favorite low-fat marinade. Turn the meat at least once and keep refrigerated.

2. Prepare the grill or broiler.

3. Alternate meat and vegetables on the skewer beginning with a mushroom, then add green pepper, cherry tomato, onion, and meat. Repeat order until there are 3 pieces of meat and 4 pieces of each vegetable on each skewer.

4. Cook 3 inches from the source of heat. Baste with marinade and turn to cook evenly—18 minutes for rare, 25 minutes for well done.

5. While these are cooking, toss wild and brown rices together until evenly mixed.

6. Serve kabobs over 1 cup of rice mixture.

Serves 4

* See "Cooking Methods" section

	RCU	FU	Cal	%Ft	P	F	C	Na
Per Serving	0	0	592	21	34	14	81	264

PIZZA

Watch the amount of cheese to keep this low in fat.

1½	C	Basic Whole Wheat Bread dough (p. 311)
1½	C	Pizza Sauce (p. 26)
1½	C	low-fat cottage cheese*
1		onion, chopped
1		green pepper, chopped
to taste		Italian seasoning
4	T	mozzarella cheese, finely grated

Gifford's Alternatives: Add:
to taste	Gifford's Italian Spice®
	OMIT Italian seasoning

WILD
ONION

1. Roll out bread dough onto a nonstick* baking sheet.

2. Mix Pizza Sauce and cottage cheese together. Spread over crust.

3. Cover with onion, green pepper, or other low-fat toppings. Sprinkle Italian seasoning to taste.

4. Top sparingly with mozzarella cheese.
   Bake at 400° for 30 minutes. Serve.

Serves 6

* See "Cooking Methods" section

	RCU	FU	Cal	%Ft	P	F	C	Na
Per Serving	0	0	246	14	17	4	37	370

VARIATION: ENGLISH MUFFIN PIZZAS

6	English muffins, toasted

1. Top ½ muffin with 2 tablespoons sauce, 2 tablespoons cottage cheese, and 1 teaspoon mozzarella cheese.

2. Broil until cheese melts, about 5 minutes. Serve.

Serves 6

	RCU	FU	Cal	%Ft	P	F	C	Na
Per Serving	0	0	236	9	17	2	37	290

PIZZA ON A POTATO CRUST

You won't be able to pick this up and eat it with your hands, but it provides a low-fat substitute for pizza lovers.

1	2 oz. can	mushrooms, chopped
4	C	mashed potatoes
2		egg whites, slightly beaten
1	tsp.	Italian seasoning
1	C	soft whole wheat bread crumbs
1	C	Tomato Sauce (p. 24)
4	oz.	lean ground beef, browned*
1		tomato, sliced
1/4	C	onion, chopped
1/4	C	green pepper, chopped
1/4	C	celery, chopped
1/2	C	pineapple chunks, optional
1/2	C	mozzarella cheese, grated

Gifford's Alternatives: Add:
1 ½ tsp. Gifford's Italian Spice®
OMIT Italian seasoning

1. Drain mushrooms and reserve the liquid.

2. Combine mashed potatoes, reserved mushroom liquid, egg whites, Italian seasoning, and bread crumbs.

3. Pat potato mixture into a nonstick* casserole. Spread tomato sauce evenly over potato mixture. Sprinkle ground beef over top.

4. Sprinkle remaining ingredients, except cheese, evenly over sauce, beginning with tomato slices.

5. Bake at 350° for 45 minutes. Top with cheese and return to oven until cheese melts, about 5 minutes. Serve.

Serves 8

* See "Cooking Methods" section

	RCU	FU	Cal	%Ft	P	F	C	Na
Per Serving	0	0	154	20	9	3	18	116

ROLLED FLANK AND DRESSING

Serve this with carrots and a green vegetable.

⅛	tsp.	paprika
¼	tsp.	dry mustard
1	tsp.	Worcestershire sauce
1	lb.	flank steak
1	C	Dressing (p. 304)
2	C	Tomato Sauce (p. 24)

Gifford's Alternatives: Add:
1	tsp.	Gifford's Basic Spice®
¼	tsp.	Gifford's Gourmet Spice®
		OMIT paprika, dry mustard

1. Combine paprika, mustard, and Worcestershire sauce.

2. Trim fat from flank. Pound above seasonings into meat.

3. Spread dressing over meat. Roll loosely and tie.

4. Place rolled meat carefully in a nonstick* casserole.

5. Pour tomato sauce over the meat. Cover and bake at 325° for 1 to 2 hours. Serve.

Serves 4

* See "Cooking Methods" section

	RCU	FU	Cal	%Ft	P	F	C	Na
Per Serving	**0**	**1**	**315**	**24**	**38**	**8**	**9**	**214**

SWISS STEAK

Brighten your plate with mixed vegetables.

1	lb.	round steak
1	clove	garlic
1	C	whole wheat flour
½	C	onion, chopped
⅓	C	carrot, finely chopped
⅓	C	green pepper, finely chopped
⅓	C	celery, finely chopped
½	C	stewed tomatoes,* drained
1	C	beef stock*
1	recipe	Basic Bouillon Gravy (p. 22)
4	C	mashed potatoes

Gifford's Alternatives: Add to flour:
1	T	Gifford's Basic Spice®

1. Trim fat from meat and rub with garlic.

2. Sprinkle meat with some of the flour and pound. Turn meat and repeat. Continue until you have used as much flour as the meat will hold.

3. Cut meat into 6 pieces. Place in a nonstick* casserole.

4. Cover with vegetables, tomatoes, and beef stock.

5. Cover casserole and cook at 300° until meat is tender, about 2 hours.

6. Strain drippings and discard. Add Basic Bouillon Gravy to meat.

7. Serve meat and gravy over mashed potatoes.

Serves 6

*See "Cooking Methods" section

	RCU	FU	Cal	%Ft	P	F	C	Na
Per Serving	0	1	357	29	28	12	49	154

THE VERY VERSATILE VEGETABLE

He who has health has hope; and he who has hope has everything.

---Arabian Proverb

THE VERY VERSATILE VEGETABLE

Presenting: "THE VERY VERSATILE VEGETABLE." It has everything. It is low in calories, fat, and price yet high in vitamins, minerals, fiber, and flavor. It is even easy to grow and a joy to prepare. So let's move the vegetable to the center stage and take a closer look at its performance.

Vegetables contain a wide variety of vitamins, minerals, enzymes, and many other food molecules that may play an important, but as yet incompletely understood, role in human nutrition. Fiber found in the cell walls and in stems, leaves, roots, and other structural parts of vegetables plays a vital role in good health.

Fiber is present in a number of different forms including cellulose, hemicellulose, lignins, and pectins. Some of the fiber is broken down by intestinal bacteria, but most of it passes through the intestines to form roughage.

Many scientists believe that a high-fiber diet is protective against bowel cancer and probably other cancers. Fiber may be protective against heart disease by limiting the uptake of cholesterol from the intestines. Fiber seems to discourage formation of gall stones. A high-fiber diet seems to encourage the growth of healthy intestinal bacteria that produce vitamins that we are unable to manufacture by ourselves and discourages the growth of harmful, toxin-producing organisms.

Vegetables contain sugar molecules lined together in various types of long chains that we call complex carbohydrates. The cell surrounding these carbohydrates must first be broken down, then the links must be broken down to release simple sugars that can then be digested. This causes a more gradual, prolonged release of sugar into the bloodstream than does ingestion of refined carbohydrates like table sugar.

Lower-carbohydrate vegetables (like lettuce and cucumbers) are usually encouraged on weight reduction programs, but the high-carbohydrate vegetables (like potatoes and corn) have usually been discouraged. Eating mainly low-carbohydrate vegetables is very unsatisfying and will usually lead to cravings for less suitable foods. Filling, nutrition-laden foods are necessary for satiety or satisfaction. We believe that the high-carbohydrate vegetables are perfectly acceptable and can be used frequently to make up a substantial part of your diet provided that high-fat toppings are not used.

Since most vegetables are easy to grow, fill your garden with them, and enjoy fresh produce from your own backyard. You may even have such a good harvest that you will want to can, freeze, or dry your surplus vegetables for use all year long. See "Home Food Preservation" on page 391 in the "Cooking Methods" section to learn how to preserve vegetables.

Baked Fish with lemon juice (p. 145) or Hen on the Nest (p. 146). Either makes an excellent main course.

Vegetable preparation is varied but easy. Eating vegetables raw is easy, and provides the most nutrition and flavor. Raw vegetables can be tossed in a salad, set in gelatin, or eaten with a low-fat dip. They are also delicious left in the refrigerator overnight in a low-calorie dressing marinade to be eaten cold.

But there are times when we want our vegetables cooked. Following are some suggestions for cooked vegetables. Steam them over boiling water or in a microwave to provide maximum vitamin and flavor retention. Then serve them, two to a platter, to enhance the appearance of each. Cook them in a wok to a "tender-crisp" stage for wonderful results. Skewer them, then brush with low-calorie dressing, and broil or grill for a real treat. Or fill your soups, stews, and casseroles with vegetables. See "Soup's On!" on page 57 for additional recipes. Season your cooked vegetables with about 1/4 teaspoon of the desired herb or spice per four servings. See "Seasoning Without Salt" on page 402 in the "Cooking Methods" section for ideas.

What more can we say about the "Very Versatile Vegetable?" No matter how you serve it, you will always get a top performance meal. So "Vegetable," take a bow and a round of applause. You deserve to be the "star of the show!"

PUMPKIN

Vegetables can be the main course or a side dish. Give Crunchy Onion Rings (p. 193), Sunshine Carrots (p. 182), Stuffed Acorn Squash (p. 197) or Apple and Acorn Squash Delight (p. 198) a try this week.

ARTICHOKES

You'll never know what you are missing until you have tried artichokes. They are fantastic and well worth the work involved to prepare them.

4		artichokes
2	cloves	garlic, halved
1		lemon, sliced
2	qts.	boiling water

Gifford's Alternatives: Add:
to taste   *Gifford's Gourmet Spice®*
to taste   *Gifford's Chinese Spice®*

1. Wash artichokes. Cut 1 inch off the top straight across with a sharp knife. Then cut off the bottom stem leaving a 1-inch stub. Pull off loose leaves and clip thorny tips from remaining leaves.

2. Add garlic and lemon slices to boiling water. Drop in artichokes. Cover and boil 20 to 45 minutes, until leaf pulls easily from the base. Drain upside down.

3. Serve with Butter Buds® and lemon juice or a low-fat dip from Fabulous Flavors (p. 19).

4. To eat, pull off leaves one at a time. Dip the light-colored end into Butter Buds® or low-calorie dip. Eat only the tender part of the leaf by drawing it between the teeth. Discard remainder of leaf. When you reach the fuzzy center or "choke," remove it with a knife and fork and discard. The heart or choicest part is now exposed. Cut it into bite-sized pieces and enjoy.

5. A wonderful stuffed artichoke can be made by combining 1 drained can of water-packed tuna with 2 cups whole wheat bread crumbs, seasonings, and 1 tablespoon Low-Calorie Italian Dressing (p. 37). Stuff artichoke before cooking, putting ½ cup stuffing per artichoke between the leaves. Cook as usual, but use a small saucepan so they will remain upright while cooking.

Serves 4

	RCU	FU	Cal	%Ft	P	F	C	Na
Per Serving	0	0	57	T	3	T	11	50

Choose ARTICHOKES that are heavy for their size with thick, tightly clinging scales. Avoid those with areas of brown on the scales. Artichokes are in season during April and May. Store them in a plastic bag in the refrigerator and eat them within three to five days.

EXTRA SPECIAL ASPARAGUS

Fresh asparagus is incredibly delicious when steamed until tender. Use it in place of frozen asparagus whenever possible. This recipe dresses up either of them.

¼	C	onion, diced
1		green pepper, chopped
½	C	mushrooms, sliced
2	10 oz. pkg.	frozen asparagus spears
2	tsp.	pimento, diced
2	tsp.	parsley, chopped

Gifford's Alternatives: Add:
to taste   Gifford's Gourmet Spice®

1. Bring to a boil onion, green pepper, and mushrooms in a saucepan. Cover and simmer for 5 minutes. Drain.

2. Steam asparagus until tender, about 12 to 15 minutes.

3. Combine asparagus with onion mixture, and garnish with pimento and parsley before serving.

Serves 6

	RCU	FU	Cal	%Ft	P	F	C	Na
Per Serving	0	0	29	6	4	T	5	6

Choose rich green ASPARAGUS with closed, compact tips. It is in season from March to May. Do not wash until ready to eat. Store in refrigerator and eat within two to three days.

FAVORITE SLICED BEETS

Fresh beets will be lower in sodium than canned beets.

1	1 lb. can	sliced beets
1	T	cornstarch*
1	dash	black pepper
¼	C	vinegar
2	tsp.	sugar*

Gifford's Alternatives: Add:
to taste   Gifford's Basic Spice®

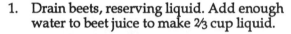

1. Drain beets, reserving liquid. Add enough water to beet juice to make ⅔ cup liquid.

2. Combine cornstarch and pepper in saucepan. Add liquid and vinegar. Whisk until smooth.

3. Cook, stirring constantly, until mixture is thickened and comes to a boil. Continue stirring and boiling for 1 minute. Add sliced beets and sugar. Heat and serve.

Serves 5

* See "Cooking Methods" section

	RCU	FU	Cal	%Ft	P	F	C	Na
Per Serving	0	0	44	6	1	T	10	214

Choose BEETS with a deep red color that are smooth, firm, and round. They are available all year. Remove the tops and store in the refrigerator. They will keep for two weeks.

PERFECTLY COOKED BROCCOLI

Everyone will love broccoli cooked this way. Try it with Hot Dill Sauce (p. 33) or other sauces from Fabulous Flavors (p. 19).

1	lb.	broccoli, fresh
2	T	onion, minced
1	clove	garlic, minced
1	T	lemon juice
to taste		seasoning without salt*

Gifford's Alternatives: Add:
to taste *Gifford's Basic Spice®*

1. Trim broccoli to uniform size. Wash. Blanch for 8 minutes. Then plunge into cold water for about 3 minutes and drain.

2. Sauté* onion and garlic. Add to broccoli. Cook gently until everything is tender-crisp, about 2 to 3 minutes. Add lemon juice. Season to taste. Serve.
Serves 4
* See "Cooking Methods" section

	RCU	FU	Cal	%Ft	P	F	C	Na
Per Serving	0	0	35	T	3	T	5	15

Choose BROCCOLI with a dark sage green to a purplish green color. Florets should be firm, compact clusters. Avoid plants with yellow leaves, thick stems, or soft spots. Broccoli is available all year. Store it in the refrigerator and use within three to five days.

BROCCOLI ITALIANO

Nice as a side dish.

2	C	broccoli, chopped
½	C	chicken bouillon
¼	tsp.	dried oregano
4	T	low-calorie mayonnaise
4	T	Romano cheese, grated

Gifford's Alternatives: Add:
1 tsp. *Gifford's Italian Spice®*
OMIT oregano

1. Combine broccoli, bouillon, and oregano in a saucepan and cook uncovered until broccoli is tender and most of liquid has evaporated, about 5 minutes.

2. Remove from heat and stir in mayonnaise and Romano cheese. Serve immediately.

Serves 4

	RCU	FU	Cal	%Ft	P	F	C	Na
Per Serving	0	1	122	22	5	3	4	171

BRUSSELS SPROUTS AS A GARNISH

Toss a few of these in a green salad for an unusual treat.

1	10 oz. pkg	frozen brussels sprouts
½	C	Low-Calorie Italian Dressing (p. 37)
½	tsp.	dill seeds
1	T	chives, chopped

1. Cook brussels sprouts until tender but still slightly firm.

BRUSSELS SPROUTS

2. Combine Italian dressing with dill seeds and chives. Pour over hot brussels sprouts.

3. Chill and serve as a garnish or relish.

Serves 6

	RCU	FU	Cal	%Ft	P	F	C	Na
Per Serving	0	0	20	6	2	T	4	17

Choose BRUSSELS SPROUTS with a bright green color, firm body, and tight-fitting outer leaves. Avoid vegetables with small holes or ragged leaves, which may indicate worms. Brussels sprouts are in season from October to January. Store in the refrigerator and use within three to five days.

EASY DOES IT BRUSSELS SPROUTS

Brussels sprouts are a member of the cabbage family. They grow on tall stems and resemble little cabbages.

5	C	brussels sprouts
½	C	Butter Buds®
to taste		seasoning without salt*
1		lemon, sliced

Gifford's Alternatives: Add:
to taste   Gifford's Basic Spice®

1. Remove loose leaves, wash, and cut a slice off the stem ends of the brussels sprouts. Cut an "X" into the stem end to speed up the cooking time.

2. Boil, uncovered, in 1 inch water for 10 to 20 minutes. Drain.

3. Serve immediately with Butter Buds®. Season. Garnish with lemon slices.

Serves 4

See "Cooking Methods" section

	RCU	FU	Cal	%Ft	P	F	C	Na
Per Serving	0	0	67	T	5	T	11	15

VARIATION: CREAMED SKILLET BRUSSELS SPROUTS

1. Soak brussels sprouts in boiling water for 5 minutes.

2. Drain and put in a nonstick* skillet with Butter Buds® and seasonings. Cover and steam for 10 minutes.

3. Add ¼ cup lemon juice and 1 cup low-fat yogurt. Heat and serve immediately.

Serves 4

See "Cooking Methods" section

	RCU	FU	Cal	%Ft	P	F	C	Na
Per Serving	0	0	103	9	7	1	16	47

APPLES AND RED CABBAGE

What a great combination!

4	C	red cabbage, shredded
2	med.	apples, cored and cut into wedges
½	C	red wine vinegar
1	T	brown sugar*
¼	tsp.	ground nutmeg

RED CABBAGE

Gifford's Alternatives: Add: *to taste*   *Gifford's Dessert Spice®*
    to taste   *Gifford's Chinese Spice®*

1. Combine cabbage, apples, vinegar, and brown sugar in saucepan over medium heat. Mix well.

2. Simmer, covered, about 10 minutes or until cabbage is tender-crisp. Add nutmeg. Mix well and serve.

Serves 6

See "Cooking Methods" section

	RCU	FU	Cal	%Ft	P	F	C	Na
Per Serving	0	0	56	3	1	T	14	16

When buying any CABBAGE, select firm heads that are heavy for their size. Look for good color free of blemishes. Cabbage is available all year. Store in refrigerator and use within one to two weeks.

STUFFED CABBAGE LEAVES

Try stuffing cabbage leaves with Savory Spanish Rice (p. 276) or Buckwheat Stuffing, listed below.

8	lg.	cabbage leaves
3	T	onion, chopped
2	T	parsley, chopped
2	T	green pepper, chopped
¼	tsp.	thyme
½	clove	garlic, pressed
3	C	brown rice,* cooked
1	C	wild rice,* cooked
1 ½	C	Tomato Sauce* (p. 24)

CABBAGE

Gifford's Alternatives: Add: to taste   *Gifford's Basic Spice®*
                                     to taste   *Gifford's Mexican Spice®*

1. Wash and blanch cabbage leaves. Drain and dry.

2. Sauté* onion, parsley, green pepper, thyme, and garlic.

3. Toss brown rice, wild rice, and sautéed vegetables together.

4. Divide into 8 equal portions and fill each cabbage leaf. Wrap leaf around filling and fasten with a toothpick. Place seam side down in a nonstick* casserole. Top with Tomato Sauce.

5. Bake covered at 350° until tender, about 45 minutes. Serve.

Yield: 8 rolls = 4 servings

* See "Cooking Methods" section

	RCU	FU	Cal	%Ft	P	F	C	Na
Per Serving	0	0	262	7	8	2	49	123

VARIATION: CABBAGE LEAVES WITH BUCKWHEAT STUFFING

1		onion, chopped
2	C	buckwheat groats

1. Sauté* onion. Add buckwheat and 1 quart water. Bring to boil. Cover and simmer 20 minutes or until water has been absorbed. Proceed from step 4 above.

	RCU	FU	Cal	%Ft	P	F	C	Na
Per Serving	0	0	213	7	9	2	40	11

COOKED CABBAGE AND VEGETABLES

A dish with interesting colors and textures. Serve with a slice of dark homemade bread.

6	med.	potatoes, peeled	8	C	cabbage, finely shredded
6	med.	carrots, peeled	2	T	whole wheat flour
3	med.	onions, halved	to taste		seasoning without salt*
1½	C	skim milk*			

Gifford's Alternatives: Add in step #2
| 1 | T | Gifford's Basic Spice® |
| 1 | tsp. | lemon juice |

1. Steam or boil halved or quartered potatoes, carrots, and onions until tender, about 1 hour.

2. While vegetables are cooking, heat 1 ¼ cups milk in a large nonstick* skillet. Add cabbage. Cover and simmer about 3 minutes.

3. Whisk flour into remaining ¼ cup milk until it is smooth. Season. Add to cooked cabbage. Boil and stir until mixture is thickened. Cover and simmer 2 to 3 more minutes.

4. Drain potatoes, carrots, and onions. Combine with cooked cabbage. Serve hot.

Serves 6

* See "Cooking Methods" section

	RCU	FU	Cal	%Ft	P	F	C	Na
Per Serving	0	0	191	1	7	T	47	101

SUNSHINE CARROTS

What a bright combination of color and taste.

2 ½	C	carrots, sliced
½	C	water
½	C	unsweetened orange juice
1	T	cornstarch*
1	med.	orange, sectioned

ORANGE SEGMENT

Gifford's Alternatives: Add:
to taste   Gifford's Dessert Spice®

1. Combine sliced carrots and water. Cover and cook until barely tender.

2. Drain liquid into measuring cup. Add orange juice and enough water to make 1 cup liquid.

3. Remove carrots from pan. Pour orange juice mixture into saucepan. Whisk in cornstarch. Cook over medium heat, stirring constantly, until it is thickened and clear.

4. Add carrots and orange sections. Coat evenly with sauce and heat thoroughly. Serve.

Serves 6

* See "Cooking Methods" section

	RCU	FU	Cal	%Ft	P	F	C	Na
Per Serving	0	0	44	11	1	1	12	22

CARROTS are available all year. Choose firm, well-shaped roots with good orange color. Avoid carrots with large green areas at the top. Store in refrigerator and use within two weeks.

BAKED CARROTS

Easy to prepare. Easy to eat.

4   C   carrots, grated
1   oz.   Butter Buds® Sprinkles

Gifford's Alternatives: Add:
to taste   Gifford's Dessert Spice®

1. Put grated carrots in a nonstick* casserole.

2. Mix Butter Buds® according to package directions. Pour over carrots. Cover and bake at 350° for 30 to 45 minutes. Serve.

Serves 6

* See "Cooking Methods" section

	RCU	FU	Cal	%Ft	P	F	C	Na
Per Serving	0	0	32	3	T	T	7	33

SAUCY CAULIFLOWER

Cauliflower loves sauces. Cheese sauce is its usual partner, but try some others like Hamburger Spaghetti Sauce (p. 164), Pizza Sauce (p. 26), or Saucy Seafood Sauce (p.28). You'll see why we call this "saucy" cauliflower.

1	med.	cauliflower
to taste		seasoning without salt*
1	C	Cheese Sauce Stand-In (p. 36)

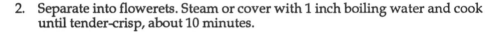

Gifford's Alternatives: Add:
to taste	**Gifford's Basic Spice®**
to taste	**Gifford's Mexican Spice®**

CAULIFLOWER

1. Wash cauliflower well, cut off the outside leaves, and core.

2. Separate into flowerets. Steam or cover with 1 inch boiling water and cook until tender-crisp, about 10 minutes.

3. Drain and season. Top with Cheese Sauce Stand-In or your favorite sauce. Serve immediately.

Serves 4

* See "Cooking Methods" section

	RCU	FU	Cal	%Ft	P	F	C	Na
Per Serving	0	0	64	15	5	1	8	66

CAULIFLOWER is in season from September to January. Choose white, compact, clean curds. Avoid plants with discolored spots. Store in refrigerator and use within two weeks.

DOUBLE CRUNCH CASSEROLE

Celery and chestnuts give this casserole its double crunch.

2	cubes	chicken bouillon
1 3/4	C	boiling water
1	bunch	celery, bias cut in 3/4-inch pieces
1	dash	black pepper
1/2	tsp.	basil
2	T	cornstarch*
1/2	C	cold water
2	5 oz. cans	water chestnuts, drained and sliced
1/3	C	dried whole wheat bread crumbs

Gifford's Alternatives: Add: to taste   *Gifford's Italian Spice®*

1. Dissolve bouillon in boiling water. Add celery and seasonings. Cover and cook until celery is tender-crisp, about 10 minutes.

2. Whisk cornstarch into ½ cup cold water. Gradually stir into celery mixture. Cook and stir until thickened. Add water chestnuts and pour into a 2-quart nonstick* casserole.

3. Sprinkle crumbs over top of casserole. Bake uncovered at 350° for 25 minutes. Serve hot.

Serves 6

* See "Cooking Methods" section

	RCU	FU	Cal	%Ft	P	F	C	Na
Per Serving	0	0	56	11	2	1	11	344

CELERY is available all year long. Choose crisp, medium green stalks that are thick and solid with a glossy surface. Store in refrigerator and use within one week.

SCRUMPTIOUS SCALLOPED CORN

This fluffy favorite and its yellow color really brighten up your dinner meal.

1	17 oz. can	cream-style corn	2	T	pimento, chopped
1	C	skim milk*	¼	C	onion, chopped
1	C	dried whole wheat bread crumbs	1	dash	black pepper
			2		egg whites, stiffly beaten

Gifford's Alternatives: Add: to taste   *Gifford's Basic Spice®*
                                        to taste   *Gifford's Mexican Spice®*

1. Combine corn and milk. Add ¾ cup of crumbs, pimento, onion, and black pepper. Mix well. Fold in stiffly beaten egg whites.

2. Pour into nonstick* 1-quart baking dish. Top with remaining ¼ cup of bread crumbs. Bake at 350° for 45 minutes. Serve hot.

Serves 8
* See "Cooking Methods" section

	RCU	FU	Cal	%Ft	P	F	C	Na
Per Serving	0	0	107	3	5	T	21	256

Fresh CORN is in season from May to September. Kernels should be small, juicy, and medium yellow color. Store, uncovered and unhusked, in the refrigerator. Use as soon as possible for sweetest flavor.

CREAMY CORN

Garnish with pimento and chopped green peppers to make a colorful side dish.

2	C	whole-kernel corn
1	C	low-fat cottage cheese
1	tsp.	whole wheat flour
1	tsp.	chicken bouillon granules*
¼	tsp.	dry mustard
2	tsp.	dried chopped chives

Gifford's Alternatives: Add:
2	T	white grape juice concentrate
½	tsp.	Gifford's Basic Spice®
¼	tsp.	Gifford's Gourmet Spice®

1. Cook corn.

2. Whip cottage cheese in blender or food processor for 2 minutes. Add flour, bouillon, mustard, and chives to cottage cheese.

3. Pour cottage cheese mixture over corn and stir gently.

4. Pour into a 1 ½-qt. nonstick* casserole. Bake at 325° for 25 to 30 minutes. Serve immediately.

Serves 6

* See "Cooking Methods" section

	RCU	FU	Cal	%Ft	P	F	C	Na
Per Serving	0	0	102	19	6	2	13	358

CORN CREOLE

A familiar vegetable goes spicy.

1	16 oz. can	stewed tomatoes, chopped
1	sm.	green pepper, chopped
1	med.	onion, chopped
1	stalk	celery, chopped
2	C	frozen corn, thawed
to taste		seasoning without salt*

Gifford's Alternatives: Add:
to taste	Gifford's Basic Spice®

1. Simmer tomatoes, green peppers, onion, and celery in a nonstick* skillet for 20 minutes.

2. Add corn. Season. Cook 5 minutes. Serve.

Serves 6

* See "Cooking Methods" section

	RCU	FU	Cal	%Ft	P	F	C	Na
Per Serving	0	0	90	1	3	1	16	114

WRENS

EGGPLANT ITALIANO

Eggplant is easy to grow and its mild flavor makes it very versatile.

1	lg.	eggplant
½	C	Low-Calorie Italian Dressing (p. 37)
½	tsp.	rosemary
½	tsp.	oregano
1	C	Tomato Sauce (p. 24)
6	T	dried whole wheat bread crumbs

Gifford's Alternatives: Add:
to taste   Gifford's Italian Spice®

1. Peel eggplant and cut crosswise in ¾-inch slices. Marinate for 1 hour in a bowl with Italian dressing, rosemary, and oregano. Be certain dressing and herbs are spread over each eggplant slice. Drain.

2. Arrange eggplant slices on a nonstick* baking sheet. Broil 3 inches from heat for about 5 minutes on each side until slices are tender and lightly browned.

3. Arrange the eggplant and tomato sauce in alternate layers in an 8" x 8" nonstick* baking dish.

4. Top with bread crumbs. Place under broiler again for about 2 minutes or until bread crumbs are toasted. Serve immediately.

Serves 6

* See "Cooking methods" section

	RCU	FU	Cal	%Ft	P	F	C	Na
Per Serving	0	0	63	18	1	1	8	221

EGGPLANT is available all year. Choose from heavy, smooth eggplants with dark purple to purple-black skin. Avoid plants with brown spots. Store at cool room temperature (60° F.). Chilling injury may occur if stored at 50° F. or below.

DILLY OF A DISH

Green beans and dill are a great combination. Plain green beans and sliced water chestnuts also make a dynamic duo.

2		beef bouillon cubes*
2	T	onion, chopped
1/4	C	green pepper, chopped
1/2	tsp.	dill seed
3	C	green beans

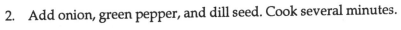

Gifford's Alternatives: Add:
to taste   Gifford's Gourmet Spice®

DILL

1. Dissolve bouillon in 2 cups boiling water.

2. Add onion, green pepper, and dill seed. Cook several minutes.

3. Add green beans. Cover and cook 8 to 10 minutes or until green beans are tender. Serve.

Serves 6

* See "Cooking Methods" section

	RCU	FU	Cal	%Ft	P	F	C	Na
Per Serving	0	0	26	3	1	T	6	135

HEAD LETTUCE

LEAF LETTUCE

GREEN BEANS IN ITALIAN SAUCE

Hmmm. Garlic toast would taste good with this.

1	9 oz. pkg	frozen green beans
2		tomatoes, diced
½	C	celery, diced
¼	C	green pepper, diced
2	T	onion, chopped
¼	tsp.	oregano
⅓	C	water

Gifford's Alternatives: Add:
to taste   *Gifford's Italian Spice®*

1. Combine all ingredients and bring to a boil.

2. Reduce heat. Cover. Simmer for 6 to 8 minutes or until green beans are tender. Serve hot.

Serves 4

	RCU	FU	Cal	%Ft	P	F	C	Na
Per Serving	0	0	41	1	2	T	9	24

GREEN BEANS are in season from April to September. Select firm, crisp, slender pods with a good green color. Store in the refrigerator and use within the week.

GREEN BEANS WITH MUSHROOMS GALORE

Perfect with so many meals as a side dish.

1	9 oz. pkg	frozen green beans
1		green onion, finely chopped
¼	lb.	fresh mushrooms, sliced
1	tsp.	lemon juice
1	tsp.	cornstarch*
1	tsp.	paprika

Gifford's Alternatives: Add:

to taste	*Gifford's Mexican Spice®*
to taste	*Gifford's Basic Spice®*

1. Cook and drain beans. Set aside.

2. Sauté* onion. Add mushrooms and lemon juice. Cook, stirring constantly, until mushrooms are tender.

3. Combine cornstarch and paprika. Sprinkle over mushrooms. Cook, stirring constantly, for 1 minute or until mixture is thickened. Add to green beans. Toss lightly. Serve hot.

Serves 4

* See "Cooking Methods" section

	RCU	FU	Cal	%Ft	P	F	C	Na
Per Serving	0	0	27	2	2	T	5	6

STUFFED MUSHROOMS

Use these as a garnish with chicken or as an appetizer.

1	lb.	large mushrooms, whole
1	10 oz. pkg	frozen chopped spinach
2	cloves	garlic, minced
2		egg whites, stiffly beaten
½	C	dried whole wheat bread crumbs

Gifford's Alternatives: Add:
to taste   *Gifford's Basic Spice®*

1. Wash mushrooms and remove caps. Heat caps in microwave oven for 2 minutes or steam briefly. Chop mushroom stems.

2. Cook spinach according to package directions along with chopped mushroom stems. Drain and squeeze to eliminate excess water.

3. Combine spinach with garlic, egg whites, and bread crumbs. Fill mushroom caps with the spinach mixture. Place caps in a nonstick* pan and bake 10 to 15 minutes at 350°. Serve hot.

Serves 6

* See "Cooking Methods" section

	RCU	FU	Cal	%Ft	P	F	C	Na
Per Serving	0	0	72	3	6	T	7	55

MUSHROOMS are available all year. Choose small to medium mushrooms with white, cream-colored, or tan caps. Caps should be closed around stem or slightly open with pink or light tan gills. Store in a paper bag in the refrigerator crisper. Use within five days.

OKRA AND TOMATOES

Okra is popular in the southern part of the United States. It is delicious when thinly sliced and fried with Hash Brown Potatoes (p. 243).

3	C	okra, sliced crosswise
½	C	Butter Buds®, optional
3	C	tomatoes, chopped
½	C	onion, chopped
⅛	tsp.	hot sauce, optional
½	C	corn, cooked, optional

Gifford's Alternatives: Add:
to taste   Gifford's Mexican Spice®

1. Wash okra. Do NOT cut off stems or tips of pods, but slice the pods thickly into rounds.

2. Boil in ½ inch water for 10 minutes. Cover the last 5 minutes. OR Cook the okra in a large nonstick* skillet with Butter Buds® until tender.

3. Add remaining ingredients and simmer about 5 minutes. Do not overcook. Serve immediately.

Serves 6

*See "Cooking Methods" section

	RCU	FU	Cal	%Ft	P	F	C	Na
Per Serving	0	0	75	2	4	T	14	59

OKRA is in season from May to September. Choose 2-inch to 4 ½-inch long, bright green pods. They should be tender and tips should bend with slight pressure. Store in a plastic bag in refrigerator. Use in three to five days.

CRUNCHY ONION RINGS

These make a crispy garnish on a casserole or enjoy them with a sandwich. Believe it or not, they are as good as deep fried onion rings.

2		egg whites
2	T	skim milk*
to taste		seasoning without salt*
2	C	whole wheat flour
2	C	skim milk*
4	T	dried whole wheat bread crumbs
4	med.	Bermuda or white onions, cut into ¼ inch slices and separated into rings.

ONIONS

Gifford's Alternatives: Add:
to taste   *Gifford's Basic Spice®*

1. Slightly beat egg whites with 2 tablespoons skim milk in a small bowl. Set aside.

2. Mix seasoning into whole wheat flour in a small bowl. Set aside.

3. Pour skim milk into a small bowl and set aside. Pour bread crumbs into a small bowl and set aside. Arrange bowls in the following order: milk, flour, egg whites, and bread crumbs.

4. Dip onion rings into bowls in the arranged order. Lightly shake off the excess.

5. Bake on a nonstick* baking sheet at 375° until tender, about 15 minutes. Cool slightly and serve.

Serves 8

* See "Cooking Methods" section

	RCU	FU	Cal	%Ft	P	F	C	Na
Per Serving	0	0	143	3	8	T	29	67

ONIONS are available all year. Choose firm globes with dry, crackly skins. Store at cool room temperature in a mesh bag. They will keep for several months.

COOKED ONIONS

Use this healthful garnish on most bean, rice, potato, or vegetable casseroles.

3	med.	onions
¼	C	Butter Buds®

1. Slice onions thinly and separate into rings. Makes about 3 cups onion rings.

2. Put 3 tablespoons water in a microwave pan. Add onions and cook in microwave until transparent. OR Sauté* onions on stove top in nonstick* skillet. Drain.

3. If desired, pour Butter Buds® over onions and coat evenly. Serve.

Serves 6

* See "Cooking Methods" section

	RCU	FU	Cal	%Ft	P	F	C	Na
Per Serving	0	0	24	T	1	T	4	4

PERFECT PARSNIP PATTIES

Parsnips sweeten after exposure to cold weather. Leave them in the ground until spring and their flavor will be at its peak when you dig them up to eat.

6		parsnips, cooked
to taste		seasoning without salt*
2	T	whole wheat flour*
½	C	low-fat yogurt*

PARSNIPS

Gifford's Alternatives: Add:
to taste   Gifford's Basic Spice®

1. Wash, peel, and quarter parsnips. Remove core and discard. Cook parsnips in boiling water for 15 minutes or until tender.

2. Drain and mash. Use cooking water to adjust consistency. Season.

3. Whisk flour into yogurt. Stir into seasoned parsnips.

4. Shape into 8 patties and brown slowly on a nonstick* griddle or skillet. Turn once. They should have a crisp crust. Serve.

Serves 5

*See "Cooking Methods" section

	RCU	FU	Cal	%Ft	P	F	C	Na
Per Serving	0	0	61	12	2	1	12	18

PARSNIPS are available from May to September. Choose smooth, firm, well-shaped roots of small to medium width. Remove tops and store in plastic bag in refrigerator. Use within two weeks.

RUTABAGA POTATO BAKE

Fill this potato nest with any of your favorite vegetables. Or how about making the nest out of sweet potatoes?

4	C	potatoes , mashed
3	C	rutabaga, diced
to taste		seasoning without salt*
garnish		parsley or chives, diced

Gifford's Alternatives: Add: **to taste**   *Gifford's Gourmet Spice®*

1. Be sure to make mashed potatoes without butter. Use skim milk.

2. Place potatoes in a 2-quart nonstick* casserole, forming a nest in the center. Bake at 400° for 20 minutes.

3. Steam or boil rutabaga until tender. Drain and season. Spoon into potato nest and garnish with parsley or chives. Serve.

Serves 6

*See "Cooking Methods" section

	RCU	FU	Cal	%Ft	P	F	C	Na
Per Serving	0	0	108	2	3	T	23	14

RUTABAGAS are in season from May to October. Choose firm, smooth plants. Size is not important. Avoid plants with cuts or punctures. Store at cool room temperature, 60° F., and they will keep for several months.

LASAGNA ROLLS

A tasty substitute for high-fat lasagna.

SPINACH

1	C	spinach
2	T	parmesan cheese, grated
1	C	dry-curd cottage cheese*
8		whole wheat lasagna noodles
2	C	Spicy Tomato Sauce (p. 25)

Gifford's Alternatives: Add:
to taste   Gifford's Italian Spice®

1. Cook spinach, drain off all excess water. Stir in cheeses. Set aside.

2. Cook lasagna noodles.

3. Spread spinach mixture evenly along the entire length of each noodle. Roll up noodle and place on its side in a nonstick* 8" x 8" casserole. Do not let noodles touch.

4. Cover lasagna with Spicy Tomato Sauce. Bake at 350° for 20 minutes. Serve hot.

Serves 4

* See "Cooking Methods" section

	RCU	FU	Cal	%Ft	P	F	C	Na
Per Serving	0	0	215	13	18	3	23	54

STUFFED ACORN SQUASH

Golden tender squash is delicious with this rice stuffing.

1 ½	C	brown rice,* cooked
½	C	dried whole wheat bread crumbs
1		onion, finely chopped
2		egg whites, slightly beaten
½	tsp.	sage
2	tsp.	parsley, chopped
1	tsp.	black pepper
3		acorn squash

Gifford's Alternatives: Add:
to taste **Gifford's Basic Spice®**
to taste **Gifford's Mexican Spice®**

1. Combine all ingredients except squash.

2. Cut squash in half. Clean out seeds and discard them.

3. Fill each squash half with rice mixture, heaping slightly.

4. Place squash in a nonstick* casserole. Seal with foil. Bake at 350° until squash is tender, about 1 hour. Serve.

Serves 6

* See "Cooking Methods" section

	RCU	FU	Cal	%Ft	P	F	C	Na
Per Serving	0	0	196	2	6	T	45	80

ACORN SQUASH is in season from September to February. Choose hard, tough-rinded squash which is heavy for its size. Avoid squash with soft areas or cuts. Store at cool room temperature, 60° F., and squash will keep several months.

 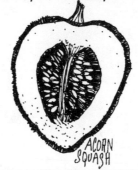 

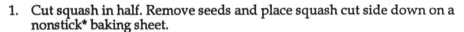
APPLE AND ACORN SQUASH DELIGHT

Acorn squash are so easy to grow and store that you can enjoy this treat all year round.

2	med.	acorn squash
4	sm.	apples, diced
¼	C	celery, diced
2	T	onion, minced
to taste		seasoning without salt*
⅓	C	water

Gifford's Alternatives: Add:
to taste   *Gifford's Basic Spice®*

1. Cut squash in half. Remove seeds and place squash cut side down on a nonstick* baking sheet.

2. In a nonstick baking dish, combine apples, celery, onion, seasonings, and water. Cover.

3. Bake both squash and apple mixture at 400° for 45 minutes or until tender. To serve, fill squash halves with apple mixture and enjoy.

Serves 4
* See "Cooking Methods" section

	RCU	FU	Cal	%Ft	P	F	C	Na
Per Serving	0	0	159	1	3	T	40	13

BRIGHT AND BEAUTIFUL

Wow! Golden yellow squash with red cranberries. What a brilliant contrast and a brilliant autumn combination!

2		egg whites, stiffly beaten
1½	C	butternut or banana squash, cooked and mashed
½	C	cranberries, chopped
1	dash	nutmeg

Gifford's Alternatives: Add:
to taste   *Gifford's Chinese Spice®*
to taste   *Gifford's Dessert Spice®*

SQUASH

---

1. Fold stiffly beaten egg whites into mashed squash.

2. Gently fold in cranberries. Pour into a 1 ½-quart nonstick* casserole. Garnish with nutmeg. Bake at 400° for 35 to 40 minutes. Serve immediately.

Serves 4

*See "Cooking Methods" section

	RCU	FU	Cal	%Ft	P	F	C	Na
Per Serving	0	0	63	T	3	T	15	15

BANANA and BUTTERNUT SQUASH are in season from September to February. Choose heavy, tough-skinned squash. Store at cool room temperature, 60° F., and they will keep for several months.

SUCCULENT SUCCOTASH

Two great companions, corn and lima beans, in creamy, seasoned yogurt.

1	12 oz. can	corn, drained
1	16 oz. can	lima beans, drained
⅓	C	low-fat yogurt*
to taste		seasoning without salt*

Gifford's Alternatives: Add:
to taste   Gifford's Basic Spice®

1. Combine all ingredients.

2. Heat over medium heat until it begins to bubble. Serve hot.

Serves 6

*See "Cooking Methods" section

	RCU	FU	Cal	%Ft	P	F	C	Na
Per Serving	0	0	107	6	5	1	22	319

SWEET POTATOES AND FRUIT JUICE

The natural goodness of fruit juice makes these sweet potatoes taste terrific without the usual butter and brown sugar.

1	lb.	sweet potatoes
1	pinch	cinnamon
1	pinch	nutmeg
1	pinch	allspice
¼	C	pineapple juice and
1	T	chopped pineapple
	OR	
½	C	orange juice and
½	tsp.	orange rind, grated

Gifford's Alternatives: Add:
to taste   Gifford's Dessert Spice®

1. Boil sweet potatoes until tender. Remove skins.

2. Mash sweet potato pulp. Add spices and juice. Whip until fluffy.

3. Place in 1-quart nonstick* baking dish. Bake at 350° until thoroughly heated. Serve.

Serves 6

* See "Cooking Methods" section

	RCU	FU	Cal	%Ft	P	F	C	Na
Per Serving	0	0	79	3	1	T	18	6

SWEET POTATOES are in season from September to April. Choose firm, medium-sized potatoes with smooth, uniformly colored skins. Avoid potatoes with cuts. Store at cool room temperature, 60° F., and they will keep for several months.

SIMPLE BROILED TOMATOES

These make a good snack as well as a side dish at lunch or dinner.

4		tomatoes
¼	C	cracker crumbs
1	T	Low-Calorie Italian Dressing (p. 37)
garnish		parsley, fresh

Gifford's Alternatives: Add:
to taste   *Gifford's Italian Spice®*

1. Slice tomatoes in half crosswise. Place on baking sheet, cut side up.

2. Combine crumbs and Italian Dressing. Sprinkle 1 tablespoon of seasoned crumbs over each tomato.

3. Broil 10 inches from source of heat for 4 minutes or until golden brown.

4. Garnish with parsley and serve.

Serves 4

	RCU	FU	Cal	%Ft	P	F	C	Na
Per Serving	0	0	75	15	3	1	14	131

It is possible to hasten the ripening time for fresh TOMATOES by placing them in a brown paper bag at room temperature.

SPINACH-STUFFED TOMATOES

Serve with a variety of Eleven Variation Dinner Rolls (p. 330) for a summer luncheon.

4	med.	tomatoes
1/4	tsp.	onion powder
1/8	tsp.	basil
1/8	tsp.	oregano
dash		black pepper
1/2	C	spinach, chopped and cooked
1/4	C	bread crumbs

Gifford's Alternatives: Add:
1 1/4	tsp.	Gifford's Italian Spice®
1/4	tsp.	Gifford's Dessert Spice®
1	pinch	ground fennel seed
		OMIT onion powder, basil, oregano, black pepper

1. Cut off the top of the tomato and scoop out a small portion of the pulp.

2. Mix the pulp with seasonings and spinach.

3. Stuff tomatoes with this mixture. Top with bread crumbs.

4. Bake at 350° for 20 to 30 minutes or until tomatoes are tender. Serve immediately.

Serves 4

	RCU	FU	Cal	%Ft	P	F	C	Na
Per Tomato	0	0	69	T	3	T	20	61

"MILD-MANNERED" TURNIPS

Turnips, rutabagas, and potatoes are great when combined in equal parts and when used interchangeably. Try it. You'll like it.

4	C	turnips, cooked and mashed
2	C	soft whole wheat bread crumbs
5		egg whites, stiffly beaten
to taste		seasoning without salt*

Gifford's Alternatives: Add:
| to taste | | Gifford's Italian Spice® |

1. Fold together turnips and remaining ingredients.

2. Place in a nonstick* 2-quart casserole. Bake at 350° for 1 hour and 15 minutes. Serve.

Serves 8

*See "Cooking Methods" section

	RCU	FU	Cal	%Ft	P	F	C	Na
Per Serving	0	0	55	T	4	T	11	108

ZUCCHINI CHEESE LAYERS

Simple to make. A wonderful way to use up this prolific plant. Also note that summer squashes are interchangeable in most recipes.

3	med.	zucchini, peeled and sliced
1/4	C	onion, chopped
1	lb.	low-fat cottage cheese*
1	T	lemon juice
1	tsp.	basil
1/4	C	parmesan cheese, grated

Gifford's Alternatives: Add:
to taste   Gifford's Italian Spice®

1. Sauté* zucchini and onion.

2. Whip cottage cheese, lemon juice, and basil in blender.

3. Alternate layers of zucchini and cottage cheese mixture in a 1 1/2-quart nonstick* casserole.

4. Top with parmesan cheese. Bake uncovered at 350° for 25 to 30 minutes. Serve hot.

Serves 6

*See "Cooking Methods" section

	RCU	FU	Cal	%Ft	P	F	C	Na
Per Serving	0	0	98	13	16	1	6	266

STUFFED ZUCCHINI BOATS

Enjoy with homemade bread.

4	med.	zucchini
1	clove	garlic, crushed
1	med.	onion, chopped
1/4	C	green pepper, chopped
1/4	C	celery, chopped
1/2	C	fresh mushrooms, chopped
1/4	tsp.	marjoram
1	tsp.	parsley, minced
2		egg whites, stiffly beaten

PEPPERS

Gifford's Alternatives: Add:
2	tsp.	Gifford's Basic Spice®
1	T	pimentos, diced (add to step #3)

1. Wash whole zucchini and parboil for 10 minutes. Drain and cool. Cut lengthwise. Scoop out the pulp and chop it finely. Set aside.

2. Sauté* garlic, onion, green peppers, celery, and mushrooms until tender. Add marjoram, parsley, and zucchini pulp. Heat. Remove from heat and cool.

3. Fold in stiffly beaten egg whites. Fill the cavity of each zucchini half with the mixture.

4. Place stuffed zucchini in a shallow nonstick* baking pan. Bake at 350° for 30 minutes. Serve.

Serves 4

* See "Cooking Methods" section

	RCU	FU	Cal	%Ft	P	F	C	Na
Per Serving	0	0	60	T	5	T	12	32

CREAMED VEGETABLES

Also try Cheese Sauce Stand-In (p. 36) or Dill Sauce (p. 33) over steamed vegetables to really dress them up.

1	recipe	Basic Low-Fat White Sauce (p. 39)
3	C	favorite vegetable
to taste		seasoning without salt*

Gifford's Alternatives: Add:
to taste   Gifford's Gourmet Spice®

1. Steam vegetables. Season.

2. Prepare white sauce and pour over vegetables. Serve.

Serves 6

*See "Cooking Method" section

	RCU	FU	Cal	%Ft	P	F	C	Na
Per Serving	0	0	67	4	4	T	14	60

COOKOUT VEGETABLES

This is a fun way to add vegetables to a backyard cookout.

4		carrots, scraped
4		onions, peeled
4		potatoes, scrubbed
4		ears corn, shucked
4	T	water
to taste		seasoning without salt*
1	pkg	Butter Buds®
		heavy-duty aluminum foil

ONIONS

Gifford's Alternatives: Add:
to taste   Gifford's Basic Spice®

1. Prepare 4 squares of foil by coating inner side with vegetable spray.

2. Cut carrots, onions, and potatoes into large chunks. Place 1 ear of corn on each square of foil with equal amounts of carrots, onions, and potatoes.

3. Sprinkle 1 tablespoon of water or powdered Butter Buds® over the vegetables. Season.

4. Wrap snugly and seal tightly. Place over hot coals for 45 to 60 minutes or until vegetables are tender. Turn occasionally to ensure even cooking. Serve.

Serves 4
* See "Cooking Methods" section

	RCU	FU	Cal	%Ft	P	F	C	Na
Per Serving	0	0	225	5	7	1	45	48

VEGETABLE FUGUE CASSEROLE

Sydette Parent

Wow! What a colorful meal.

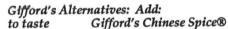

3	med.	tomatoes
2	lb.	zucchini
3	med.	green peppers
¾	C	green onions, sliced
½	C	celery, diced
2	C	fresh mushrooms, sliced
½	tsp.	tarragon, dried
⅛	tsp.	black pepper
1	C	brown rice,* cooked
2	oz.	Swiss cheese, shredded
1 ½	C	chicken stock*

Gifford's Alternatives: Add:
to taste   *Gifford's Chinese Spice®*

1. Cut tomatoes in half and scoop out seeds and pulp, leaving nicely walled shells. Put the pulp into a large skillet.

2. Cut zucchini in half lengthwise and scrape out centers leaving "canoes." Mix zucchini pulp with tomato pulp in skillet. Cook, cutting these up somewhat with a spoon.

3. Slice green peppers in half lengthwise and discard seeds. Arrange tomato, zucchini, and green pepper halves in two 9" x 13" pans. Set aside.

4. Sauté* green onions, celery, and mushrooms until wilted. Add to zucchini and tomato mixture along with tarragon, black pepper, and rice. Let cool to just warm and stir in shredded cheese.

5. Spoon this stuffing into vegetable shells. Pour ¾ cup chicken stock into bottom of both pans. Bake at 375° for 45 to 60 minutes. Serve hot.

Serves 6

* See "Cooking Methods" section

	RCU	FU	Cal	%Ft	P	F	C	Na
Per Serving	0	0	137	22	8	3	21	270

BASIC ONE-SKILLET VEGETABLES

This tastes wonderful as is. But it can be made into a stew or casserole by adding your favorite sauce and rice or potatoes. Or you can cook it in a wok with bits of chicken.

4	C	zucchini, thinly sliced
1	C	carrot, coarsely shredded
1	C	onion, chopped
¾	C	celery, bias-sliced
1	C	mushrooms, sliced
½	med.	green pepper, cut into thin strips
½	tsp.	garlic powder
¼	tsp.	basil
1	dash	black pepper
1	C	chicken stock*
¼	C	chili sauce
2	tsp.	prepared mustard
2	med.	tomatoes, cut into wedges

Gifford's Alternatives: Add:
to taste   Gifford's Italian Spice®

1. In a large nonstick* skillet, place zucchini, carrot, onion, celery, mushrooms, green pepper, garlic powder, basil, and black pepper. Cover with chicken broth and cook over medium heat until vegetables are tender. Stir occasionally.

2. Combine chili sauce and mustard. Stir into vegetable mixture. Add tomato wedges and cook about 5 minutes longer. Season to taste and serve.

Serves 8

See "Cooking Methods" section

	RCU	FU	Cal	%Ft	P	F	C	Na
Per Serving	0	0	50	T	2	T	11	190

WONDERFUL RATATOUILLE

Serve this wonderful dish with French bread. Hmmm!

2		tomatoes, cut in wedges
⅛	tsp.	thyme
1		onion, sliced
1		green pepper, cut in strips
2	C	eggplant, peeled, sliced crosswise, then cut into strips
2	C	zucchini, same as above
2	cloves	garlic, crushed
1		bay leaf
to taste		black pepper
¼	C	parmesan cheese, grated

Gifford's Alternatives: Add:
to taste   Gifford's Italian Spice®

1. Sprinkle tomatoes with thyme and let stand.

2. Sauté* remaining vegetables and garlic until barely tender. Add bay leaf.

3. Pour into a 1-quart nonstick* casserole. Arrange tomato wedges on top. Sprinkle with black pepper and cheese.

4. Bake at 350°, covered, for 30 minutes. Remove bay leaf before serving.

Serves 8

* See "Cooking Methods" section

	RCU	FU	Cal	%Ft	P	F	C	Na
Per Serving	0	0	48	16	3	1	7	36

WOK TALK

*Wisdom is knowing what to do;
virtue is doing it.*

WOK TALK

Let's talk "wok!" A wok is an all-purpose cooking pan used for Oriental cooking. It is 12 inches to 24 inches in diameter and is shaped like a wide, stubby cone. It was traditionally made of thin tempered iron but woks are now also made of aluminum or stainless steel. We recommend a wok with a nonstick surface to reduce the need for oil in Oriental cooking.

The wok's cone shape allows a certain control over cooking temperatures. Liquids will puddle in the bottom of the wok where the temperature is hottest. Foods can be cooked quickly in the bottom portion and then pulled up to cook more slowly, out of the liquid, on the wok's sides.

Stir-frying involves this method of wok cooking. With some minor adjustments, it is an excellent cooking method for a high-complex carbohydrate, low-fat diet since you will use little or no oil and lots of vegetables and rice. There are two main steps in stir-frying: preparation and cooking. They each take about the same amount of time, since the preparation time is relatively long and the cooking time is relatively short.

Oriental cooks have mastered the artistic impact of food preparation. Foods are selected for their color, texture, shape, and size as well as for their taste. And the results are beautiful to behold. Imagine bias-cut celery and carrots, green pepper strips, and pink curved shrimp all tossed together on a bed of fluffy rice. A splash of dark soy sauce provides flavor and contrast. Outstanding!!

Following is a list of some stir-fry ingredients and how to prepare them.

BAMBOO SHOOTS are slightly sweet and crisp. They are available canned and add an ivory color, an interesting shape, and a crunch to your recipe. Rinse before using.

BEAN CURD or TOFU is made from soybeans that have been cooked, puréed, and formed into a white semi-solid cube. It is a good source of protein but is 53 percent fat, so it needs to be used in moderation. Its increasing popularity has made it available at many supermarkets as well as in Oriental or health food stores. Store tofu in the refrigerator, covered with water. To use, cut it into cubes and cook in your wok along with your favorite meats and vegetables. Since tofu tastes quite bland, it takes on the added seasonings very well.

BEAN SPROUTS can be purchased canned or you can grow your own. See "Sprouts" in the Cooking Methods section on page 406. Traditionally, mung beans are used, but any type of sprout can be used in stir-frying. They add a remarkable texture to your meal.

BROCCOLI should be washed and the florets cut into equal, bite-sized pieces.

CARROTS should be scrubbed or peeled and then thinly sliced on the diagonal.

CAULIFLOWER should be washed and the florets cut into equal, bite-sized pieces.

CELERY should be washed and bias-cut.

CHINESE CABBAGE has a white stalk and green crinkly leaves. Buy it fresh and finely chop or shred it. Add to soups or to stir-fry dishes. It does not require much cooking.

CHINESE EGG NOODLES are a very thin pasta made of flour, eggs, water and salt. We recommend the use of brown rice in place of egg noodles but if you use egg noodles, boil or stir-fry rather than deep fry them. Use sparingly since they are high in RCUs.

GINGER ROOT is a light brown gnarled root. It is grated fresh and used for its flavor. Ground ginger powder can be used in place of fresh ginger, but it is rather inadequate by comparison. Fresh ginger root will keep in the refrigerator for months if wrapped in plastic.

GREEN BEANS should be washed and cut into 1- to 1 ½-inch diagonal pieces.

GREEN PEPPERS should be washed, have their seeds removed, and then chopped or cut into long, thin strips.

MEATS: Choose only one meat for your recipe. Allow 2 ounces of raw meat per person. Choose from the following:

CHICKEN or TURKEY white meat should be skinned and chopped into bite-sized pieces.

SHRIMP, fresh or thawed, should be quartered, shelled, and deveined.

WHITE FISH FILET should be skinned and chopped into 1- to 1 ½-inch squares.

LEAN HAM should be trimmed of fat and chopped into small pieces.

LEAN PORK should be carefully trimmed of fat and chopped into small pieces.

LEAN BEEF, such as flank, rump, or round, should be trimmed of fat and chopped into small pieces.

MUSHROOMS should be washed, then used whole or sliced.

ONIONS should be peeled and then sliced into rings or diced. Green onions and leeks can be sliced, using both the white and green parts.

PEANUT OIL is the traditional oil used in wok cooking because of its high smoking point. If peanut oil is used, add only enough to keep ingredients from sticking.

SNOW PEAS are also called pea pods or Chinese peas. They are pods which have been picked before the peas have fully developed. They can be purchased fresh or frozen or you may grow your own. Their flat shape and green color add visual as well as actual "snap" to your recipe.

SOY SAUCE is a dark brown liquid made from soybeans, wheat, yeast, and salt. It is the most common seasoning used in Oriental cooking. It is not as high in sodium (439 mg per teaspoon) as salt (1890 mg. per teaspoon), but it should still be used carefully. It adds color and contrast as well as flavor.

WATER CHESTNUTS are available fresh or canned. They resemble a bulb with a tough, dark skin and a crisp, white interior. Only the interior is sliced and eaten. Its crispness and delicate sweetness are unsurpassed in Oriental cooking.

ZUCCHINI can be peeled and sliced diagonally or into strips.

Cooking the prepared vegetables is a show in itself. In fact, it is often done right at the dinner table so that the family or guests can watch. The wok must be very hot and then brushed with peanut oil. We recommend using one-half cup bouillon, chicken stock, or water in place of the peanut oil, adding more liquid if necessary during the cooking process. Most recipes will tell exactly which ingredients to add first and how long to cook them, but the rule of thumb is to begin cooking the slowest-cooking vegetables first (i.e., carrots). Most vegetables are cooked to a "tender-crisp" stage, which means that they are tender on the outside and still crisp on the inside. Serve vegetables over cooked brown rice. Perfect!!

So let's not talk wok anymore. Grab a pair of chopsticks or a fork, and let's eat.

ENDLESS SUKIYAKI

The combinations are endless. Only your taste and imagination set the limits. Before long, friends and family members will want to try out their own ideas for recipes in the wok, too. Let them, and have fun.

1. Take a look at the list of ingredients on pages 210-211. Choose your favorites, experiment, or just use what you have on hand. Remember to use only 1-2 ounces of meat per person so that any combination will be under 20% fat.

2. Cook the brown rice (p. 281). Allow 1/2 cup cooked rice per person.

3. Prepare ingredients by washing and chopping into small pieces.

4. Heat your wok or a heavy nonstick* skillet and pour in chicken stock, water, or a VERY THIN coat of peanut oil.

5. Add ingredients according to length of cooking time, slowest first. Cook until all ingredients are tender-crisp. Five to 10 minutes is average. Season. Serve immediately over rice.

CHINESE FRIED RICE

This is a great way to use leftover rice.

4		green onions, chopped
1/4	C	green peppers, diced
1/4	C	celery, chopped
3	C	day-old cooked rice
1/4	C	chicken bouillon*
4	oz.	cooked ham, diced -OR-
8	oz.	cooked shrimp
4		egg whites
1/4	C	bean sprouts*
1/2	C	snow peas
1/4	C	parsley, minced
1 1/2	T	soy sauce, optional

Gifford's Alternatives: Add:

1/2	tsp.	Gifford's Chinese Spice®
1/4	tsp.	Gifford's Gourmet Spice®
1/8	tsp.	Gifford's Dessert Spice®

1. Sauté* onions, green peppers, and celery until tender.

2. Sauté rice in chicken bouillon until hot and golden.

3. Add onion mixture and ham or shrimp. When these ingredients are well mixed, hollow a center in the rice. Pour 4 egg whites into the hollow and scramble until semi-cooked. Stir cooked eggs into the rice.

4. Add bean sprouts and snow peas. Cook for 5 minutes. Stir in parsley. Serve at once with soy sauce.

Serves 8

* See "Cooking Methods" section

With Ham

	RCU	FU	Cal	%Ft	P	F	C	Na
Per Serving	0	0	134	11	7	2	22	292

With Shrimp

	RCU	FU	Cal	%Ft	P	F	C	Na
Per Serving	0	0	130	1	9	T	22	322

SPINACH STIR-FRY

Unique and uniquely delicious!

¼	lb.	boneless beef round steak, fat trimmed
1	T	soy sauce
1-2	C	chicken stock*
1	tsp.	ginger root, grated
2	tsp.	cornstarch*
¼	tsp.	beef bouillon granules*
¼	C	water
8	oz.	small spinach leaves, fresh
½	C	water chestnuts, sliced
3	C	brown rice,* cooked

Gifford's Alternatives: Add:
¼	tsp.	*Gifford's Chinese Spice®*
¼	tsp.	*Schilling® Orange Peel*
1	tsp.	*unsweetened apple juice concentrate*

1. Partially freeze beef; slice it thinly into bite-sized strips. Combine with soy sauce and marinate at room temperature for 15 minutes.

2. Heat wok or large nonstick* skillet. Pour in chicken stock and stir-fry ginger root for 30 seconds. Add beef and stir-fry for 3 minutes until browned.

3. Whisk cornstarch and bouillon granules into ¼ cup water. Add to wok. Cook and stir until thickened.

4. Stir in spinach and water chestnuts. Cook, covered, for 2 minutes. Serve immediately over rice.

Serves 6

*See "Cooking Methods" section

	RCU	FU	Cal	%Ft	P	F	C	Na
Per Serving	0	0	198	17	9	4	30	418

VEGGIE STIR-FRY

A meatless stir-fry or a side dish.

1	C	broccoli
1	C	yellow squash
1	C	carrots
1	sm.	onion
2	tsp.	oil*
½	C	chicken bouillon*

Gifford's Alternatives: Add:
| 1 | small | orange, peeled, quartered, sliced |
| 1 | tsp. | Gifford's Chinese Spice® |

1. Break broccoli into pieces and thinly slice stems. Slice squash, carrots, and onions.

2. Pour oil and bouillon in wok or nonstick* skillet. Add vegetables and simmer uncovered until bouillon has cooked away.

3. Lightly brown vegetables in remaining oil. Season and serve.

Serves 6

* See "Cooking Methods" section

	RCU	FU	Cal	%Ft	P	F	C	Na
Per Serving	0	0	42	21	2	1	6	54

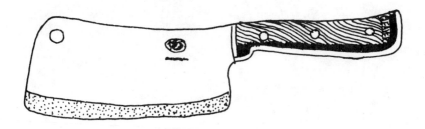

ZUCCHINI PINEAPPLE STIR-FRY

What a combination!

1	sm.	zucchini, sliced
1	med.	onion, chopped
½	C	crushed pineapple
1 ½	C	bean sprouts*
½	C	pineapple juice, drained from canned pineapple
1 ½	T	soy sauce
3	C	brown rice*, cooked

SQUASH

Gifford's Alternatives: Add:
1	tsp.	*Gifford's Chinese Spice®*
1	tsp.	*Schilling® Orange Peel*
1		*carrot, shredded*

1. Sauté* zucchini and onions in wok or nonstick* skillet until tender.

2. Add pincapple, sprouts, juice, and soy sauce. Cook, uncovered, until thoroughly heated. Serve over rice.

Serves 6

* See "Cooking Methods" section

	RCU	FU	Cal	%Ft	P	F	C	Na
Per Serving	0	0	177	T	6	T	38	344

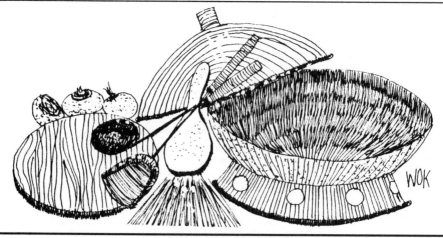

WOK

SAUCY SHRIMP SAUCE AND RICE

Saucy indeed! But everybody will love this shrimp dish.

1	T	diet margarine
1 ½	C	shrimp, cooked
½	C	celery, chopped
2	T	onion, chopped
1	C	fresh mushrooms, sliced
½	tsp.	beef bouillon granules*
½	C	water
1	T	cornstarch*
¼	tsp.	ginger
1	tsp.	soy sauce
2	C	brown rice,* cooked

Gifford's Alternatives: Add:
1	*tsp.*	*Gifford's Chinese Spice®*
¼	*tsp.*	*Gifford's Dessert Spice®*
		OMIT ginger

1. Melt margarine in a large nonstick* skillet. Add shrimp and cook 4 to 6 minutes, stirring often.

2. Add celery, onions, and mushrooms. Stir together over high heat for 2 minutes.

3. Dissolve bouillon in ¼ cup boiling water. Set aside.

4. Whisk cornstarch into ¼ cup cold water. Add bouillon mixture, ginger, soy sauce.

5. Combine with shrimp mixture. Cook, stirring until thickened and shiny.

6. Serve ⅔ cup sauce over ½ cup cooked rice.

Serves 4

* See "Cooking Methods" section

	RCU	FU	Cal	%Ft	P	F	C	Na
Per Serving	0	T	246	12	24	3	29	225

VEGETABLES ORIENTAL

When zucchini and tomatoes are in season, let them "star" in this great meal.

2	C	chicken stock*
2	med.	onions, chopped
3	cloves	garlic, minced
½	bunch	broccoli florets, chopped
1		large carrot, chopped
½	lb.	mushrooms, sliced
8	C	brown rice,* cooked
¼	C	mung bean sprouts*
¼	C	alfalfa sprouts*
1	T	soy sauce

Gifford's Alternatives: Add:
1	*med.*	*pear, peeled, diced*
1 ½	*tsp.*	*Gifford's Chinese Spice®*

1. Prepare all ingredients.

2. Heat wok or large nonstick* skillet. Add chicken stock and cook onions, garlic, broccoli, and carrots until tender-crisp.

3. Add mushrooms. Cook 2 to 3 minutes more.

4. Add rice, stir as it is reheated. Sprinkle sprouts and soy sauce over rice mixture and heat 3 minutes longer. Serve immediately.

Serves 12.

* See "Cooking Methods" section

	RCU	FU	Cal	%Ft	P	F	C	Na
Per Serving	0	0	181	4	5	1	38	199

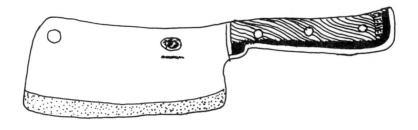

GINGER CHICKEN STIR-FRY

This can also be made with turkey strips instead of chicken.

WILD GINGER

1	T	soy sauce
2	tsp.	ground ginger
4	T	water
2		chicken breasts, boned, skinned, and cut into ¼-inch strips
1	16 oz. can	bean sprouts*
2	T	cornstarch*
6		green onions, sliced
1	4 oz. can	mushrooms, drained and sliced
1	6 oz. can	bamboo shoots, drained
1	10 oz. pkg	frozen green beans
1	C	water
3	C	brown rice,* cooked

1. Prepare all ingredients.

2. Make a sauce by mixing soy sauce, ginger, and 4 tablespoons water.

3. Heat wok or large nonstick* skillet. Add soy sauce mixture and chicken pieces. Cook on high heat for 4 minutes. Remove meat after cooking.

4. Drain bean sprouts and save liquid. Whisk cornstarch into liquid and heat in wok until thickened.

5. Add vegetables, chicken, and 1 cup water. Simmer until chicken is done. Vegetables should remain tender-crisp.

6. Serve immediately over ½ cup cooked rice.

Serves 6

See "Cooking Methods" section

	RCU	FU	Cal	%Ft	P	F	C	Na
Per Serving	0	0	231	6	17	2	38	260

ORIENTAL CHICKEN OVER BULGUR

Cracked wheat or brown rice can be used in place of bulgur.

3 ½	C	chicken stock*
1	C	Chinese pea pods, cut in fourths
½	C	water chestnuts, sliced
1 ½	C	mushrooms, sliced
⅛	tsp.	white pepper
2	T	cornstarch*
½	C	water
2	C	chicken, cooked and sliced
1	C	Basic Bulgur (p.273)
1	T	soy sauce

Gifford's Alternatives: Add:
½	C	red bell pepper, diced (add to step #2)
½	C	pineapple chunks, drained (add to step #2)
1	tsp.	Gifford's Chinese Spice®
1	pinch	ground cinnamon

1. Prepare all ingredients.

2. Heat nonstick* wok and add ½ cup chicken stock. Add pea pods, water chestnuts, and mushrooms. Sauté* over moderate heat for 2 minutes.

3. Add 1 ½ cups chicken stock and pepper. Cover and cook for 6 minutes.

4. Whisk cornstarch into water. Stir into wok.

5. Add chicken. Heat, stirring frequently, until mixture thickens.

6. Serve over bulgur that has been heated with 1 ½ cups chicken stock until liquid has been absorbed. Add soy sauce just before serving.

Serves 6

* See "Cooking Methods" section

	RCU	FU	Cal	%Ft	P	F	C	Na
Per Serving	0	0	159	16	17	3	14	488

SHRIMP APPLE CURRY

Chicken or fish filets can be used in place of shrimp.

1	C	chicken stock*
½	C	onion, chopped
½	C	apple, diced
1	clove	garlic, minced
½	C	green pepper, chopped
2	C	low-fat yogurt*
2	tsp.	lemon juice
½	tsp.	curry powder
1	dash	chili powder
2	C	shrimp, cooked
3	C	brown rice,* cooked

1. Prepare vegetables and shrimp.

2. Heat wok or nonstick* skillet and add chicken stock. Sauté* onion, apple, and garlic. Cook until tender but not brown.

3. Add green pepper, yogurt, and remaining ingredients. Cook on low heat, stirring constantly, until heated thoroughly. Do not boil or yogurt will curdle. Serve over cooked rice.

Serves 6

* See "Cooking Methods" section

	RCU	FU	Cal	%Ft	P	F	C	Na
Per Serving	0	0	224	9	16	2	33	122

TUNA

PINTO BEAN STIR-FRY

Beans in a wok? Sure, why not? Superb!

2/3	C	pinto beans, dry
1		green pepper, cut into thin strips
4	stalks	celery, thin bias-cut
2	med.	onions, sliced
1	10 oz. pkg	frozen French-cut green beans
3	med.	tomatoes, cut in wedges
1	T	cornstarch*
1	T	soy sauce
1	tsp.	beef bouillon granules*
1/2	C	water
2	C	chicken stock*
1/2	tsp.	fresh ginger root, grated
1/8	tsp.	black pepper
1/2	tsp.	curry powder
1/4	C	parsley, chopped
3	C	brown rice,* cooked

WILD TEA

1. Cook pinto beans.

2. Prepare vegetables.

3. Combine cornstarch, soy sauce, bouillon granules, and water. Set aside.

4. Heat wok or nonstick* pan and add chicken stock, ginger root, black pepper, curry powder, and parsley.

5. Add the celery and onion and stir-fry until tender-crisp.

6. Add cornstarch mixture, stirring until thickened and shiny.

7. Add cooked pinto beans, green pepper, French-cut green beans, parsley, and tomato. Cook until all of the vegetables are heated thoroughly. Serve over cooked brown rice.

Serves 6

* See "Cooking Methods" section

	RCU	FU	Cal	%Ft	P	F	C	Na
Per Serving	0	0	267	3	11	1	54	475

PINEAPPLE HAM STIR-FRY

Sweet and succulent! Your family will love this dish.

1	16 oz. can	pineapple chunks, juice-packed
½	C	orange juice
1	T	soy sauce
¼	tsp.	chicken bouillon granules*
1	clove	garlic, minced
⅛	tsp.	black pepper
4	tsp.	cornstarch*
¼	C	cold water
1	C	chicken stock*
6	oz.	lean ham, diced
1	med.	green pepper, cut into 1-inch squares
3	C	brown rice,* cooked

1. Drain pineapple, reserving juice. Combine orange juice, soy sauce, bouillon granules, garlic, black pepper, and reserved pineapple juice. Set aside.

2. Whisk cornstarch into ¼ cup cold water. Set aside.

3. Heat wok or nonstick* skillet until very hot. Add chicken stock, ham, and green pepper. Cook until ham is just browned, about 4 minutes. Remove from wok.

4. Combine orange juice mixture and pineapple chunks in wok. Cover and cook 2 minutes. Remove pineapple with slotted spoon.

5. Return ham to juice in wok. Add cornstarch mixture. Cook and stir until thickened. Adjust thickness with chicken stock or water.

6. Return pineapple to wok. Heat. Serve over ½ cup brown rice.

Serves 6

* See "Cooking Methods" section

	RCU	FU	Cal	%Ft	P	F	C	Na
Per Serving	0	0	204	19	8	4	33	323

CHOP SUEY

Stop! You can't top this chop suey!

1	10 oz. pkg	frozen green beans
2	T	soy sauce
6	oz.	lean ham, diced
2	lg.	Bermuda onions, sliced ¼-inch thick and separated into rings
4	C	broccoli florets
2	C	fresh mushrooms, sliced
4	T	potato flakes
4	C	brown rice,* cooked

BROCCOLI

Gifford's Alternatives: Add:
2	tsp.	*Gifford's Chinese Spice®*
1	T	*Butter Buds® Sprinkles*
2	T	*low-fat evaporated milk*

1. Cook frozen green beans until tender. Reserve cooking liquid and add water to equal 1 ½ cups.

2. Sauté* soy sauce, ham, green bean liquid, onions, broccoli, and mushrooms until tender.

3. Add green beans and, for thickening, dry potato flakes. Heat until everything is warm and tender. Serve over ½ cup cooked rice.

Serves 8

* See "Cooking Methods" section

	RCU	FU	Cal	%Ft	P	F	C	Na
Per Serving	0	0	229	15	13	4	40	371

CANTON BEEF

This dish is great anytime for family or friends.

BLACK
MUSTARD

8	oz.	flank steak
1	T	soy sauce
1	tsp.	vinegar
1	clove	garlic, minced
½	tsp.	dry mustard
1	C	chicken stock*
3	C	broccoli florets
1	10 ½ oz. can	tomato soup
1	C	green onion, sliced
½	C	water chestnuts, sliced
3	C	brown rice*, cooked

1. Trim fat from beef. Freeze and slice into thin strips cut diagonally across the grain.

2. Combine ¼ cup water, soy sauce, vinegar, garlic, and mustard. Add steak strips. Marinate in refrigerator for 1 hour.

3. Heat wok or heavy nonstick* skillet. Add chicken stock, marinated steak and marinade. Cook about 5 minutes, stirring often. Add broccoli, soup, onions, and water chestnuts. Adjust consistency with water, if necessary. Heat, stirring often. Serve hot over ½ cup brown rice.

Serves 6

*See "Cooking Methods" section

	RCU	FU	Cal	%Ft	P	F	C	Na
Per Serving	0	0	245	14	17	4	35	493

AMERICAN STIR-FRY

Watch out! This will fast become a family favorite and there will never be leftovers.

4	oz.	lean hamburger*
½	C	onion, chopped
½	C	celery, sliced
1	10 ½ oz. can	cream of mushroom soup
½	C	carrots, sliced
¼	C	green pepper, chopped
2	C	water
3	C	brown rice,* cooked

Gifford's Alternatives: Add:
1 ½	tsp.	chicken bouillon granules*
1	tsp.	onion powder
2	T	diced pimentoes

1. Brown* hamburger and drain.

2. Prepare vegetables.

3. Heat wok or nonstick* skillet. Combine all ingredients except rice. Cook until vegetables are tender-crisp.

4. Serve over ½ cup brown rice.

Serves 6

* See "Cooking Methods" section

	RCU	FU	Cal	%Ft	P	F	C	Na
Per Serving	0	0	206	22	9	5	30	293

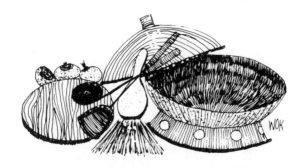

"THE POTATO, FRIEND OR FOE?"

*"We need not pray for great opportunities,
but rather the willingness to do little things in a great way."*
---Ethel F. Lord

THE POTATO, FRIEND OR FOE?

Potatoes are an excellent food. They contain 11 percent protein, 88 percent carbohydrate, and only one percent fat. They are high in potassium, fiber, and vitamins B and C. Because they are low in fat, high in fiber, delicious to eat, and inexpensive to buy, they should become a major part of our low-fat diet.

There are three classes of potatoes: new potatoes, baking potatoes, and all-purpose potatoes. New potatoes are freshly harvested, not fully mature, small, and thin-skinned. They are excellent when eaten boiled. Baking potatoes are medium to large in size with a thicker skin. They do not become mealy or dry when baked. Idaho potatoes are among the best baking potatoes. All-purpose potatoes can be used for boiling, baking, mashing, salads, etc. But all classes of potatoes are generally easy to prepare.

When buying potatoes, choose ones that are firm, well-shaped, and reasonably smooth. Avoid any with green discoloration or sprouts. Store potatoes in a dark, dry place with good ventilation and a temperature of about 45°- 50°. They are available year round.

Potatoes are a very versatile vegetable. They can be served for breakfast, lunch, dinner, or snacks. They could be served every day for months and never be eaten the same way twice. They can be baked, boiled or mashed. They can be eaten as the main course, a side dish, a salad, a soup, a snack, or a casserole. They can even be used to make breads and rolls.

Potatoes are quite tasty. They have a pleasant flavor of their own that does not overpower other foods. They are especially good with carrots. Potatoes and onions seem inseparable. Cheese and potatoes are a popular combination, but cheese must be used sparingly because of its high fat content. The traditional meat and potatoes as well as potatoes and gravy must also be watched closely because of the usual high fat in the meat and the gravy.

Potatoes are best when baked with the skins left on and enjoyed for what they are. A baked potato, topped with any number of low-fat toppings or with a variety of meat and vegetable mixtures, makes a nutritious, low-fat meal. Surprisingly, potatoes taste fine without any toppings once you develop the taste. But when potatoes are prepared by peeling off the skin, then adding fat in the form of frying, butter, cheese, gravy, or sour cream, they become a high-fat, undesirable food.

This doesn't mean that you must give up the potato's versatility by only eating baked potatoes. It simply means you need to follow certain guidelines to receive the maximum benefit of this wonderful food.

1. Leave the skins on whenever possible.
2. Never deep fry potatoes. Deep frying always makes potatoes too high in fat, so try the substitutes for French fries (p. 241).
3. Hash browns can be made in a nonstick* pan with vegetable spray to keep the percentage of fat low (p. 243).
4. Use Butter Buds® Sprinkles or reduced fat spreads instead of butter.
5. Replace high-fat gravies with low-fat gravies (p. 22).

6. Yogurt or cottage cheese make perfectly acceptable replacements for sour cream.

With these guidelines, you will only be giving up fat, not taste.

Boiled potatoes should become a staple item in soups, salads, and casseroles. Save the water in which potatoes have been boiled for use in soups or casseroles. See "Soup's On!" on page 57 for several hearty potato soup recipes. There are a variety of potato salad and casserole recipes in this section. Refer to The Bread Spread on page 297 for potato bread recipes.

Boiled potatoes are quickly turned into mashed potatoes by whipping them with potato water or skim milk. Without the addition of salt, butter, or high-fat milk, mashed potatoes remain a low-fat potato variation. There are many unique and exciting recipes in this section using mashed potatoes. Instant mashed potatoes are not quite as nutritious as your own mashed potatoes made with potato water, but there will be times when you will want to use them. Go ahead. They are quick and easy. Just remember to leave out the butter and to use skim milk.

The potato, is it friend or foe? You'll have to agree, when prepared without fats, the potato is the best friend your low-fat diet ever had!

Potato soup recipes, see:
"Soup's On!" on page 57
Potato bread recipes, see:
The Bread Spread on page 297

SAGE

CHIVES

CHIVES

BASIC BAKED POTATOES

Baked potatoes are filling, nutritious, full of fiber, and low in fat. They can be eaten as a side dish or turned into the main course with a variety of toppings.

4   med.   potatoes

1. Scrub potatoes to remove all dirt. Dry.

2. Wrap in foil, if desired, and poke holes in the potato with a fork. Bake at 375° for 1 hour or until thoroughly cooked.

3. To serve, cut an "X" across the top and pull back the skin slightly. Top freely with chopped celery, chives, green peppers, or parsley since they are so low in calories and fat, or serve with any of the other low-fat toppings listed below.

Serves 4

	RCU	FU	Cal	%Ft	P	F	C	Na
Per Serving	0	0	90	T	3	T	21	4

LOW-FAT BAKED POTATO TOPPINGS

2   T   Barbecue Sauce (p. 24)

Barbecue	RCU	FU	Cal	%Ft	P	F	C	Na
Per Serving	0	0	28	T	T	T	8	6

¼   C   Butter Buds®, liquid

Butter Buds	RCU	FU	Cal	%Ft	P	F	C	Na
Per Serving	0	0	24	T	0	0	2	0

¼   C   carrots, cooked

Carrots	RCU	FU	Cal	%Ft	P	F	C	Na
Per Serving	0	0	11	T	T	T	1	6

2   T   cheddar cheese

Cheddar	RCU	FU	Cal	%Ft	P	F	C	Na
Per Serving	0	1	56	72	4	5	T	99

½   C   chili

Chili Per Serving	RCU	FU	Cal	%Ft	P	F	C	Na
	0	0	119	18	10	2	13	63

½   C   corn, cooked

Corn Per Serving	RCU	FU	Cal	%Ft	P	F	C	Na
	0	0	95	9	3	1	18	T

½   C   low-fat cottage cheese*

Cottage Cheese Per Serving	RCU	FU	Cal	%Ft	P	F	C	Na
	0	0	100	2	20	T	4	336

½   C   mixed vegetables, cooked

Mixed Veg. Per Serving	RCU	FU	Cal	%Ft	P	F	C	Na
	0	0	58	3	3	T	12	48

2   T   mozzarella cheese, grated

Mozzarella Per Serving	RCU	FU	Cal	%Ft	P	F	C	Na
	0	1	42	71	33	4	T	113

2   T   onion, chopped

Onion Per Serving	RCU	FU	Cal	%Ft	P	F	C	Na
	0	0	10	T	T	T	2	3

½   C   peas, cooked

Peas Per Serving	RCU	FU	Cal	%Ft	P	F	C	Na
	0	0	55	T	3	T	10	1

¼   C   Salsa (p. 27)

Salsa Per Serving	RCU	FU	Cal	%Ft	P	F	C	Na
	0	0	16	T	1	T	4	2

½   C   favorite soup

Soup Per Serving	RCU	FU	Cal	%Ft	P	F	C	Na
	0	0	150	5	8	1	15	200

½ C   Spanish Rice (p. 276)

Span. Rice Per Serving	RCU	FU	Cal	%Ft	P	F	C	Na
	0	0	123	18	7	3	18	116

½ C   low-fat yogurt*

Yogurt Per Serving	RCU	FU	Cal	%Ft	P	F	C	Na
	0	0	63	1	4	2	7	64

Serves 1

See "Cooking Methods" section

SWAP MEET

When company comes, dress up your dinner with these.

4		potatoes
1		onion, sliced
4	tsp.	Butter Buds® OR diet margarine*
to taste		seasoning without salt*

Gifford's Alternatives: Add:
to taste   **Gifford's Basic Spice®**
   OMIT seasoning without salt

1. Cut each potato into 4 crosswise slices. Brush Butter Buds® or diet margarine between slices and over top of potatoes.

2. Reassemble potato, with onion slices between potato slices. Hold together with toothpicks. Season to taste. Wrap in heavy-duty foil.

3. Arrange on a baking sheet. Bake at 400° for 45 minutes, or until potatoes are tender. Serve hot.

Serves 4

See "Cooking Methods" section

	RCU	FU	Cal	%Ft	P	F	C	Na
Per Serving	0	0	113	16	3	2	22	85

HAMBURGER CREOLE OVER BAKED POTATOES

Try this over cooked brown rice instead of potatoes.

½	C	onion, chopped	½	C	celery, chopped
½	lb.	lean hamburger	½	tsp.	chili powder
1	16 oz. can	stewed tomatoes*	sprinkle		dried red peppers, crushed
½	C	green pepper, chopped	4	med.	potatoes, baked

Gifford's Alternatives: Add all ingredients to hamburger while sautéeing:

1	T	*Gifford's Mexican Spice®*
¼	tsp.	*Gifford's Dessert Spice®*
1	tsp.	*Worcestershire sauce*
1	tsp.	*apple juice concentrate*

1. Sauté* onions until transparent. Set aside. Sauté hamburger. Drain and add to onions.

2. Purée stewed tomatoes. Add tomatoes, green peppers, celery, and spices to meat. Cook. Celery and green peppers should be slightly crisp.

3. Serve over a hot baked potato.

Serves 4

* See "Cooking Methods" section

	RCU	FU	Cal	%Ft	P	F	C	Na
Per Serving	**0**	**1**	**281**	**22**	**20**	**7**	**30**	**213**

POTATOES

SCALLOPED POTATOES

Rene Mortensen

A half cup of diced lean ham turns this into a main course with only seven percent fat.

6		potatoes, sliced
1		onion, sliced
1	1/2 oz. pkg	Butter Buds®
2	T	whole wheat flour*
1/4	tsp.	black pepper
2	C	skim milk,* heated

Gifford's Alternatives: Add in step #1:

1 1/2	tsp.	*chicken bouillon granules**
1 1/2	tsp.	*onion powder*
2	T	*diced pimentos*
1/2	tsp.	*dry ground mustard*

1. Combine Butter Buds®, flour, and pepper.

2. Layer potatoes and onions with flour mixture in a nonstick* casserole.

3. Pour heated skim milk over potato layers.

4. Cover and bake at 350° for 1 1/2 hours. Serve hot.

Serves 6

* See "Cooking Methods" section

	RCU	FU	Cal	%Ft	P	F	C	Na
Per Serving	0	0	131	T	5	T	28	46

GARLIC

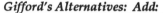

FIVE-LAYER POTATO CASSEROLE

Five fun, filling, fantastic, flavorful foods fix a fanciful meal for your family.

2	med.	onions, sliced
½	lb.	lean ground beef, browned*
8	med.	potatoes, cooked and sliced
1	C	frozen corn, cooked
1	10 ½ oz. can	cream of mushroom soup

Gifford's Alternatives: Add:

1	tsp.	*Gifford's Basic Spice®*
½	tsp.	*Gifford's Mexican Spice®*
1	tsp.	*Worcestershire sauce*

1. In a nonstick* 9"x13" pan, layer the following: sliced onions, lean ground beef, sliced precooked potatoes, corn, and cream of mushroom soup combined with 1 soup can water.

2. Cover with foil and bake at 350° for 30 minutes.

3. There are as many variations to this basic recipe as there are vegetables. Replace the corn with peas, broccoli, zucchini, or carrots. Serve hot.

Serves 8

* See "Cooking Methods" section

	RCU	FU	Cal	%Ft	P	F	C	Na
Per Serving	0	1	197	20	11	5	30	287

ONIONS

CREAMED PEAS AND NEW POTATOES

This fancy favorite tastes so rich you'll never believe it's low-fat, but it is.

10		new potatoes
1	10 oz. pkg	frozen peas OR
1	lb.	fresh peas
12		pearl onions OR

Gifford's Alternatives: Add:

3	T	green onions, sliced
½	pkg	Butter Buds®
1 ½	T	cornstarch*
1	C	skim milk*
1	tsp.	*chicken bouillon granules**
½	tsp.	*thyme*
⅛	tsp.	*black pepper*

1. Peel potatoes. Cover with water. Boil and cook until tender. Drain.*

2. Cook peas and onions together until tender. Drain.

3. While vegetables are cooking, mix Butter Buds®, cornstarch, and milk together until smooth. Heat until thickened, stirring constantly.

4. Pour sauce over combined hot vegetables. Serve immediately.

Serves 6
* See "Cooking Methods" section

	RCU	FU	Cal	%Ft	P	F	C	Na
Per Serving	0	0	102	4	5	T	20	71

BARBECUED POTATO KABOBS

Try these over the grill this summer.

3		chicken breasts
12	small	potatoes
3		onions, halved
6	large	fresh mushrooms
1		green pepper, cut into wedges
½	C	Barbecue Sauce (p. 24)

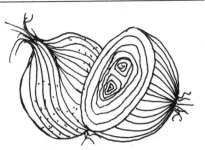

Endless Sukiyaki (p. 212) will bring endless pleasure to your family. See "Wok Talk" (p. 209) for more wok recipes.

1. Skin chicken. Cut each breast in half lengthwise. Thread onto separate skewers.

2. Thread potatoes and onions on skewers also.

3. Lay skewers across foil-lined pan. Bake at 400° for 25 minutes or until potatoes are tender.

4. Thread mushrooms and green peppers on additional skewers.

5. Preheat broiler. Brush all kabobs with barbecue sauce. Cook under broiler, turning and basting frequently, for 10 minutes. Remove from skewers to serve.

Serves 6

	RCU	FU	Cal	%Ft	P	F	C	Na
Per Serving	0	0	226	8	32	2	18	89

GERMAN HOT POTATO SALAD

Warm and wonderful potato salad. Serve with a kosher dill pickle and a sandwich.

5	med.	potatoes	½	tsp.	salt
1	tsp.	sugar*	¼	tsp.	black pepper
¼	C	vinegar	½	C	onion, chopped
¼	C	water	2	T	imitation bacon bits*
1		egg white	1	T	green pepper, diced

Gifford's Alternatives: Add:
1	T	apple juice concentrate
2	tsp.	onion powder
½	tsp.	whole pickling spice, ground fine (use blender's grind speed)
¼	tsp.	ground caraway seed

1. Peel, halve, and boil potatoes. Slice when cool.
2. Combine sugar, vinegar, water, egg white, salt, and black pepper. Heat and stir until thickened.
3. Add potatoes, onion, bacon bits, and green pepper. Mix, heat, and serve.

Serves 8

*See "Cooking Methods" section

	RCU	FU	Cal	%Ft	P	F	C	Na
Per Serving	0	0	61	T	2	T	14	125

Cottage cheese, chives, bacon bits, chopped onions or green peppers, chili or a little grated cheese are only a few of the many possible toppings for Basic Baked Potatoes (p. 230).

SUIT YOURSELF POTATO SALAD

Create the potato salad that is tailor-made for your family's taste.

6		potatoes
½	C	onion, chopped
½	C	celery, chopped
¼	C	green pepper, chopped
¼	C	radishes, sliced
1	tsp.	parsley, minced
¼	C	frozen peas, cooked and cooled
2	T	pimento, chopped
1	large	dill pickle, chopped

1. Boil, cool, and peel potatoes.

2. Combine with any or all of the remaining ingredients. (Omit pickle to reduce salt content.)

3. Stir in dressing (see below). Chill before serving.

Serves 8

	RCU	FU	Cal	%Ft	P	F	C	Na
Per Serving	0	0	72	2	2	T	16	182

Try any of the following Dressings:

EASY POTATO SALAD DRESSING

1	C	low-fat cottage cheese,* blended
1	tsp.	prepared mustard
to taste		seasoning without salt*

Gifford's Alternatives: Add:

2	tsp.	*chicken bouillon granules**
2	tsp.	*onion powder*
1	tsp.	*dry ground mustard*
½	tsp.	*ground celery seed*
¼	tsp.	*ground sage*
⅛	tsp.	*ground white pepper*
1	pinch	*ground coriander*

OMIT seasoning without salt

1. Combine ingredients and fold into potato salad.

*See "Cooking Methods" section

	RCU	FU	Cal	%Ft	P	F	C	Na
Per Serving	0	0	25	3	5	T	1	91

ITALIAN POTATO SALAD DRESSING

½	C	low-fat cottage cheese,* blended
¼	C	Low-Calorie Italian Dressing (p. 37)
1	tsp.	prepared mustard

1. Combine ingredients and fold into potato salad.

*See "Cooking Methods" Section

	RCU	FU	Cal	%Ft	P	F	C	Na
Per Serving	0	0	17	T	3	T	2	131

THICK AND CREAMY POTATO SALAD DRESSING

1	C	mashed potatoes
¼	C	low-fat cottage cheese,* blended
to taste		skim milk* OR pickle juice
1	tsp.	prepared mustard
to taste		seasoning without salt*

1. Combine ingredients and fold into potato salad.

*See "Cooking Methods" section

	RCU	FU	Cal	%Ft	P	F	C	Na
Per Serving	0	0	19	9	2	T	3	30

SAVORY BOILED POTATOES

Remarkable!

½	C	onion, chopped
1	clove	garlic, crushed
¾	C	parsley, chopped
4	oz.	pimento, chopped
⅛	tsp.	black pepper
1	cube	chicken bouillon
1	C	water
6	med.	potatoes, thinly sliced

1. Sauté* onion and garlic until soft.

2. Combine onion mixture, parsley, pimento, pepper, chicken bouillon, and water in large soup pot.

3. Add sliced potatoes. Bring to a boil.

4. Reduce heat, cover, and simmer until potatoes are tender, about 20 minutes.

5. Serve, undrained, with a sprinkle of parsley.

Serves 8

* See "Cooking Methods" section

	RCU	FU	Cal	%Ft	P	F	C	Na
Per Serving	0	0	71	1	2	T	15	60

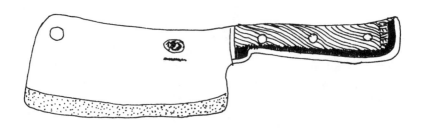

LOW-FAT FRENCH FRIES

One or two minutes under the broiler will make these extra crisp.

4		potatoes
1	T	Barbecue Sauce (p. 24) OR
2	T	apple juice
1	tsp.	seasoned salt

Gifford's Alternatives: Add:
to taste   **Gifford's Basic Spice® OR**
                   Gifford's Mexican Spice®
                   OMIT seasoned salt

1. Boil potatoes in skins until just tender.

2. Remove from water and chill.

3. Peel and slice into French fries or leave skins on and cut lengthwise into 8 wedges.

4. Place in a bowl and toss with 1 tablespoon barbecue sauce and seasoned salt OR sprinkle with fruit juice and seasoned salt.

5. Bake at 400° for 10 to 15 minutes on a nonstick* baking sheet. Turn with spatula and continue baking for 10 to 15 minutes longer. Serve hot.

Serves 4

	RCU	FU	Cal	%Ft	P	F	C	Na
Per Serving	0	0	98	T	3	T	20	165

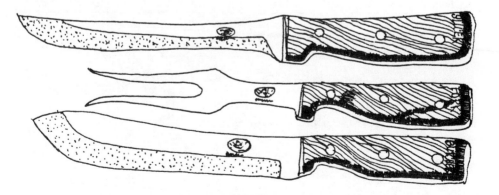

GOLDEN POTATO BALLS

A terrific "pinch hitter" for French fries.

½	tsp.	prepared mustard
2	drops	Tabasco sauce
¼	C	Butter Buds®, optional
3	C	mashed potatoes
2		egg whites, stiffly beaten
½	C	evaporated skim milk*
1	C	corn flake crumbs

Gifford's Alternatives: Add:
1 ½   tsp.   Gifford's Basic Spice®

1. Add mustard, Tabasco sauce, and Butter Buds® to mashed potatoes and beat.

2. Fold in stiffly beaten egg whites.

3. Shape into 8 to 12 potato balls.

4. About 15 minutes before serving, brush potato balls with evaporated milk, and roll in crumbs.

5. Bake at 425° for 5 to 6 minutes on a nonstick* baking sheet. Serve at once.

Serves 6

* See "Cooking Methods" section

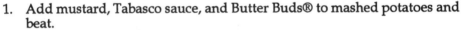

	RCU	FU	Cal	%Ft	P	F	C	Na
Per Serving	**0**	**0**	**118**	**2**	**5**	**T**	**25**	**68**

POTATO CRISPS

Another low-fat alternative to French fries.

4	large	potatoes
3		egg whites, lightly beaten
to taste		seasoning without salt*

Gifford's Alternatives: Add:
1 ½   tsp.   Gifford's Basic Spice®

1. Peel potatoes, if desired, and finely grate them.

2. Add egg whites and seasonings.

3. Heat a nonstick* fry pan to 300°- 350°. Spoon batter into heated skillet and spread into 4-inch pancakes.

4. Cook until potatoes are tender. Turn and brown on other side. Serve.

Serves 6

* See "Cooking Methods" section

	RCU	FU	Cal	%Ft	P	F	C	Na
Per Serving	0	0	100	1	4	0	21	19

HASH BROWNS

You don't need to give up hash browns—only the oil.

4		potatoes, boiled
1		onion, chopped
½	C	chicken bouillon
to taste		seasoning without salt*

Gifford's Alternatives: Add:
| 1 ½ | tsp. | Gifford's Basic Spice® |

1. Shred boiled potatoes (preferably with skins on). Combine with chopped onion.

2. Cook in a heated nonstick* pan using chicken bouillon instead of oil.

3. Season. Turn potatoes often, until golden brown. Serve.

Serves 4

* See "Cooking Methods" section

	RCU	FU	Cal	%Ft	P	F	C	Na
Per Serving	0	0	91	T	3	T	21	106

POTATO MISH MASH

This is a basic recipe for mashed potatoes. It can also be used as a base for a variety of casseroles. Add bits of ham, vegetables, or a sprinkle of grated cheese and you have a quick meal.

4	med.	potatoes
1/3	C	skim milk*
1/4	C	Butter Buds®, optional

Gifford's Alternatives: Add:

1 1/4	tsp.	chicken bouillon granules*
1	tsp.	onion powder
1/8	tsp.	ground white pepper

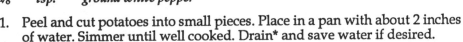

1. Peel and cut potatoes into small pieces. Place in a pan with about 2 inches of water. Simmer until well cooked. Drain* and save water if desired.

2. Mash potatoes with reserved water or milk. Add Butter Buds®. Beat until fluffy. Serve.

3. To make a potato pie crust, pat mashed potatoes into a pie pan. Bake at 350° until golden brown. Fill with cooked vegetables, thick stew, soup, or chili. Serve.

4. To make a potato nest for cooked vegetables, put mashed potatoes in a 2-quart nonstick* pan. Form a "nest" in the center. Bake at 400° for 20 minutes or until lightly browned. Spoon vegetables into "nest" and serve.

Serves 4

* See "Cooking Methods" section

	RCU	FU	Cal	%Ft	P	F	C	Na
Per Serving	0	0	102	2	3	T	21	14

SLOW-COOK POTATOES

These can be cooked in your crock pot during the afternoon.

1/4	C	cornstarch	1/4	C	onions, finely chopped
1/2	C	Butter Buds®	1/4	tsp.	white ground pepper
4	C	skim milk*	7	lg.	potatoes, grated

Gifford's Alternatives: Add:

½	tsp.	chicken bouillon granules*
½	tsp.	onion powder

1. Blend cornstarch and Butter Buds® with a little milk until smooth. Add remaining milk and boil 1 minute, stirring constantly.

2. Add onions, pepper, and grated potatoes.

3. Pour into nonstick* shallow casserole, about 16"x11"x1". Bake at 300° for 3 hours. Serve hot.

Serves 10

* See "Cooking Methods" section

	RCU	FU	Cal	%Ft	P	F	C	Na
Per Serving	0	0	121	3	6	1	24	53

STUFFED POTATO BOATS

For variety, try stuffing potato skins with The Dynamic Duo (p. 247) or Bashful Blushing Potatoes (p. 246).

4	large	baking potatoes
½	C	evaporated skim milk*
1	tsp.	chives, chopped
1	tsp.	parsley, chopped
⅛	tsp.	sage
¼	tsp.	black pepper
¼	C	Butter Buds®
1	dash	paprika

1. Bake potatoes at 400° for about 45 minutes. Cut in half lengthwise.

2. Scoop out insides and mash with remaining ingredients except paprika. Mix thoroughly.

3. Spoon mashed potatoes into shells on baking sheet. Sprinkle with paprika.

4. Return to oven for 10 minutes or until lightly browned. Serve.

Serves 8

* See "Cooking Methods" section

	RCU	FU	Cal	%Ft	P	F	C	Na
Per Serving	0	0	61	1	3	T	13	2

POTATO ROLL-UPS

Wow!! What a good idea. Fun for children, company, or family parties.

3	C	mashed potatoes, cold
¾	C	whole wheat flour
to taste		seasoning without salt*
½	C	Butter Buds®

1. Combine potatoes, flour, seasonings, and Butter Buds®. Knead by hand to blend thoroughly and divide into 12 equal parts.

2. Pat or roll each part into a 7-inch circle on a floured board.

3. Heat nonstick* griddle or skillet. Cook patties over medium heat, turning once, until golden brown spots appear on both sides. Pierce bubbles with a fork.

4. Remove from griddle, spread with Butter Buds® and fill with applesauce or another low-fat filling. See Low-fat Baked Potato Toppings on pages 230-232 for ideas. Roll up and place, seam side down, in shallow pan. Keep warm in 275° oven until all pancakes are cooked. Serve.

Serves 12

See "Cooking Methods" section

	RCU	FU	Cal	%Ft	P	F	C	Na
Per Serving	**0**	**0**	**66**	**1**	**2**	**T**	**14**	**10**

BASHFUL BLUSHING POTATOES

Quick and colorful.

6	med.	potatoes
¼	C	Butter Buds®, optional
1	10 ½ oz. can	tomato soup, undiluted
¼	C	cheddar cheese, grated

TOMATOES

1. Cook and mash potatoes. Mix in Butter Buds®.

2. Heat soup and add to potatoes. Mixture will be thin but will thicken during baking.

3. Spoon into 1 ½-quart casserole and sprinkle with cheese. Bake at 350° for 25 minutes or until top is browned. Serve.

Serves 6

See "Cooking Methods" section

	RCU	FU	Cal	%Ft	P	F	C	Na
Per Serving	0	0	124	14	4	2	22	201

THE DYNAMIC DUO

This can become either a colorful variation of mashed potatoes or a glowing, thick soup by simply adjusting the consistency.

6	potatoes, peeled
5	carrots, cut up
3	onions, chopped
to taste	seasoning without salt*

SUNFLOWERS

Gifford's Alternatives: Add:
to taste Gifford's Basic Spice®
OMIT seasoning without salt

1. Boil all ingredients together until tender.

2. Drain and reserve the water. Mash together, adding reserved water to achieve the proper consistency. Season and serve.

Serves 10

See "Cooking Methods" section

	RCU	FU	Cal	%Ft	P	F	C	Na
Per Serving	0	0	75	2	2	T	17	22

SURPRISE PACKAGE

There's a splendid surprise under this wrapping of mashed potatoes.

4	oz.	lean hamburger OR rump roast, diced
½	C	onion, chopped
½	C	celery, sliced
½	C	carrots, sliced
1	10 oz. pkg	frozen peas
1	10 ½ oz. can	tomato soup
4	C	mashed potatoes

Gifford's Alternatives: Add ingredients with step #1:

3	tsp.	lime juice
½	tsp.	Gifford's Gourmet Spice®
½	tsp.	Gifford's Basic Spice®

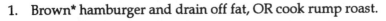

1. Brown* hamburger and drain off fat, OR cook rump roast.

2. Sauté* onion, celery, and carrots until tender.

3. Mix meat, onion, celery, carrots, peas, and tomato soup together. Put in the bottom of a casserole dish.

4. Top with mashed potatoes. Garnish with paprika.

5. Bake at 350° for about 1 hour or until golden brown.

6. This can be served with Basic Bouillon Gravy (p. 22).

Serves 6

See "Cooking Methods" section

	RCU	FU	Cal	%Ft	P	F	C	Na
Per Serving	0	0	180	15	11	3	27	250

POTATO PUFF

You can add vegetables to this for color and variety.

¼	C	lean ham, diced
½	C	onion, minced
2	C	mashed potatoes
4		egg whites
¼	C	mozzarella cheese, grated
1	dash	paprika
2	C	Basic Bouillon Gravy (p. 22)

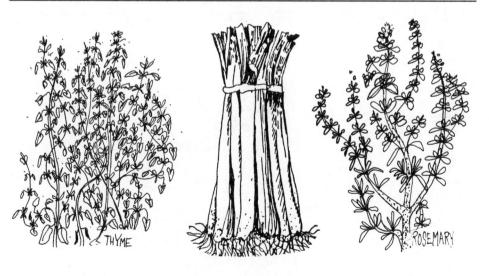

1. Mix ham, onion, and mashed potatoes together.

2. Beat egg whites until stiff and fold into potatoes.

3. Sprinkle cheese on top, if desired. Garnish with paprika.

4. Bake at 350° for 1 hour or until puffy and golden brown.

5. While potatoes are baking, make gravy. Serve over potatoes.

Serves 4

	RCU	FU	Cal	%Ft	P	F	C	Na
Per Serving	0	0	140	20	10	3	19	378

POTATO BROCCOLI CASSEROLE

Substitute your favorite vegetable for the broccoli and create your own potato casserole.

4	small	potatoes
1/4	C	Butter Buds®, optional
1/4	C	skim milk*
1	10 oz. pkg	frozen chopped broccoli
1/4	C	cheddar cheese, grated

BROCCOLI

Gifford's Alternatives: Add:
1	T	peach juice concentrate
1	tsp.	Gifford's Basic Spice®
1	pinch	sage
1	pinch	nutmeg

1. Cook, drain, and mash potatoes with milk and Butter Buds®.

2. Cook broccoli according to package directions. Drain well. Fold into mashed potatoes.

3. Put in nonstick* pan. Sprinkle with cheese.

4. Bake at 350° for 15 minutes or until cheese melts. Serve hot.

Serves 4

* See "Cooking Methods" section

	RCU	FU	Cal	%Ft	P	F	C	Na
Per Serving	0	0	142	15	7	2	23	70

THE BEAN BAG

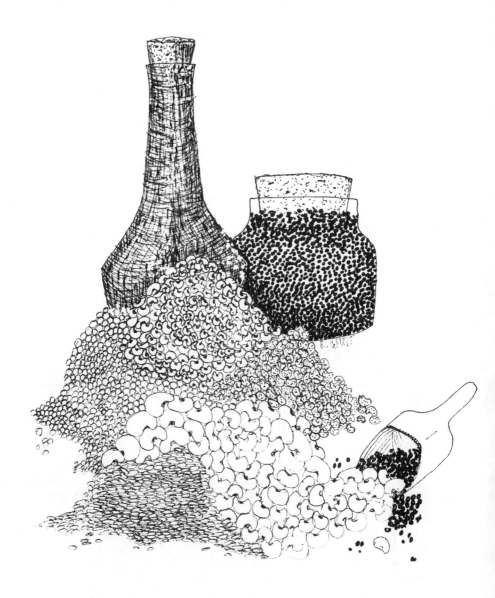

"Good health is often a matter of good judgment."

---Marion D. Hanks

THE BEAN BAG

Until now, you may have thought beans were good only for filling bean bags. Well, read on. You may be surprised at what you learn about this humble food.

Beans are high in iron, phosphorus, magnesium, calcium, potassium, thiamine (B1), pyridoxine (B6), folic acid, riboflavin (B2), and niacin. They are very low in fat, contain no cholesterol, and are high in fiber and complex carbohydrates. They will fill you up after only 250 calories.

Beans are inexpensive, easy to store, and versatile. They are easy to prepare in spite of the fact it takes some planning to accommodate the lengthy cooking time. See "Beans" on page 385 in the "Cooking Methods" section for directions on how to cook them.

Beans, lentils, and peas are part of a larger group known as legumes. There is such a wide variety of legumes that sometimes confusion results, especially among the bean group. Following is a brief description of the most popular legume varieties along with some common uses for each.

BLACK BEANS are also known as turtle beans or black turtle beans. They have a tender, sweet taste. They are popular in South American, Oriental, and Mediterranean dishes. Select these beans for thick soups.

BLACK-EYED PEAS are also known as black-eyed beans or cowpeas. They are small, oval-shaped, and creamy white with a black spot on the side. They are a staple in the southern United States. They are popular in soul food cooking, served as a main dish vegetable or with ham hocks. Give them a try with chicken.

GARBANZO BEANS are also known as chickpeas. Since they require a lengthy cooking time, canned garbanzos may be more convenient. They are enjoyed in Spain, Italy, and the Middle East. Their flavor is nutlike and they are often cooked, seasoned, and served cold for snacking or on a salad bar. Try them as a main dish vegetable or puréed for a dip.

GREAT NORTHERN BEANS have a delicate flavor. They are used in salads, soups, and main dishes.

KIDNEY BEANS are also known as red kidney beans because of their red color and kidney shape. They have almost worldwide popularity but are commonly used in chili and Mexican dishes. Use them as a substitute for pink or red beans.

LENTILS are one of the oldest and most nutritious of foods. They are not actually a bean but are a separate category of the legume family. They are not well known in the United States but are very popular in Europe. Fabulous as a soup, lentils also team up well with other vegetables, grains, meats, or fish. Use them to replace noodles, potatoes, beans, rice, or meat in many recipes. They make a great meat extender, too.

LIMA BEANS are also known as butter beans. They are broad, flat, and come in large and small sizes. The small-sized limas are commonly called baby limas, and they are traditionally combined with corn to make succotash. Large limas make a rich soup, an excellent main dish vegetable, an exceptional side dish with chicken and curry, or a nice addition to a variety of casseroles.

MUNG BEANS are used almost exclusively for sprouting. They have become the common bean sprouts we associate with Oriental dishes.

NAVY BEANS is the general name given to the family of white beans including great northern, pea beans, and small white beans.

PEAS are a separate category in the legume family. They are used both whole and split. Dried whole peas are soaked, cooked, and served as an accompaniment to main dishes. They are also used mashed or puréed. Dry split peas come in a yellow or green color. The skins are removed by a machine from specially grown whole, dried peas and the result is split peas. Their realm of excellence is split pea soup. But they can also be cooked right along with rice or other grains for a rich protein dish.

PINTO BEANS are a relative of the kidney bean and are used in the same way. Beige with brown speckles, they are a staple in Mexican cooking.

SMALL WHITE BEANS are much like pea beans and can be used interchangeably. They are most commonly used to make baked beans.

Some people avoid eating this versatile, nutritious food because of the embarrassment and discomfort of gas, or flatulence. Gas is created when naturally occurring bacteria in the digestive tract react with certain chemical compounds in beans. Some of these compounds are water-soluble and will be removed when the water used to soak the beans is discarded. The problem is also lessened if you introduce beans into your diet slowly. As your system becomes used to beans, the flatulence problems subside.

SOYBEANS are unique and require special attention. They are one of the oldest known sources of protein, dating back to 2000 B.C. in China. They were, in fact, China's main source of protein for hundreds of years. But they are not only the food of the past, they are also the food of the future. They have calcium, iron, phosphorus, vitamins A, D, E, and some of the B vitamins. Soybeans are also the least expensive protein available to man. Soybeans are 40 percent fat. This is much higher than any other bean; however, it is lower than cheese, eggs, and most meats. So when soybeans are used and in place of animal products, they can be a benefit to your low-fat diet. They can be eaten many ways: whole, boiled, or baked; made into soy milk or tofu; sprouted; ground into grits or flour; or made into Texturized Vegetable Protein (TVP), a meat substitute.

SPROUTING is another wonderful way of using beans. All beans can be sprouted and used at this stage. Their nutrition soars with this simple act. "Sprouts" (p. 406) in the "Cooking Methods" section of this book contains information on how to sprout beans and the advantages of doing so.

Well, what do you think? We hope you are convinced that this humble food is one of the most important foods you'll eat on your low-fat diet.

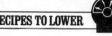
Bean soup recipes, see:
    "Soup's On!" on page 57

Bean salad recipes, see:
    The Garden Spot on page 97

Other bean casserole recipes, see:
    The Sweep of the Scythe on page 269

BOSTON BAKED BEANS

Everyone loves this classic bean favorite.

4	C	navy beans,* cooked
½	C	lean ham, diced
1		onion, chopped
½	tsp.	salt
1	T	brown sugar*
¼	C	dark molasses*
1	tsp.	dry mustard
½	tsp.	Worcestershire sauce

1. Put cooked beans into a bean or baking casserole dish. Add diced ham and onions.

2. Mix salt, brown sugar, molasses, mustard, Worcestershire sauce, and 1 cup boiling water. Pour over beans.

3. Cover and bake at 300° for 6 to 8 hours, adding additional water, if necessary. Uncover during last ½ hour to brown beans and meat. Serve hot.

Serves 6

* See "Cooking Methods" section

	RCU	FU	Cal	%Ft	P	F	C	Na
Per Serving	1	0	142	8	8	1	24	281

EASY CHILI

This spicy dish is great with or without meat. For a "racy" variation, add a half cup cooked brown rice.

1		onion, chopped	½	T	green pepper, diced
½	lb.	lean hamburger,	to taste		chili powder
		optional	to taste		Tabasco sauce, optional
4	C	kidney beans,* cooked	to taste		jalapeno peppers, optional
2	C	tomatoes,*stewed			

Gifford's Alternatives: Add:

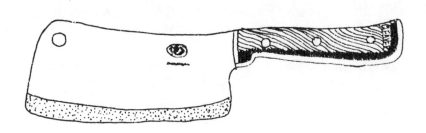

TOMATOES

1	tsp.	*Worcestershire sauce*
1	tsp.	*apple juice concentrate*
1	tsp.	*Kitchen Bouquet®*
2	tsp.	*Gifford's Mexican Spice®*
¼	tsp.	*Gifford's Dessert Spice®*
½	C	*tomato purée*
1	drop	*Wright's® Liquid Smoke*
		OMIT chili powder

1. Sauté* onions.

2. Brown* hamburger.

3. Mix all ingredients together. Season to taste.

4. Simmer for 15 minutes. Serve hot. Like most bean recipes, this will taste better the second day.

Serves 6

* See "Cooking Methods" section

	RCU	FU	Cal	%Ft	P	F	C	Na
Per Serving	0	0	257	16	20	5	30	128

KIDNEY BEAN AND CORN CHOWDER

A clever combination.

2	C	cream-style corn
1		onion, chopped
1	clove	garlic, minced
1	C	kidney beans,* cooked
2	C	skim milk*
2	tsp.	prepared mustard
1	small	potato, cooked and diced
1	C	beef stock*
1	T	imitation bacon bits*

1. Combine all ingredients except bacon bits. Simmer for 15 minutes. Do not boil.

2. Top with imitation bacon bits before serving.

Serves 4

* See "Cooking Methods" section

	RCU	FU	Cal	%Ft	P	F	C	Na
Per Serving	**0**	**0**	**227**	**4**	**11**	**1**	**42**	**467**

HAM AND BEANS

Gretchen Gaunt

You'll want a lot of this traditional bean recipe on hand to keep everyone happy.

5	C	white beans,* cooked	1	C	lean ham, cooked and diced
2	C	chicken bouillon*	to taste		seasoning without salt*
1		onion, chopped			

Gifford's Alternatives: Add:

2-3	drops	Tabasco sauce
1	tsp.	chicken bouillon granules*
1	tsp.	onion powder
¼	tsp.	thyme
to taste		pepper

1. Combine cooked beans, chicken bouillon, and enough water to create desired consistency. For a creamier consistency, remove 1 cup of beans, and purée. Return to mixture.

2. Sauté* onion and ham. Add to beans. Season to taste. Serve hot.

Serves 10

* See "Cooking Methods" section

	RCU	FU	Cal	%Ft	P	F	C	Na
Per Serving	0	0	143	11	11	2	21	214

RED BEANS AND RICE

For a change of pace, replace kidney beans with lentils, pinto, garbanzo, or black beans.

1		onion, chopped
2	T	green pepper, chopped
1/2	C	fresh mushrooms, chopped
2	stalks	celery, chopped
2	C	kidney beans,* cooked
8	oz.	lean ham, chopped
to taste		seasoning without salt*
4	C	brown rice,* cooked

Gifford's Alternatives: Add: 2 tsp. *Gifford's Basic Spice®*
1 tsp. *peach juice concentrate*

1. Sauté* onion, green pepper, mushrooms, and celery.

2. Combine all ingredients, except rice, and cook until tender. Adjust consistency with water or bouillon, if necessary.

3. Remove 1 cup beans and blend in blender. Return to bean mixture and stir until liquid is thickened.

4. Serve over 1/2 cup hot brown rice.

Serves 8

* See "Cooking Methods" section

	RCU	FU	Cal	%Ft	P	F	C	Na
Per Serving	0	0	322	12	17	4	50	38

KOSHERY

The Egyptians consume this in great quantities.

1	C	onions, sliced
1	C	whole wheat macaroni,* cooked
1	C	brown rice,* cooked
1	C	lentils,* cooked
2	C	Spicy Tomato Sauce (p. 25)

1. Sauté* onions.

2. Combine macaroni, rice, and lentils in a bowl. Top with sautéed onions.

3. Pour tomato sauce over rice combination or serve separately. Enjoy.

Serves 4

* See "Cooking Methods" section

	RCU	FU	Cal	%Ft	P	F	C	Na
Per Serving	0	0	233	2	11	1	43	62

LENTILS IN TOMATO SAUCE

This is marvelous over whole wheat spaghetti or brown rice.

1	med.	onion, chopped
1	clove	garlic, minced
1 ½	C	lentils,* dried
½	tsp.	black pepper
¼	tsp.	basil
¼	tsp.	oregano
1	C	fresh mushrooms, chopped
2	C	water
2	C	beef bouillon*
2	C	tomatoes,* stewed
1	6 oz. can	tomato paste
1	T	vinegar

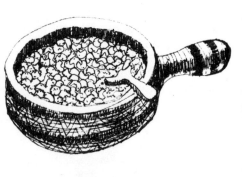

Gifford's Alternatives: Add:

¼	C	*pear juice*
1	T	*Gifford's Italian Spice®*
⅛	tsp.	*ground fennel*

1. Sauté* onions and garlic until onions are transparent.

2. Add remaining ingredients and simmer, uncovered, about 1 hour, stirring occasionally. Serve hot.

Serves 12

* See "Cooking Methods" section

	RCU	FU	Cal	%Ft	P	F	C	Na
Per Serving	0	0	107	4	7	T	20	133

LENTIL POTATO STEW

This is a thick, mild-tasting meal.

1	C	lentils,* dried
4	C	chicken stock
1	C	potatoes, diced
1		carrot, grated
1	T	cornstarch*
to taste		seasoning without salt*

Gifford's Alternatives: Add:
1	T	Butter Buds®Sprinkles
1	T	onion powder
1	tsp.	garlic powder
½	tsp.	dry ground mustard
½	tsp.	thyme
to taste		black pepper
		OMIT other seasonings

1. Cover lentils with 4 cups chicken stock in a large pot. Bring to a boil and cook 1 hour.

2. Add potatoes and carrots. Cook 20 minutes, or until vegetables are tender.

3. Whisk cornstarch into ½ cup water until smooth and add to lentils. Bring to a boil. Season to taste. Serve hot.

Serves 4

* See "Cooking Methods" section

	RCU	FU	Cal	%Ft	P	F	C	Na
Per Serving	0	0	205	3	13	1	36	26

LIMA BEANS AND TOMATOES

For a unique taste, add a sprinkle of dried, crushed mint leaves.

¼	C	fresh mushrooms, sliced
1	clove	garlic, minced
¼	C	onion, chopped
1	10 oz. pkg	frozen lima beans
¼	C	celery, chopped
¼	C	carrots, chopped
1	C	tomatoes,* stewed

Gifford's Alternatives: Add: 1 ½ tsp. *Gifford's Basic Spice®*

1. Sauté* mushrooms, garlic, and onion until transparent.

2. Cook lima beans, celery, and carrots.

3. Combine tomatoes, including juice, with onion mixture and lima bean mixture. Adjust consistency by adding water. Simmer. Serve.

Serves 4

* See "Cooking Methods" section

	RCU	FU	Cal	%Ft	P	F	C	Na
Per Serving	0	0	98	3	6	T	19	165

MEXICAN SPICE MIX

Mariteresa Bergerson

This will be at its flavor peak for 2 months.

5	tsp.	cumin	5	T	minced onions, dried
5	tsp.	chili powder	5	T	minced garlic, dried
2 ½	tsp.	black pepper	2 ½	tsp.	salt

1. Combine spices and store in a covered bottle.

2. Use 3 tablespoons mix for every cup of dry beans.

GARLIC

Yield: 17 Tablespoons

	RCU	FU	Cal	%Ft	P	F	C	Na
Per Tablespoon	0	0	7	T	T	T	1	301

REFRIED BEANS

This recipe can be made without mashing the beans to create a spicy side dish.

| 3 | T | Mexican Spice Mix (p. 261) |
| 3 | C | pinto beans,* cooked |

1. Add Mexican Spice Mix to drained, cooked pinto beans, and 1 cup reserved bean liquid.

2. Cook for 20 minutes.

3. Mash with an electric mixer or potato masher. Add more water, if necessary.

4. Serve hot or reheat. Great on tacos, enchiladas, burritos, or as a dip.

Serves 6

* See "Cooking Methods" section

	RCU	FU	Cal	%Ft	P	F	C	Na
Per Serving	0	0	136	3	7	T	25	158

MEXICAN BEAN STEW

Mariteresa Bergerson

Serve this with hot corn bread.

3	C	pinto beans,* cooked and drained
3	T	Mexican Spice Mix (p. 261)
1/2	C	corn
2		carrots, cut in 2-inch chunks
1/2	C	zucchini, cut in 2-inch chunks
6 1/2	C	water

Gifford's Alternatives: Add:
1	T	*Gifford's Mexican Spice®*
1/4	tsp.	*Gifford's Dessert Spice®*
		OMIT Mexican Spice Mix

1. Combine pinto beans, Mexican Spice Mix, and vegetables in a soup pot. Add water.

2. Simmer, covered, for 30 to 60 minutes. Serve hot.

Serves 6

* See "Cooking Methods" section

	RCU	FU	Cal	%Ft	P	F	C	Na
Per Serving	0	0	161	3	9	T	28	220

SOFT TACOS

To reduce the fat percentage even more, replace cheese with rinsed cottage cheese.

1	recipe	Refried Beans (p. 261)	8	T	mozzarella cheese, grated
2		tomatoes, diced			
3	C	lettuce, shredded	8	T	Salsa (p. 27)
1	C	onions, chopped	8		corn tortillas

1. Prepare all ingredients except tortillas.

2. Heat corn tortillas quickly in a dry, nonstick* frying pan. If desired, spray pan with vegetable spray first.

3. Layer ingredients into folded tortilla beginning with refried beans. Repeat for each remaining tortilla. Serve.

Serves 8

See "Cooking Methods" section

	RCU	FU	Cal	%Ft	P	F	C	Na
Per Serving	0	0	204	14	9	3	35	339

TOSTADAS

Low-fat cooking can really be delicious, can't it?

12		corn tortillas
1	recipe	Refried Beans (p. 261)
4	C	lettuce, shredded
1½	C	onions, chopped
2	med.	tomatoes, chopped
1	C	Salsa (p. 27)
12	T	mozzarella cheese, grated, optional

1. Place tortillas on a nonstick* baking sheet and bake at 350° for 8 to 10 minutes. Turn once and watch closely to prevent burning.

2. Assemble tostada by placing tortilla on a plate, spread with ⅓ cup refried beans, top with lettuce, onions, tomatoes, salsa, and 1 tablespoon cheese. Enjoy!

Serves 12

See "Cooking Methods" section

	RCU	FU	Cal	%Ft	P	F	C	Na
Per Serving	0	0	157	15	6	3	26	289

TAMALE PIE

Fun and filling.

1	C	yellow corn meal
4	C	water
1	med.	onion, chopped
1	med.	green pepper, chopped
1	clove	garlic, minced
1	T	chili powder
2	16 oz. can	kidney beans, drained
1	16 oz. can	stewed tomatoes,* chopped
1	16 oz. can	corn, drained

Gifford's Alternatives: Add:
1   T   Gifford's Mexican Spice®
*   OMIT chili powder*

CORN

1. Combine corn meal and water in a skillet. Cook on low heat until thick, stirring often. Remove from heat and set aside.

2. Sauté* onions, green peppers, and garlic in a nonstick* skillet until transparent. Add chili powder, beans, tomatoes, and corn. Simmer for 10 minutes.

3. In a nonstick* 9" x 13" baking pan, layer corn meal mixture with tomato-bean mixture in 3 layers, beginning with corn meal.

4. Bake at 350° for 45 minutes. Serve warm.

Serves 8

* See "Cooking Methods" section

	RCU	FU	Cal	%Ft	P	F	C	Na
Per Serving	0	0	187	7	7	1	34	271

MEXICAN BARBECUED BEANS

Rene Mortensen

Picturesque and appealing! Serve with your favorite tossed green salad.

6	C	pinto beans,* cooked
1		carrot, shredded
2	large	onions, chopped
1	clove	garlic, minced
2	C	beef bouillon*
2	T	chili powder
¾	tsp.	cumin
¼	tsp.	dried red hot pepper, crushed
4	C	Basic Tomato Sauce (p. 24)

Gifford's Alternatives: Add:
1 ¼	T	*Gifford's Mexican Spice®*
1	tsp.	*Worcestershire sauce*
2	tsp.	*apple juice concentrate*
		OMIT chili powder, cumin

1. Place cooked beans in a pot. Cover with 2 inches of water.

2. Add carrots, onion, garlic, bouillon, chili powder, cumin, and red pepper.

3. Bring to a boil. Reduce heat, cover, and simmer for 1 hour.

4. Stir in tomato sauce. Cover and simmer for 2 hours or until tender. Uncover the last hour for a thicker consistency. Serve.

Serves 12

* See "Cooking methods" section

	RCU	FU	Cal	%Ft	P	F	C	Na
Per Serving	0	0	183	3	9	1	29	120

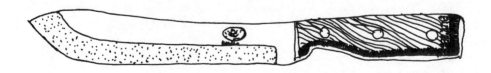

BEANS AND BARLEY

What an outstanding combination of textures, colors, and taste!

1	C	pinto beans,* cooked	1/4	C	lentils, dried
1	C	small white beans,* cooked	1/4	C	pearl barley
			1		onion, chopped
4	C	beef bouillon*	1/2	C	mushrooms, chopped
1/2	tsp.	prepared mustard	1		carrot, chopped
2	T	parsley, minced			
1/4	C	split peas, dried			

Gifford's Alternatives: Add:

1	T	*Gifford's Basic Spice®*
1	12 oz. can	*tomato juice*
1/2	tsp.	*ground cinnamon*

1. Combine drained beans with beef bouillon, mustard, and parsley. Adjust consistency with water, if necessary.

2. Bring to a boil. Reduce heat, cover, and simmer 45 minutes.

3. Add split peas, lentils, and barley. Cover and simmer another hour until all beans are tender.

4. Sauté* onion, mushrooms, and carrots until tender. Add to bean mixture and serve.

Serves 6
* See "Cooking Methods" section

	RCU	FU	Cal	%Ft	P	F	C	Na
Per Serving	0	0	186	3	10	T	34	288

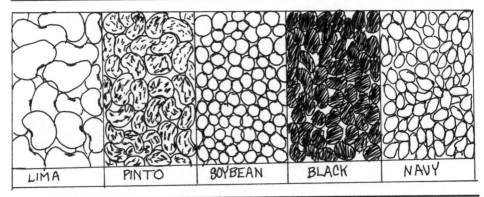

LIMA   PINTO   SOYBEAN   BLACK   NAVY

BEANS AND PINEAPPLE

Serve this sweet-and-sour treat over cooked rice.

2	C	pineapple chunks, juice-packed	2	T	cornstarch*
2	T	vinegar	2	C	pinto beans,* cooked
2	tsp.	soy sauce	1		green pepper, chopped
1	tsp.	chicken bouillon granules*	1/4	C	fresh mushrooms, sliced
2	T	brown sugar*	1/2		onion, sliced into rings
			3	C	brown rice,* cooked

Gifford's Alternatives: Add:

2	T	*peach juice concentrate*
1	tsp.	*Gifford's Chinese Spice®*
2	tsp.	*Butter Buds® Sprinkles*
2	T	*diced pimentos*

1. Drain pineapple, reserving juice. Mix pineapple juice, vinegar, soy sauce, and bouillon granules.

2. Combine brown sugar and cornstarch. Add to pineapple juice mixture. Heat until thickened, stirring constantly.

3. Remove from heat. Add drained beans, pineapple, green pepper, mushrooms, and onion slices.

4. Cook over low heat until vegetables are tender-crisp. Serve immediately over 1/2 cup cooked rice.

Serves 6

* See "Cooking Methods" section

	RCU	FU	Cal	%Ft	P	F	C	Na
Per Serving	0	0	253	5	9	1	56	233

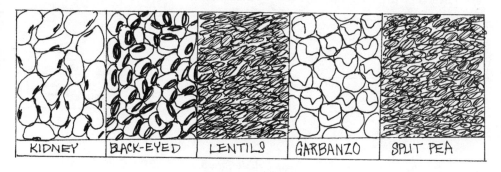

KIDNEY   BLACK-EYED   LENTILS   GARBANZO   SPLIT PEA

BEAN-MAC SOUP

Healthy, hearty, and children love it.

1	C	potatoes, chopped
2	C	carrots, chopped
2	C	onions, chopped
2	C	green beans
1	C	macaroni, uncooked
1/4	C	tomato paste
1/2	C	tomato sauce
2	cloves	garlic, pressed
2	tsp.	dry basil
1/3	C	Parmesan cheese, grated
1	T	oil*
1	16 oz. can	white beans, drained

Gifford's Alternatives: Add:
1	T	*Gifford's Basic Spice®*
1 1/4	tsp.	*Gifford's Italian Spice®*
1	tsp.	*Schilling® Orange Peel*
1	small	*shallot, minced*
		OMIT basil

1. Boil potatoes, carrots, and onions in 3 quarts of water until almost done. Add green beans and macaroni. Cook until tender.

2. While vegetables are cooking, combine tomato paste, tomato sauce, garlic, basil, and cheese in a bowl. Beat in the oil very slowly.

3. Add 2 cups of the cooked vegetables and broth. Beat vigorously.

4. Pour mixture back into the soup pot and mix well. Add white beans. Serve.

Serves 6

* See "Cooking Methods" section

	RCU	FU	Cal	%Ft	P	F	C	Na
Per Serving	T	1	283	22	12	7	46	777

HMMM! Boston Baked Beans (p. 254) and Golden Corn Bread (p. 294) are delicious old favorites.

THE SWEEP
OF THE SCYTHE

Whatsoever a man soweth, that shall he also reap.

--Galatians 6:7

Haystacks (p. 285) is only one of the many wonderful recipes using whole grains found in Sweep of the Scythe (p. 269)

THE SWEEP OF THE SCYTHE

In less hurried, less modern times, grains were harvested with a scythe. As the farmer walked through his field, he swung the sharp single-edged blade that was set at an angle in a long wooden shaft. The long grasses fell and grains, which were the mainstay of his diet, were reaped.

Today we harvest grains with large machinery and whole grains have been replaced by meat in the American diet. But in other parts of the world, grains still provide people with their main source of protein. In India and Asia, people eat rice and millet; in Africa and the Middle East, cracked wheat; and in Europe, barley. As Americans, we are again being influenced by the "sweep of the scythe" and our eating trends are swinging back to low-fat whole grains.

Wheat, rice, corn, barley, rye, oats, millet, and buckwheat are the most common grains for our use.

WHEAT is called the staff of life and indeed it is. It is one of the oldest and most basic foods known to man. The whole wheat kernel consists of three parts: bran, germ, and endosperm. The bran is the outer covering that is made up of layers. These are rich in vitamins, minerals, and high-quality protein. They are also an excellent source of fiber in our diets. The wheat germ is the part of the kernel from which the plant sprouts. It is one of the richest sources of vitamins B and E. It also contains protein, fat, minerals, organic phosphates, and calcium. Wheat germ can be added to baked goods and cereals, as well as sprinkled on fruits, vegetables, and yogurt. The endosperm is the main part of the wheat kernel. It is mainly starch with almost no vitamins or minerals. White flour is made principally from this part of the kernel. You can see why it has little food value. Whole wheat flour, however, contains all of the germ and much of the bran in addition to endosperm.

It is clear that we must eat the complete wheat kernel to receive the full value of it. Grains are low in fat and high in fiber and therefore should be a substantial part of our diet. Meats are high in fat, contain no fiber, and should be used in smaller amounts (four ounces per day). By reducing high-fat, high-calorie meat intake, we can enjoy the filling effect of grains. It isn't the breads or cereals that are fattening, it is the butter, jams, sugars, etc., that we are eating with them.

There are five main ways to use wheat so that the complete kernel can be taken advantage of: whole wheat flour, cracked wheat, bulgur, gluten, and sprouts. See The Bread Spread on page 297 for recipes using whole wheat flour and "What Shall I Have For Breakfast?" on page 41 for wheat cereals. Cracked wheat recipes are contained in this chapter. Recipes using sprouts are found in Bizarre Bazaar on page 375 and The Garden Spot on page 97. See "Sprouts" in the "Cooking Methods" section on page 406 of this book to learn how to sprout wheat. Bulgur and gluten require more explanation.

BULGUR has been a staple in the Armenian diet for centuries. Bulgur is sometimes called "wheat berries" because of its sweet, nutlike flavor and slightly chewy texture. It has the advantage of cooking more rapidly than whole or cracked wheat. It is also versatile enough to use as cereal, in breads, soups, casseroles, stuffing, salads, or as an extender for hamburger. Since it closely resembles brown rice, it can also be used in any way that rice is used, including as a pilaf. Bulgur can be made ahead and stored in an air-tight container in the refrigerator for two weeks. Recipes using bulgur can be found in this chapter.

GLUTEN is a meat substitute made from wheat. It appears naturally in the whole wheat kernel. Since it is insoluble, it can be separated from the rest of the kernel with water, after it has been ground into flour. The starch is washed away and the results are long shreds of wheat protein that are tough and elastic. Gluten is easy to make but it is somewhat messy and time-consuming. It provides an inexpensive meat substitute or extender. Consult cookbooks specializing in gluten for recipes.

Wheat is one of the best additions you can make to your low-fat diet. It is important to note that whole wheat should be introduced gradually into your diet. The increase in fiber may cause diarrhea until your system becomes used to it.

RICE is the principal food for more than half the human race. When it is first harvested, it is covered by an indigestible hull. When this is removed, the result is known as BROWN RICE. Because it retains its bran coat and germ, it is slower to tenderize and requires longer cooking time. But it is well worth the time since it is filled with protein, calcium, phosphorous, iron, vitamin E, and most of the B vitamins. Brown rice comes in long and short varieties. Short-grain types are more tender and moist when cooked and can be used with sauces. They have a wetter, heavier quality. Long-grain types are best for soups, moldings, or stuffing. Their consistency is dry and fluffy.

WHITE RICE is made by polishing and debranning brown rice. White rice has a fluffy texture and white appearance but is greatly lacking in nutrition. Even though white rice is usually enriched, we cannot emphasize enough the nutritional gap between white and brown rice.

CONVERTED RICE is cooked and dried before being polished, which forces much of the vitamin B into the grain before the bran is removed. It is, therefore, a little better than white rice.

Quick-cooking varieties save time but provide almost no nutrition to your meal.

We recommend the use of brown rice. It is easy to learn to enjoy its full, nutlike taste. Cook large amounts and then reheat it in a steamer or in the microwave for the convenience of quick-cooking varieties.

WILD RICE is not a true rice. A seed, it comes from a grass that grows in the northern United States. It remains a luxury because of the difficulty of harvesting it. This luxury becomes affordable by combining wild rice with cooked brown rice.

A pilaf was originally an Oriental dish of rice boiled with meat or fish and then spiced. Now there are as many variations for this basic dish as there are Asian or Mid-Eastern countries. The use of different herbs and spices can help your pilaf take on a wide variety of international flavors.

So learn to enjoy rice. Eat it alone or with beans, poultry, vegetables, or even fruit.

CORN is an important grain to the people of South America. Its most common use is in the form of corn meal. It is often eaten in combination with beans. Recipes using corn meal are in this section.

PEARL BARLEY is another grain that can be combined with other foods for increased nutrition. It is most often added to soups. See "Soup's On!" on page 57. Barley can also be purchased in flour form and used as a thickening agent.

MILLET is a tiny, round, light-colored grain. It grows on a long grass and is sometimes used as hay in America. It is not well known here but it is popular in India and Asia. It makes a good, hot cereal for breakfast. Millet meal or flour can be used in breads or muffins, and as a thickener in casseroles.

BUCKWHEAT is a plant with triangular seeds. These seeds are usually ground into a dark flour. Its claim to fame is that it stays with you and is most often used to make pancakes. See "What Shall I Have For Breakfast?" on page 41. It was especially popular in the mid 1800s.

Buckwheat is also called kasha or groats. It is a favorite in Russia, Eastern Europe, and among some Jewish communities. It can be used as a base for meat and vegetables, as a hot breakfast cereal, or in breads. If groats seem too unusual for your taste, combine one-third groats with two-thirds bulgur.

RYE has a unique taste. It is the only grain besides wheat that contains some gluten. Its most common form is flour, which is used with whole wheat, rice, corn, or buckwheat flours to make bread. It can also be used as a thickener for gravies. See The Bread Spread on page 297 for recipes using rye flour.

OATS are a favorite grain of the Scottish. We are most familiar with oats in the form of rolled oats as a breakfast cereal. Oatmeal also makes moist tasty breads. Oat flour can be used with soy, barley, rice, or rye flours for an interesting change in wheat bread. See The Bread Spread on page 297 for recipes.

The sweep of the scythe provides us with grains that represent endless eating possibilities. They are inexpensive, readily available, and filling. Their nutrition, fiber, and taste make them essential in a low-fat diet.

Additional rice recipes, see:
    The Very Versatile Vegetable on page 171
    The Bean Bag on page 251
    "Just For Fun!" on page 347

Additional rye recipes, see:
    The Bread Spread on page 297

Additional oat recipes, see:
    The Bread Spread on page 297
    "What Shall I Have For Breakfast?" on page 41

Additional buckwheat recipes, see:
    "What Shall I Have For Breakfast?" on page 41

BASIC BULGUR WHEAT

To make dried, cracked bulgur, spread Basic Bulgur on a baking sheet for two hours at 200° and then run it through a grinder.

| 1 | C | whole wheat |
| 1 | C | water |

METHOD 1:

1. Combine wheat and water in a heavy saucepan. Cover and bring to a boil. Reduce heat and simmer 1 hour.

METHOD 2:

1. Combine wheat and water in a small pot. Set pot on a rack in a large pot which has water in it. The water should come almost to the level of the rack. Cover the larger pot and put on high heat for 15 minutes. Reduce heat and steam until wheat absorbs water, about 45 minutes longer. Serve as a breakfast cereal or as you would rice.

Serves 8

	RCU	FU	Cal	%Ft	P	F	C	Na
Per Serving	0	0	75	3	2	T	16	T

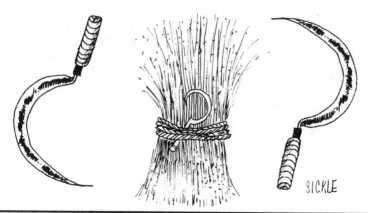

SICKLE

KASHA

This can be used as you would use cooked cracked wheat or brown rice.

1		egg, slightly beaten
1	C	buckwheat groats
½	C	onion, chopped
2½	C	chicken or beef stock*
¼	tsp.	salt
3	T	parsley, chopped

1. Combine egg and groats in a nonstick* frying pan. Heat over low heat until grains become separated.

2. Add remaining ingredients. Bring to a boil. Reduce heat, cover, and simmer until groats are tender, about 25 minutes.

3. Fluff with a fork before serving.

Serves 6

* See "Cooking Methods" section

	RCU	FU	Cal	%Ft	P	F	C	Na
Per Serving	0	0	77	16	3	2	13	254

TABBOULI

This tossed bulgur salad has as many variations as your taste buds allow.

½	C	bulgur
1	C	water
1	C	parsley, chopped
½	C	onion, chopped
1		tomato, chopped
3	T	lemon juice
1	tsp.	oil*
¼	tsp.	salt
½	C	celery, chopped
1		cucumber, chopped

BUCKEYE

1. Soak bulgur in water for ½ hour. Drain well.

2. Combine bulgur, parsley, onion, and tomato.

3. Mix lemon juice, oil, and salt. You can try replacing half the lemon juice with vinegar. Also consider basil, garlic, or mint.

4. Toss dressing with bulgur mixture, celery, and cucumbers. Mix together until all ingredients are lightly coated.

5. Refrigerate for 24 hours. This stores extremely well in the refrigerator.

6. Serve this historical salad on lettuce leaves.

Serves 6

*See "Cooking Methods" section

	RCU	FU	Cal	%Ft	P	F	C	Na
Per Serving	0	0	54	13	2	1	15	96

CRACKED WHEAT PILAF

Serve this as you would rice pilaf.

1		onion, chopped
1	C	cracked wheat
2	T	chicken stock*
2	C	water, boiling
2	T	soy sauce, optional
to taste		seasoning without salt*

Gifford's Alternatives: Add:
1 ¼   tsp.   Gifford's Basic Spice®

1. Sauté* chopped onion and cracked wheat in chicken stock until onion is transparent.

2. Add 2 cups boiling water. Reduce heat, cover, and cook until liquid is absorbed, about 15 minutes.

3. Add soy sauce, if desired. To reduce sodium content, omit soy sauce and season with other herbs or spices. Serve.

Serves 4

* See "Cooking Methods" section

	RCU	FU	Cal	%Ft	P	F	C	Na
Per Serving	0	0	122	5	5	1	26	664

SAVORY SPANISH RICE

You'll find lots of uses for this flavorful dish.

1	med.	onion, chopped
1	sm.	green pepper, chopped
1/4	lb.	lean ground beef
3	C	brown rice,* raw
1	clove	garlic, minced
2	C	tomatoes, chopped
1		bay leaf
1/8	tsp.	red pepper
4	C	water

Gifford's Alternatives: Add:
2	*tsp.*	*Gifford's Mexican Spice®*
1/4	*tsp.*	*Gifford's Dessert Spice®*
1	*tsp.*	*Kitchen Bouquet®*
2	*T*	*cucumber, peeled, seeds removed, diced*

1. Sauté* onion and green pepper until tender.

2. Brown* beef and drain.

3. Combine all ingredients. Bring to a boil, stir, and reduce heat. Simmer 45 to 60 minutes or until rice is tender. Stir often to prevent sticking. Remove bay leaf before serving.

Serves 6
* See "Cooking Methods" section

	RCU	FU	Cal	%Ft	P	F	C	Na
Per Serving	0	0	123	19	7	3	18	20

LIMA PINTO SOYBEAN BLACK NAVY

THE BRONCO BUSTER

This dish is so filling. It is a perfect example of a delicious, low-fat meal.

6		potatoes, baked
1 ½	C	Savory Spanish Rice (p. 276)
1 ½	C	peas, cooked

1. Cut open each baked potato.

2. Top with ¼ cup Savory Spanish Rice and ¼ cup peas. Serve.

Serves 6

	RCU	FU	Cal	%Ft	P	F	C	Na
Per Serving	0	0	178	7	8	1	35	15

RACY RICE AND CHILI

This wild combination will tame your taste buds right away.

| 3 | C | Easy Chili (p. 255) |
| 1 ½ | C | Savory Spanish Rice (p. 276) |

1. Combine these 2 recipes. Serve hot.
Serves 6

	RCU	FU	Cal	%Ft	P	F	C	Na
Per Serving	0	0	182	18	13	4	22	73

HOT PEPPERS

PEPPERS

HOT PEPPERS

STUFFED BELL PEPPERS

Replace rice filling with Bulgur Stuffing or Millet Stuffing. See following recipes.

PEPPERS

6	med.	green bell peppers
3	C	Savory Spanish Rice (p. 276)
1	C	Tomato Sauce (p. 24)

1. Wash and core peppers. Steam for 20 minutes.

2. Fill each with ½ cup Savory Spanish Rice.

3. Place in a casserole and top with tomato sauce. Bake at 350° for 30 to 40 minutes, or until tender. Serve.

Serves 6

* See "Cooking Methods" section

	RCU	FU	Cal	%Ft	P	F	C	Na
Per Serving	0	0	149	16	7	3	21	28

VARIATION: BULGUR STUFFING

2	C	bulgur wheat
1	C	beef bouillon*
to taste		seasoning without salt*

1. Fill each bell pepper with ⅓ cup bulgur. Place peppers in casserole and top with beef bouillon.

2. Cover and bake at 375° for 30 minutes. Uncover and continue baking for 15 more minutes. Serve.

*See "Cooking Methods" section

	RCU	FU	Cal	%Ft	P	F	C	Na
Per Serving	0	0	78	4	2	T	14	75

VARIATION: MILLET STUFFING

3	C	water
1	C	millet
1½	C	onion, chopped
1	clove	garlic, chopped
½	C	fresh mushrooms, sliced
to taste		seasoning without salt*
2		egg whites, stiffly beaten
½	C	low-fat cottage cheese*

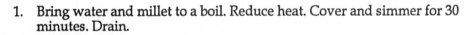

1. Bring water and millet to a boil. Reduce heat. Cover and simmer for 30 minutes. Drain.

2. Sauté* onion, garlic, and mushrooms. Season.

3. Combine millet, egg whites, and cottage cheese with onion mixture.

4. Fill green pepper halves with millet mixture. Bake at 350° for 30 minutes. Serve.

*See "Cooking Methods" section

	RCU	FU	Cal	%Ft	P	F	C	Na
Per Serving	0	0	158	3	8	T	31	74

PLAIN BUT PERFECT PILAF

Sprinkle cinnamon over this to give it a Middle-Eastern flavor.

1	C	vermicelli, raw
5	C	chicken broth,* hot
2	C	brown rice,* raw
sprinkle		cinnamon, optional

1. Break vermicelli into 1-inch or 2-inch pieces and brown in ½ cup chicken broth until it takes on a golden color.

2. Add rice and stir lightly until rice is crisp.

3. Pour in hot chicken broth. Cover. Simmer over low heat for about 60 minutes. Serve.

Serves 6

* See "Cooking Methods" section

	RCU	FU	Cal	%Ft	P	F	C	Na
Per Serving	0	0	252	4	5	1	53	339

BROWN RICE OLE'

Three choices of seasonings let you decide how spicy to make this Mexican brown rice dish.

HOT PEPPERS

1	med.	onion, chopped
1/4	C	green pepper, chopped
4	oz.	fresh mushrooms, sliced
2		tomatoes, diced
2	C	beef bouillon*
1	C	brown rice,* raw
1	clove	garlic, minced
2/3	C	diced green chilies OR
1	tsp.	chili powder OR
1/4	tsp.	basil AND
1/4	tsp.	oregano

Gifford's Alternatives: Add:
2	tsp.	Gifford's Mexican Spice®
1/4	tsp.	Gifford's Dessert Spice®
		OMIT chili powder, basil, oregano

1. Sauté* onion, green pepper, and mushrooms until tender.

2. Add tomatoes and bouillon. Bring to a boil.

3. Add remaining ingredients.

4. Reduce heat. Simmer 45 to 60 minutes or until tender. Serve.

Serves 6

* See "Cooking Methods" section

	RCU	FU	Cal	%Ft	P	F	C	Na
Per Serving	0	0	141	4	4	1	30	77

SPICE RACK

FAVORITE BROWN RICE

You'll never have leftovers when you make this simple dish.

1	pkg.	dry onion soup mix
3	C	water
1	2 oz. can	mushrooms and juice
3	cubes	beef bouillon*
1¼	C	brown rice,* raw

1. Combine all ingredients in a saucepan and bring to a boil.

2. Pour into a baking dish. Cover and bake at 325° until rice is tender, about 1 hour. Stir occasionally. Serve hot.

Serves 6

* See "Cooking Methods" section

	RCU	FU	Cal	%Ft	P	F	C	Na
Per Serving	0	0	146	4	3	1	30	272

CRACKED RICE AND RAISINS

Serve this for breakfast or as a side dish.

1	C	brown rice,* raw
4	C	skim milk*
½	C	raisins

Gifford's Alternatives: Add:

1 ¼	tsp.	*vanilla*
2	tsp.	*Gifford's Dessert Spice®*
2	T	*peach juice concentrate*

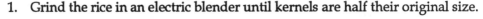

1. Grind the rice in an electric blender until kernels are half their original size.

2. Combine all ingredients in a saucepan. Cover and simmer until rice is cooked, about 15 to 20 minutes. Serve.

Serves 4

* See "Cooking Methods" section

	RCU	FU	Cal	%Ft	P	F	C	Na
Per Serving	1	0	311	2	12	1	63	132

LIGHTLY CURRIED RICE

This subtle curried flavor will enhance a variety of meals.

2	C	hot water
½	C	brown rice,* raw
½	C	tomatoes,* stewed
¼	C	onion, finely sliced
¼	C	green pepper, finely sliced
¾	tsp.	curry powder

1. Pour hot water over rice and let sit for 45 minutes.

2. Add remaining ingredients and bake, covered, at 350° for 1 ½ hours or until done. Stir occasionally until the liquid is absorbed. Remove while it is still moist. Serve.

Serves 3

* See "Cooking Methods" section

	RCU	FU	Cal	%Ft	P	F	C	Na
Per Serving	0	0	134	3	3	1	29	8

BEEF AND RICE CASSEROLE

Serve this with a couple of your favorite vegetables.

½	lb.	lean ground beef
¼	C	green pepper, chopped
½	C	onion, chopped
1	C	celery, chopped
1	C	brown rice,* raw
2	C	beef bouillon*
¼	tsp.	Tabasco sauce
to taste		seasoning without salt*

1. Brown* and drain meat.

2. Add vegetables and rice. Cook until rice is golden brown.

3. Add beef bouillon, Tabasco sauce, and seasoning. Heat to boiling. Stir well.

4. Pour into 2-quart casserole. Cover and bake at 350° for 50 minutes. Serve.

Serves 6

* See "Cooking Methods" section

	RCU	FU	Cal	%Ft	P	F	C	Na
Per Serving	0	0	223	20	13	5	26	182

ALOHA RICE

Garnish this with pineapple rings.

2	6 ½ oz. cans	tuna, water-packed
1	16 oz. can	pineapple tidbits, juice-packed
3	C	brown rice,* cooked
1	T	soy sauce
1	2 oz. can	mushrooms, sliced

1. Drain tuna and mix it in a casserole dish with pineapple, including juice.

---

2. Add rice, soy sauce, and mushrooms. Mix well.

3. Bake at 325° for 60 minutes. Serve.

Serves 6

See "Cooking Methods" section

	RCU	FU	Cal	%Ft	P	F	C	Na
Per Serving	0	0	230	8	20	2	33	273

HAYSTACKS

Kids love to fill their plates and stomachs with this low-fat meal.

3	T	cornstarch*
3	C	chicken bouillon*
1 ½	C	chicken, cooked and diced
3	C	brown rice,* cooked
6		green onions, chopped
1	C	celery, chopped
2		tomatoes, chopped
6	T	yellow cheese, grated
1	C	crushed pineapple, drained
8	oz.	mushrooms, sliced

1. Whisk cornstarch into cool chicken bouillon. Heat until thickened. Use as a gravy.

2. Prepare remaining ingredients and place each in a separate container.

3. Start with the brown rice and build yourself a "haystack." Top with gravy. Enjoy!

Serves 6

See "Cooking Methods" section

	RCU	FU	Cal	%Ft	P	F	C	Na
Per Serving	0	0	228	20	17	5	30	315

TURKEY MOUNTAIN

This is a different and colorful way to use leftover turkey.

¾	C	brown rice,* raw
3	T	cornstarch*
3	C	chicken bouillon*
8	oz.	turkey, cooked
to taste		seasoning without salt*
½	C	corn, steamed
½	C	carrots, steamed
½	C	peas, steamed

Gifford's Alternatives: Add:

1	tsp.	chicken bouillon granules*
2	tsp.	onion powder
¼	tsp.	thyme
1	pinch	white pepper
1	pinch	ground nutmeg

1. Cook rice until tender, about 60 minutes. Set aside.

2. Whisk cornstarch into chicken bouillon. Heat until thickened.

3. Add turkey, which has been cut into bite-sized pieces. Season to taste.

4. Steam vegetables separately. Serve vegetables, rice, and gravy in separate bowls. Start with rice, add gravy, and top with vegetables. Enjoy!

Serves 6

* See "Cooking Methods" section

	RCU	FU	Cal	%Ft	P	F	C	Na
Per Serving	0	0	213	13	14	3	29	287

VERY "VARIED" VEGETABLES AND RICE

This could be served as a meatless meal with whole wheat bread and yogurt, or add six ounces browned* lean hamburger.

2		carrots, finely diced
1		onion, sliced
2	stalks	celery, diced
1	lb.	zucchini, diced
8	oz.	fresh mushrooms, sliced
1/2		green pepper, diced
1		tomato, chopped
1/4	C	boiling water
4	C	brown rice,* cooked

1. Place carrots, onion, celery, zucchini, mushrooms, and green pepper in a saucepan with the tomato and water. Cover tightly, bring to a boil, and simmer gently over low heat until carrots are tender, about 15 minutes.

2. Add rice and stir to mix. Reheat over low heat and serve.

Serves 8

* See "Cooking Methods" section

	RCU	FU	Cal	%Ft	P	F	C	Na
Per Serving	0	0	206	4	6	1	44	51

SWEET-AND-SOUR LENTIL CASSEROLE

If you do not like sweet-and-sour sauce, use Basic Bouillon Gravy (p. 22).

6	T	barley
1	C	lentils, dried
3 ½	C	water
1		onion, chopped
2		carrots, diced
½	C	fresh mushrooms, sliced
½	tsp.	salt
1		bay leaf
3	T	sugar
2	T	vinegar
1	clove	garlic, pressed
1	tsp.	prepared mustard

1. Wash and drain barley and lentils. Combine lentils, barley, water, onion, carrots, mushrooms, salt, and bay leaf. Bring to boil, cover, reduce heat, and simmer 45 minutes.

2. Strain and reserve liquid. Remove bay leaf. Put cooked mixture into a 2 quart casserole.

3. Combine sugar, vinegar, ⅓ cup reserved liquid, garlic, and mustard. Pour over lentil mixture.

4. Bake at 350° for 20 minutes or until liquid is absorbed. Serve.

Serves 6

	RCU	FU	Cal	%Ft	P	F	C	Na
Per Serving	1	0	200	3	11	T	41	193

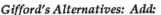

BARLEY AND MUSHROOM PILAF

This pilaf replaces the usual rice with barley for an unusual change.

1	C	onions, sliced
16	oz.	fresh mushrooms, sliced
2	C	pearl barley
5	C	chicken or beef stock*
to taste		seasoning without salt*
2	tsp.	dill seed

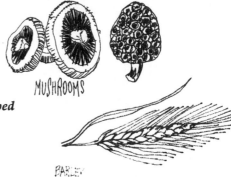

MUSHROOMS

Gifford's Alternatives: Add:

3		*egg whites, cooked and chopped*
1	*T*	*Butter Buds® Sprinkles*
½	*tsp.*	*chicken bouillon granules**
½	*tsp.*	*thyme*
¼	*tsp.*	*Gifford's Gourmet Spice®*
		OMIT 1 tsp. dill seed

BARLEY

1. Sauté* onions and mushrooms until transparent.

2. Add barley to onion mixture. Then add stock, seasonings, and dill. Mix well.

3. Pour into a nonstick* casserole. Cover and bake at 350° for 30 minutes. Keep moist with additional stock or water. Serve.

Serves 6

* See "Cooking Methods" section

	RCU	FU	Cal	%Ft	P	F	C	Na
Per Serving	0	0	273	2	8	1	59	351

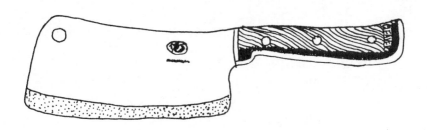

SPLIT PEA AND BARLEY CASSEROLE

Perk up this basic dish with your favorite vegetables.

1		onion, chopped
½	C	yellow split peas
2½	C	chicken stock*
½	C	pearl barley
2	T	parsley, chopped
1	tsp.	dill seed
4	oz.	fresh mushrooms, sliced

1. Saute* onions until transparent. Add split peas and cook for 5 minutes.

2. Add ½ cup stock. Add barley and cook for 2 minutes, stirring occasionally.

3. Add remaining stock, parsley, and dill. Bring to a boil. Reduce heat, cover, and simmer 55 minutes or until liquid is absorbed.

4. Add mushrooms and cook 5 minutes longer. Serve.
Serves 4

See "Cooking Methods" section

	RCU	FU	Cal	%Ft	P	F	C	Na
Per Serving	0	0	196	2	9	T	39	268

AMAZING MILLET LENTIL PATTIES

This could be made with lean hamburger replacing one cup of the lentil millet mixture.

¾	C	millet	to taste		seasoning without salt*
1½	C	water	3		egg whites, beaten
2	C	lentils,* cooked	¼	C	wheat germ
1		onion, chopped	2	C	Tomato Sauce (p. 24)

1. Cover millet with 1 ½ cups water. Bring to a boil. Reduce heat, cover, and simmer 30 minutes, or until tender.

2. Add cooked, drained lentils to cooked millet. Add onion and seasoning.

3. Form into patties, dip in beaten egg whites, and then dip in wheat germ.

4. Bake in nonstick* baking dish at 350° for 20 minutes until thoroughly heated. Turn once. Serve with tomato sauce.

Serves 6

*See "Cooking Methods" section

	RCU	FU	Cal	%Ft	P	F	C	Na
Per Serving	0	0	215	5	12	1	35	25

VEGETABLE MILLET STEW

A thick, golden treasure with whole wheat bread.

1	C	carrots, chopped
½	C	onion, chopped
1	C	potato, chopped
1	C	cabbage, shredded
½	C	celery, chopped
¼	C	fresh mushrooms, chopped
2	T	parsley, chopped
½	C	millet
4	C	water

Gifford's Alternatives: Add:

1 ¼	T	*Gifford's Basic Spice®*
½	C	*tomato juice*
juice of		*1 small lemon*

1. Combine all vegetables in a soup pot.

2. Sprinkle parsley and millet over vegetables. Add 3 to 4 cups water.

3. Bring to a boil, reduce heat, cover, and simmer for 45 to 60 minutes. Keep moist with additional water. Serve.

Serves 6

*See "Cooking Methods" section

	RCU	FU	Cal	%Ft	P	F	C	Na
Per Serving	0	0	103	2	3	T	23	31

RICE PIE SHELL

Fill this with hot stew or your favorite meat, vegetable, and gravy combination.

| 2 | C | brown rice,* cooked | ⅔ | C | evaporated skim milk* |

1. Put rice in bowl. Mash partially with fork.

2. Whip evaporated skim milk. Add to rice. Mix with fork to blend thoroughly.

3. Spoon into glass or nonstick* pie pan. Press with a fork. It will be about ½-inch thick.

4. Bake at 350° for 25 minutes by setting pie pan in a deep broiler pan. Cover with a baking sheet.

5. Fill and serve.

Yield: 1 crust = 6 slices

* See "Cooking Methods" section

	RCU	FU	Cal	%Ft	P	F	C	Na
Per Serving	0	0	99	3	4	T	19	6

LEFTOVERS PIE

You won't recognize your leftovers when they are baked in this "custardy" pie.

1½	C	cooked brown rice, cooled	¾	C	nonfat yogurt*
			1	med.	onion, chopped
2		eggs	1	tsp.	garlic powder
1	C	cottage cheese*	1	C	leftover meat, diced
1	C	leftover vegetables			

1. Press rice into a nonstick* pie pan and bake at 375° for 5 minutes. Set aside to cool slightly before adding filling.

2. Sauté* onions in a nonstick skillet until transparent. Combine with remaining ingredients.

3. Pour filling into rice pie crust. Bake at 375° until a knife inserted in the center comes out clean, about 25 minutes. Serve warm.

Serves 6

See "Cooking Methods" section

	RCU	FU	Cal	%Ft	P	F	C	Na
Per Serving	0	0	171	3	17	5	13	278

"WILD" WILD RICE LOAF

Adventuresome? Try this in place of meat loaf.

½	C	whole buckwheat
½	C	brown rice,* raw
½	C	wild rice,* raw
4	C	water
2	med.	onions, chopped
1	C	celery, chopped
½	C	mushrooms, chopped
¼	C	fresh parsley, chopped
2	tsp.	cumin

1. Bring buckwheat, rice, and wild rice to a boil in 4 cups of water. Cover and simmer about an hour. Add more water, if necessary.

2. Saute* onion, celery, and mushrooms until tender.

3. Combine all ingredients, including parsley and cumin.

4. Pour into a nonstick* loaf pan. Bake at 350° for 1 hour. Serve.

Serves 6

See "Cooking Methods" section

	RCU	FU	Cal	%Ft	P	F	C	Na
Per Serving	0	0	173	3	7	1	42	37

GOLDEN CORN BREAD

This is the perfect partner for your favorite bean recipe.

1	C	whole wheat flour	1	C	skim milk*
1	C	corn meal	2		egg whites
4	tsp.	baking powder	2	T	oil
2	T	sugar	1/4	tsp.	salt

1. Combine flour, corn meal, baking powder, and sugar.

2. Add milk, egg whites, oil, and salt. Mix well.

3. Bake in a nonstick* 9-inch square pan at 425° for 20 to 25 minutes. Serve.

Serves 12

See "Cooking Methods" section

	RCU	FU	Cal	%Ft	P	F	C	Na
Per Serving	1	0	106	23	4	3	18	193

CORN MEAL PIE CRUST

Remember to add the numbers for both the pie crust and the filling together to obtain the correct total calories, etc.

2	C	yellow corn meal	1	T	oil*
1/4	tsp.	salt	1/2	C	chicken stock*
2	T	dry yeast			

1. Combine all ingredients. Adjust with chicken stock to make a stiff batter.

2. Pat into a nonstick* pie pan. Fill with your favorite stew or thick bean soup.

3. Bake at 350° for 30 minutes. Serve.

Serves 8

See "Cooking Methods" section

	RCU	FU	Cal	%Ft	P	F	C	Na
Per Serving	1	0	139	18	3	3	23	86

BASIC CORN MEAL POLENTA

Polenta is a gourmet version of corn meal mush.

1	C	yellow corn meal
½	C	cold water
½	tsp.	salt
2 ½	C	boiling water

1. To keep polenta from becoming lumpy,
   stir corn meal, cold water, and salt until smooth.

2. Slowly stir in boiling water, cover, and cook over low heat for 20 minutes.
   As the water is absorbed, the corn meal becomes thick.

3. Spread polenta in a nonstick* baking dish so that it is about 1-inch thick.
   Allow it to cool.

4. Cut into squares and top with a spicy tomato sauce, Beef Stroganoff, stew,
   or other favorite sauces. Serve.

Serves 4

* See "Cooking Methods" section

	RCU	FU	Cal	%Ft	P	F	C	Na
Per Serving	1	0	115	7	2	1	22	238

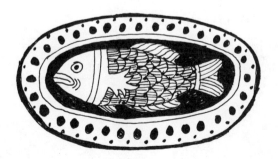

ELEGANT WILD RICE AND ALMONDS

A royal side dish fit for the most elegant meal.

1	C	wild rice,* raw OR	6		green onions, chopped
½	C	brown rice,* raw AND	¼	tsp.	black pepper
½	C	wild rice,* raw	1	T	parsley, chopped
1	C	mushrooms, sliced	12		almonds, slivered

1. Cook rice.

2. Sauté* mushrooms and onions until tender.

3. Combine rice and vegetables. Season with freshly ground pepper.

4. Garnish with parsley and slivered almonds before serving.

Serves 6

* See "Cooking Methods" section

	RCU	FU	Cal	%Ft	P	F	C	Na
Per Serving	0	0	279	7	10	2	56	6

VARIATION: APPLE RICE TOSS

½	C	apple, chopped
1	recipe	Elegant Wild Rice and Almonds

1. Toss apples into rice just before serving.

	RCU	FU	Cal	%Ft	P	F	C	Na
per serving	0	0	284	7	10	2	58	6

THE BREAD SPREAD

"Whatever is worth doing at all is worth doing well."

---Chesterfield

THE BREAD SPREAD

Nothing makes a home seem cozier than the smell of bread baking in the oven. You gain a sense of pride every time you serve a warm loaf of bread and the matchless taste leaves everyone wanting seconds. But the best reason for baking bread is the opportunity to select and control the ingredients that will ensure good nutrition for your family.

Following is a list of the various bread ingredients. Understanding the fine points of each basic ingredient will help you make wise choices when making or buying bread.

FLOUR is the main ingredient in bread. Whole wheat flour contains the entire whole wheat kernel including the bran, germ, and endosperm. See Sweep of the Scythe on page 269 for more details on the structure of the whole wheat kernel. This flour is high in fiber as well as nutrition. It produces a heavier, more compact loaf with a nutlike flavor.

Unbleached flour has had the bran and germ removed but no chemicals are added during the milling. It is slightly higher in gluten than all-purpose flour.

All-purpose flour has had the bran and germ removed. It is made only from the endosperm, which is predominately starch. Even though it is enriched with iron and B-vitamins, it is still lacking in fiber and nutrition. Chemicals have also been added to bleach the flour and improve its handling and baking properties.

Rice, oat, soy, buckwheat, millet, rye, potato, or barley flours all provide their own wonderful and unique flavor and texture to the basic bread recipe.

Our recommendation is to use 100 percent whole wheat flour or whole wheat flour in combination with some of the other flours. Bread recipes need some form of wheat flour, because wheat flour contains a protein called gluten. The basic structure of a loaf of bread is dependent on the amount of gluten it contains. When the flour is mixed with liquids and kneaded, the gluten develops an elastic framework that holds the gas bubbles produced by the yeast. This causes the bread to rise.

Other factors that affect the wheat gluten are the type of wheat, where it is grown, and how it has been milled. Hard, red, winter wheat is generally the highest in protein and gluten. Deaf Smith Co., Texas, has the reputation for growing the best hard winter wheat. Soft wheat contains less gluten and is not satisfactory for making yeast breads.

There are three basic methods of milling: roller, burr, and stone grinding. ROLLER milling removes the bran and germ and then mills the endosperm into a white powder. Bleach, preservatives, and some nutrients are usually added during this process. BURR milling cuts up the whole kernel and makes wonderful cereals. The flour, however, is quite coarse. STONE GRINDING rubs the entire kernel between two stones and produces a fine flour with the wheat germ evenly distributed. This is the recommended milling technique for maximum fiber and nutrition.

Since there is no question about the full flavor, fiber, and nutrition of freshly ground whole wheat flour, you may consider purchasing a stone grinding home mill. This is an excellent investment. And having several 50-pound bags of whole wheat on hand, ready to grind into fresh flour, gives a sense of security. It is important to note that freshly ground flour that is not used immediately can be frozen or refrigerated to help retain its food value. If this idea does not appeal to you, then purchase whole wheat stone-ground flour for use in your breadmaking.

YEAST is a living, microscopic plant. It grows on the sweeteners in the dough and produces carbon dioxide. These gas bubbles are caught in the gluten framework and cause the bread to rise. Active dry yeast and compressed yeast cakes are the two most common forms of yeast and can be used interchangeably. Both must be kept cool or refrigerated, and both may be frozen and used when brought up to room temperature. Dry yeast can be purchased in small, scant one-tablespoon packages or in bulk. In these recipes, one tablespoon yeast and one small package of yeast can be used interchangeably.

Brewers yeast is different from dry and compressed yeast. It has no leavening power and is therefore not used for breadmaking. It is primarily used to add nutritional value.

SWEETENERS, such as honey, molasses, or granulated sugar, provide the food on which the yeast grows. Honey is twice as sweet as sugar, so you can use half as much. Molasses has trace minerals in it and a stronger taste. Either of these sweeteners may require a slight reduction of liquid in the recipe. They both make a stickier dough and a moister loaf than bread made with granulated sugar. Since bread requires such a small amount of sweetener, granulated sugar is acceptable.

An alternative sweetener you may wish to try in your bread making is diastatic malt, made from sprouted wheat. This will add a natural, maltlike sweetness without the addition of sugar. See "Sprouts" on page 406 in the "Cooking Methods" section for instructions on sprouting wheat. Then dry the sprouts on a baking sheet in the oven. When they have cooled, grind them to powder in your blender. This mixture is called diastatic malt. To use, omit regular sweetener and add one tablespoon diastatic malt to the lukewarm liquid of a four loaf recipe.

LIQUIDS used in bread making include milk, water, potato water, or fruit juice. Milk is an excellent liquid addition and provides nutrients as well as creating a smooth, light bread. Water keeps the bread moist and the crust crisp. Potato water gives the bread an incredible lightness while fruit juices create a sweet, fruity flavor.

FATS help the dough stretch and produce a more tender loaf. We recommend polyunsaturated oils in place of butter, margarine, shortening, or lard. See "Fats" on page 390 in the "Cooking Methods" section for more information on the various types and properties of fats.

SALT adds flavor. It also controls the action of the yeast by slowing the rising of the bread.

EGGS help the color, texture, and nutrition of breads. Since egg yolks are high in fats, we recommend using two egg whites in place of each whole egg. Whole eggs have been omitted in most recipes in this section.

TIME is the next important ingredient to consider. Certainly one of the following methods of making bread will allow you the time to enjoy the taste and nutrition of homemade bread. The three basic breadmaking methods are conventional, quick mix, and batter; and the four time-saving methods are refrigerator, freezer, sourdough, and brown-and-serve.

The conventional method involves sprinkling dry yeast over warm water (105°-115°) and allowing it to grow for 10 to 20 minutes. The liquids, salt, and half the flour are then added and beaten either by hand or with a standard or heavy-duty mixer. This beating develops the gluten in the flour. Then the remaining flour is added.

A variation of this method allows the yeast to rise with the sugar, liquid, and part of the flour. This is known as the sponge method. Both require careful monitoring of the temperature. If it is too hot, it will kill the yeast; if it is too cool, it will slow down the yeast's action. A thermometer is helpful in making sure the liquid is between 105° and 115°.

The quick mix method mixes the dry yeast with some of the flour, which then acts as a protection for the yeast. An equal amount of hot liquid (120°-130°) is added. Not only is time saved, but the dough rises faster. Add remaining ingredients after the hot liquid and beat for three minutes with an electric mixer or about 300 strokes by hand. This develops the gluten so that the kneading time is shorter.

The batter method requires no kneading. Since it is wetter, it is simply beaten or stirred to develop the gluten. Allow it to rise in the bowl or in a nonstick pan and bake. The texture of bread made by this method is open and coarse.

The refrigerator method allows you to mix, knead, and shape the dough all at once. Then let it rest 20 minutes and keep it in the refrigerator for two to 24 hours. Before baking, allow the dough to warm up to room temperature.

The freezer method requires you to mix, knead, and shape the dough without letting it rise. Freeze it in moisture-proof wrapping and it will keep for one to two weeks. When you are ready to use it, let it rise until double in bulk, about four hours, and bake as usual.

The sourdough method involves both a unique preparation method and a unique flavor. See the recipe for Sourdough Starter on page 340 in this chapter.

The brown-and-serve method lets you prepare the recipe as usual, then bake it until almost done but not browned. Cool, package, and refrigerate the bread or rolls for up to one week. When you are ready for piping hot bread or rolls for dinner, simply brown them in the oven and serve.

Breadmaking technology and terminology is basically the same for all bread-making methods. KNEADING is the single most important step in turning out a light loaf of bread. It develops the gluten and transforms a sticky dough into a smooth, elastic ball.This is done by turning the dough onto a floured surface (wood or canvas is excellent), then folding the dough towards you with your fingers and pushing it away from you with the palms of your hands. Turn the dough one-quarter turn with each push. This process usually takes five to 10 minutes.

The dough must then RISE in a warm, draft-free place. There are several ways to accomplish this: (1) Heat oven to 150° for one minute. Turn it off and place the bowl of dough inside to rise. (2) Cover bowl with a wet, hot towel that has been completely wrung out. (3) Set the bowl of dough in a sink that is partly full of hot water. (4) Set the bowl inside a cupboard. OR (5) Place the bowl of dough on an electric heating pad turned on low.

Always allow the dough to rise until double in bulk, which takes about one hour. Letting the dough rise too long is a common problem, so watch it closely. A simple test will tell you when it has risen enough. Press two fingers about one inch into the dough and if the dent remains, it is ready.

PUNCH down the dough with your fist. This will release the gas and allow you to do the final shaping of the dough.

SHAPE the dough into loaves by rolling the dough into a rectangle and then rolling it up like a jelly roll from the narrow side. Pinch the lengthwise seam and tuck under the ends. To make a round loaf, simply make a smooth ball and place it on a nonstick baking sheet. There is actually no limit to the number of shapes you can create for rolls, so enjoy yourself, and try new ideas.

Place all breads and rolls in nonstick pans to avoid adding extra fats by greasing the pans. See "Nonstick" on page 399 in the "Cooking Methods" section. The bread must then rise a second time in a warm, draft-free place.

You can ensure a shiny crust by brushing the dough with a mixture of one egg white and one tablespoon water. For a hard, crisp crust on French or sourdough breads, brush with plain water, salt water, or cornstarch water before and during baking.

When baking breads at altitudes over 4,000 feet, you must make a few minor changes. Dough rises faster in high altitudes so you may use slightly less yeast and a little more liquid. Also use shorter rising periods and more of them---two is usually sufficient. And lower the baking temperature slightly.

Bread will turn a golden brown color when it is done. It will also slightly pull away from the sides of the pan and will have a hollow sound when thumped on the bottom.

Cool the bread slightly, then cut with a serrated knife using a gentle sawing motion. Allow bread to cool on a rack and then store in a plastic bag in a cool, dry place. Storage in the refrigerator encourages mold. To freeze homemade bread, wrap tightly in a moisture-proof, airtight wrapping. It will stay fresh for three to six months.

There are many wonderful, whole-grain breads currently on the market. When buying them, read the list of ingredients carefully so you will get the most nutritious bread available.

As you can see, breads should become one of our main protein sources. They are high in fiber and nutrition. There are endless combinations of flavors, textures, shapes, and sizes to choose from. They make any soup or salad a filling, low-fat meal. So whether you decide to make or buy your bread, take advantage of that great "bread spread" available for your good health.

Additional bread recipes, see:
    The Sweep of the Scythe on page 269

CROUTONS

Sydette Parent

Add these "crunchies" to soup or a tossed green salad.

6   slices   whole wheat bread

1. Cut bread in ½-inch cubes.

2. Place on nonstick* baking sheet and broil until browned on one side. Then turn cubes over and brown other side.

    OR

3. Brown on medium high heat in electric fry pan with nonstick* surface.

VARIATION: GARLIC CROUTONS

1. Sprinkle cubes with apple juice concentrate* and garlic powder. Bake at 225° for 2 hours.

Serves 12

* See "Cooking Methods" section

	RCU	FU	Cal	%Ft	P	F	C	Na
Per Serving	0	0	33	T	2	T	6	70

DRESSING

This is great to use as a side dish or stuffing with chicken or turkey. It is a delicious food that can be enjoyed all year round instead of just during the holidays. Try this as a baked casserole with peas and chopped chicken.

24	slices	white bread
10	slices	rye bread
4	cubes	chicken bouillon
to taste		seasoning without salt*
to taste		garlic powder
to taste		poultry seasoning
5	stalks	celery, chopped
2		onions, chopped

1. Break bread into pieces and allow to dry.

2. Dissolve bouillon cubes in 4 cups boiling water. Pour over dried bread. Mix well. Dressing should be moist. Add more water, if necessary. Season to taste.

3. Sauté* celery and onions. Add to dressing mixture.

4. Bake at 350° until thoroughly heated, about 30 minutes. Serve.

Serves 24

* See "Cooking Methods" section

	RCU	FU	Cal	%Ft	P	F	C	Na
Per Serving	1	0	99	T	3	T	17	261

APPLE DRESSING

Something a little different for that Thanksgiving meal.

12		slices whole wheat bread
½	C	onion, chopped
½	C	celery, chopped
1	T	parsley, chopped
1		egg
1 ½	C	skim milk
1	med.	apple, chopped
¼	C	raisins

Gifford's Alternatives: Add during step #4:
3	T	apple juice concentrate
½	tsp.	vanilla

Add during step #5:
1	T	Butter Buds® Sprinkles
1	T	onion powder
½	tsp.	Gifford's Dessert Spice®

1. Cut bread into ½-inch cubes. Spread on baking sheets and bake at 375° until dry, about 5 minutes. Put cubes in a large bowl.

2. Sauté* onions, celery, and parsley.

3. Pour over bread.

4. Lightly beat egg and add milk. Stir. Add to bread mixture.

5. Gently stir in apples and raisins.

6. Spoon into 2-quart nonstick* casserole. Bake at 350° for 1 hour. Serve.

Yield: 12 (½ cup) servings

* See "Cooking Methods" section

	RCU	FU	Cal	%Ft	P	F	C	Na
Per Serving	2	0	71	1	3	1	14	114

WHOLE WHEAT NOODLES

These noodles make incredible chicken or turkey noodle soup.

1 ½	C	whole wheat flour
¼	tsp.	salt
1	C	low-fat yogurt*

1. Mix flour and salt. Add enough yogurt to make a stiff dough.

2. Knead the dough for about 3 minutes.

3. Heavily flour the counter top. Press dough out with hands.

4. Sprinkle more flour on top of dough and roll out with a floured rolling pin. IT IS ESSENTIAL THAT THE DOUGH BE VERY THIN. Let rest 5 minutes.

5. Cut into ¼-inch slices for noodles. Spread on paper and let dry until hard, about 3 hours.

6. Cook noodles by dropping them in boiling water or bouillon. Cook 10 to 15 minutes. Serve.

Serves 6

* See "Cooking Methods" section

	RCU	FU	Cal	%Ft	P	F	C	Na
Per Serving	**0**	**0**	**108**	**10**	**5**	**1**	**21**	**101**

PITA BREAD

Fill this pocket bread with salads or cut it into wedges and serve it as an appetizer with a dip.

1	T	dry yeast		1/4	tsp.	salt
1 1/4	C	warm water		3	C	whole wheat flour

1. Sprinkle yeast onto warm water and let stand for 5 minutes.

2. Add salt and flour. Knead 5 minutes. Let rest 15 minutes.

3. Divide into 8 equal parts and shape into round balls with hands.

4. Stick a 24-inch strip of waxed paper to the countertop with water. Spread thin layer of flour over waxed paper. Using a floured rolling pin, roll each ball into a 6-inch circle.

5. Place on nonstick* baking sheets. Let rise uncovered for 20 to 25 minutes.

6. Bake at 500° for 5 minutes. Allow to cool. Cut in half, fill with salad and enjoy.

Serves 8

	RCU	FU	Cal	%Ft	P	F	C	Na
Per Serving	0	0	135	4	6	1	28	61

VARIATION: PITA BREAD SANDWICHES

1		pita bread
2	C	alfalfa sprouts*
1/4	C	mushrooms, chopped
1/4	C	chicken, cooked and chopped
1/4	C	apple, chopped

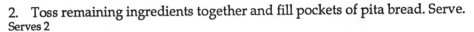

1. Cut pita bread in half.

2. Toss remaining ingredients together and fill pockets of pita bread. Serve.

Serves 2

*See "Cooking Methods" section

	RCU	FU	Cal	%Ft	P	F	C	Na
Per Serving	0	0	75	6	8	T	9	47

ONION FLAT BREAD

Different! Delicious!

2	small	onions, chopped
2	stalks	celery, chopped
to taste		garlic powder
1	C	warm water
1	T	oil*
3	C	whole wheat flour

ONIONS

1. Sauté* onions, celery, and garlic powder until tender.

2. Add warm water and oil to onion mixture.

3. Stir in flour and let stand 10 minutes.

4. Divide the dough into 12 balls. Roll each ball into a 14-inch circle.

5. Cook on a nonstick* griddle until brown on both sides. Serve.

Serves 12

See "Cooking Methods" section

	RCU	FU	Cal	%Ft	P	F	C	Na
Per Serving	0	0	106	14	4	2	21	11

SAGE

CHIVES

SAGE

WHOLE WHEAT BREAD STICKS

Susan Johnson

You may make bread sticks from any bread recipe whose dough handles well. They are especially decorative with soups, salads, or spaghetti.

1	T	dry yeast
1 ½	C	warm water
3 ½	C	whole wheat flour
1	T	malted milk powder
1	T	honey*
¼	tsp.	salt
1	T	gluten flour, optional
1		egg white

1. Sprinkle yeast onto warm water. Let set about 10 minutes.

2. Add remaining ingredients except egg white and mix well.

3. Divide dough into 12 balls. Roll each ball between hands to form a bread stick. If desired, pinch in half to form 24 short bread sticks.

4. Place on a nonstick* baking sheet. Let rise ½ hour.

5. Beat egg white and 2 tablespoons water until frothy. Brush on bread sticks and sprinkle with topping.

Possible Toppings:
 Salad Supreme
 Garlic powder
 Onion powder
 Italian Dressing Mix
 Any low-calorie topping

6. Bake at 400° for 12 to 15 minutes. Serve hot.

Serves 24

* See "Cooking Methods" section

	RCU	FU	Cal	%Ft	P	F	C	Na
Per Serving	0	0	52	5	2	T	12	3

FAST AND EASY WHOLE WHEAT BREAD

This bread has a heavy moist texture with a wonderful sweet taste. The best!!

2	tsp.	honey*
2 ⅔	C	lukewarm water
4	tsp.	dry yeast
3	T	honey*
5	C	whole wheat flour
½	tsp.	salt
¼	C	wheat germ
1	T	sesame seeds, optional

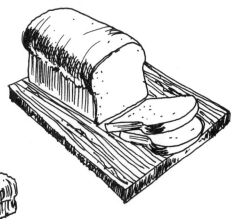

1. Stir 2 teaspoons honey into ⅔ cup lukewarm water. Sprinkle yeast over the mixture. Set aside for 10 minutes.

2. Combine 3 tablespoons honey with ⅔ cup warm water and combine with yeast mixture.

3. Stir into flour. Add salt, wheat germ, and 1⅓ cups warm water. Dough will be sticky.

4. Pour dough into a nonstick* loaf pan. Smooth top with wet spatula. Sprinkle sesame seeds over top of loaf, if desired. Allow to rise to top of pan.

5. Bake at 400° for 30 to 40 minutes. Cool 10 minutes on a rack, then turn out of pan. Cool before slicing.

Yield: 1 loaf = 20 slices

* See "Cooking Methods" section

	RCU	FU	Cal	%Ft	P	F	C	Na
Per Slice	0	0	109	4	4	1	23	49

DILLY BREAD

This is a "dilly" of a bread to serve with soups or salads!

1	T	dry yeast
1/4	C	warm water
1	C	low-fat cottage cheese*
1	T	onion, minced
2	T	sugar*
1	T	oil*
2	tsp.	dill seed
1/2	tsp.	salt
1/4	tsp.	baking soda
1 1/4	C	whole wheat flour
1 1/4	C	unbleached flour

DILL

1. Sprinkle yeast on warm water.

2. Heat cottage cheese to lukewarm and combine with yeast mixture.

3. Add all other ingredients except flours. Stir well.

4. Gradually mix in flours to form a stiff dough. Let rise until double in bulk, about 1 hour.

5. Punch down. Put into nonstick* loaf pan or form a round loaf on a nonstick* baking sheet.

6. Cover. Let rise 40 minutes. Bake at 350° for 40 to 50 minutes. Cool 5 minutes before removing from pan. Slice and serve.

Yield: 1 loaf – 20 slices

* See "Cooking Methods" section

	RCU	FU	Cal	%Ft	P	F	C	Na
Per Slice	0	0	69	11	4	1	11	94

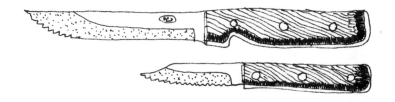

BASIC WHOLE WHEAT BREAD

This bread has a firm, even texture. You can double or triple the recipe and freeze the extra dough.

1	T	dry yeast	2	T	honey*
2 ½	C	warm water	6-8	C	whole wheat flour
1	tsp.	salt	3	T	oil*

1. Dissolve yeast in 2 cups water. Mix in salt, 1 tablespoon honey and 4 cups whole wheat flour until smooth. Keep warm until light and bubbly, about 45 minutes.

2. Add ½ cup hot water, oil, 1 tablespoon honey, and 2 to 4 cups flour. Knead for 10 minutes.

3. Keep covered in a warm place until double in size, 1 hour.

4. Punch down and form 2 loaves. Let rise in nonstick* loaf pans until double in size. Bake at 350° for 30 minutes. Cool and slice.

Yield: 2 loaves = 32 slices

* See "Cooking Methods" section

	RCU	FU	Cal	%Ft	P	F	C	Na
Per Slice	0	0	105	15	4	2	20	60

VARIATION: CELERY BREAD

2	T	celery seeds

1. Add to basic bread recipe before kneading.

VARIATION: GARLIC BREAD

3-5	cloves	garlic, crushed

1. Add to basic bread recipe before kneading.   GARLIC

VARIATION: SPROUTED WHEAT BREAD

1	C	sprouted wheat, chopped

1. Add to basic bread recipe before kneading.

VARIATION: CRACKED WHEAT OR SEVEN-GRAIN BREAD

2   C   cracked wheat OR seven-grain cereal

1. Replace 2 cups of whole wheat flour with 2 cups cracked wheat or **seven-grain cereal.**

VARIATION: ONION BREAD

1   pkg   dry onion soup mix

1. Add onion soup mix to dough just before second addition of flour.

	RCU	FU	Cal	%Ft	P	F	C	Na
Per Slice	0	0	105	15	3	2	20	69

For all the above recipes.

VARIATION: POTATO BREAD

1   med.   potato

1. Dissolve yeast in ½ cup warm water.

2. Scrub potato, cut up, and blend with the remaining 2 cups water. Liquify.

3. Mix with the flour.

4. Bake as directed. This dough can be shaped into 4 small, round **loaves and** baked on a nonstick* baking sheet.

	RCU	FU	Cal	%Ft	P	F	C	Na
Per Slice	0	0	108	15	4	2	21	61

VARIATION: RAISIN BREAD

| 1 | C | raisins |

1. Add to basic bread recipe in step 2.

	RCU	FU	Cal	%Ft	P	F	C	Na
Per Slice	0	0	120	13	4	2	23	62

See "Cooking Methods" section

WILD
ONION

WHOLE WHEAT PRETZELS

These make a good snack, but go easy on the salt.

½	recipe	Whole Wheat Bread (p. 311)
1		egg white
1	T	water
1	tsp.	salt

1. Divide dough into 16 pieces. Roll each piece into 20-inch ropes and make into a pretzel shape.

2. Whisk egg white and water together until foamy. Brush onto pretzels. Sprinkle with a minimum of salt.

3. Bake on a nonstick* baking sheet at 425° for 15 minutes. Cool before serving.

Yield: 16 pretzels

See "Cooking Methods" section

	RCU	FU	Cal	%Ft	P	F	C	Na
Per Serving	0	0	105	15	4	2	20	172

PILGRIM BREAD

A delicious blend of corn and grains.

3	C	whole wheat flour
1 ½	C	unbleached flour
¾	C	rye flour, light
½	C	yellow corn meal
3	T	honey*
2	T	dry yeast
1	tsp.	salt
2 ½	C	hot water
¼	C	oil*
1		egg white

1. Mix flours and corn meal. Set aside.

2. Mix 2 ½ cups combined flour mixture, honey, yeast, and salt in a large bowl.

3. Stir water, oil, and egg white into yeast mixture. Beat for 3 minutes with electric mixer. Gradually add enough of the combined flours to make a soft dough.

4. Knead until smooth and elastic, 8 to 10 minutes. Cover; let rise until double in bulk, about 1 hour.

5. Punch down. Divide in half and shape into loaves. Place in nonstick* loaf pans. Cover; let rise until double, about 30 minutes.

6. Bake at 375° for 35 to 40 minutes. Cool before slicing.

Yield: 2 loaves = 32 slices

* See "Cooking Methods" section

	RCU	FU	Cal	%Ft	P	F	C	Na
Per Slice	1	0	94	21	3	2	16	61

HERB LOAF

Subtle, superb taste.

3	C	whole wheat flour
2	C	unbleached flour
1	T	dry yeast
2	tsp.	celery flakes
2	tsp.	parsley flakes
½	tsp.	thyme, crushed
1	C	skim milk*
1	T	sugar
2	T	oil*
1	tsp.	onion powder
1		egg white

1. Mix flours and set aside.

2. Combine 1 cup of mixed flour, dry yeast, celery flakes, parsley flakes, and thyme.

3. Heat milk, sugar, oil, and onion powder. Add to flour mixture.

4. Stir in egg white. Beat with mixer for 3 minutes.

5. Stir in about 3 cups of remaining mixed flours. Knead until smooth and elastic, 5 to 8 minutes.

6. Shape into ball. Cover; let rise in warm place until double in bulk, about 1 hour.

7. Punch down. Let rest 10 minutes. Shape into round loaf. Place on nonstick* baking sheet. Slash a large "X" on the top. Cover and let double in bulk, 30 to 45 minutes.

8. Bake at 375° for 30 to 35 minutes. Cool before slicing.

Yield: 1 round loaf = 20 slices

* See "Cooking Methods" section

	RCU	FU	Cal	%Ft	P	F	C	Na
Per Slice	1	0	113	14	4	2	21	8

FRENCH BREAD A LA CORN MEAL

What a sweet, moist bread. This also makes great bread sticks.

1	C	cooked corn meal (p. 317)
2	T	dry yeast
½	C	warm water
1	T	sugar*
½	tsp.	salt
1	C	skim milk,* scalded
3	C	unbleached flour
2	C	whole wheat flour

1. Prepare cooked corn meal recipe and cool slightly.

2. Sprinkle yeast over warm water.

3. Put sugar and salt in a large bowl. Add scalded milk. Stir. Add cooked corn meal. Mix well and cool to lukewarm.

4. Add 1 cup flour to yeast mixture. Stir. Add remaining flour 1 cup at a time until dough can be handled. Turn dough onto a floured surface and knead until smooth and elastic, 10 minutes.

5. Put in a bowl, cover, and let rise until double in bulk, about 1 hour.

6. Punch down. Let rest 10 minutes and form into a long loaf. Gash top diagonally with sharp knife, ¼-inch deep every 2 ½ inches apart. Cover; let rise until double, about 45 minutes.

7. Bake at 400° for 15 minutes. Reduce temperature to 350° and bake for 30 to 35 minutes longer. Put a pan of water on the bottom rack of the oven. The additional moisture causes a hard crust to form on the bread. Cool before slicing.

   HINT: For a crisper crust, baste with salt water (¼ cup water and 1 tablespoon salt) after shaping into a loaf and again 5 minutes before bread is finished baking.

Yield: 1 loaf = 16 slices
* See "Cooking Methods" section

	RCU	FU	Cal	%Ft	P	F	C	Na
Per Slice	1	0	137	3	5	T	28	83

COOKED CORN MEAL:

3	C	water
1	C	corn meal
½	tsp.	salt
1	C	cold water

1. Bring 3 cups water to a boil.

2. Mix corn meal, salt, and cold water together. Pour into boiling water and cook until thickened, stirring frequently. Cover; continue cooking over low heat 10 minutes.

Yield 4 cups

	RCU	FU	Cal	%Ft	P	F	C	Na
Per Cup	1	0	115	7	3	1	22	239

WONDERFUL RYE BREAD

This recipe can be mixed up and kept in the refrigerator until baking time.

1	T	dry yeast
1½	C	warm water
1	C	warm skim milk*
1	T	honey*
½	tsp.	salt
1	T	caraway seeds
2	C	rye flour, dark
4	C	whole wheat flour
2	T	orange rind, freshly grated, optional

1. Sprinkle yeast into warm water. Let sit 10 minutes.

2. Mix remaining ingredients with yeast. The dough will be sticky.

3. Shape into 1 large loaf or 3 small loaves. Place on nonstick* baking sheet. Let rise until double. Bake at 375° for 50 minutes. Cool before slicing.

Yield: 1 large or 3 small loaves ▪ 20 slices

* See "Cooking methods" section

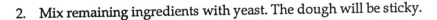

	RCU	FU	Cal	%Ft	P	F	C	Na
Per Slice	0	0	119	5	5	1	24	54

WHOLE WHEAT-CARROT BREAD

Carrots add vitamin A to this great bread.

5	C	whole wheat flour
2	C	unbleached flour
2	T	dry yeast
½	tsp.	salt
2	C	skim milk*
½	C	water
¼	C	oil*
¼	C	honey*
1	C	carrot, grated

1. Combine flours, dry yeast, and salt in a large mixing bowl.

2. Heat milk, water, oil, and honey until very warm (120°).

3. Add liquid gradually to flour mixture. Beat with an electric mixer for 3 minutes.

4. Stir in grated carrots and enough flour to make a soft dough.

5. Allow dough to rest for 10 minutes on a floured surface. Knead until smooth and elastic. Cover; let rise until double in bulk, about 1 hour.

6. Punch down. Divide in half. Shape into 2 round loaves or place into 2 non-stick* loaf pans. Cover; let rise until double in bulk, about 30 minutes.

7. Bake at 375° for 40 to 45 minutes. Cool before slicing.

Yield: 2 loaves = 32 slices

* See "Cooking Methods" section

	RCU	FU	Cal	%Ft	P	F	C	Na
Per Slice	1	0	111	16	4	2	20	40

GINGER BATTER BREAD

This quick bread has a "ginger-snappy" taste.

2	C	unbleached flour	1	C	water
1	T	dry yeast	2	T	oil*
½	tsp.	salt	1	T	honey*
¼	tsp.	ginger, ground	2	C	whole wheat flour
1	13 oz. can	evaporated skim milk*			

1. Combine unbleached flour, yeast, salt, and ginger in a large bowl.

2. Add warm (120°) milk, water, oil, and honey to flour mixture. Beat with an electric mixer for 2 minutes. Cover. Let rise 15 minutes.

3. Stir in whole wheat flour by hand.

4. Divide dough in half and shape into loaves.. Let rise in nonstick* loaf pan for 40 minutes.

5. Bake at 375° for 40 to 45 minutes. Cool on rack before slicing. Serve.

Yield: 2 loaves = 28 slices

* See "Cooking Methods" section

	RCU	FU	Cal	%Ft	P	F	C	Na
Per Slice	1	0	72	15	3	1	13	34

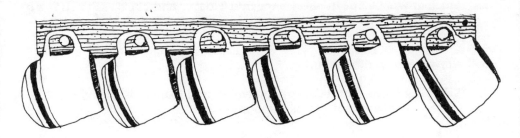

PUMPERNICKEL BREAD

Wow! Now this is what you call a hearty loaf of bread!

2	T	dry yeast
½	C	lukewarm water
¾	C	corn meal
3	C	cold water
2	T	molasses*
2	T	caraway OR sesame seeds
2	T	oil*
1	tsp.	salt
2	C	mashed potatoes
1	C	wheat germ
3	C	rye flour, dark
5 ½	C	whole wheat flour
1		egg white, slightly beaten
1	T	water

1. Sprinkle yeast over ½ cup lukewarm water.

2. Sprinkle corn meal into cold water. Stir constantly to prevent lumps and bring to a boil. Cook until thickened.

3. Add molasses, 1½ tablespoons seeds, oil, and salt to corn meal. Allow mixture to cool to lukewarm.

4. Add mashed potatoes, wheat germ, and yeast to corn meal mixture. Let stand 5 minutes.

5. Gradually add rye flour, then enough whole wheat flour to make a stiff dough.

6. Knead 10 to 15 minutes until smooth and satiny. Place in a large bowl, cover with a damp cloth, and allow to rise until double in bulk.

7. Punch down. Divide in half. Shape into 2 loaves and place each in a 9" x 5" x 3" nonstick* pan or place both round loaves on a nonstick* baking sheet.

8. Allow to rise another hour.

9. Whisk egg white with 1 tablespoon water until foamy. Brush over loaf tops. Sprinkle tops with ½ tablespoon seeds.

10. Bake at 375° for an hour or until the loaves sound hollow when tapped on the bottom.

11. Cool on racks. Slice and enjoy!

Yield: 2 loaves = 28 slices

* See "Cooking Methods" section

	RCU	FU	Cal	%Ft	P	F	C	Na
Per Slice	0	0	167	13	7	3	30	71

HAMBURGER BUNS

Broil or grill four-ounce lean hamburger patties to go with these.

½   recipe   Basic Whole Wheat Bread (p. 311)

1.   Roll dough out to ½ -inch thickness.

2.   Cut 16 circles with a clean, empty tuna can. Place on nonstick* baking sheet and let rise until double in bulk. Sprinkle with sesame seeds, if desired.

3.   Bake at 425° for 10 minutes. Cool before serving.

Serves 8

* See "Cooking Methods" section

	RCU	FU	Cal	%Ft	P	F	C	Na
Per Bun	0	0	105	15	4	2	20	60

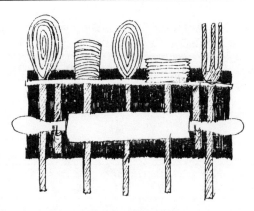

BASIC OATMEAL BREAD

For variety, add one cup raisins OR one cup cracked wheat OR one cup cooked rice.

2	T	dry yeast
½	C	warm water
2 ¼	C	skim milk *
1	C	rolled oats
3	T	honey*
3	T	oil*
½	tsp.	salt
¾	C	wheat germ
5	C	whole wheat flour
2		egg whites, lightly beaten

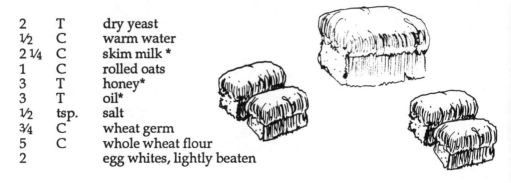

1. Sprinkle yeast into warm water.

2. Scald milk and mix with oats, honey, oil, and salt.

3. Cool to lukewarm and add wheat germ and 2 cups of whole wheat flour. Beat well.

4. Add yeast mixture and egg whites. Beat well.

5. Add enough flour to make a soft dough. Turn onto floured surface and knead until smooth and elastic, 10 minutes.

6. Place in bowl. Cover; let rise until double, about 1 hour.

7. Punch down. Divide in half and let rest 10 minutes. Shape into loaves and place in nonstick* loaf pans. Let rise until double, about 1 hour.

8. If you like, brush loaf tops with 1 beaten egg white and 1 tablespoon water. Then sprinkle rolled oats lightly over the tops.

9. Bake 375° for 40 minutes. Cover with foil for last 20 minutes to prevent burning. Cool on racks before slicing.

Yield: 2 loaves ▪ 32 slices

* *See "Cooking Methods" section*

	RCU	FU	Cal	%Ft	P	F	C	Na
Per Slice	0	0	101	19	4	2	17	42

RAISIN MOLASSES BREAD

This bread is high in protein and iron.

2	T	dry yeast
2 ½	C	warm water
4 ½	C	unbleached flour
3	C	whole wheat flour
1	C	rolled oats
½	C	wheat germ
1	tsp.	salt
1 ½	C	low-fat cottage cheese*
¼	C	molasses OR honey
2	T	oil*
1	C	raisins
½	tsp.	cinnamon

1. Sprinkle yeast into warm water.

2. Combine flours and oats. Mix 3 cups of flour-oat mixture, wheat germ, and salt in a large bowl. Add yeast mixture.

3. Blend cottage cheese in blender. Add cottage cheese, molasses, and oil. Beat until smooth, about 3 minutes.

4. Stir in raisins, cinnamon, and enough of the flour-oat mixture to make a soft dough.

5. Knead 10 minutes on floured surface. Cover; let rise in bowl until double, about 1 hour.

6. Punch down. Divide into thirds and shape into loaves. Place in nonstick* loaf pans, 9" x 5" x 3". Cover; let rise until double, about 30 minutes.

7. Bake at 375° for 30 to 35 minutes, or until done. Cool before slicing.

Yield: 3 loaves = 48 slices

* See "Cooking Methods" section

	RCU	FU	Cal	%Ft	P	F	C	Na
Per Slice	1	0	97	9	4	1	18	63

BRAN CEREAL BATTER BREAD

No kneading keeps this recipe quick and easy.

1 ½	C	unbleached flour
1	T	dry yeast
½	tsp.	salt
½	C	hot water
½	C	skim milk*
2	T	oil*
3	T	honey*
2		egg whites
1	C	whole bran cereal
½	C	wheat germ
1	C	whole wheat flour

1. Combine 1 cup unbleached flour, dry yeast, and salt in a mixing bowl.

2. Add water, milk, oil, honey, and egg whites. Beat with an electric mixer for 3 minutes at high speed.

3. Stir in bran, wheat germ, and remaining flour by hand.

4. Divide dough in half. Form into loaves. Let rise in nonstick* loaf pans for 40 minutes.

5. Bake at 375° for 35 minutes or until done. Cool on racks before slicing.

Yield: 2 loaves = 24 slices

See "Cooking Methods" section

	RCU	FU	Cal	%Ft	P	F	C	Na
Per Slice	1	0	76	19	3	2	11	69

MUSHROOM ONION BREAD

This bread has a unique taste and texture. You'll love it.

1	C	mushrooms, chopped
1	C	onion, chopped
2	C	skim milk*
2	T	honey*
2	T	oil*
1	tsp.	salt
1/4	tsp.	black pepper
2	T	dry yeast
1/2	C	warm water
2		egg whites
1/2	C	wheat germ
5	C	unbleached flour
3	C	whole wheat flour

1. Sauté* mushrooms and onion.

2. Heat milk; stir in honey, oil, salt, and pepper. Cool to lukewarm.

3. Sprinkle yeast over warm water. Add milk mixture, egg whites, wheat germ, and 2 cups unbleached flour. Add sauteed mushrooms and onions. Beat until smooth. Stir in enough flour to make a stiff dough. Knead on a floured surface until smooth and elastic, 10 minutes. Cover; let rise until double in bulk.

4. Punch down. Divide into 3 parts and shape into loaves. Cover and let rise in nonstick* loaf pans until double in bulk.

5. Bake at 400° for 40 minutes. Cool on racks before slicing.

Yield: 3 loaves = 48 slices

* See "Cooking Methods" section

	RCU	FU	Cal	%Ft	P	F	C	Na
Per Slice	1	0	84	10	3	1	16	42

CARAWAY RYE ROLLS

Crusty companions for a crisp green salad.

4	C	rye flour, dark
2	T	dry yeast
2	T	caraway seeds
2	C	skim milk*
1	tsp.	salt
2	T	honey
2	T	oil
2		egg whites
2	C	whole wheat flour
1	C	unbleached flour

1. Combine 3 cups rye flour, yeast, and caraway seeds. Set aside.

2. Heat milk, salt, honey, and oil until lukewarm. Add to flour mixture.

3. Add lightly beaten egg whites. Beat for about 3 minutes.

4. Add remaining 1 cup rye flour, 2 cups whole wheat flour, and 1 cup unbleached flour. Dough will be stiff. Knead 10 minutes. Cover; let rise 1 hour.

5. Punch down. Shape into 24 rolls and place on nonstick* baking sheet. Cover; let rise 30 minutes.

6. Brush with water; sprinkle with caraway seeds. Bake at 375° for 15 to 20 minutes. Serve hot.

Yield: 24 rolls

* See "Cooking Methods" section

	RCU	FU	Cal	%Ft	P	F	C	Na
Per Roll	1	0	139	12	6	2	25	92

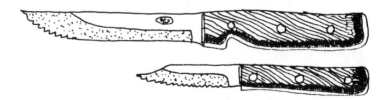

SURPRISE "NO OIL" ROLLS

Roll out, cut into four-inch rounds, and use as hamburger buns, also.

2	T	dry yeast
½	C	warm water
1	C	low-fat cottage cheese,* small curd
1	T	sugar*
¼	tsp.	baking soda
½	tsp.	salt
1		egg white
2½	C	whole wheat flour

1. Sprinkle yeast over warm water. Set aside.

2. Warm cottage cheese.

3. Add cottage cheese, sugar, baking soda, salt, egg white, and ½ cup flour to yeast mixture. Beat for 2 minutes.

4. Gradually add remaining flour to form a soft dough. Knead for 10 minutes on a floured surface. Cover; let rise until double, about 1 ½ hours.

5. Punch down. Divide into 12 equal parts and roll into balls.

6. Place in 9-inch round nonstick* baking pan. Cover; let rise until double, about 30 minutes.

7. Bake at 350° for 20 minutes. Serve hot.

Yield: 12 rolls.

See "Cooking Methods" section

	RCU	FU	Cal	%Ft	P	F	C	Na
Per Roll	0	0	98	3	7	T	17	159

CRUNCHY HARD ROLLS

Hot rolls and fruit salad make a quick lunch.

2	T	dry yeast
1	C	warm water
2	C	unbleached flour
1	T	sugar*
½	tsp.	salt
2	T	oil*
1		egg white
2	C	whole wheat flour

1. Sprinkle yeast onto warm water.

2. Add 1 cup unbleached flour, sugar, salt, oil, and 1 egg white. Beat about 3 minutes.

3. Gradually add more flour until it forms a soft dough. Knead 5 minutes on a floured surface. Cover; let rise 20 minutes.

4. Divide into 18 pieces and shape into rolls. Place on a nonstick* baking sheet. Slash tops lengthwise with a sharp knife. Let rise until double in bulk, about 15 minutes.

5. Brush with an egg white which has been lightly beaten with 1 tablespoon water.

6. Bake at 400° for 15 to 20 minutes with a shallow pan of water on the bottom shelf of the oven. The additional moisture creates a crisp crust on the rolls. Serve hot.

VARIATION: KAISER ROLLS

1. Flatten each of the 18 pieces of dough into 4-inch rounds. Lift 1 edge of the circle and press it to the center. Then lift the corner of the fold and press it into the center. Continue clockwise for 5 or 6 folds. Place on nonstick* baking sheet and let rise. Bake as directed.

Yield: 18 rolls

See "Cooking Methods" section

	RCU	FU	Cal	%Ft	P	F	C	Na
Per Roll	1	0	103	16	3	2	18	55

NO NEED TO KNEAD ROLLS

No kneading necessary! What could be easier?

VANILLA

2	T	dry yeast
1	C	water
1 ½	C	whole wheat flour
½	tsp.	salt
2	T	oil*
3	T	honey*
1		egg white
1 ½	C	unbleached flour

1. Sprinkle yeast on warm (120°) water.

2. Add whole wheat flour, salt, oil, honey, and egg white. Beat until smooth, about 2 minutes.

3. Add unbleached flour.

4. Cover. Let rise 30 minutes, optional.

5. Stir and spoon into nonstick* or paper-lined muffin pans and fill cups half full. Let rise 30 minutes.

6. Bake at 400° for 12 to 18 minutes. Serve hot.

Yield: 12 rolls

* See "Cooking Methods" section

	RCU	FU	Cal	%Ft	P	F	C	Na
Per Roll	1	0	67	18	2	1	12	41

ELEVEN VARIATION DINNER ROLLS

Changing the shape of these rolls can make a meal elegant or casual.

2	T	dry yeast
½	C	warm water
1	C	whole wheat flour
2	T	oil*
2	T	sugar*
½	tsp.	salt
1	C	skim milk*
1		egg white
3	C	unbleached flour

1. Sprinkle yeast on warm water.

2. Add whole wheat flour, oil, sugar, salt, milk, and egg white to yeast mixture. Beat about 3 minutes.

3. Stir in enough remaining flour to make a soft dough. Knead for 10 minutes on a floured surface. Cover; let rise for 20 minutes.

4. Shape (see variations below). Cover and let rise until doubled, about 15 minutes.

5. Bake at 425° for about 12 minutes. Cool on wire racks before serving.

SIMPLE ROLLS:
1. Divide dough into 24 equal pieces and roll into balls. Place in a 9"x 13" nonstick* baking pan.

CLOVERLEAF:
1. Form dough into 1-inch balls. Place 3 balls in each nonstick* muffin pan section.

CRESCENT:
1. Divide dough in half. Roll out each half into a 12-inch circle about ¼ inch thick. Cut into 12 wedges. Roll up wedge from the wide end. Place point side down on a nonstick* baking sheet; curve ends.

SNAILS:

1. Roll dough into a ¼-inch thick rectangle. Cut into strips ½ inch wide and 5 inches long. Roll each piece into a rope about 10 inches long. Shape into a flat coil and tuck the ends under. Place on a nonstick* baking sheet.

FIGURE EIGHTS:

1. Follow directions for snails, except pinch the ends of each 10-inch strip together. Twist once to form a figure 8. Place on a nonstick* baking sheet.

TWISTS:

1. Give Figure Eights an additional twist.

BOWS:

1. Follow directions for snails, except tie each 10-inch piece into a single or double knot. Place on a nonstick* baking sheet.

PARKER HOUSE ROLLS:

1. Roll dough ¼ inch thick. Cut with a 2 ½-inch round cutter. Press a knife handle across each circle slightly off center to make a crease. Fold short side onto long side and press edges together. Place on a nonstick* baking sheet or next to each other in a 9" x 13" nonstick* pan.

BRAIDS:

1. Form several ropes, ½ inch in diameter. Braid 3 ropes together into a long braid and cut into 3-inch lengths. Pinch together at the ends. Place on a nonstick* baking sheet.

BUTTERFLIES:

1. Divide dough in half. Roll each half into a 24" x 6 "x ¼" rectangle. Starting with the long side, roll up like a jelly roll. Cut off 2-inch pieces. Press across the center of each roll with the handle of a knife to form a deep crease and spiral sides become visible. Place on a nonstick* baking sheet.

FANTAILS:

1. Roll dough into a rectangle ¼ inch thick. Cut into 1-inch strips. Stack 6 or 7 strips; cut into 1 ½-inch sections. Place on end in nonstick* muffin pan.

Yield: 24 rolls.

* See "Cooking Methods" section

	RCU	FU	Cal	%Ft	P	F	C	Na
Per Roll	1	0	84	14	3	1	15	46

BAGELS

Bagels have no oil in them. Make them into sandwiches or eat them with soups and salads.

1	T	dry yeast
1	C	warm water
1	tsp.	honey*
½	tsp.	salt
2 ¾	C	whole wheat flour
2	qts.	water

1. Sprinkle yeast over warm water.

2. Stir in honey, salt, and 1 ¼ cups flour. Beat until smooth.

3. Stir in remaining flour. Knead for 10 minutes on floured surface. Cover; let rise until double, about 15 minutes.

4. Punch down and divide into 8 equal portions. Shape each piece into a smooth ball; punch hole in the center and pull gently to enlarge hole and make uniform shape. Let rise 20 minutes.

5. Heat 2 quarts of water to boiling in large kettle. Reduce heat; add 4 bagels. Simmer 7 minutes, turning once.

6. Drain on kitchen towel. Repeat with remaining bagels. If desired, sprinkle bagels with chopped onion, poppy seeds, sesame seeds, or caraway seeds.

7. Bake at 375° on nonstick* baking sheet until bagels are golden brown, 30 to 35 minutes. Enjoy them warm or cold.

Yield: 8 bagels

* See "Cooking Methods" section

	RCU	FU	Cal	%Ft	P	F	C	Na
Per Bagel	0	0	128	4	5	T	27	122

Nothing tastes better than warm bread from the oven. Try Eleven Variation Dinner Rolls (p. 330), Fast and Easy Whole Wheat Bread (p. 309), Crunchy Banana Muffins (p. 335) or Dilly Bread (p. 310) for a real dinner treat.

ENGLISH MUFFINS

Fresh fruit and an English muffin make a nice breakfast.

1	T	dry yeast
¾	C	skim milk,* warm
2	T	oil*
2		egg whites
½	tsp.	salt
1	T	sugar*
1	C	whole wheat flour
2	C	unbleached flour

1. Sprinkle yeast over warm milk. Set aside for 5 minutes.

2. Add oil and egg whites to yeast mixture.

3. Beat in salt, sugar, and 1 cup flour until smooth.

4. Stir in enough flour to make a soft dough. Knead 10 minutes on a floured surface. Cover; let rest 20 minutes.

5. Roll out dough to ½-inch thickness. Cut out circles with a clean, empty tuna can. Sprinkle with corn meal. Cover; let rise until double in bulk, about 45 minutes.

6. Bake on nonstick* electric griddle or fry pan at 275° for 8 to 10 minutes per side. Turn once.

7. Cool and store in an airtight bag. To serve, split with a knife, then toast them. Serve hot.

Yield: 12 muffins

* See "Cooking Methods" section

	RCU	FU	Cal	%Ft	P	F	C	Na
Per Muffin	1	0	129	19	4	3	22	92

The bounties of the harvest, fresh fruits and vegetables, milk, beans and whole grains, are all for our use and good health.

BRAN MUFFINS

This is a quick, filling snack.

2		egg whites
2	T	honey*
1¾	C	skim milk
1	T	oil*
2	C	whole bran cereal
1	C	whole wheat flour
1	T	baking powder

1. Beat egg whites until foamy.

2. Add honey, milk, and oil. Beat well. Stir in bran cereal and let stand for 2 minutes.

3. Stir in flour and baking powder.

4. Fill nonstick* or paper-lined muffin pans ⅔ full. Bake at 400° for 25 to 30 minutes or until done. Cool before serving.

Yield: 12 muffins

* *See "Cooking Methods" section.*

	RCU	FU	Cal	%Ft	P	F	C	Na
Per Muffin	1	0	102	13	4	2	13	130

WHOLE WHEAT DROP BISCUITS

Try these topped with tuna in a seasoned white sauce. Hmmm!

1	C	whole wheat flour
1	C	unbleached flour
1	T	oil*
1	T	baking powder
¾	C	skim milk*

1. Mix all ingredients together. Adjust milk, if necessary, to obtain desired consistency.

2. Drop by spoonfuls onto a nonstick* baking sheet.

3. Bake at 350° for 10 to 15 minutes. Serve.

Yield: 14 biscuits

See "Cooking Methods" section

	RCU	FU	Cal	%Ft	P	F	C	Na
Per Biscuit	0	0	68	16	2	1	12	89

CRUNCHY BANANA MUFFINS

What a treat! These are sure to become a family favorite for breakfast, snacks, or dessert.

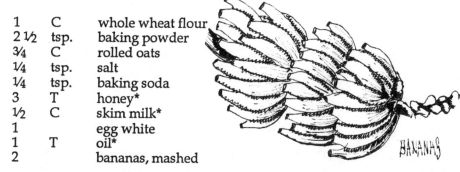

1	C	whole wheat flour
2 ½	tsp.	baking powder
¾	C	rolled oats
¼	tsp.	salt
¼	tsp.	baking soda
3	T	honey*
½	C	skim milk*
1		egg white
1	T	oil*
2		bananas, mashed

1. Combine flour, baking powder, oats, salt, and baking soda.

2. Add honey, milk, egg white, oil, and bananas. Stir with fork just until dry ingredients are moistened.

3. Use nonstick* muffin pan or muffin papers and fill cups ⅔ full. Bake at 400° for 18 to 20 minutes. Let cool before removing muffin papers. Serve.

Yield: 12 muffins

See "Cooking Methods" section

	RCU	FU	Cal	%Ft	P	F	C	Na
Per Muffin	1	0	86	20	2	2	16	170

SPICY PUMPKIN ROLLS

Delicious with a fresh fruit salad.

1	T	dry yeast	2	T	brown sugar*
¼	C	warm water	½	tsp.	cinnamon
1	C	skim milk*	¼	tsp.	nutmeg
¾	C	canned pumpkin	⅛	tsp.	ground cloves
1		egg white	⅛	tsp.	ground ginger
2	T	oil	2	C	unbleached flour
2	C	whole wheat flour			

Gifford's Alternatives: Add:
1 ¼   tsp.   *Gifford's Dessert Spice®*
            OMIT cinnamon, nutmeg, cloves, ginger

1. Sprinkle yeast into warm water. Set aside.

2. Heat milk, pumpkin, egg white, and oil until very warm. Set aside.

3. Combine whole wheat flour, brown sugar, and spices. Add pumpkin mixture. Stir well.

4. Add yeast mixture and beat until smooth, about 3 minutes.

5. Stir in enough unbleached flour to make a soft dough. Knead 5 minutes on floured surface.

6. Cover; let rise 20 minutes.

7. Shape into 2-inch balls. Place each ball in nonstick* muffin pan. Cover; let rise until double, about 20 minutes.

8. Bake at 375° for 20 minutes or until done. Serve hot.
Yield: 24 rolls

* See "Cooking Methods" section

	RCU	FU	Cal	%Ft	P	F	C	Na
Per Roll	0	0	82	16	3	1	15	7

WHOLE WHEAT-RAISIN MUFFINS

A healthy, hearty treat.

1	C	grape-nuts cereal
¾	C	apple juice
¼	C	skim milk*
1	C	whole wheat flour
¼	tsp.	salt
2	tsp.	baking powder
2	T	oil*
2		egg whites
½	C	raisins

1. Combine grape-nuts, apple juice, milk, flour, salt, baking powder, and oil in a large bowl.

2. Beat egg whites for 1 minute. Combine with grape-nuts mixture.

3. Stir in raisins.

4. Spoon batter into nonstick* or paper-lined muffin pan and fill cups ⅔ full.

5. Bake at 400° for 20 minutes. Cool. Remove papers and serve.

Yield: 12 muffins

* See "Cooking Methods" section

	RCU	FU	Cal	%Ft	P	F	C	Na
Per Muffin	T	T	116	19	3	3	20	158

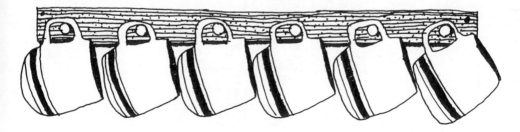

SPROUTED WHEAT MUFFINS

Wheat is easy to sprout but if allowed to grow longer than three days it becomes bitter.

2	C	whole wheat flour
2	tsp.	baking powder
2	T	honey
1	C	skim milk*
2		egg whites
2	T	oil*
½	C	sprouted wheat*

1. Mix flour and baking powder.

2. Add honey, milk, egg whites, and oil. Mix well.

3. Stir in sprouted wheat until evenly mixed.

4. Bake at 425° for 15 minutes in nonstick* or paper-lined muffin pans. Cool before serving.

Yield: 18 muffins

* See "Cooking Methods" section

	RCU	FU	Cal	%Ft	P	F	C	Na
Per Muffin	0	0	67	23	2	2	11	33

SUNFLOWERS

APPLESAUCE MUFFINS

Line a basket with a gingham cloth, load it up with muffins, and you have a warm, neighborly treat.

1		egg
2	T	oil*
1 ½	C	applesauce, unsweetened
1 ½	C	whole wheat flour
½	C	bran buds cereal
½	tsp.	baking soda
2	tsp.	baking powder
½	tsp.	nutmeg
½	tsp.	cinnamon
½	C	raisins

Gifford's Alternatives: Add:
1	tsp.	*Gifford's Dessert Spice®*
		OMIT nutmeg, cinnamon

1. Mix egg, oil, and applesauce in a bowl. Add flour, bran buds cereal, baking soda, baking powder, and spices. Stir in raisins.

2. Spoon batter into a nonstick* or paper-lined muffin pan, filling the cups ¾ full.

3. Bake 375° until slightly brown, about 20 to 25 minutes. Serve.

Yield: 12 muffins

* See "Cooking Methods" section

	RCU	FU	Cal	%Ft	P	F	C	Na
Per Muffin	T	T	107	25	3	3	18	134

SOURDOUGH STARTER

Sourdough breads are wonderful for your low-fat diet since they are made without oil.

1	C	whole wheat flour
1	tsp.	dry yeast
1	tsp.	sugar*
1 ½	C	warm water

1. Mix all ingredients in a crock or glass container. DO NOT USE METAL. Leave overnight at room temperature.

2. In the morning, add 1 cup flour and enough water to make a thick batter.

3. Repeat second step for 2 or 3 days.

4. Allow the starter to sit for 1 to 3 days until it becomes active and bubbly.

5. It is now ready to use or to cover and store in the refrigerator.

6. To replenish: Each time you use your starter, replenish it with a mixture of equal parts of milk and flour (i.e. ½ cup flour and ½ cup milk). Leave it at room temperature several hours or overnight, until it again becomes full of bubbles, then cover and store in the refrigerator.

7. The starter is best if used at least once a week. If not used for 2 or 3 weeks, it may become too sour. Freshen it with a small amount of baking soda OR discard half of the starter and replenish it with 1 cup water and 1 cup flour.

8. You may freeze a good starter and allow it to stand at room temperature for 24 hours after it has thawed.

	RCU	FU	Cal	%Ft	P	F	C	Na
Per Cup	0	0	150	4	6	1	32	3

SIMPLE SOURDOUGH BREAD

One cup rye flour or corn meal can be substituted for one cup flour to add variety to this basic recipe.

1	C	Sourdough Starter (p. 340)
2	C	warm water
2	C	unbleached flour
2	C	skim milk*
2	tsp.	honey*
1	T	dry yeast
2	C	whole wheat flour
¼	C	wheat germ, optional
1	tsp.	salt
2	tsp.	baking soda

1. Combine starter, 2 cups warm water and 2 cups unbleached flour in a large bowl. Cover and let stand 8 to 12 hours. This is called a "sponge." It will be bubbly when ready to use.

2. Scald milk. Stir in honey and allow to cool to lukewarm. Sprinkle yeast onto milk and stir until dissolved. Combine this with the "sponge."

3. Add 2 cups of the whole wheat flour and the wheat germ. Mix well.

4. Sprinkle salt and baking soda into dough and stir gently.

5. Cover and let rise about 30 minutes.

6. Add enough unbleached flour until dough is very stiff. Knead 8 minutes on a floured surface.

7. Divide in half and shape into loaves. Place in nonstick* loaf pans. Let rise until double.

8. Bake at 400° for 20 minutes. Reduce heat to 325° and bake until done. Bread will pull away from the sides of the pan and sound hollow when thumped on top. Cool on a rack before serving.

Yield: 2 loaves = 32 slices

See "Cooking Methods" section

	RCU	FU	Cal	%Ft	P	F	C	Na
Per Slice	1	0	110	4	4	T	23	88

"SAN FRANCISCO" SOURDOUGH

This is as close as possible to the "real" thing.

1 ½	C	water
1	T	dry yeast
1	C	Sourdough Starter (p. 340)
3 ½	C	whole wheat flour
1	T	sugar*
1	tsp.	salt
½	tsp.	baking soda
2	C	unbleached flour

1. Combine water and yeast until bubbly. Do not stir.

2. Combine sourdough starter, whole wheat flour, sugar, and salt with yeast mixture. Stir until smooth, about 3 minutes. Let sit until double in bulk.

3. Add baking soda and unbleached flour. Knead about 5 to 8 minutes on a floured surface.

4. Shape into 2 round or oblong loaves and place on a nonstick* baking sheet. Cover; let rise until double in bulk.

5. Brush with 1 tablespoon water and 1 egg white which have been lightly beaten together.

6. Bake at 400° for 40 to 55 minutes with a shallow pan of water on the bottom shelf of the oven. The additional moisture will create a crisp crust on the bread.

Yield: 2 loaves = 36 slices

* See "Cooking Methods" section

	RCU	FU	Cal	%Ft	P	F	C	Na
Per Slice	0	0	39	6	2	T	13	56

SOURDOUGH ENGLISH MUFFINS

Toasted or plain, English muffins make great sandwiches.

½	C	Sourdough Starter (p. 340)
5	T	dry powdered milk*
1	C	water
1½	C	unbleached flour
1	C	whole wheat flour
1	T	sugar*
¼	tsp.	salt
½	tsp.	baking soda

1. Combine starter, dry powdered milk, water, and unbleached flour in a large bowl. Stir, cover, and let sit at room temperature for 8 hours.

2. Sprinkle whole wheat flour, sugar, salt, and baking soda over first mixture and stir. Dough will be stiff. Knead on a floured surface until no longer sticky, about 3 minutes.

3. Roll dough out to ½-inch thickness and cut 12 muffins with clean, empty tuna can.

4. Sprinkle top and bottom with corn meal. Cover; let rise for 45 minutes.

5. Bake on nonstick* electric griddle or fry pan at 275° about 10 minutes per side. Turn once. Cool before serving.

Yield: 12 muffins

* See "Cooking Methods" section

	RCU	FU	Cal	%Ft	P	F	C	Na
Per Muffin	1	0	103	2	4	T	21	100

HOAGIE SANDWICHES "AU JUS"

"Au Jus" sandwiches are usually dipped in meat drippings which are high in fat. Replace drippings with a low-fat barbecue sauce or French onion soup and enjoy this old favorite.

1	loaf	"San Francisco" Sourdough bread (p. 342)
3	T	prepared mustard
3	T	catsup
12	oz.	chicken OR turkey, sliced
2		tomatoes, sliced
6		leaves lettuce
1		onion, sliced
18	slices	cucumber pickle
2	C	Barbecue Sauce (p. 24) OR
		French Onion Soup (p. 82)

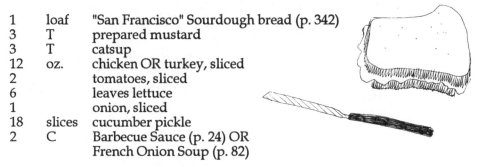

1. Slice loaf of sourdough bread lengthwise. Spread one side with mustard and one side with catsup.

2. Layer chicken or turkey, tomatoes, lettuce, onion, and pickle slices on 1 side of the loaf. Top with the rest of the loaf of bread.

3. Slice crosswise into 6 sections.

4. Pour barbecue sauce or warm French onion soup into 6 small bowls. Dip sandwich into sauce as you eat it. Hmmm!

Serves 6

	RCU	FU	Cal	%Ft	P	F	C	Na
Per Serving	0	0	263	6	23	2	57	549

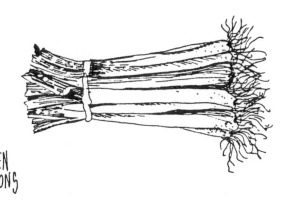

GREEN
ONIONS

TURKEY ASPARAGUS OPEN-FACE SANDWICH

A light dinner for a warm summer evening.

4	T	low-calorie French dressing
2	T	onion, finely chopped
1/8	tsp.	black pepper
1	10 oz. pkg	asparagus, frozen
2		English muffins
8	1 oz.	slices cooked turkey
8	tsp.	mozzarella cheese, grated

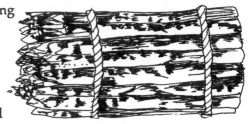

1. Mix French dressing, onions, and pepper.

2. Cook and drain asparagus. Pour French dressing mixture over asparagus and refrigerate for 2 hours.

3. Use a slotted spoon to remove asparagus and set it aside.

4. Cut English muffins in half and toast them. Spread a light coat of the French dressing mixture on the bread. Layer a slice of turkey, more French dressing, and asparagus.

5. Broil 4 inches from heat for about 4 minutes.

6. Sprinkle 2 teaspoons of mozzarella cheese over asparagus and broil for 1 minute. Serve.

Serves 4

	RCU	FU	Cal	%Ft	P	F	C	Na
Per Serving	0	0	180	23	16	4	17	335

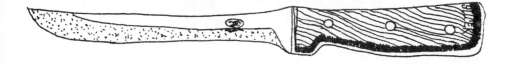

MOZZARELLA SPROUT SANDWICH

The name alfalfa comes from the Arabs, meaning "father of all foods." Eat this sandwich with soup or a salad and your meal's overall percentage of fat will be under 20 percent.

1	C	cucumber, thinly sliced
½	C	carrot, shredded
2		green onions, chopped
5	T	Low-Calorie Italian Dressing (p. 37)
¼	C	skim mozzarella cheese, shredded
2		English muffins
½	C	alfalfa sprouts

1. Combine cucumber, carrot, green onions, and low-calorie Italian dressing.

2. Sprinkle 1 tablespoon mozzarella cheese on each English muffin half. Broil until melted.

3. Spoon ⅓ cup of vegetable mixture atop each half.

4. Add 2 tablespoons of sprouts. Serve.

Serves 4

	RCU	FU	Cal	%Ft	P	F	C	Na
Per Serving	0	0	102	20	4	2	24	42

"JUST FOR FUN!"

*The chief cause of failure and unhappiness
is trading what we want most for what we want at the moment.*

"JUST FOR FUN!"

There are times when we all eat just for fun. We may want an elegant dessert for company, a special treat for a special occasion, a cool drink on a hot afternoon, cake and ice cream for a birthday party, or we may just have the "munchies." Once in a while, it's okay to eat just for fun as long as we make good choices about what we eat. This section is filled with good choices. Flip through these pages of low-fat, low-sugar desserts, drinks, and snacks and you'll be surprised at how many beautiful, tasty treats there are within the guidelines of a low-fat, low-sugar diet.

Also included are some recipes that do not fall exactly within the guidelines, since there may be times when they are needed. Simply watch the serving size and frequency. Remember, they are still much better for you than their high-fat, high-sugar counterparts.

Does your family have a favorite dessert or treat? Most families do. Experiment with the following suggestions and see if you can adapt your recipe to a low-fat, low-sugar format. Most can be adapted with only a slight difference in the taste or texture.

1. Almost all recipes can reduce the amount of fat by half without a noticeable difference.
2. Replace all or half of the white flour with whole wheat flour. The consistency may need to be adjusted with more liquid, since whole wheat flour is heavier and more absorbent.
3. Use skim or one percent milk instead of whole milk, cream, or half-and-half.
4. Replace sour cream and cream cheese with low-fat yogurt or cottage cheese.
5. Omit or reduce the amount of salt by half.
6. Use two egg whites instead of a whole egg.
7. Reduce white sugar by half.

Since honey is twice as sweet as sugar, you may replace the sugar with half as much honey. You may need to adjust the consistency with flour.

Any or all of the above adjustments will help make your desserts and snacks more nutritious. While not every change is possible, most recipes are still acceptable after some alterations have been made. If you don't enjoy your family favorite after experimenting with the above changes, then you must consider one of two options: either get along with a very small serving, or learn to love another dessert that is within the guidelines.

These changes will become easier as you decrease your need for very sweet, rich desserts. Your taste and tolerance for sugar may have been slowly increased in an upward direction but it can be decreased in a downward direction. Replacing baked goods and snacks with fresh fruits will become more natural and satisfying to you. And believe it or not, the sweets you once loved will begin to taste too sweet to you.

We have also included some recipes for drinks because there will be times when you will want to use them. Like desserts, it's okay once in a while.

Remember that the goal is to drink six to eight glasses of water a day, and to get away from soda pop and drinks that cause your blood sugar to rise rapidly. This is not always easy for some people to do. So as you work toward this goal, enjoy some of these refreshing drinks.

Well, as you can see, low-fat, low-sugar eating doesn't have to be dry or dull. Search until you find just the recipes that allow you to make a permanent lifestyle change for your own good health. Enjoying desserts, drinks, and snacks can be part of that lifestyle, especially when you occasionally need to eat just for fun.

FRESH STRAWBERRY PIE

Isn't it nice to know that you can eat a slice of this beautiful pie without feeling guilty? Follow this same recipe using peaches or raspberries in place of strawberries for other delicious fruit pies.

1		Grape-Nuts Pie Crust (p. 350)
5	C	strawberries, fresh
½	C	fruit juice concentrate*
2	T	cornstarch*
¼	C	cold water

1. Prepare pie crust. Cool.

2. Mash 2 cups fresh strawberries. Add fruit juice concentrate.

3. Whisk cornstarch into cold water and pour into mashed fruit.

4. Heat to boiling, stirring constantly. Mixture will become a thick, shiny glaze.

5. Fill pie crust with remaining whole strawberries. Pour glaze over the top. Chill and serve.

Serves 6

* See "Cooking Methods" section

	RCU	FU	Cal	%Ft	P	F	C	Na
Per Serving	2	0	260	4	5	1	189	149

GRAPE-NUTS PIE CRUST

Joyce Nixon
Mariteresa Bergerson

Isn't this a great idea? Only a trace of fat and a terrific taste.

| 1 | 6 oz. can | apple juice concentrate* |
| 1 ½ | C | grape-nuts cereal |

1. Mix juice with grape-nuts and let stand for a few minutes until moisture is absorbed.

2. Press into a 9-inch nonstick* pie pan.

3. Bake at 350° for 12 minutes.

4. Cool. Fill with fruit and yogurt or a pudding recipe from this chapter. Serve.

Serves 6

* See "Cooking Methods" section

	RCU	FU	Cal	%Ft	P	F	C	Na
Per Serving	0	0	164	T	4	T	36	148

OATMEAL BIRD NESTS

Sydette Parent

This can be used as a low-fat pie crust. Fill crust or "bird nests" with fruit and yogurt or other puddings in this chapter.

⅓	C	raisins
1 ½	C	rolled oats
1	C	apples, finely shredded
¼	tsp.	salt

Gifford's Alternatives: Add:
| 1 | tsp. | Gifford's Dessert Spice® |

1. Soften raisins in 4 tablespoons warm water.

2. Add remaining ingredients to raisins and water.

3. Put a small portion into nonstick* muffin pan cups and, using fingers, press dough along bottom and part way up the sides to form a "nest."

4. Bake at 375° for 25 minutes. Remove when warm or they will stick. Fill and serve.

Yield: 16 nests

* See "Cooking Methods" section

	RCU	FU	Cal	%Ft	P	F	C	Na
Per Serving	0	0	41	13	1	1	8	30

WHOLE WHEAT PIE SHELL

Joyce Nixon
Mariteresa Bergerson

Fill this with a double recipe of Frothy Fruit Fluff (p. 369) and the percentage of fat will drop to under 20 percent.

3	T	diet margarine*
1 ½	C	whole wheat flour
5	T	ice water
1	T	fruit juice concentrate*

1. Cut margarine into flour.

2. Add ice water and fruit juice concentrate.

3. Knead and wrap in plastic. Let rest 30 minutes

4. Press dough into pie pan and bake at 375° for 10 minutes or until lightly browned. Cool before filling.

Serves 6

* See "Cooking Methods" section

	RCU	FU	Cal	%Ft	P	F	C	Na
Per Serving	0	0	118	32	4	4	20	69

STRAWBERRY CHEESECAKE

Joyce Nixon
Mariteresa Bergerson

A fabulous low-fat variation of this all-time favorite dessert.

2	C	fresh strawberries	2		egg whites
2		bananas	1	env.	unflavored gelatin
2	C	low-fat yogurt*	2	T	boiling water
1	tsp.	vanilla	1		baked Grape-Nuts Pie Crust (p. 350)

1. Dissolve gelatin in boiling water. Combine 1 cup strawberries, bananas, yogurt, vanilla, egg whites, and gelatin in blender on high speed for 2 minutes.

2. Pour into baked Grape-Nuts Pie Crust.

3. Bake at 350° for 1 hour.

4. Refrigerate for 3 hours. Top with remaining 1 cup fresh strawberries before serving.

Serves 6

See "Cooking Methods" section

	RCU	FU	Cal	%Ft	P	F	C	Na
Per Serving	0	0	254	5	9	1	51	200

BANANA PINEAPPLE PUDDING

Joyce Nixon
Mariteresa Bergerson

Double this recipe and pour over sliced bananas in a Grape-Nuts Pie Crust (p. 350) for an outstanding low-sugar, low-fat pie.

2 ½	C	unsweetened pineapple juice
5	T	cornstarch*
4		bananas

1. Blend pineapple juice, cornstarch, and 2 peeled bananas until smooth.

2. Cook banana mixture over medium heat until thickened, stirring constantly.

3. Pour over 2 sliced bananas in dessert dishes. Chill before serving.
Serves 5
* See "Cooking Methods" section

	RCU	FU	Cal	%Ft	P	F	C	Na
Per Serving	0	0	137	7	2	1	33	2

LEMON FLUFF PIE FILLING

This pie is too good to be true, but it is! This can be enjoyed as a pudding or layered with Whipped Topping (p. 357) in parfait glasses.

1	env.	unflavored gelatin	1	tsp.	lemon rind, grated
1	T	cold water	1	C	boiling water
2	T	sugar*	½	C	ice water
¼	C	lemon juice	½	C	nonfat dry milk*
½	C	cold water	1		egg white

Gifford's Alternatives: Add:

1	C	*boiling pineapple juice*	1	tsp.	*lemon rind, grated*
1 ½	T	*honey*	½	tsp.	*vanilla extract*
2	T	*Butter Buds® Sprinkles*			*OMIT 1 C boiling water*
¼	tsp.	*cream of tarter*			

1. Combine gelatin and 1 tablespoon cold water. Add sugar, lemon juice, ½ cup cold water, and 1 teaspoon grated lemon rind to boiling water. Stir until gelatin and sugar are dissolved. Freeze until almost firm.

2. Put deep metal bowl and mixer beaters into freezer for 30 minutes.

3. Put ice water into cold bowl, whisk dry milk into water, and add egg white. Beat until stiff. Chill.

4. Break up frozen lemon mixture and combine with chilled milk mixture. Beat well with an electric mixer until fluffy, but not too soft. Spoon into a cold pie shell (see index) and chill. Garnish with more grated lemon rind and serve.
Serves 6
* See "Cooking Methods" section

	RCU	FU	Cal	%Ft	P	F	C	Na
Per Serving	1	0	63	T	4	T	8	59

BANANA YOGURT DELIGHT

Fabulous!

2		bananas, very ripe
1	C	low-fat yogurt*
¾	C	instant rolled oats
garnish		cinnamon

STRAWBERRY PLANT

1. Peel and chop the bananas.

2. Blend bananas and yogurt until smooth.

3. Stir in oatmeal. Serve chilled in individual glasses, topped with banana slices or cinnamon.

Serves 4

See "Cooking Methods" section

	RCU	FU	Cal	%Ft	P	F	C	Na
Per Serving	0	0	136	13	4	2	24	38

RICE PUDDING

This is just as delicious warm as it is chilled.

2		egg whites
2	C	skim milk*
2	T	sugar
1 ½	C	brown rice,* cooked
1	tsp.	vanilla
¼	C	raisins
1	dash	cinnamon

VANILLA

Gifford's Alternatives: Add:
| 1 | tsp. | Gifford's Dessert Spice® |

1. Beat egg whites until stiff. Add milk and sugar.

2. Stir in rice, vanilla, and raisins. Pour into a nonstick* baking pan. Garnish with cinnamon.

3. Bake at 325° for 25 minutes. Stir and add more cinnamon, if desired. Continue baking for 20 to 25 more minutes. Garnish with a few raisins and serve.

Serves 6

* See "Cooking Methods" section

	RCU	FU	Cal	%Ft	P	F	C	Na
Per Serving	1	0	123	T	5	T	25	57

A "BERRY" SPECIAL TREAT

Yummy!

2	C	brown rice,* cooked and cooled
1	C	crushed pineapple
½	C	dates, chopped
2	T	brown sugar*
½	C	Whipped Topping (p. 357)
4	C	fresh berries

1. Combine rice, pineapple, dates, and brown sugar. Chill.

2. Serve in 4 decorative bowls. Top each serving with a dollop of Whipped Topping and 1 cup fresh berries.

Serves 4

* See "Cooking Methods" section

	RCU	FU	Cal	%Ft	P	F	C	Na
Per Serving	1	0	313	4	7	2	66	60

TAPIOCA PUDDING

This recipe can be made without orange juice by replacing the juice with a half cup of skim milk. Then add any fresh fruit in place of the orange segments.

1 ½	C	skim milk*
1	T	sugar*
3	T	quick-cooking tapioca
2		egg whites
½	C	orange juice
½	tsp.	vanilla
½	C	orange segments, diced OR
½	C	dates, quartered

ORANGES

1. Combine milk, sugar, and tapioca in a saucepan. Let stand 5 minutes.

2. Beat egg whites until stiff. Set aside.

3. Bring tapioca mixture to boil over medium heat, stirring constantly. Add orange juice.

4. Cool, stirring occasionally. Add vanilla. Fold in egg whites and diced orange segments. Chill and serve.

5. When dates are used, omit sugar and orange segments. Add dates to boiling tapioca mixture BEFORE orange juice is added. Cook about 6 minutes. Add orange juice and proceed as above.

Serves 6

* See "Cooking Methods" section

With oranges	RCU	FU	Cal	%Ft	P	F	C	Na
Per Serving	0	0	47	T	4	T	9	41

With dates	RCU	FU	Cal	%Ft	P	F	C	Na
Per Serving	0	0	95	T	3	T	20	41

BREAD PUDDING

This dessert is nutritious as well as tasty.

3		slices whole wheat bread, day old and cubed			
½	C	raisins	1	T	sugar*
2	C	skim milk*	1	tsp.	cinnamon
3		egg whites, slightly beaten	1	tsp.	vanilla

Gifford's Alternatives: Add: 1   tsp.   *Gifford's Dessert Spice®*

1. Mix bread cubes and raisins in a 1 ½-quart nonstick* baking pan.

2. Combine milk, egg whites, sugar, cinnamon, and vanilla. Pour over bread and raisins. Stir.

3. Place in oven with a shallow pan of water. Bake at 350° for 45 to 55 minutes OR until an inserted knife comes out clean. Serve warm.

Serves 6

* See "Cooking Methods" section

	RCU	FU	Cal	%Ft	P	F	C	Na
Per Serving	0	0	113	T	6	T	21	130

WHIPPED TOPPING

You'll be surprised at how stiff this low-fat topping becomes because of the egg whites.

2		egg whites	to taste		vanilla extract
1	C	ice water	2	T	sugar OR fruit juice
1	C	nonfat dry milk*			concentrate*

1. Everything must be ice cold! Chill a deep metal bowl and electric mixer beaters in the freezer for 30 minutes.
2. Beat egg whites until stiff peaks form.
3. Add ice water, dry milk, and vanilla. Beat 10 minutes.
4. Add sugar or fruit juice concentrate, if desired.
5. Beat another 10 minutes or until stiff. Use within the hour.

Serves 12

* See "Cooking Methods" section

	RCU	FU	Cal	%Ft	P	F	C	Na
Per Serving	0	0	49	T	4	T	6	63

CREPES

Preparing this recipe two hours before cooking allows time for the flour particles to expand. This will ensure tender crepes.

4		egg whites
1 ½	C	skim milk*
1	C	whole wheat flour
1		egg yolk

1. Beat egg whites until they stand in stiff peaks. Set aside.

2. Whisk remaining ingredients together. Fold in egg whites.

3. If there is time, allow batter to sit in the refrigerator for 2 hours before cooking.

4. Heat nonstick* crepe pan to 400°. Spoon 2 tablespoons batter into pan. Tilt to thinly coat pan. When cooked on one side, carefully peel crepe from pan and turn over. Cook on second side and remove from pan.

5. Place squares of waxed paper between finished crepes to prevent sticking together. Cover to keep warm.

6. Fill these with yogurt, fresh fruit, Whipped Topping (p. 357), or other low-fat fillings. These are perfect to serve as an elegant dessert or to guests on social occasions. They are also nice for breakfast.

7. Hint: Crepes may be prepared a day ahead and frozen with waxed paper between each crepe. This will save time when you need to use them. Allow them to thaw at room temperature. Use as you would freshly made crepes.

Yield: 14 6-inch crepes

* See "Cooking Methods" section

	RCU	FU	Cal	%Ft	P	F	C	Na
Per Crepe	0	0	42	12	3	T	6	22

RAISIN CARROT CAKE

Add ¼ cup of drained chunky pineapple to this recipe for a delightful change.

2	C	whole wheat flour
1 ½	tsp.	baking powder
1 ½	tsp.	baking soda
1	tsp.	cinnamon
3	med.	carrots
½	C	orange juice concentrate*
⅓	C	oil*
2		eggs
½	C	raisins

Gifford's Alternatives: Add:
| 1 | tsp. | Gifford's Dessert Spice® |
| ¼ | tsp. | peach juice concentrate |

1. Combine flour, baking powder, baking soda, and cinnamon. Set aside.

2. Grate carrots in food processor or dice by hand. Combine orange juice concentrate, oil, and eggs with grated carrots.

3. Add carrot mixture to dry ingredients. Mix well. Stir in raisins.

4. Pour batter into nonstick* 9" x 13" baking pan. Bake at 350° for 25 to 30 minutes. Cool. Cut into 16 pieces. Serve.

Serves 16

* See "Cooking Methods" section

	RCU	FU	Cal	%Ft	P	F	C	Na
Per Serving	T	1	143	37	3	6	19	143

APPLESAUCE COOKIES

What a sweet treat!

2		eggs	2	C	whole wheat flour
2	T	oil*	1	tsp.	baking powder
1	C	applesauce,	1 ½	tsp.	cinnamon
		unsweetened	½	C	rolled oats
1 ¼	C	apple juice concentrate*	½	C	raisins

Gifford's Alternatives: Add:

½	tsp.	*vanilla*
1	T	*chopped walnuts, optional*
1	T	*Butter Buds® Sprinkles*
2	tsp.	*Gifford's Dessert Spice®*

1. Combine eggs, oil, applesauce, and apple juice in a bowl. Mix well.

2. Add flour, baking powder, and cinnamon. Stir in oatmeal and raisins.

3. Drop by teaspoonfuls onto nonstick* baking sheet. Bake at 350° for 7 to 10 minutes.

Yield: 36 cookies

* See "Cooking Methods" section

	RCU	FU	Cal	%Ft	P	F	C	Na
Per Cookie	T	T	55	33	2	2	9	24

GINGER SNAPS

This soft ginger snap cookie is wonderful, but limit yourself to two per day.

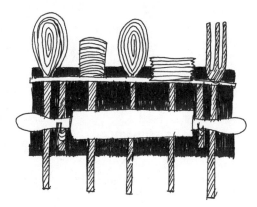

¼	C	light molasses
¼	C	oil*
¼	C	honey
⅓	C	hot water
½	tsp.	baking soda
1	tsp.	ground ginger
¼	tsp.	ground cloves
¼	tsp.	nutmeg
⅛	tsp.	allspice
1½	C	whole wheat flour

1. Combine molasses, oil, honey, water, and baking soda.

2. Stir all the spices into the whole wheat flour and add to molasses mixture. Blend well.

3. Chill dough half an hour. Drop dough by teaspoonfuls onto nonstick* baking sheet, then flatten with the bottom of a glass. Bake at 375° for 10 minutes. Serve.

Yield: 25 small cookies

* See "Cooking Methods" section

	RCU	FU	Cal	%Ft	P	F	C	Na
Per Cookie	0	0	62	33	1	2	10	20

BANANA OATMEAL COOKIES

Limit yourself to two cookies per day.

BANANAS

¼	C	oil*
½	C	brown sugar*
2		egg whites
1½	tsp.	vanilla
3		bananas, mashed
1	C	whole wheat flour
½	tsp.	ground cloves
1	tsp.	baking soda
½	tsp.	salt
1	tsp.	cinnamon
¼	tsp.	nutmeg
3	C	rolled oats
1	C	raisins OR
¾	C	dates, chopped

1. Mix oil, sugar, egg, vanilla, and bananas in a large bowl.

2. Stir in flour, cloves, soda, salt, cinnamon, nutmeg, and rolled oats.

3. Add raisins or dates and drop by rounded teaspoonsful 1 inch apart onto a nonstick* baking sheet.

4. Bake at 375° for 12 to 15 minutes. Enjoy! Store in airtight container.

Yield: 50 cookies

* See "Cooking Methods" section

	RCU	FU	Cal	%Ft	P	F	C	Na
Per Cookie	0	0	65	16	2	2	11	30

NATURALLY SWEET APPLESAUCE

Applesauce can also be made by cooking apples and then blending them into a purée with a blender. Season and chill. This applesauce can be frozen or canned for use throughout the year.

4	lg.	apples, peeled	1	tsp.	lemon juice
½	C	water	¼	tsp.	cinnamon

1. Blend all ingredients in a blender at medium speed until smooth, about 1 minute. Serve chilled.

2. For a "frothy" variation, fold 2 stiffly beaten egg whites into the applesauce and serve in a decorative glass with a sprinkle of cinnamon on top.

Serves 4

	RCU	FU	Cal	%Ft	P	F	C	Na
Per Serving	0	0	70	T	T	T	18	1

TORTILLA TRIANGLES

These make a crunchy taco salad or a fun snack. Sprinkle with chili powder, garlic powder, or cumin for different flavors.

12   corn   tortillas

1. Leave tortillas whole for tostadas or cut into 6 pie-shaped pieces for chips.

2. Place on nonstick* baking sheet and bake at 300° for 8 to 10 minutes.

3. WATCH CLOSELY! These burn easily. Cool before serving. Store in air-tight container.

Serves 6

* See "Cooking Methods" section

	RCU	FU	Cal	%Ft	P	F	C	Na
Per Serving	0	0	110	16	2	2	20	316

FRESH FRUIT FONDUE

A sprinkle of lemon juice will prevent cut fruit from turning dark.

1	16 oz. can	peach halves, juice-packed
1	tsp.	cornstarch*
¼	tsp.	cinnamon
⅛	tsp.	allspice
1	tsp.	lemon juice
½	tsp.	vanilla
1	C	cantaloupe, cubed
1	sm.	apple, cored and wedged
¾	C	fresh strawberries
½	sm.	banana, cut into chunks

Gifford's Alternatives: Add:

2	T	peach juice concentrate
½	tsp.	Gifford's Dessert Spice®

1. Blend undrained peaches, cornstarch, cinnamon, allspice, and lemon juice until smooth. Transfer to a saucepan. Cook, stirring until thickened. Add vanilla.

2. Pour into a fondue pot to keep warm. Dip cantaloupe, apple, strawberry, or banana pieces into warm fondue and enjoy.

Serves 5

* See "Cooking Methods" section

	RCU	FU	Cal	%Ft	P	F	C	Na
Per Serving	0	0	77	T	T	T	19	6

For low-sugar desserts, try Banana Pineapple Pudding (p. 352), Melon Balls in Lemon Sause (p. 365), or Fresh Strawberry Pie (p. 349). They are scrumptious!

BAKED APPLES

Pour chilled evaporated skim milk over hot apples for a delightful change.

| 6 | | apples | ⅓ | C | apple juice |
| 6 | T | raisins | 1 | dash | cinnamon |

1. Wash, core, and halve apples. Place in glass baking dish. Stuff apples with 1 tablespoon raisins and sprinkle with apple juice or fill cavity with applesauce.
2. Cover the bottom of the dish with ¼ inch water.
3. Sprinkle apples with cinnamon.
4. Cook, covered, in oven at 400° until apples are tender, 30 to 60 minutes. Serve hot.

Serves 6

	RCU	FU	Cal	%Ft	P	F	C	Na
Per Serving	0	0	116	T	T	T	28	2

MELON BALLS IN LEMON SAUCE

Beautiful to behold. Even better to eat.

2	C	ripe melon, honeydew or cantaloupe
2		lemons
1	T	sugar*

1. The melon must be absolutely ripe for this dessert. Halve it and remove the seeds. Using a melon baller, make as many melon balls as possible. Chill them thoroughly while making the sauce.

2. Grate the rind of the lemons into a small pan. Squeeze the juice from the 2 lemons and measure it, adding enough water to make ⅔ cup. Add this to the rind, with sugar and remaining melon pieces that have not been balled. Bring to boil and allow to simmer for 5 minutes.

3. Blend this mixture, chill it, and put it in the bottom of a glass dish. Top it with melon balls, a sprig of mint, and a lemon slice. Serve.

Serves 4

	RCU	FU	Cal	%Ft	P	F	C	Na
Per Serving	0	0	49	T	T	T	15	12

For special occasions, try Artic Sunshine (p. 367), Sparkling Grape Soda (p. 366), Hot Holiday Cider (p. 373), Grapefruit Razzle Dazzle (p. 366), or Frozen Fruit Slush (p. 367).

GRAPEFRUIT RAZZLE DAZZLE

This is just as good with orange juice or pineapple juice as with grapefruit juice.

⅓	C	frozen strawberries, unsweetened
1	C	grapefruit juice, unsweetened
1 ½	C	club soda

1. Blend strawberries and fruit juice in a blender until smooth. Pour into pitcher.

2. Pour club soda slowly down the side of pitcher and stir gently.

3. Serve over crushed ice.

Serves 3

	RCU	FU	Cal	%Ft	P	F	C	Na
Per Serving	0	0	36	T	T	T	8	T

SPARKLING GRAPE SODA

Fill grape juice with bubbles and children will drink it like pop.

1	T	lemon juice
2	C	grape juice, unsweetened
2	C	club soda

1. Combine lemon juice and grape juice in a pitcher.

2. Slowly pour club soda down the side of a pitcher. Stir gently.

3. Serve over crushed ice.

Serves 3

	RCU	FU	Cal	%Ft	P	F	C	Na
Per Serving	0	0	63	T	T	T	14	T

FROZEN FRUIT SLUSH

This healthful treat makes a versatile snack for you and your children. For an unusual twist, try this for breakfast.

| 3 | | bananas, ripe | 1 | C | orange juice |
| ½ | C | lemon juice | 4 | C | pineapple juice |

1. Blend all ingredients in a blender until smooth, and set aside.

2. Combine crushed ice and water to the desired consistency ending up with a total of 5 cups.

3. Add the blended fruit juices and serve.

4. OR freeze the blended fruit juices in a wide unbreakable bowl or pan. Scrape frozen fruit mixture out with an ice cream scoop or spoon and put it into a glass. Pour clear diet soda over the top to achieve the desired consistency and serve. OR freeze into popsicles.

Serves 12

	RCU	FU	Cal	%Ft	P	F	C	Na
Per Serving	0	0	82	T	T	T	20	1

ARCTIC SUNSHINE

Milk can be frozen in an ice cube tray and these cubes used in place of ice. This drink can also be made with other frozen juice concentrates such as grape or apple.

1	6 oz. can	orange juice concentrate*	1		egg
			5		ice cubes, crushed
2 ¼	C	skim milk*			

1. Blend orange juice, ¼ cup milk, and egg until smooth.

2. Add crushed ice. Fill blender with remaining milk. Blend briefly.

3. Pour into glasses and serve immediately.

Serves 3

* See "Cooking Methods" section

	RCU	FU	Cal	%Ft	P	F	C	Na
Per Serving	1	0	210	9	10	2	38	107

FRESH FRUIT FLIP-OUT

A blender and crushed ice turn fresh fruit into a sherbet-like dessert.

1	C	orange juice
1		banana
1	C	strawberries OR raspberries
		crushed ice

1. Blend all ingredients in blender until smooth, except ice.

2. Add crushed ice and blend briefly. Serve.

Serves 2

	RCU	FU	Cal	%Ft	P	F	C	Na
Per Serving	0	0	135	3	2	T	31	3

PINEAPPLE BANANA TREAT

Delicious!

3		eggs	2 ½	C	whole wheat flour
⅓	C	oil*	2	tsp.	baking powder
1	C	pineapple juice	1	tsp.	baking soda
		(drain chunks)	1	tsp.	cinnamon
1	C	mashed banana	1	20 oz.	pineapple chunks,
				can	juice reserved

Gifford's Alternatives: Add:

1	tsp.	*banana flavor extract*
1	tsp.	*pineapple flavor extract*
½	tsp.	*vanilla*
1	T	*Butter Buds® Sprinkles*
1 ½	tsp.	*Gifford's Dessert Spice®*

1. Mix eggs, oil, pineapple juice, and banana in a bowl.

2. Add flour, baking powder, baking soda, and cinnamon. Mix well. Stir in drained pineapple.

3. Pour into a nonstick* 9" x 13" baking pan. Bake at 350° for 20 to 25 minutes. Cool and cut into 16 bars. Enjoy!

Yield: 16 bars

See "Cooking Methods" section

	RCU	FU	Cal	%Ft	P	F	C	Na
Per Bar	0	0	145	37	4	6	21	93

FROTHY FRUIT FLUFF

Be creative! Fold cottage cheese or pieces of fruit such as pineapple, strawberries, or raspberries into this whipped fruit gelatin and enjoy the wide variety of possibilities. It makes good pie filling. Your children will love it!

1	env.	unflavored gelatin
½	C	cold water
1 ½	C	fruit juice (apple, orange, grape, etc.)
2	T	sugar*
1		egg white
1	C	low-fat yogurt*

1. Sprinkle gelatin into cold water. Add fruit juice and sugar. Boil until gelatin and sugar are dissolved. Cool in refrigerator.

2. When gelatin is partially set, beat egg white into stiff peaks. Set aside.

3. Whip partially set gelatin with an electric mixer until light and fluffy.

4. Fold in egg white and yogurt. Chill in parfait glasses, a pie shell (see index), or freeze in paper cups with a popsicle stick.

Serves 6

See "Cooking Methods" section

	RCU	FU	Cal	%Ft	P	F	C	Na
Per Serving	0	0	61	10	3	1	11	22

SIMPLE SOFT ICE CREAM

This can be made into a milk shake by blending with crushed ice and serving immediately. Try blending in a ripe banana for a delicious milk shake.

1	C	nonfat dry milk*
3	C	water
2	T	sugar*
to taste		vanilla extract

1. Blend all ingredients in a blender until smooth. For a variety of flavors, replace vanilla extract with banana, cherry, or maple extract.

2. Freeze in a shallow pan.

3. Just before serving, thaw slightly and break into small chunks. Whip until soft. Spoon into 4 dishes. Top with fresh fruit and enjoy.

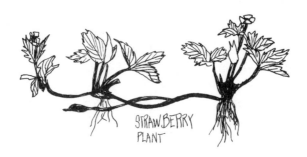

STRAWBERRY PLANT

VARIATION: FUDGESICLES

1	recipe	Simple Soft Ice Cream
to taste		artificially sweetened chocolate drink powder

1. Stir artificially sweetened chocolate drink powder into Simple Soft Ice Cream recipe. Pour into paper cups with popsicle sticks and freeze. Serve to eager children.

Serves 4

* See "Cooking Methods" section

	RCU	FU	Cal	%Ft	P	F	C	Na
Per Serving	1	0	143	T	12	0	18	177

FROZEN FRUIT SHAKE

Do you love ice cream? This thick, icy treat will thrill you.

| 1 | C | skim milk* |
| 2 | C | frozen peaches |

1. Pour milk into blender.

2. Add slightly thawed frozen fruit slowly.

3. Blend until fruit is thoroughly mixed. HINT: You may prefer to use milk frozen in ice cube trays and fresh fruit. It will be easier on your blender. Serve immediately.

Serves 2
* See "Cooking Methods" section

	RCU	FU	Cal	%Ft	P	F	C	Na
Per Serving	0	0	75	T	5	T	15	63

FRUIT SNOW

This recipe has many variations. Replace grated pears with other grated or chopped fruits or one-and-one-half cups fruit juice, and enjoy a wide variety of fruit snows.

1	env.	unflavored gelatin	1/4	C	lemon juice
2	C	raw pears, peeled	2		egg whites
		and grated	2	T	sugar

1. Sprinkle gelatin into 1/2 cup water. Heat until dissolved. Cool slightly.

2. Combine pears and lemon juice and add to gelatin.

3. Beat egg whites until foamy. Add sugar and beat until stiff peaks form.

4. Fold in grated pear mixture.

5. Garnish with fresh fruit. Serve cold.

Serves 8

	RCU	FU	Cal	%Ft	P	F	C	Na
Per Serving	0	0	54	T	1	T	13	8

PINEAPPLE SHERBET

Janice Bohling

Pineapple can be replaced with strawberries, raspberries, peaches, or pears.

1½	C	buttermilk*
1	C	crushed pineapple, drained
1	tsp.	vanilla
½	tsp.	lemon juice
2	T	sugar*

1. Blend all ingredients in a blender.

2. Freeze in a shallow pan or in paper cups with popsicle sticks.

3. Before serving, break into pieces and whip until soft. Spoon into dishes and top with a spoonful of crushed pineapple before serving.

Serves 3

* See "Cooking Methods" section

	RCU	FU	Cal	%Ft	P	F	C	Na
Per Serving	1	0	103	T	5	T	21	154

CRUNCHY TOMATO TEASER

Sydette Parent

Serve this treat hot or cold. If served hot, do not allow celery or onion to cook. They must remain crisp.

¼	C	celery, chopped
2		green onions and tops
1	tsp.	green pepper, chopped
1	T	zucchini, chopped
2½	C	tomato juice
1½	tsp.	soy sauce
1½	tsp.	Worcestershire sauce
¼	tsp.	red hot taco sauce

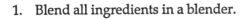

TOMATOES

1. Finely chop vegetables.

2. Combine all ingredients. Heat or chill. Serve.

Serves 5

	RCU	FU	Cal	%Ft	P	F	C	Na
Per Serving	0	0	28	5	1	T	6	392

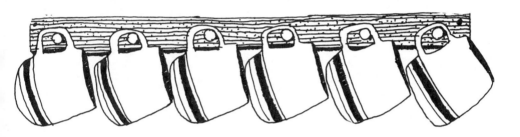

HOT HOLIDAY CIDER

This drink will warm up holiday parties during the snowy Christmas season.

3	C	apple cider	
1	C	water	
1		cinnamon stick	
½	tsp.	whole cloves	
1		orange, sliced	

1. Combine cider and water. Stir in cinnamon stick and cloves.

2. Simmer for 10 minutes. Strain.

3. Serve hot. Garnish with orange slices and cinnamon stick.

Serves 8

	RCU	FU	Cal	%Ft	P	F	C	Na
Per Serving	0	0	50	T	T	T	12	1

CRUNCHY MUNCHIES

This can be made in a microwave by cooking at full power for six minutes. Stir every two minutes.

1	C	Cheerios
1	C	Wheat Chex
2	C	Rice Chex
1	C	Corn Chex
2	C	pretzel sticks
1/3	C	apple juice
4	tsp.	Worcestershire sauce
1/2	tsp.	garlic powder
1	tsp.	onion powder

GARLIC

1. Combine dry cereals to make 5 cups and add pretzel sticks.

2. Combine apple juice, Worcestershire sauce, and seasonings. Toss with the cereals.

3. Place in a shallow nonstick* baking pan. Bake at 275° for 1 hour. Stir every 10 minutes. Cool before serving.

Serves 8

*See "Cooking Methods" section

	RCU	FU	Cal	%Ft	P	F	C	Na
Per Serving	0	0	90	T	2	T	32	222

BIZARRE
BAZAAR

Necessity is the mother of invention.

BIZARRE BAZAAR

Do you enjoy the unusual? Do you like to try new ideas? Do you like a bit of adventure in your life? If you do, then this is the section for you. Bizarre bazaar is a collection of a few delicious, nutritious, low-fat recipes which are unique. Take a look through these and then have a little fun by making them for your family. Don't be shy! Give them a try!

WHEAT GRASS

Keep growing, clipping, and eating wheat grass as long as it tastes sweet. If it becomes bitter, replant your wheat.

1. Plant whole wheat in a flower pot about ¼ inch deep. Keep watered.

2. When wheat has grown into a very thin grass blade, clip with scissors.

3. Use wheat grass in salads. Sprouting wheat increases vitamin C by 600 percent. All B-complex vitamins also increase dramatically.

EGGPLANT AND CRACKED WHEAT SALAD

Sydette Parent

Serve for supper.

EGGPLANT

1	lb.	eggplant
3	cloves	garlic, minced
1	T	lemon juice
¼	tsp.	chili powder
⅛	tsp.	black pepper
1	C	cracked wheat, cooked with ⅛ tsp. salt
¼	C	low-fat yogurt*
2		tomatoes, sliced
1		lemon, wedged

1. Wash eggplant and puncture with fork every few inches, on all sides. Bake at 350° for 1 ½ hours, until very soft. Cool.

2. Cut eggplant in half. Remove "meat" and chop into ½-inch pieces.

3. Combine remaining ingredients except tomatoes and lemon wedges with eggplant in a large bowl. Chill.

4. Place ⅓ cup mound of eggplant mixture on top of tomato slice. Tuck a lemon wedge on the side and serve.

Serves 8

* See "Cooking Methods" section

	RCU	FU	Cal	%Ft	P	F	C	Na
Per Serving	0	0	41	7	2	T	8	36

POTATO BEET SALAD

Joyce Nixon
Mariteresa Bergerson

This is a colorful variation of potato salad. Great for your next summer outing since there is no mayonnaise to spoil in the heat.

4	C	potatoes, cooked and sliced
2	C	green beans, cooked
1	C	beets, cooked
½	C	celery, sliced
½	C	green onions, sliced

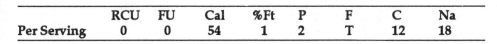

BEETS

1. Gently mix all ingredients.

2. Chill and serve.

Serves 10

	RCU	FU	Cal	%Ft	P	F	C	Na
Per Serving	0	0	54	1	2	T	12	18

ESSENE BREAD

This bread takes its name from an ancient brotherhood in Palestine.

| 3 | C | sprouted wheat* |
| 1/4 | C | raisins |

1. Grind sprouts in meat grinder. Add raisins.

2. Form into a loaf on a nonstick* baking sheet.

3. Bake at 225° for 2-2 1/2 hours. Cool before serving.

Yield: 8 slices

* See "Cooking Methods" section

	RCU	FU	Cal	%Ft	P	F	C	Na
Per Serving	0	0	241	4	7	1	52	1

CREAMY COTTAGE CHEESE SANDWICH

A creamy, crunchy sandwich.

1 1/2	C	low-fat cottage cheese,* dry curd
1 1/2	T	nonfat dry milk*
2	T	water
1	tsp.	lemon juice
1/2	C	mushrooms, chopped
1	T	onion, chopped
1/3	C	carrot, chopped
1/4	C	celery, chopped
1	dash	garlic powder
1	dash	Worcestershire sauce

1. Place the cottage cheese, nonfat dry milk, water, and lemon juice in a blender and blend until smooth.

2. Scrape out of blender and add vegetables, garlic powder, and Worcestershire sauce.

3. Spread ½ cup of mixture on 2 slices of whole wheat bread to make a sandwich. Experiment with other breads such as rye or pumpernickel. This is delicious with lettuce and tomatoes, too. Enjoy!

Serves 5

*See "Cooking Methods" section

	RCU	FU	Cal	%Ft	P	F	C	Na
Per Serving	0	0	62	8	12	T	4	25

UNUSUAL OATMEAL SOUP

This is actually just a vegetable soup with oatmeal.

1		onion, sliced
½	C	mushrooms, sliced
2	cloves	garlic, minced
1	C	rolled oats
7	C	chicken stock*
2 ½	C	tomatoes,* stewed
to taste		seasoning without salt*
1	C	skim milk*

Gifford's Alternatives: Add:
1 ¼   T   *Gifford's Basic Spice®*
Top off with Butter Buds® Sprinkles

1. Sauté* onion, mushrooms, and garlic until tender.

2. Stir in oats, stock, and tomatoes.

3. Bring to a boil, reduce heat, and simmer for 5 minutes.

4. Season and stir in milk. Serve hot.

Serves 8

* See "Cooking Methods" section

	RCU	FU	Cal	%Ft	P	F	C	Na
Per Serving	0	0	82	8	5	T	14	375

CREAMY SPROUT SOUP

Deliciously different.

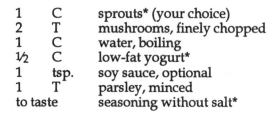

1	C	sprouts* (your choice)
2	T	mushrooms, finely chopped
1	C	water, boiling
½	C	low-fat yogurt*
1	tsp.	soy sauce, optional
1	T	parsley, minced
to taste		seasoning without salt*

1. Add sprouts and mushrooms to boiling water.

2. Lower heat and simmer for 3 to 5 minutes.

3. Stir in yogurt and seasoning. Serve hot.

Serves 4

See "Cooking Methods" section

	RCU	FU	Cal	%Ft	P	F	C	Na
Per Serving	0	0	38	12	3	1	6	130

WHAT A "COOL" SURPRISE!

Sound unusual? Well, try it and you'll be pleasantly surprised.

1	C	tomato soup, condensed
6	oz.	cranberry juice cocktail
6	oz.	water
1	tsp.	lemon juice
6	T	low-fat yogurt*

1. Combine all ingredients except yogurt.

2. Chill.

3. Serve in glass bowls with a tablespoon of yogurt on top.

Serves 6

See "Cooking Methods" section

	RCU	FU	Cal	%Ft	P	F	C	Na
Per Serving	0	0	48	19	1	1	9	180

WATERMELON SOUP

Colorful, delicious, and fun for company on a summer afternoon.

2 ½	C	chicken stock*
¾	C	chicken, cooked and diced
½	C	mushrooms, sliced
½	C	bamboo shoots
½	C	lean ham, cooked and diced
¾	C	green peas
1	4 lb.	watermelon

1. Bring chicken stock to a boil. Add chicken and simmer for 10 minutes.

2. Add mushrooms, bamboo shoots, ham, and peas.

3. Cut the top from the melon. Scoop out the seeds and some of the pulp. Pour the soup into the melon and replace the top.

4. Steam the melon in or over a large pan of boiling water for about 1 ½ hours or until melon is cooked.

5. To serve the soup, place the melon on the table and scoop out watermelon along with the soup. Cut down rind as the level of the soup is lowered.

Serves 6

See "Cooking Methods" section

	RCU	FU	Cal	%Ft	P	F	C	Na
Per Serving	0	0	147	15	11	2	18	290

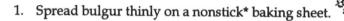

CRUNCHY BULGUR SNACKS

This will help when you get the "munchies."

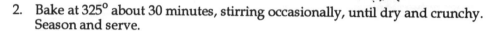

| 2 | C | Basic Bulgur (p. 273) |
| to taste | | seasoning without salt* |

1. Spread bulgur thinly on a nonstick* baking sheet.

2. Bake at 325° about 30 minutes, stirring occasionally, until dry and crunchy. Season and serve.

Serves 8

* See "Cooking Methods" section

	RCU	FU	Cal	%Ft	P	F	C	Na
Per Serving	0	0	50	4	2	T	11	T

WALKING ON AIR

Edward Parent

This fluffy, puffy combination can be eaten for breakfast or a snack.

1	6 oz. carton	low-fat plain yogurt*
1	tsp.	sugar*
1-2	C	puffed wheat

1. Pour yogurt into a bowl and stir in sugar.

2. Add puffed cereal and stir gently. Eat immediately.

Serves 1

* See "Cooking Methods" section

	RCU	FU	Cal	%Ft	P	F	C	Na
Per Serving	0	0	328	8	10	3	36	98

ONION PIE

Unusual and unusually savory.

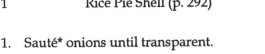

2	C	onion wedges
½	C	water
2	T	cornstarch*
2	C	chicken stock*
to taste		seasoning without salt*
1		Rice Pie Shell (p. 292)

1. Sauté* onions until transparent.

2. Add water to onions and bring to a boil.

3. Whisk cornstarch into cool chicken stock. Add to onions. Heat until thickened. Season to taste.

4. Fill Rice Pie Shell and bake at 350° for 25 minutes. Serve.

Serves 6

* See "Cooking Methods" section

	RCU	FU	Cal	%Ft	P	F	C	Na
Per Serving	0	0	137	4	5	1	28	146

APPENDIX 1

COOKING METHODS

Apple Juice Concentrate, see "Fruit Juice Concentrate"

Artificial Sweeteners, see "Sweeteners"

BAKING POWDER

Baking powder substitute can be made from ½ teaspoon cream of tartar plus ¼ teaspoon baking soda for each teaspoon baking powder.

BEANS

Beans, also see "Soybeans"

Beans are convenient, easy to store, and nutritious. They provide an inexpensive source of protein. They are a staple food for more than half the world's population. But some people are discouraged from using beans because of the lengthy cooking time. Following are several cooking methods for beans. Hopefully, you will find one of these methods that will work for you.

The first step in preparing beans is to rinse them in cold water. Then sort them before cooking by removing any foreign matter such as dirt or rocks, beans that are wrinkled, too large, too small, or with holes in them.

The next step is to soak the beans. This is not necessary if you plan to cook them all day but soaking is usually more convenient. Soaking also shortens the cooking time and removes some of the water-soluble chemical compounds which cause flatulence or gas. Beans will double in size as a result of soaking. We will describe both the long and short methods of soaking.

The long method takes less effort but more time. Cover the sorted beans with water and allow them to soak overnight, about 8 to 10 hours, at room temperature. Use 6 to 8 cups water for 2 cups dry beans. If you work, start the process in the morning and they will be ready to cook when you come home. Discard the water after soaking. Most would prefer the loss of some nutrients over the discomforts of gas.

The short method is more convenient for some cooks. Cover beans with water (2 cups beans with 6 to 8 cups water). Bring them to a boil. Boil for 3 minutes. Remove from heat, cover, and soak for 1 hour. Discard the water.

Cooking the beans can be accomplished by a variety of methods.

No-Soak Method: Add twice as much water as the recipe calls for to dry, sorted beans. Bring them to a boil. Cover and reduce heat to maintain a simmer. This method takes 2 to 3 hours. You will need to watch them carefully and add more water when needed.

Stove-Top Method: Use heavy metal pots of stainless steel, cast aluminum, or cast iron. The pot must have a tight fitting lid. Cover soaked beans with water, bring to a boil, cover, and reduce heat. Simmer until beans are tender, 30 minutes to 3 hours, depending on the type of beans.

The Pressure Cooker Method: Combine beans and water in the pressure cooker (do not fill more than half full) OR combine the beans and water in a stainless steel bowl and set it in about 3 inches of water in the pressure cooker. Follow directions for the use of your pressure cooker and cook soaked beans for 5 to 8 minutes. If you live more than 3,500 feet above sea level, double the cooking time in the pressure cooker. This is the fastest cooking method but it requires your constant attention because of the potential danger if the pressure cooker is misused.

Oven Method: This method is used in combination with other methods to make baked beans. Be sure to use cooked beans which are not over-cooked. Do not use metal baking pans; use glass, ceramic, or earthenware. Combine ingredients, cover, and bake for 1½ hours at 300°. To brown beans, remove the cover and bake 15 to 30 minutes longer.

Crock Pot Method: This method is not as easy as it might seem. You will need to experiment with times and settings. Try cooking soaked beans on **high** for 2 to 3 hours and then continue cooking on **low** for 6 to 8 hours. Check during the cooking time on **high** to make sure the beans are continually covered with water.

Whatever method is most convenient for you, simply cook the beans until they are tender. Do not overcook. Most soaked beans require 1½ hours cooking time on the stove top or 5 to 8 minutes in a pressure cooker. That includes black, garbanzo, great northern, pea, small white, pink, pinto, red, or kidney beans. Black-eyed peas can be cooked on the stove top, unsoaked, for 1½ hours but not in a pressure cooker. Lentils and split peas can also be cooked unsoaked and require only 30 to 45 minutes cooking time on the stove top. They cannot be cooked in a pressure cooker. Lima beans do not work well in a pressure cooker, either, but soaked lima beans will cook in 45 to 60 minutes on the stove top. HINT: High-acid foods, such as tomatoes, tend to slow the cooking time. If you need to add vinegar or tomatoes, be sure to add them near the end of the cooking time.

Microwave ovens are not satisfactory for cooking beans. But they are wonderful for thawing frozen cooked beans, finishing soups, casseroles, or reheating bean dishes.

Cooked beans store well. They will keep in an airtight container in the refrigerator for at least four days. In fact, bean soups and casseroles actually taste better the second day because the flavors and seasonings continue to blend. Beans also freeze well. You may want to undercook them a little if you are planning to freeze them but it isn't necessary. Thaw beans slowly in the refrigerator overnight or at room temperature. Then simmer until warm.

Beef Bouillon, see "Beef Stock"

BEEF STOCK

These sources of beef stock are interchangeable.

1. HOMEMADE beef stock is made by cooking beef chunks or a beef bone in about 2 quarts of water, so that the meat is covered. Onions and celery can be added to the meat as it cooks. Bring it to a boil, then simmer for 2 to 3 hours. Remove from heat, strain, and cool. When stock is completely cool, remove all remaining fat from the top of the stock. Store stock in refrigerator or freezer.

2. CANNED beef bouillon or beef stock is convenient and low in fat but it is high in sodium (900 mg per 4 oz.).

3. BOUILLON granules or cubes are low in fat but high in sodium (400 mg in 8 oz.). Dissolve 1 cube or 1 teaspoon of bouillon granules in 1 cup boiling water. It is possible to buy low-sodium bouillon. HINT: If you must use several cups of canned broth or bouillon cubes, dilute them (2 cans water to 1 can broth or 2 cups water to 1 cube bouillon). This will weaken the flavor a little but it will reduce the amount of fat and sodium by half.

BROWN LEAN HAMBURGER

Always buy the leanest ground beef possible. Remember to keep individual serving sizes at 2 to 4 ounces. Cook the hamburger in your microwave oven or in a nonstick frying pan. Stir so that it cooks evenly and becomes crumbly. When it is completely browned, drain off all the grease. Pour the hamburger into a strainer and rinse it in very hot water. Allow it to drain. Blot any remaining grease off the meat with a paper towel.

Brown Sugar, see "Sweeteners"

BUTTER BUDS®, MOLLY McBUTTER®, AND OTHERS

These are brand names for no-fat, low-calorie butter-flavored granules. They are made from natural ingredients. Since they are fat-free, they cannot be used for frying or baking, but they can be used to give cooked foods a buttery flavor. Sprinkle them dry over mashed potatoes, popcorn, pasta, or vegetables. Use them in liquid form and pour over cooked vegetables, potatoes, fish, rice, or pancakes. Mix them in casseroles, sauces, or gravies.

Buttermilk, see "Milk"

CANNED FRUITS

It is best to buy fruits which are packed in water or their own juices when buying canned fruits. They also come packed in light, medium, or heavy syrups, each with an increasing amount of sugar. To reduce the sugar in these syrup-packed fruits, empty the can into a strainer and rinse the fruit with cold water. See "Home Food Preservation" page 391 for instructions on home canning of fruits.

CATSUP

One tablespoon of catsup has 16 calories, a trace of protein, a trace of fat, 4 grams of carbohydrate, and 147 mg of sodium. It is only 3 percent fat, about 8 percent sugar, and high in sodium. Low-sodium catsup reduces the level of sodium from 147 mg to 4 mg. It is good to be aware of this so that you will only use catsup in very small amounts.

CHEESE

Cheese is a high-protein food but it is also high in fat (60 percent to 94 percent). Buy part-skim or all-skim cheese when possible and use it sparingly.

COTTAGE CHEESE is the exception. It is made from skim milk and allowed to curdle. Most cottage cheese is creamed, which means that cream or milk has been added to the curds. Always buy the lowest-fat cottage cheese you can find, preferably skim. It is also possible to buy dry-curd cottage cheese, which is simply the curd with no milk added. Regular creamed cottage cheese is 36 percent fat and it can be rinsed off in a strainer to reduce the fat content. Low-fat cottage cheese made with skim milk is 4 percent fat and dry-curd cottage cheese is 11 percent fat. There are many recipes where cheese can be successfully replaced by cottage cheese. You can make your own delicious cottage cheese by following these easy directions.

1. Dissolve a rennet tablet or ¼ Junket tablet in warm water.
2. Heat 1 gallon skim milk in a large, heavy pot to 90°. Add 2 cups buttermilk live-culture yogurt, and stir until thoroughly mixed. Then add dissolved rennet tablet.
3. Remove from heat. Cover and leave overnight in a warm place.
4. In the morning, you will find a gelatinous mass in the pot. This is the curd. Cut through the curd with a silver knife to break it into small pieces. Set the bowl of curd in a pan of warm water on the stove and heat until the curd is up to 110°. It is essential that you have a thermometer. After it reaches 110°, turn off the heat but leave the curd bowl in the pan of water for about ½ hour.
5. Pour the curd into a cloth bag or several layers of cheese cloth and hang it up to drain. Use a bowl to catch the whey, which can be used in cooking, if desired.
6. When it is drained, mash the curds with a fork and add a little low-fat yogurt to moisten it. Store this delicious cottage cheese in your refrigerator.

CHICKEN

Many recipes call for cooked chicken pieces. Following are recommendations for cooking chicken. Wash chicken pieces and put them into a large pot. Cover with water. Cook until meat is tender and remove pot from heat. Strain chicken broth from cooked chicken and set it aside. Allow chicken to cool, then remove the skin, since most of the fat is contained between it and the meat. Pick the chicken meat off the bones and cut it into bite-sized pieces. Store meat in refrigerator until needed. See "Chicken Stock" for suggestions for chicken broth.

Chicken Bouillon, see "Chicken Stock"

CHICKEN STOCK

These sources of chicken stock are interchangeable.

1. HOMEMADE chicken stock is made by cooking chicken parts in about 2 quarts of water, so that the meat is covered. Onions or celery can be added to the meat as it cooks. Bring it to a boil, then simmer for 2 to 3 hours. Remove from heat, strain, and cool. When the stock is completely cooled, remove all the remaining fat from the top of the stock. Store stock in your refrigerator or freezer. This is the best source of chicken stock because it is low in both fat and sodium. It is also called "de-fatted chicken broth."

2. CANNED chicken stock or chicken broth is convenient but it is high in fat. Skim off as much fat as possible. When it is used in combination with other foods, such as in a soup, the total percentage of fat can be kept under 20 percent. It is also high in sodium (830 mg in 4 oz.).

3. BOUILLON granules or cubes are low in fat but high in sodium (400 mg in 8 oz.). Dissolve 1 cube or 1 teaspoon of bouillon granules in 1 cup boiling water. It is possible to buy low-sodium bouillon. HINT: If you must use several cups of canned broth or bouillon cubes, double dilute them (2 cans water to 1 can broth or 2 cups water to 1 cube bouillon). This will weaken the flavor a little but it will reduce the amount of fat and sodium by half.

Cornstarch, see "Thickenings"

Corn Syrup, see "Sweeteners"

Cottage Cheese, see "Cheese" and "Milk"

De-fatted Chicken Broth, see "Chicken Stock"

DIET MARGARINE

Diet margarine has about ⅔ the calories and grams of fat as regular margarine and about half the calories and grams of fat as real butter. We recommend using polyunsaturated oils when fats are called for in a recipe. But there are times when oils cannot be used as a substitute. In these cases, diet margarine will reduce the total grams of fat. It should be remembered that there is a lot of water in diet margarine so it is not suitable for frying or sautéing. See "Sauté" on page 401.

DRAIN

Save the water from boiled potatoes or vegetables. It can be used in soups to add flavor and nutrition. When mashing potatoes, use the reserved liquid instead of water.

EGGS

Egg yolks are high in fat (6 grams per yolk). We recommend that you use 2 egg whites in place of each whole egg whenever possible.

Evaporated Milk, see "Milk"

FATS

Animal and plant products are the two sources of fat in our diet. Animal products consist of meat, eggs, milk, and milk products such as yogurt and cheese. Plant products consist of nuts, seeds, and oils.

A fat is never completely saturated, polyunsaturated, or monosaturated, but for practical purposes, it is labeled one of these three.

SATURATED means filled to capacity. Saturated fats harden at room temperature and are found in all animal products. Changing liquid fats into solid fats is called HYDROGENATION. Hydrogenated oils behave like saturated fats—they both tend to raise the level of cholesterol in the blood and should therefore be avoided.

POLYUNSATURATED: **Poly** means many and **unsaturated** means not filled to capacity. Polyunsaturated fats are liquid oils of plant origin. COLD PRESSING is the preferable method of extracting these oils. When using fats, cold-pressed oil is one of the best choices.

MONOUNSATURATED: **Mono** means one and **unsaturated** means not filled to capacity. Monounsaturated fats are also liquid oils of plant origin and provide a rich flavor. Olive oil is an excellent choice and can be used in place of cold-pressed oil.

All animal products contain saturated fats. Some animal products which are especially high in saturated fats are beef, lamb, pork, ham, lard, butter, cream, whole milk, and whole-milk cheeses. Animal products which are lower in saturated fats are fish, chicken, turkey, skim and low-fat milk, cottage cheese, as well as, Swiss, hoop, and mozzarella cheeses.

Animal products also contain CHOLESTEROL, which is not present in plant products. Cholesterol is a waxy material used in many of the body's chemical processes. Everyone requires it, but too much cholesterol in the blood encourages the development of heart and blood vessel diseases. It can be manufactured by the body or it can be absorbed directly into the body from the foods you eat. Egg yolks and organ meats are especially high in cholesterol.

Plant products fall into all categories.

Polyunsaturated plant products consist of liquid vegetable oils. The oils, listed in order of polyunsaturation, are safflower, soybean, sunflower, corn, cottonseed, and sesame seed.

Plant products which contain saturated fats are coconut oil, palm oil, and cocoa butter. These oils are also used commercially in cookies, pie fillings, and nondairy milk and cream substitutes.

Olive oil, peanut oil, and canola (rapeseed) oil are the most common monounsaturated oils. Avocados and walnuts also contain monounsaturated oils.

Hydrogenated plant products come in the form of shortening or stick, diet, and tub margarines. Tub margarine is more polyunsaturated than stick margarine, since it is not required to hold stick form. Diet margarine contains water and has only half the fat found in other solid margarines. It can be used for seasoning or as a spread but its high water content makes it unsuitable for cooking.

Fats can be a deceptive group of foods. They pack a lot of calories into beguilingly small parcels. They are often hidden in foods, so read the labels on packaged foods. The first ingredient appears in the largest amount in the product. When cooking, reduce the amount of fats called for by half and replace solid fats with polyunsaturated oils. We need to reduce our intake of fats drastically. So watch the kinds and amounts of fats you eat and don't let the fats make you fat.

Flour, see "Thickenings" (p. 409) and The Bread Spread (p. 297)

Fructose, see "Sweeteners"

FRUIT JUICE CONCENTRATES

Frozen fruit juices such as orange or apple juice are quite sweet. This undiluted concentrate can be used to sweeten many recipes in place of sugar.

Garlic Powder, see "Seasonings"

Hamburger, see "Brown Lean Hamburger"

HOME FOOD PRESERVATION

This allows you to control exactly what you are eating. Food additives and preservatives are eliminated. Salt and sugar can be reduced or omitted.

There are three basic methods of home food preservation: canning, freezing, and drying. There is not adequate space in this book to explain all the details concerning the advantages and disadvantages of these three methods, or the details of how to do each method. We recommend that you read cookbooks which deal specifically with canning, freezing, or drying foods if the idea of home food preservation appeals to you. IT IS VERY IMPORTANT TO KNOW

EXACTLY WHAT YOU ARE DOING SINCE ERRORS CAN RESULT IN FOOD POISONING OR BOTULISM. Botulism is a deadly poison associated with improper canning. Even a small taste can be fatal. For this reason, we recommend the use of a pressure canner in home canning.

Following are simple charts which briefly give instructions on canning, freezing, or drying fruits or vegetables.

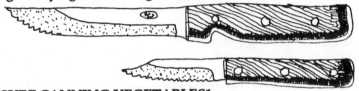

PRESSURE CANNING VEGETABLES*

Asparagus: Wash. Grade. Trim off scale. Pack raw and cover with boiling water. Leave 1/2-inch head space. Adjust lids. Process quarts for 30 minutes at 10 pounds pressure.

Lima Beans: Shell. Grade. Pack raw and cover with boiling water. Leave 1½-inch head space. Adjust lids. Process quarts for 25 minutes at 10 pounds pressure.

String Beans: Wash. Cut in pieces. Pack raw and cover with boiling water. Leave 1/2-inch head space. Adjust lids. Process quarts for 25 minutes at 10 pounds pressure.

Carrots: Slice or cut as desired. Pack raw and cover with boiling water, leaving 1-inch head space. Adjust lids. Process quarts for 30 minutes at 10 pounds pressure.

Corn: Cut kernels from cob. To each quart of corn, add 2 cups boiling water and boil 1 minute. Pack loosely and cover with boiling water. Leave 1-inch head space. Adjust lids. Process quarts for 85 minutes at 10 pounds pressure.

Green Peas: Shell. Use only young, fresh peas. Pack raw loosely and cover with boiling water. Leave 1-inch head space. Adjust lids. Process quarts 40 minutes at 10 pounds pressure.

Pumpkin: Peel and cut into 1-inch cubes. Cook until tender. Strain. Pack hot. Leave 1/2-inch head space. Adjust lids. Process quart jars for 80 minutes at 10 pounds pressure.

Tomatoes: See fruit chart.

*At altitudes of 2,000 feet or higher, use 15 pounds pressure instead of 10.

PRESSURE CANNING FRUITS*

We suggest that you process fruits in their own juice, pineapple juice, or with water using little or no sugar. Honey is twice as sweet as sugar and can be used to process fruit, but it has a distinctive taste of its own. Pack the jars with as much fruit as possible. Applesauce needs no additional liquid or sweetener. Add lemon extract, spices, or ascorbic acid, if desired.

Apples: Wash, pare, core and cut in pieces. Pack. Fill with liquid to within ½ inch of top. Adjust lids. Process quarts 10 minutes at 5 pounds pressure.

Applesauce: Cook applesauce (not in pressure cooker). Pack hot to within ¼ inch of top. Adjust lids. Process quarts for 15 minutes at 5 pounds pressure.

Apricots or Apricot Nectar: Wash. Pack whole or halve and pit. Fill with liquid to within ½ inch of top. For nectar, cook after pitted until soft and run through a food mill. Fill jars to within ½ inch of top. Adjust lids. Process quarts for 10 minutes at 5 pounds pressure.

Berries (except strawberries): Wash. Stem. Fill with liquid to within ½ inch of top. Adjust lids. Process quarts or pints for 8 minutes at 5 pounds pressure.

Cherries: Wash and stem. Pit. Pack jars. Fill with liquid to within ½ inch of top. Adjust lids. Process quarts for 10 minutes at 5 pounds pressure.

Grapes: Wash and stem. Pack jars. Fill with liquid to within 1½ inches of top. Adjust lids. Process quarts for 8 minutes at 5 pounds pressure.

Grape Juice: Wash and stem. Pack quart jar half full of grapes. Fill with boiling water to within 1 inch of top. Adjust lids. Process quarts for 8 minutes at 5 pounds pressure. Allow to sit for 6 weeks before using. To use, pour juice through a strainer into a pitcher and dispose of grape pulp. Adjust sweetness.

Peaches: Wash. Dip peaches in boiling water, then cold water. Remove skins. Cut in halves and remove pits. Pack jars. Fill with liquid to within ½ inch of top. Adjust lids. Process quarts for 10 minutes at 5 pounds pressure.

Pears: Wash. Peel. Halve and core. Pack jars. Fill with liquid to within ½ inch of top. Adjust lids. Process quarts for 10 minutes at 5 pounds pressure.

Plums: Wash. Prick skins. Pack. Fill with liquid to within ½ inch of top. Adjust lids. Process for 10 minutes at 5 pounds pressure.

Rhubarb: Wash. Cut in pieces. Pack. Add liquid to within ½ inch of top. Adjust lids. Process quarts for 5 minutes at 5 pounds pressure.

Tomatoes: Scald for 30 seconds. Place in cold water. Remove skins. Core and quarter. Pack tightly to within ½ inch of top. Adjust lids. Process quarts for 10 minutes at 5 pounds pressure.

Tomato Juice: Cook tomatoes and put through food press. Bring to a boil. Fill jars to within ¼ inch of top. Adjust lids. Process quarts for 10 minutes at 5 pounds pressure.

Tomato Sauce: Simmer tomato juice until it cooks down to desired consistency. This may take several hours. Fill pint or quart jars to within ½ inch of top. Adjust lids. Process for 10 minutes at 5 pounds pressure.

*At altitudes of 2,000 feet or higher, use 10 pounds pressure instead of 5.

PRESSURE CANNING DRIED BEANS: SOYBEANS, LIMA BEANS, GARBANZO BEANS, KIDNEY BEANS, OR PINTO BEANS

Soak beans overnight at least 12 hours. Put 3 ½ cups of the soaked beans into a clean quart jar. Fill with hot water to within 1 inch of top. Adjust lids. Process quarts for 60 minutes at 15 pounds pressure.

PRESSURE CANNING GRAINS

Use clean quart jars. Fill with dry grain using 1 ½ cups wheat, or ¾ cups millet, or 1 cup split peas, or 1½ cups dry lentils, or 1 cup rice per quart jar. Fill with hot water to within 1 inch of the top. Adjust lids. Process for 60 minutes at 15 pounds pressure.

OVEN CANNING OF RAISINS OR DATES

Buy raisins or dates when they are on sale and process them. They will keep for a couple of years. Fill clean quart jars to within 1 inch of top. Adjust lids. Place in oven for 1 hour at 225°. Adjust lid again, if necessary, when removing from the oven. The jars do not need to seal.

FREEZING FRUITS

Select firm, ripe fruit. Wash. If necessary, slice and immerse in a solution of 3 tablespoons lemon juice and 1 quart water. Drain on a paper towel. Berries are, of course, frozen whole. Apples and blueberries can be steam-blanched to keep the skins tender. Pears and bananas do not freeze well. (Mashed bananas can be frozen to be used in cooking.) The following fruits all freeze well without sugar: apples, blackberries, blueberries, cherries, cranberries, currants, figs, gooseberries, loganberries, melons, peaches, pineapple, plums, prunes, rhubarb, raspberries, and strawberries. Use plastic or glass airtight containers. Frozen fruit is especially delicious if eaten while still partially frozen.

FREEZING VEGETABLES

Enzymes remain active in vegetables even after they are harvested. Blanching is imperative before freezing to lessen the activity. There are two methods of blanching: boiling or steaming. The boiling method involves submerging the vegetables in boiling water for the allotted time and then immediately removing them and plunging them into cold water. The steaming method involves suspending the vegetables over boiling water for the allotted time and then immediately removing them and plunging them into cold water. Drain all vegetables on several thicknesses of paper toweling, covering them also. Store in airtight plastic or glass containers. Vegetables may be cooked directly upon removal from the freezer.

Asparagus: Parboil 3 to 12 minutes. Chill 12 to 15 minutes.

Green Beans: Parboil 2 minutes. Chill 5 minutes.

Lima Beans: Parboil 1 ½ minutes. Chill 3 minutes.

Broccoli: Steam 3 to 5 minutes. Chill 4 to 5 minutes.

Cabbage: Cook until tender, then steam 3 or 4 minutes. Cool over, but not in, cold water.

Celery, diced: Steam until tender. Cool over, but not in, cold water.

Corn: Steam 3 to 5 minutes off the cob or 8 minutes on the cob. Cool over, but not in, cold water for 15 minutes.

Green Peas: Steam 1 to 3 minutes. Chill 2 to 5 minutes.

Tomato Sauce: Prepare and freeze.

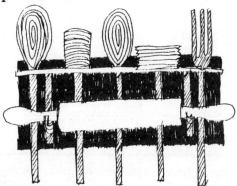

DRYING VEGETABLES

Select vegetables in their prime. When preparing them by peeling, slicing, mashing, or blending, use a stainless steel knife to prevent discoloration. Vegetables are generally precooked before drying. They must also be drier than fruits to store well. Store dried foods in airtight plastic bags.

Green Beans: Cut in 1-inch pieces. Steam 15-20 minutes. Dry. Test: Brittle, dark greenish to brownish color.

Lima Beans: Steam 15-20 minutes. Dry. Test: Shatter when crushed.

Carrots: Cut ⅛-inch slices or strips. Steam 8 to 10 minutes. Dry. Test: Brittle, deep orange color.

Corn: Steam whole ears 10-15 minutes. Cut corn from ears. Steam an additional 20 minutes. Dry. Test: Dry, brittle.

Mushrooms: No steaming required. Slice or leave whole. Dry. Test: Leathery to brittle.

Onions: No steaming required. Slice, chop ⅛-inch to ¼-inch pieces. Dry. Test: Brittle.

Peas, Green: Steam shelled peas for 10 minutes. Dry. Test. Shatter when crushed.

Peppers: Remove seeds, cut into ⅛-inch to ¼-inch strips, rings, or cubes. Scald in boiling water. Steam 3 to 5 minutes. Dry. Test: Pliable to brittle.

Potatoes: Peel and cut into ⅛-inch to ¼-inch strips. Rinse in cold water, then steam for 4 to 6 minutes. Dry. Test. Brittle.

DRYING FRUITS

Select fruits in their prime. When preparing them by peeling, slicing, pitting, coring, mashing, or blending, use a stainless steel knife to prevent discoloration. Fruits are easier to dry than vegetables. Store dried foods in airtight plastic bags.

Apples: Pare, core, and cut in ⅛-inch to 1 ¼-inch slices or rings. Dry. Test: Leathery to brittle.

Apricots: Peel, if desired. Cut in halves, remove pits. Turn inside out. Dry. Test: Pliable to leathery.

Bananas: Peel and slice across length. Dry. Test: Leathery and pliable but not sticky.

Berries: Leave whole. Dry. Test: Hard, without visible moisture when squeezed.

Cherries: Remove stems and pits. Drain. Dry. Test: Leathery, but sticky. These can also be dried after being cut in half.

Grapes: Use only seedless grapes. Leave whole but remove stems. Dip in boiling water to remove skins. Dry. Test: Pliable, dark brown color.

Peaches: Peel. Cut in halves and remove pits. Quarter, or slice, if desired. Dry. Test: Pliable and leathery.

Pears: Pare, core, and cut into quarters. Cut into ½-inch slices or rings. Dry. Test: Pliable or leathery.

Plums: Leave whole. Blanch, if desired — it will speed drying. Dry. Test: Pliable and leathery.

Strawberries: Remove stems and leaves. Cut in half. Dry. Test: Dry with no visible moisture when crushed.

REHYDRATION OF DRIED FRUITS AND VEGETABLES

Cover dried foods with water and soak for 30 minutes. Add more water, if necessary. Use as you would fresh. Do not boil rehydrated foods.

Honey, see "Sweeteners"

Hydrogenation, see "Fats"

IMITATION BACON BITS

These contain no animal fat because they are a soybean byproduct. They are very high in sodium.

Macaroni, see "Pasta"

Maple Sugar and Maple Syrup, see "Sweeteners"

MILK

Milk is an excellent source of protein, calcium, vitamins A, D, E, and K. It is available in several grades: namely, whole, 2 percent, 1 percent, and skim, and is the source of many milk products.

Blended Cottage Cheese: Cottage cheese blended with a small amount of milk until smooth makes a wonderful substitute for sour cream. It can even replace mayonnaise in many instances. See Fabulous Flavors on page 19 for recipes, and "Cheese" on page 388 to learn to make cottage cheese.

Buttermilk: Originally, buttermilk was the milk remaining after the butter had been churned, but now buttermilk is made from cultures added to skim or nonfat milk. It is also possible to buy buttermilk in powdered form, which is convenient for cooking. Following are two recipes for making buttermilk.

1. Add 1 tablespoon lemon juice to 1 cup lukewarm nonfat milk. Let it stand for 5 minutes and then stir briskly.

2. OR mix 3 ¾ cups water with1 ⅓ cups instant powdered milk. Stir in 1 cup buttermilk. Cover with waxed paper and clean towel. Let stand at room temperature overnight until clabbered. Stir until smooth. Store in refrigerator. Makes 1 quart.

Evaporated Milk: Evaporated Milk is made by removing the water from fresh whole milk. It is then pasteurized, homogenized, fortified with vitamin D, sealed in cans, and heat-sterilized. Evaporated whole milk is 32 percent fat while evaporated skim milk has only a trace percentage of fat. Sweetened condensed milk is simply evaporated milk, which is 40 percent sugar. There is no place for it in this program.

Milk: Milk varies in the amount of fat it contains. Whole milk is 53 percent, 2 percent milk is 38 percent fat, 1 percent milk is 18 percent fat, skim and

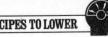

buttermilk are both 3 percent fat. Two glasses of 1 percent, skim, or buttermilk per day is sufficient for most adults.

Nonfat Dry Milk: Nonfat dry milk is a useful form of milk. It can be stored for several months, reconstituted, and used for drinking or cooking. It comes either as an instant or a noninstant powder. Noninstant is slightly superior nutritionally since it is prepared by a low-heat process. Use instant if something is to be cooked since it mixes more easily and the advantage of the noninstant is lost in the cooking. Dried whole milk is 45 percent fat and nonfat dry milk is 2 percent fat.

Sour Cream Substitute: An equal amount of yogurt is a wonderful substitute for sour cream. For a more sour flavor, pour homemade yogurt into a strainer lined with cheesecloth and allow it to drain until it is the consistency of sour cream. This will take several hours at room temperature.

Whipped Topping: Real whipped cream, as well as imitation nondairy topping, are high in fat (89 percent to 96 percent). We suggest that you make your own low-fat whipped topping to use on fruits or gelatin salads. See "Just for Fun!" on page 347, for a surprisingly good recipe for whipped topping.

Yogurt: Yogurt is a highly valuable food made from milk and special bacterial cultures that make the milk more digestible. Commercial yogurts are often laced with heavy amounts of fat or sugar or both. Read the ingredients carefully. Since plain, unflavored yogurt may well be the most versatile food in your kitchen and since it is very easy to make, we suggest you learn to make your own yogurt. This recipe has an especially creamy texture.

1. Add 1 cup nonfat dry milk to 3 1/3 cups skim milk and whisk until smooth.
2. Heat in microwave to 190° or in the top of a double boiler until it just begins to boil.
3. Remove from heat and allow to cool to 110°. Add 1 heaping tablespoon starter. You may purchase a starter at a health food store or buy plain yogurt that states on the carton it contains active yogurt cultures. Stir gently until smooth.
4. Pour into the 5 cups of an electric yogurt maker and heat for 6 to 10 hours. The longer the time, the more tart the taste.
5. Refrigerate and be sure to save 1 heaping tablespoon for your next batch.
6. If you do not have an electric yogurt maker, there are several other methods for making yogurt. a) Use a wide-mouth thermos. b) Cover the jars tightly with plastic wrap and place them in a clean shoe box lined with paper towels. Wrap the shoe box with a thick towel and leave it undisturbed in a warm place for 3 to 5 hours. c) Set the yogurt in your gas oven with only the pilot light on. d) Place pint jars, sealed tightly with plastic wrap or lids, on top of an electric heating pad which has been set on medium. You may have other ideas but the goal is to keep the yogurt, at 110° for 3 to 5 hours.
7. REMEMBER, EVERYTHING YOU USE DURING THE PROCESS MUST BE IMMACULATELY CLEAN.
8. 1 cup equals 175 calories, 18 grams of protein, a trace of fat, 21 grams of carbohydrate, 256 mg of sodium, and is 4 percent fat.

Molasses, see "Sweeteners"

Monounsaturated, see "Fats"

NONSTICK

Pans that do not need to be greased are an important investment for low-fat cooking. Teflon, Baker's Secret, or Silverstone are all excellent choices. Suggested pans include: a 9" x 9" casserole; a 9" x 13" casserole; two to four loaf pans; two baking sheets; a large soup pot; three various-sized saucepans; and two frying pans, one small and one large. An electric nonstick wok is nice for stir-fry but not essential.

Vegetable cooking spray is another means of keeping food from sticking to pans without greasing them. It is made from lecithin, a natural vegetable compound extracted from soybeans. It contains no cholesterol or salt. One spray has 10 calories, 1 gram of fat, and no carbohydrates or protein.

It is also possible to buy liquid lecithin at a health food store and use it in place of grease. It is marked **unrefined** and looks terrible, but it has no flavor and works perfectly.

De-fatted chicken broth or bouillon are also good substitutes for oil when sauteing or cooking in a wok.

A microwave oven can cook many of your favorite foods without using oil. Experiment with your favorite recipes and see in how many your microwave oven can reduce the fat.

Noodles, see "Pasta"

Orange Juice Concentrate, see "Fruit Juice Concentrate"

VANILLA

PASTA

Pasta products are not especially nutritious, but they are filling. They are basically a high-starch, low-protein food with a small amount of vitamin enrichment. Most adults and children love pasta, and when it is used as a base for other nutritious foods it can be of great value. Whenever possible, buy whole wheat pasta.

Pasta can be divided into two main groups: noodles and macaroni. Noodles are characterized by the addition of eggs to flour. This increases the protein, but it also increases the amount of fat. Why not try making your own whole wheat noodles with yogurt instead of eggs by using the recipe on page 280. Sometimes vegetable purée is added to noodles, spinach being the most common. This provides some variety in taste, color, and nutrition.

The macaroni group includes spaghetti, lasagna, macaroni, shells, and other macaroni shapes. These are usually enriched with vitamins or wheat germ. Our suggestion is to use these products in small amounts with high-nutrition foods. Fill out soups with a handful of whole wheat macaroni or noodles. Top whole wheat pasta with creamed chicken or tuna or a vegetable-tomato sauce. Since cheese is so high in fat, macaroni and cheese would not be a good choice.

If whole wheat pasta is difficult to find, be creative; substitute brown rice, potatoes, or whole wheat bread in the recipe.

Polyunsaturated Fats, see "Fats"

RICE

Brown rice is unprocessed and therefore highly nutritious. It has high-quality protein, calcium, phosphorous, iron, vitamin E, and most B vitamins. When brown rice is processed, most of the nutrition is lost and white rice, converted rice, or quick-cooking rice are the results. Since there is quite a nutritional gap between processed and unprocessed rice, we encourage the eating of brown rice or wild rice.

Brown rice requires a longer cooking time but there's no extra work involved on your part. There are three basic methods of cooking brown rice: boiling, pressure cooking, or baking.

BOILING: Wash rice and drain. Put 1 cup rice into a saucepan large enough to allow rice to triple in volume. Add 2 cups boiling water and bring the mixture to a boil again. Do not add salt to the water or the rice will be tough. Reduce heat to the lowest possible setting, cover, and simmer for 45 minutes. Do not stir, since that causes the rice to become sticky and pasty. Remove from heat after 45 minutes and let it stand unopened for several minutes. This will allow it to steam. The result will be perfect brown rice with its full, nutlike taste.

PRESSURE COOKING: Wash rice and drain. Place 1 cup rice and 2 cups water in the pressure cooker. Put pressure regulator in place and heat until the regulator jiggles evenly or reaches 15 pounds pressure. Reduce heat so that the regulator jiggles slowly, and cook for 40 minutes. A shorter cooking time results

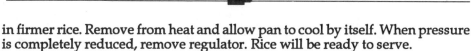

in firmer rice. Remove from heat and allow pan to cool by itself. When pressure is completely reduced, remove regulator. Rice will be ready to serve.

BAKING: Wash rice and drain. Place 1 cup rice and 2 cups water in a casserole. Cover and bake at 350° for 60 minutes.

HINTS: (1) Chicken or beef broth, tomato juice, or vegetable broth can be substituted for water in any of these recipes. OR (2) Line a ring mold with plastic wrap and pack cooked rice firmly into the mold. Cover and allow it to stand several minutes. Invert it onto a serving plate. Remove the mold and plastic wrap. Fill the center with chicken a la king, chicken salad, or another favorite dish.

SALT

Oversalting is a serious problem in this country. Almost all commercial products have salt added. Since salt is a natural ingredient in all foods, our need for more salt is an acquired taste. There are several solutions to this problem.

Salt can be omitted entirely in almost all recipes. If you want to do it gradually, simply cut the amount of salt in half.

Use a salt substitute, if desired, but some people notice a difference in taste.

Compensate for the decrease in salt by increasing the use of herbs and spices. See "Seasoning Without Salt" on page 402 for a complete list of herbs and spices, including spice blends by Chef Howard Gifford. Try using some of the sauces and dressings in Fabulous Flavors (p. 19).

Canned vegetables are usually high in sodium. Use fresh vegetables, frozen vegetables, or try low-sodium canned vegetables. You could also process your own fresh vegetables and omit the salt. See "Home Food Preservation" on page 391 for instructions on home canning of vegetables.

Bouillon is a mainstay in low-fat cooking but it is high in sodium. Buy low-sodium bouillon or double dilute regular bouillon.

Processed tomato products are also high in sodium. Make your own tomato juice, tomato sauce, or tomato paste and omit the salt. See "Home Food Preservation" on page 391 for instructions on home canning of tomatoes. It is also possible to buy some tomato products which are low-sodium.

Sea salt is still salt and should be used just as sparingly as table salt. It is not highly refined or treated so it is rich in minerals which replace about 20 percent of the sodium chloride in table salt.

SAUTÉ

Sauté means to fry quickly and turn frequently in a little fat. It is possible to sauté without this unnecessary addition of fat to a recipe. Following are two suggested methods:

1. Microwave: Use 2 tablespoons of water and a covered glass or Corning Ware dish. Cook at full power until tender, about 5 or 10 minutes.

2. Stove Top: Use a nonstick frying pan. Sauté with vegetable spray, defatted chicken broth, or chicken or beef bouillon until tender.

Saturated Fats, see "Fats"

Season to Taste, see "Seasoning Without Salt"

SEASONING WITHOUT SALT

There is a wide variety of herbs and spices that can be used to enhance the taste of our food. This is especially important in the low-sodium, low-sugar cooking encouraged in this program. We all like our food to taste good and with the proper use of herbs and spices it can be done without the use of high-fat, high-sodium, or high-sugar recipes. Read about the various seasonings, try some of the suggestions, and then experiment until you find just the right combination to suit your family's taste buds.

Many recipes include spice and flavor alternatives using commercial spice blends created by Master Chef Howard Gifford. See the order form at the end of this book to purchase a set of these six mixed spices.

Allspice: The flavor resembles a blend of cinnamon, nutmeg, and cloves but it is actually the product of only one plant. Add 2 whole allspice to the pot when stewing chicken. Try a dash over fruit salad or in baked goods.

Anise Seed: This gives food a licorice flavor. Perhaps you might enjoy muffins or a loaf of bread with this delightful flavor.

Basic Spice: A blend of basic spices including onion powder, garlic powder, beef bouillon, thyme, paprika, and other spices, by Chef Howard Gifford. (To order, see form at end of this book.)

Basil: This herb is a natural companion for tomatoes and potatoes. Use it in tomato juice and tomato sauce, vegetable or potato casseroles, potato salads, or in hamburger patties.

Bay Leaves: These are not eaten but are added to soups while cooking and removed before serving. They add zest to almost any dish. When making potato salad, try cooking the potatoes with a bay leaf and onion.

Caraway Seeds: These seeds have a distinctive flavor. They are commonly used in rye bread but are also delicious in sauerkraut, cooked cabbage, potatoes, coleslaw, or cottage cheese.

Cayenne: This fiery spice is made from ground red peppers. It can be added to almost any recipe but use it sparingly. It will not taste as hot if it is added to cooked food.

Celery Leaves and Seeds: Celery is naturally high in sodium and therefore adds a great deal of flavor to casseroles, beans, vegetables, and soups. Fresh celery leaves are excellent cooked in soups and especially good in homemade chicken broth. Celery seeds perk up relishes, pickles, and potato salads. Of course, chopped celery stalks are used extensively in the recipes throughout this book.

Chervil: This is not a common American herb but the French are especially fond of it. Use it as you would parsley. It is excellent in salad dressings and when cooking peas.

Chili Powder: This spice is made from chili peppers blended with other spices. It can be either mild or hot. It is most commonly used with beans and in Mexican dishes. Try a sprinkle over cooked corn.

Chinese Spice: A blend of onion powder, chicken bouillon, ginger, and other spices, by Chef Howard Gifford. (To order, see form at end of this book.)

Chives: This member of the onion family is much smaller and milder than its big brother. It is best with cottage cheese, dips, sauces, cream soups, and on baked potatoes. One tablespoon fresh chopped chives is equal to 1 teaspoon freeze-dried chives.

Cinnamon: This spice makes simple dishes exciting. Try a sprinkle on rice to give it that special touch. It is also good over applesauce.

Cloves: Whole cloves are highly fragrant and can be used in stews as well as with fruits. Ground cloves go especially well in lentil recipes. They are also used in combination with cinnamon and nutmeg in baked goods.

Curry: This spice has an unusual flavor which is generally associated with Indian cooking. It can be added to white sauce and used in leftovers. It is also delicious in chicken recipes.

Dessert Spice: A blend of dry banana, orange peel, cinnamon, allspice, and other spices, by Chef Howard Gifford. (To order, see form at end of this book.)

Dill: Dill's fresh taste perks up any recipe: use it in potato or white bean soup; sprinkle it in salads; combine it with lemon and use it over fish; add it to white sauce; or mix it with coleslaw or potato salad.

Extracts: Pure extracts provide a wide variety of flavorings. Vanilla, almond, banana, maple, and mint are just a few of the delightful tastes which await you in the wonderful world of extracts. Use them in hot cereals, breads, muffins, sauces, salad dressings, carrots, yams, squash, or fruit salads.

Fennel: If you like licorice flavor, you will enjoy adding fennel to some of your favorite dishes. Try it in boiled fish dinners or in baked apples.

Garlic: This is one of the most popular seasonings in use today. Fresh garlic can be chopped, minced, grated, or pressed. One quarter teaspoon of garlic powder is equal to 1 clove of garlic. Garlic powder is preferable to garlic salt since it is lower in sodium. Garlic can be used in soups, casseroles, salads, dressings, breads, and beans.

Gourmet Spice: A blend of onion powder, chicken bouillon, tarragon, dill, and other spices, by Chef Howard Gifford. (To order, see form at end of this book.)

Horseradish: This root is commonly grated, mixed with vinegar, and sold in a jar. It is not used in cooking as much as it is used alongside fish or meat. It can be added to a white sauce or sour cream substitute and used on vegetables.

Hot Peppers: Be careful when you use these ferocious pods. They are not only hot to the taste but fresh pulp can burn your skin, too. These are definitely an acquired taste.

Italian Spice: A blend of onion powder, garlic powder, beef bouillon, chicken bouillon, basil, and other spices, by Chef Howard Gifford. (To order, see form at end of this book.)

Lemon: This fresh-tasting juice can be added to sauces, soups, salad dressings, fish, fruit, and vegetable dishes to enliven their flavor.

Marjoram: This unique herb is good on green beans, lima beans, mushrooms, rice, and poultry dressing.

Mexican Spice: A blend of onion powder, paprika, garlic powder, cumin, chili powder, chicken bouillon, beef bouillon, and other spices, by Chef Howard Gifford. (To order, see form at end of this book.)

Mint: What has a fresher taste than mint? Mix it with yogurt for a refreshing salad. Add it to fruit salads. Try it in hot cooked rice or simmer a few flakes with a pan of peas. It also makes a wonderful tea to settle an upset stomach.

MSG: Monosodium glutamate is a flavor enhancer which has no taste of its own but brings out natural food flavors and helps them to blend into one another. There is evidence which links MSG to negative physical reactions. It would seem wise to avoid the use of MSG when possible, as well as the use of seasoned, garlic or onion salts which are largely MSG.

Mustard: Use either dry or prepared mustard. It gives salad dressings an extra tang and is perfect in place of mayonnaise on sandwiches.

Nutmeg: Use it in the ground form. Sprinkle it over vegetables like cauliflower, spinach, broccoli, or onions. Combine it with cinnamon for use on berries or sliced bananas.

Oregano: This herb gives recipes that Italian flavor. It gives character to stews, chili, potatoes, tomatoes, or baked beans. Sprinkle it over seafood.

Onion: This is certainly one of the most popular seasonings, whether used fresh, as flakes, or as powder. One tablespoon chopped onion is equal to 1/4 teaspoon onion powder, and 1 cup chopped onion is equal to 1 tablespoon instant minced onion. Use it in soups, stews, casseroles, salads, vegetables, or baked goods.

WILD ONION

Paprika: This popular spice is used more for its bright red color than for its taste. It is made from sweet red peppers but has a very mild flavor. Use it in sauces, salads, vegetables, rice, or potatoes for an artistic contrast. To give baked poultry a golden brown color, mix paprika with flour when coating chicken or turkey prior to cooking.

Parsley: This seasoning is usually used as a garnish but it is actually a fine source of vitamins A and C. It is also rich in chlorophyll, which makes an excellent breath freshener. It adds color and nutrition to soups, casseroles, salads, stuffings, vegetables, and even fruit.

Pepper: There is nothing like the taste of freshly ground pepper on almost any dish. Buy a pepper mill and whole peppercorns and treat your palate to the great flavor of fresh ground pepper.

Poppy Seeds: These tiny black seeds make an attractive garnish for cooked pasta. Sprinkle them over homemade bread or rolls before cooking.

Poultry Seasoning: This seasoning allows you to make dressing as a side dish for any meal. This seasoning also tastes especially good in chicken casseroles.

Rosemary: This herb has a sweet taste and is nice in combination with basil, oregano, and marjoram in Italian dishes. It is quite potent, so use sparingly and taste as you cook so that you don't use too much. Garlic powder and parsley are also good complements to rosemary. It can be used in soups, stews, chicken dishes, and with cauliflower or corn.

Sage: This herb has a strong but appetizing flavor. It is best in stuffings for chicken or turkey. Add a dash to tomato soup.

Sesame Seeds: These are an excellent source of amino acids. They can be toasted by heating in a shallow pan for 10 minutes at 350°. Sprinkle them on bread or rolls before baking, or on vegetables or fish. Like all seeds and nuts, sesame seeds are high in fat, so use them sparingly.

Soy Sauce: This product is also known as tamari sauce. It is the traditional seasoning of Oriental food. It is made from soybeans, water, wheat, and salt. It is high in sodium (1319 mg per tablespoon) but not as high as salt (1819 per teaspoon).

Tabasco: Usually 1 or 2 drops of this extremely hot sauce is enough to perk up any dish. It is made from mashed red-hot peppers blended with vinegar.

Tarragon: This is an important herb with seafood, chicken, or tomato dishes. It gives a tang to tartar sauce or creamed chicken.

Thyme: This herb blends well with other herbs, including "parsley, sage, rosemary, and . . . ." It is wonderful with chicken, soups, carrots, green beans, peas, onion, tomato slices, green salads, or seafood.

Worcestershire Sauce: This flavoring adds dark color as well as majestic taste to soups, casseroles, gravies, and stews.

Sour Cream Substitute, see "Milk"

SOYBEANS

Soybeans are not especially low in fat (40 percent) but are acceptable when used in place of animal products. They can be purchased in health food stores and some supermarkets. You may even want to plant some of your own easy-to-grow plants. Plant "Giant Green" for its flavor.

Soybeans require longer soaking and cooking time than other legumes, but because of their incredible nutrition and versatility, it is well worth the extra time.

Method 1: Soak soybeans for 8 hours. You can soak them in the refrigerator to prevent them from souring, sprouting, or forming gases. Drain and rinse well. Cover with fresh water and cook for 2 to 3 hours.

Method 2: Soak soybeans for 1 hour. Drain and rinse well. Freeze overnight. This will shorten the cooking time. Boil for 2 to 3 hours the next day. With both of these methods, watch closely so they do not boil over.

Method 3: The pressure cooker method is the fastest way to cook soybeans. Always read and follow the instructions carefully before using your pressure cooker. Cover the soybeans with water and season. Cook at 15 pounds pressure for 30 minutes.

Method 4: The oven method is used in combination with any 1 of the other 3 methods. Place cooked soybeans in a baking dish. Season and cover with liquid. Cover dish and bake at 350° for 1 to 2 hours or until done. Bake uncovered the last half hour for a crisper surface.

If you want to know more about this distinctive bean and its products, we suggest reading cookbooks that specialize in soybean cooking.

SPROUTS

It's time you discovered the exciting world of sprouts. They are an inexpensive, highly nutritious, easy-to-grow food. Depending on the kind of dried seed you use, the vitamins, minerals, amino acids, and protein can increase from three to 60 times when sprouted. There is more nourishment contained in a plant's sprout than at any other stage of its life-cycle. Eat sprouts raw or cooked. Add them to salads, sandwiches, cooked vegetables, and even baked goods. Here's how to do it:

1. Soak seeds in 2 cups warm water for 12 hours in a quart jar. DO NOT USE TOMATO, POTATO, OR TREATED SEEDS. ALL ARE POISONOUS.

2. Secure a gauze or nylon fabric over the mouth of the jar with a rubber band and DRAIN THE SEEDS WELL.

3. Shake the seeds along the bottom and sides of the jar and then lay the jar on its side. Cover the jar with a towel to keep it dark, but allow the air to circulate through the top.

4. Rinse the seeds at least 3 times a day. The water should be between 50 and 80 degrees. Drain well after each rinsing and replace the towel.

5. When sprouts reach proper length, place them in the refrigerator. They are at their peak 60 to 80 hours after soaking.

Kind & Amount	Length	# of Days	Hints
1 T ALFALFA	1"-2"	3-5	These only need to be soaked for 15 minutes. Also rinse them during storage to prevent mold.
½ cup BARLEY	¼"	3-4	Rinse often.
½ cup BEANS	¼"	2-3	Kidney, lima, navy, pinto, and white beans are all acceptable.
½ cup CORN	¼"	2-3	Do not over-sprout.
½ cup GARBANZO	2"	2-3	
½ cup LENTILS	2"	1-2	Use as soon as sprouts are visible.
¼ cup MUNG	2"-3"	3-4	Commonly known as Chinese bean sprouts.
½ cup PEAS	2"	2-3	
½ cup RYE	¼"	2-3	
¼ cup SESAME	½"	3-4	
½ cup SOYBEANS	4"	2-3	Rinse 3 to 4 times during soaking. Rinse often while sprouting and do not over-sprout.
¼ cup SUNFLOWER	¼"	2-3	
¼ cup WHEAT	¼"	2-3	Becomes bitter if over-sprouted.

Sugar, see "Sweeteners"

SWEETENERS

Artificial Sweeteners are very low in calories, however, we do not recommend their use. Most of them are made from coal tar derivatives. The following observations need further study but the implications are that any sweetener, natural or artificial, raises the setpoint. Rats given artificial sweeteners in their

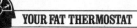

water actually increased their food intake and gained weight. Dieters who drink diet soft drinks have a more difficult time losing weight.

Brown Sugar and Raw Sugar do contain traces of nutrients that white sugar lacks, but they both react in the same way in the body as white sugar.

Corn Syrup is made from cornstarch. It is a highly refined simple carbohydrate and therefore causes a rapid increase, then rapid drop, in blood sugar.

Fructose is a high-calorie sweetener. It occurs naturally in fruit. The body handles it a little differently from other sugars so that it does not cause such a rapid rise and decrease in blood sugar.

Honey contains traces of protein and small amounts of several vitamins and minerals. It is easily digested. It has about twice the sweet taste that sugar has, therefore only half as much is needed. It has an interesting flavor of its own and it also brings out the flavors of other foods. It is 82 percent carbohydrate compared to processed sugars, which are over 99 percent carbohydrate. However, it is still a simple carbohydrate and it is broken down in the body the same way as white sugar.

Replacing dry sugars with honey in baking is generally a good change to make. To do this, simply use half as much honey as you would sugar, and then slightly reduce the amount of liquids.

Maple Sugar and Maple Syrup are both simple carbohydrates. Maple sugar is maple syrup which has been boiled down to evaporate the remaining liquid. Maple syrup is the boiled-down sap of the sugar maple tree. These two sweeteners are not quite as sweet as honey and they are about 15 percent lower in calories. They contain no vitamins but they do have a surprisingly broad sampling of minerals. They also have a more distinctive flavor than honey or sugar.

Molasses is the cooked liquid which remains after the crystallization of granulated sugar. There are several layers within the remaining molasses, each with a different color and food value. Blackstrap molasses, the last layer, has a very strong taste but contains the most iron, calcium, and potassium as well as several of the B vitamins.

White Sugar is a highly refined carbohydrate made from sugar cane and sugar beets. It has little food value. It is responsible for a dramatic increase and then dramatic decrease in blood sugar. This cycle stimulates hunger and a craving for more sugar. It also encourages the setpoint to rise.

As you reduce your consumption of sweets, you will lose your taste for them. In the meantime, remember that there are only minimal differences in the various sweeteners and all of them will tend to raise your setpoint. When you want to satisfy your sweet tooth, be safe instead of sorry and enjoy a piece of fresh fruit.

THICKENINGS

The following thickenings can be used interchangeably.

Arrowroot starch contains some vitamins and minerals. It will make a thicker mixture than cornstarch and it is quite easily digested.

Cornstarch is a good thickening agent. There are no RCUs or FUs in a tablespoon of cornstarch but there are 30 calories, 1 gram of fat, and 7 grams of carbohydrates. It will mix smoothly with cool liquids, 1 tablespoon to 1 cup of liquid. When it is heated, it thickens and becomes shiny and clear. You need to use only half as much cornstarch as flour.

Flour, All-Purpose is the traditional thickening agent. There are no RCUs, no FUs, 25 calories, no fat grams, and 5 grams carbohydrates in 1 tablespoon.

Flour, Whole Wheat is also a good thickening agent. There are no RCUs, no FUs, 22 calories, a trace of fat, and 5 grams of carbohydrates in 1 tablespoon. Put flour and water in a small jar with a tight lid and shake until the mixture is smooth. Use twice as much flour as you would cornstarch.

Oat Bran is an excellent thickening agent.

TOMATOES

Processed tomato juice, tomato sauce, tomato paste, and canned tomatoes are high in sodium. There are two possible solutions.

First, buy low-sodium tomato products whenever possible.

Second, process your own tomatoes. See "Home Food Preservation" on page 391 for directions on home canning of tomatoes. Salt can be omitted. All recipes in the book are computed with low-sodium tomato products.

It is not difficult to grow your own tomatoes. Tomatoes are ready to be harvested when they are a uniform red color but before they become soft. Green tomatoes can be harvested just before a killing frost and kept in a dark place. Stack them no more than two deep or wrap them in newspaper. They will ripen in 4 to 6 weeks if held between 55° to 70° in moderate humidity.

VEGETABLE JUICE COCKTAIL

Note that vegetable juice cocktail is high in sodium, 872 mg sodium in 8 ounces, but low-sodium, vegetable juice cocktail has only 60 mg sodium in eight ounces. This can be an excellent occasional snack.

White sugar, see "Sweeteners"

Whipped Topping, see "Milk"

Whole Wheat Macaroni or Noodles, see "Pasta"

Yogurt, see "Milk"

APPENDIX 2

HOW TO COMPUTE THE PERCENTAGE OF FAT IN YOUR OWN RECIPES

1. List all of the ingredients in your recipe. Include the amount of each ingredient, i.e. Frozen Fruit Shake :

1 cup whole milk
1 cup frozen sliced peaches
½ frozen sliced pear

2. Look up each ingredient in the Table of Food Composition on pages 187-208 in *How to Lower Your Fat Thermostat* or on the food labels. Calculate the number of calories and the number of grams of fat for each ingredient.

1 cup whole milk	170 cal	10 grams fat
1 cup peaches	65 cal	T of fat
½ pear	50 cal	T of fat

(i.e. 1 pear = 100 calories and a T of fat so ½ pear = 50 calories and a T of fat.)

3. Total the number of calories in the entire recipe (i.e. 170 + 65 + 50 = 285 calories total).

4. Total the number of grams of fat in the entire recipe (i.e. 10 + T + T = 10 grams of fat total).

5. Multiply the total number of grams of fat by 9, because there are 9 calories in 1 gram of fat (i.e. 10 grams of fat x 9 calories per gram = 90 calories in 10 grams of fat).

6. To determine the percentage fat in the recipe, divide the total number of calories (i.e. 285 calories) into the total number of calories in the grams of fat (i.e. 90 calories).

90 divided by 285 = .31
Move the decimal point two spaces to the right, and it becomes 31%. Thus 31% of the calories in the recipe come from the fat.

7. Now you have a clear picture of which ingredients are causing your recipe to be filled with fats. You may now either reduce the amount of that ingredient or replace it with a low-fat substitute. In some cases, it can be eliminated altogether without a noticeable effect on the recipe. In our example, replace the whole milk with skim milk and you will change the percent of fat from 31% to simply a trace of fat.

NOTE: All calculations in this book have been performed using fifteen decimal place precision. Data in the tables have been rounded off for your convenience. Calculations using rounded numbers will yield different results.

APPENDIX 3

HOW TO COMPUTE REFINED CARBOHYDRATE UNITS (RCUs) AND FAT UNITS (FUs)

1   RCU   = 6 grams of sugar or honey
             = 12 grams of white flour
             = 24 grams of raisins or dates
             = 48 grams of fruit juice concentrate
You are allowed 2 RCUs per day.
1   FU   = 6 grams of refined fat such as oil or margarine
             = 8 grams of naturally-occurring fat such as meat, milk, or eggs.
You are allowed 4 FUs per day if your ideal weight is less than 140 pounds and 5 FUs per day if your ideal weight is more than 140 pounds.

1. Look up the number of grams of carbohydrates (RCUs) or grams of fat (for FUs). This information can be found on the package, in some calorie-counting booklets, or in the Table of Food Composition (pp. 187-208) in *How to Lower Your Fat Thermostat.*
2. Divide by the number of grams in 1 RCU or 1 FU.

FOR EXAMPLE:
ONE CUP SUGAR equals 176 grams of carbohydrate. Since 6 grams of sugar equal 1 RCU, divide 6 into 176. The answer is 29.3 rounded off to 29 RCUs in a cup of sugar.
ONE CUP OF WHITE FLOUR equals 84 grams of carbohydrate. Since 12 grams of white flour equal 1 RCU, divide 12 into 84. The answer is 7 RCUs in a cup of white flour.
ONE CUP OF RAISINS equals 116 grams of carbohydrate. Since 24 grams of raisins equal 1 RCU, divide 24 into 116. The answer is 4.8 rounded off to 5 RCUs in a cup of raisins.
ONE-FOURTH CUP OF OIL equals 54 grams of fat. Since 6 grams of refined fat equal 1 FU, divide 6 into 54. The answer is 9 FU in ¼ cup of oil.
ONE EGG has 6 grams of fat. Since 8 grams of naturally-occurring fat equal 1 FU, divide 8 into 6. The answer is .75 rounded off to 1 FU per egg.

APPENDIX 4

RECIPES SUITABLE FOR USE WITH A
YEAST-MANAGEMENT PROGRAM

There is a type of yeast living in the body that is generally harmless in controlled numbers. When overgrowth occurs, however — often following the use of antibiotics, birth control pills, cortisone, Prednisone, or chemotherapy — you may suffer with a number of unpleasant symptoms, including depression, insomnia, anxiety, irritability, fatigue, intestinal gas, bloating, constipation, diarrhea, heartburn, muscle stiffness, muscle cramps, pounding heart, shortness of breath, hypoglycemia, excessive hunger cravings for sugar, and weight gain.

Overgrowth of this yeast, called Candida albicans, can also interfere with weight loss. In their book, *Back to Health*, physician Dennis Remington and registered dietician Barbara Higa outline an effective yeast-control program, including a diet that avoids foods that encourage yeast overgrowth.

Phase I of the diet eliminates all refined sugars, refined flour products, yeast breads, aged cheese, fermented products (like alcoholic beverages and vinegar), fruit, fruit juices, coffee, tea, herbal teas, mushrooms, sprouts, peanuts and peanut products, and processed meats.

After you start feeling better, generally in about one month, you can begin Phase II of the diet, which allows you to gradually reintroduce many foods, watching for unpleasant reactions. You should continue to avoid sugar, fruit juice, and alcoholic beverages.

Most of the recipes in this book can be used on Phase II of the yeast management diet. For Phase I, make these changes to the following recipes: 1. Omit ham, sprouts, mushrooms, raisins, cheese, and any pickles. 2. Use lemon juice instead of vinegar. 3. Substitute rolled oats for bread crumbs.

PHASE 1 YEAST CONTROL RECIPES

If you suspect that you might have a yeast problem, you can find *Back to Health* in bookstores or health food stores. It can also be ordered through Vitality House International, Inc., 1675 N. Freedom Blvd, 11-C, Provo, Utah 84604. Send $10.95 plus $2.50 for postage and handling or simply use the coupon on the last page of this book.

APPENDIX 5

SIMPLIFIED LIST OF FOODS

Following is a simplified list of foods divided into two columns. The first column is of foods which are low in refined carbohydrates (RCUs) and are under 20 percent fat. They are foods which can be used on this program. The second column is of foods which are either high in refined carbohydrates (RCUs) or contain over 20 percent fat or both. They are foods which should be avoided for your own good health.

USE	AVOID
FRUITS:	
Most fruits are under 20% fat. Limit dried fruit such as raisins to 1 oz. a day and prunes and other dried fruits to 2 oz. a day.	Olives are 89% fat. Avocadoes are 82% fat.
VEGETABLES:	
All vegetables are under 20% fat.	None.
FATS AND OILS:	
Butter Buds® Imitation butter flavor	Butter, lard, meat fat, margarine, and all oils are 100% fat. Mayonnaise and salad dressings
NUTS:	
	Almonds are 81%, cashews are 70%, pecans are 90% and walnuts are 71% fat.
LEGUMES: (Beans, Peas, Peanuts, and Lentils)	
Almost all beans are under 20% fat, i.e. kidney, pinto, navy, lima, garbanzo, white, red, calico, red Mexican, and black.	Soybeans contain 40% fat and are the only bean over 20% fat.
Peas are all under 20% fat, i.e. split, green, etc. Lentils	Peanuts are 77% fat.

USE	AVOID

MILK PRODUCTS:

1% or skim milk
Buttermilk
Canned evaporated skim milk
Plain, low-fat yogurt
Low-fat cottage cheese
Cheeses made with skim milk

Whole milk is 53% fat.
2% milk is 38% fat.
Yogurt made from whole milk is 50% fat.
Most hard cheeses are between 69% and 80% fat; i.e. cheddar cheese is 72%.

Cream cheese is 91% fat.

Nondairy creamer is 59% fat.
Sour cream is 91% fat.

BREADS, GRAINS, AND CEREALS:

Most whole-grain breads are under 20% fat
Sourdough breads

Whole grains such as whole wheat, barley, rye, rolled oats, millet, buckwheat, corn, and both brown and wild rice.

Flours, i.e. whole wheat, rye, oat, buckwheat, rice, or barley.

Whole grain cereals, i.e. Shredded Wheat, Roman Meal, grape-nuts, Cream of Wheat, Quaker Oats, Quaker Grits, corn meal, Wheat Hearts, Wheat Nuts, Wheatena, cracked wheat, and farina.

Baked goods, i.e. cakes, pies, crackers, doughnuts, sweet rolls, quick breads, commercial mixes, and cookies are too high in both fats and sugars.

White bread

White rice

White flour

Most cold cereals are too high in sugar. Check the labels to determine the RCUs or use only those cereals which have less than 3 grams of sugar per serving.

MEAT, FISH, POULTRY AND EGGS:

Most items in this group are over 20 percent fat. Limit yourself to 3 or 4 ounces of meat per day. They are divided into acceptable and unacceptable groups rather than over 20 percent fat and under 20 percent fat.

Lean beef, i.e. lean hamburger 15% flank 33%, round roast and rump roast 53%

Beef, i.e. marbled and fatty cuts corned beef 73%, fatty hamburgers 64%

Fish, i.e. bluefish 29%, red snapper 9%, flounder 1%, haddock 40%, halibut 41%, mackerel 58%, and boiled shrimp 10%.

Poultry without skin, i.e. chicken white meat 12%, chicken dark meat 25%, turkey white meat 18%, and turkey dark meat 35%. Water-packed tuna 8%

Egg whites, no fat

Fish, i.e. salmon 68%, whitefish 69%

Frankfurters 80%, luncheon meats 76% Organ meats, i.e. liver 42%, kidney 43%, sweetbreads 68%. Duck 43%, goose 77%, Lamb 79%, mutton 73%, Pork 51%, ham 69%, bacon 78%, Spareribs 81%, sausage 93%

Oil-packed tuna 67% Egg yolks 77%

DESSERTS, BEVERAGES, SNACKS, AND CONDIMENTS:

Fresh fruit
Canned fruit, water- or juice-packed
Whole-grain crackers, breads, and rolls
Catsup, mustard, horseradish, vinegar
Pepper, herbs, spices

Unflavored gelatin
Herb teas
Nonfat bouillon

Canned fruits packed in syrup
Puddings, ice cream, sherbets

Bakery items containing white flour, white sugar, and more than 20% fat.
Candy and chocolate
Fried foods such as potato chips
Salt, limit yourself to 800 mg per meal or 2-2½ grams per day.
Gelatin desserts
Sugared drinks

APPENDIX 6

ABBREVIATIONS

RCU = Refined Carbohydrate Unit
RCUs come mainly from sugar and white flour.
FU = Fat Unit
FUs come mainly from animal products such as meat, eggs, milk, cheese, or butter. They also come from vegetable oils, nuts, and seeds.
Cal = Calories
% Ft = Percent Fat
The percentage of the total calories in the recipe which are fat. All meals should be under 20 percent fat.
P = Protein in grams (1 gram = 4 calories)
F = Fat in grams (1 gram = 9 calories)
C = Carbohydrates in grams (1 gram = 4 calories)
Na = Sodium in milligrams. You are allowed 2000-2500 milligrams per day.
T = Trace (less than one-half)

INDEX

Recipes for Kids to Lower Their Fat Thermostats®

LaRene Gaunt and Edward A. Parent, Ph.D.
Illustrated by Dick Brown

Introducing *Recipes for Kids to Lower Their Fat Thermostats*, a fun, creative, full-color recipe book and guide to healthy eating, just for kids! This book uses an interactive approach to teach children about basic nutrition and exercise. Through activities such as coloring, games and cooking. Your child will learn to choose and make lower-fat foods that help her grow, have lots of energy and help her be strong. The "Tips for Mom and Dad" chapter shows how you can help your child develop life-long freedom from overweight.

12 Steps to Lower Your Fat Thermostat®

Dennis Remington, M.D.; Garth Fisher, Ph.D.;Edward Parent, Ph.D.; Barbara Higa Swasey, R.D.

Distilled from years of personal visits and seminars with people like you, this audiotape and workbook program works. You'll feel like you're having a private consultation with Dr. Remington, Dr. Fisher, Dr. Parent and Barbara Higa Swasey on every tape. Listen to each step as many times as you want. By doing the activities suggested you'll be lowering your Fat Thermostat for comfortable, lifelong weight control.

MasterCook II

MASTERCOOK II by Arion Software, makes it easier than ever to prepare delicious, wholsesome meals with all your favorite recipes. You get: A powerful RECIPE FILER, INSTANT NUTRITIONAL ANALYSIS, a 31-DAY MENU AND DIET PLANNER, and over 1000 delicious recipes including those in *Recipes to Lower Your Fat Thermostat*. Use your computer to analyze and print out your recipes or to help plan your meals, shopping and food budget. For PC Windows or Macintosh.

How To Lower Your Fat Thermostat®

Dennis Remington, M.D.; A. Garth Fisher, Ph.D.; Edward A. Parent, Ph.D.

Diets don't work and you know it! The less you eat, the more your body clings to its fat stores. This best-selling book contains the original program that teaches you to lose weight by giving yourself plenty of nutrients to convince the control centers in your brain to release excess fat stores. Your weight will come down naturally and comfortably, and stay at that lower level permanently.

Recipes To Lower Your Fat Thermostat®

LaRene Gaunt
Second Edition NEW for the 1990's

Companion cookbook to *How To Lower Your Fat Thermostat* and *The New Neuropsychology of Weight Control*. Now you can put principles of the Fat Thermostat program to work in your daily diet with this beautifully illustrated cookbook. It contains over 400 of your favorite recipes, a 14-day menu plan, and 16 full-color pictures. You'll find breakfast ideas, soups and salads, meats and vegetables, wok food, potatoes, beans, breads, desserts and treats. All are designed to please and satisfy while lowering your fat thermostat.

Acrylic Cookbook Holder

This acrylic cookbook holder is the perfect companion to your new cookbook. Designed to hold any cookbook open without breaking the binding, it allows you to read recipes without distortion while protecting pages from splashes and spills.

Desserts to Lower
Your Fat Thermostat®
Barbara Higa, R.D.

If you think you have to say goodbye to desserts, think again. At last there's a book that lets you have your cake and eat it, too. *Desserts to Lower Your Fat Thermostat* is filled with what you thought you could never find: recipes for delicious desserts, snacks, and treats that are low in fat and free of sugar, salt, and artificial sweeteners. The 200 delectable ideas packed between the covers of this book meet the guidelines of both the American Heart Association and the American Diabetes Association. They will meet your own tough standards, too -- especially if you've been longing for winning ideas that will delight your family without destroying their health.

Back to Health:
A Comprehensive Medical and Nutritional Yeast-Control Program
Dennis Remington, M.D. and Barbara Higa, R.D.

UPDATED FOR THE 1990's WITH AN
EXPANDED PHYSICIAN SECTION
If you suffer from anxiety, depression, memory loss, heartburn, or gas . . . if weight control is a constant battle . . . if you are tired, weak, and sore all over . . . this book was written for you. While yeast occurs naturally in the body, when out of control it becomes the body's enemy, manifesting itself in dozens of symptoms. Getting yeast back under control can correct many conditions once considered chronic. More than 100 yeast-free recipes, plus special sections on weight control, hypoglycemia, and PMS.

Pocket Progress Guide

A pocket-sized summary of the Fat Thermostat program that includes food composition tables, daily records, and a progress summary for quick and easy reference and record-keeping anytime, anywhere.

Easy Gourmet Menus
To Lower Your
Fat Thermostat®
Chef Howard Gifford

Feeling deprived? Has your diet become boring? Do you crave those wonderful foods you used to eat? Then you'll love *Easy Gourmet Menus.* TV's Chef Howard Gifford makes preparing healthy meals fun and exciting. Create everything from Crispy Fried Chicken to Razzleberry Cheesecake and enjoy to your heart's content. Over 150 low-fat, high-nutrition, irresistible recipes with shopping lists.

Gifford's Gourmet
De-Lites
Chef Howard Gifford

You'll exclaim **"This can't be low-fat! It tastes too good!"** Professional Chef Howard Gifford's meals have astonished guests at weight loss health resorts, students at his Cooking school, and television viewers. *Gifford's Gourmet De-Lites* has two weeks of breakfast, lunch, and dinner menus with complete shopping lists. The recipes are a breeze to prepare. Learn how to organize your kitchen and time for the long-term solution to your weight loss questions.

The Health Deck
Chef Howard Gifford

Deal yourself a complete breakfast, lunch, dinner, and dessert. The Health Deck is perfect for those on the run who demand excellence in the food they eat. It has 52 vibrantly full-colored cards and over 175 low-fat, great tasting recipes. You also get an 80-minute cooking tips video, a 48-page Achieving Success manual, and an instant recipe finder computer program. Each card has shopping lists for 1, 2 or 4 people, so it is ideal for today's smaller sized families.

Gifford's Spice Mixes

Chef Howard Gifford has just made your cooking easier. Now the unique flavors created by Chef Gifford can be had at the shake of a bottle. Eliminate the cupboard full of spices that are seldom used and the time of mixing and measuring spices. No more guess-work to create a desired taste. These new spice mixes are conveniently packaged with six inviting flavors. Use these spice mixes with the delicious recipes in *Recipes to Lower Your Fat Thermostat, 2nd Edition; Easy Gourmet Menus to Lower Your Fat Thermostat* and Gifford's *Gourmet De-Lites*, or flavor your own meals with the desired spice mix. You'll be delighted by the results.

Maintaining the Miracle:
An Owner's Manual for the Human Body
Ted Adams, Ph.D.; A. Garth Fisher, Ph.D.; Frank G. Yanowitz, M.D.

Unlike most health books that teach you how to treat a problem, *Maintaining the Miracle* addresses the kind of bodily upkeep necessary to head off problems. By following the daily, monthly, and periodic suggestions for your age group you will enjoy years of trouble-free living. This is the owner's manual that should have come with your body.

Five Roadblocks to Weight Loss (Audiocassette)
Dennis Remington, M.D. and Edward Parent, Ph.D.

If you have a serious weight problem that has resisted your best efforts, you could be suffering from any of the five roadblocks to weight loss: food addictions, artificial sweeteners, food allergies, yeast overgrowth, and stress. Learn what these roadblocks are and what to do about them—in an exclusive interview with Drs. Dennis Remington and Edward Parent.

QTY	CODE	DESCRIPTION	RETAIL	SUBTOTAL
	A	How to Lower Your Fat Thermostat	$9.95	
	B	Recipes to Lower Your Fat Thermostat#	$15.95	
	C	Acrylic Cookbook Holder	$9.95	
	D	New Neuropsychology of Weight Control (8 cassettes & guide)*	$79.95	
	E	Back to Health (Yeast/Candida Guide)	$10.95	
	F	Maintaining the Miracle	$16.95	
	H	Five Roadblocks to Weight Loss (Audiocassette)	$7.95	
	I	Pocket Progress Guide	$2.95	
	K	Recipes for Kids to Lower Their Fat Thermostats	$15.95	
	M	MasterCook II (Computer Recipe and Nutrition Program)@	$39.95	
	N	Desserts to Lower Your Fat Thermostat	$12.95	
	O	Gifford's Gourmet De-Lites#	$12.95	
	P	Easy Gourmet Menus to Lower Your Fat Thermostat#	$13.95	
	Q	Chef Howard Gifford's Health Deck	$59.95	
	R	Chef Howard Gifford's Menu of the Month Cards (6 cards)+	$14.95	
	S	Gifford's Gourmet De-Lites Spice Mix Set (6 bottles)#	$18.95	
	S3	Individual Spices - Basic (SB), Chinese (SC), Dessert (SD), Gourmet (SG), Italian (SI), Mexican (SM) — Circle the spice of your choice (three 2 oz. containers of same spice per package).	$9.95	
	T	12 Steps to Lower Your Fat Thermostat (6 cassettes, workbook)*	$79.95	

Shipping & Handling, $2.50 for the 1st item, $.50 each additional item.	+	
Canadian: $6.00 (U.S. dollars) for 1st item, $2.00 each additional item.	+	
For faster delivery, usually under five days, by UPS, add $1.50.(Excludes Alaska & Hawaii)	+	
* Buy D or T and get 1 book free! Utah residents add 6.125% sales tax.	+	
# Buy B, O, or P, and receive $5.00 off item S. @ Buy M and receive $10.00 off another item. + Buy any Gifford product and recieve R for $5.95. (Limited to product on hand.) **TOTAL**		

Prices subject to change without notice

Name_____DayPhone_____

Address_____

City_____State_____Zip_____

☐ Check ☐ Money Order - Make payable to: Vitality House Publishing
☐ MasterCard ☐ VISA ☐ American Express ☐ Discover Card

Card Number_____Expiration_____

Signature_____

How did you hear about our products? ☐ Friend ☐ Book ☐ Other _____

Mail to: Vitality House Publishing, 1675 No. Freedom Blvd. #11-C, Provo, UT 84604-2570 (801)373-5100
Copyright© 1994 Vitality House International, Inc. Orders shipped upon receipt. Allow 2-3 weeks shipping.
TO ORDER CALL TOLL FREE: 1-800-748-5100
OR FAX YOUR ORDER TO: 801-373-5370

RTL794